How Institutions Evolve

The Political Economy of Skills in Germany, Britain, the United States, and Japan

The institutional arrangements governing skill formation are widely seen as constituting a key element in the institutional constellations that define distinctive "varieties of capitalism" across the developed democracies. This book explores the origins and evolution of such institutions in four countries – Germany, Britain, the United States, and Japan. It traces cross-national differences in contemporary training regimes back to the nineteenth century and, specifically, to the character of the political settlement achieved among employers in skill-intensive industries, artisans, and early trade unions. The book also tracks evolution and change in training institutions over a century of development. It uncovers important continuities through putative "breakpoints" in history, but also – more important perhaps – it provides insights into modes of institutional change that are incremental but cumulatively transformative. The study underscores the limits of the most prominent approaches to institutional change, and it identifies the political processes through which the form and functions of institutions can be radically reconfigured over time.

Kathleen Thelen is Professor of Political Science at Northwestern University. She is the author of *Union of Parts: Labor Politics in Postwar Germany* and co-editor of *Structuring Politics: Historical Institutionalism in Comparative Analysis*. Her work on labor politics and on historical institutionalism has appeared in *World Politics*, *Comparative Political Studies*, *The Annual Review of Political Science*, *Politics & Society*, and *Comparative Politics*. She is chair of the Council for European Studies, and she serves on the executive boards of the Comparative Politics, European Politics and Society, and Qualitative Methods sections of the American Political Science Association. She has received awards and fellowships from the Max Planck Society, the Institute for Advanced Study in Berlin, the National Science Foundation, the Alexander von Humboldt Foundation, the American Scandinavian Foundation, and the German Academic Exchange Program.

Cambridge Studies in Comparative Politics

Other Books in the Series

Lisa Baldez, *Why Women Protest: Women's Movements in Chile*
Stefano Bartolini, *The Political Mobilization of the European Left, 1860–1980: The Class Cleavage*
Mark Beissinger, *Nationalist Mobilization and the Collapse of the Soviet State*
Nancy Bermeo, ed., *Unemployment in the New Europe*
Carles Boix, *Democracy and Redistribution*
Carles Boix, *Political Parties, Growth, and Equality: Conservative and Social Democratic Economic Strategies in the World Economy*
Catherine Boone, *Merchant Capital and the Roots of State Power in Senegal, 1930–1985*
Catherine Boone, *Political Topographies of the African State: Territorial Authority and Institutional Choice*
Michael Bratton and Nicolas van de Walle, *Democratic Experiments in Africa: Regime Transitions in Comparative Perspective*
Valerie Bunce, *Leaving Socialism and Leaving the State: The End of Yugoslavia, the Soviet Union, and Czechoslovakia*
Daniele Caramani, *The Nationalization of Politics: The Formation of National Electorates and Party Systems in Western Europe*

Continued after the Index

How Institutions Evolve

THE POLITICAL ECONOMY OF SKILLS IN GERMANY, BRITAIN, THE UNITED STATES, AND JAPAN

KATHLEEN THELEN

Northwestern University

CAMBRIDGE UNIVERSITY PRESS

CAMBRIDGE UNIVERSITY PRESS
Cambridge, New York, Melbourne, Madrid, Cape Town, Singapore, São Paulo

Cambridge University Press
40 West 20th Street, New York, NY 10011–4211, USA

www.cambridge.org
Information on this title:www.cambridge.org/9780521837682

First published 2004
Reprinted 2006

Printed in the United States of America

A catalogue record for this book is available from the British Library.

Library of Congress Cataloguing in Publication Data
Thelen, Kathleen Ann.
How institutions evolve : the political economy of skills in German, Britain,
of the United States, and Japan / Kathleen Thelen.
p. cm. — (Cambridge Studies in comparative politics)
Includes bibliographical references and index.
ISBN 0-521-83768-5 — ISBN 0-521-54674-5 (pbk.)
1. Employees — Training of — Europe — Case studies. 2. Employees – Training of—
United States — Case studies. 3. Employees – Training of—Japan — Case studies.
4. Occupational training — Europe — Case studies. 5. Occupational training —
United State — Case studies. 6. Occupational training — Japan — Case studies.
I. Title. II. Series.
HF5549.5.T445 2004
331.25'92—dc22 200404785

ISBN-13 978-0-521-83768-2 hardback
ISBN-10 0-521-83768-5 hardback

ISBN-13 978-0-521-54674-4 paperback
ISBN-10 0-521-54674-5 paperback

To Ben

Contents

Preface *page* xi

1 THE POLITICAL ECONOMY OF SKILLS IN COMPARATIVE-HISTORICAL PERSPECTIVE 1
Skills and Skill Formation 8
The Argument in Brief 20
Theories of Institutional Genesis and Change 23
The Origins and Evolution of Institutions: Lessons from the Present Study 31
Outline for the Book 37

2 THE EVOLUTION OF SKILL FORMATION IN GERMANY 39
The Importance of the Artisanal Economy in the Evolution of Skill Formation in Germany 42
Strategies of the Large Machine and Metalworking Companies 55
Political Coalitions and the Evolution of the System 63
The Political Coalition against Reform 79

3 THE EVOLUTION OF SKILL FORMATION IN BRITAIN 92
State Policy and the Fate of the British Artisanate 93
Union and Employer Strategies in the Metalworking/Engineering Industry 104
Reform Efforts before World War I 118
The Impact of War and Its Aftermath 133
Comparisons and Conclusions 145

4 THE EVOLUTION OF SKILL FORMATION IN JAPAN AND THE UNITED STATES 148
The Evolution of Skill Formation in Japan 149
The Role of the State and the Fate of the Japanese Artisanate 151
Strategies of the Large Metalworking Companies 163
The Evolution of the Japanese Management System 166
Germany and Japan Compared 174
The Evolution of Skill Formation in the United States 177
Skill Formation in Early Industrial America 178
Union and Employer Strategies in the Metalworking Industry before World War I 186
The Politics of Training during and after World War I 202
Comparisons and Conclusions 212

5 EVOLUTION AND CHANGE IN THE GERMAN SYSTEM OF VOCATIONAL TRAINING 215
The Evolution of the System under National Socialism 219
Vocational Training in Postwar Germany 240
Contemporary Developments in the German Training System: Erosion through Drift? 269

6 CONCLUSIONS, EMPIRICAL AND THEORETICAL 278
Cross-National Comparisons: The Origins of Divergent Skill Regimes 278
Institutional Complementarities 285
Institutional Evolution and Change 292

Bibliography 297
Index 323

Preface

I am well aware that vocational training is not going to strike some readers as the most scintillating of topics, but I hope they persevere long enough for me to make the case that this subject holds many valuable insights for political economy and comparative politics generally. I myself became interested in skill regimes as an offshoot of my interest in what defines and sustains different models of capitalism. Wolfgang Streeck's pioneering work first drew my attention to the importance of training in Germany's successful manufacturing economy in the 1980s. In the meantime, a broad consensus has emerged that skill formation is a crucial component in the institutional constellations that define distinctive "varieties of capitalism" in the developed democracies and very possibly beyond. This literature has made it very clear that different skill formation regimes have important consequences for a variety of contemporary political economic outcomes, but it had nothing to say about where these institutions had come from in the first place. This is what I wanted to find out.

The cross-national component of this book, therefore, explores the genesis of some striking institutional differences across four countries – Germany, Britain, the United States, and Japan – asking the question: "Why did these countries pursue such different trajectories with respect to skill formation and plant-based training?" My research led me back to the nineteenth century and pointed specifically to differences in the coalitional alignments among three key groups – employers in skill-intensive industries (especially metalworking), traditional artisans, and early trade unions. Along the way, I discovered how the development of skill formation in the early industrial period interacted with the development of collective bargaining institutions and nascent labor unions and employer organizations in ways that set countries on different political-economic paths. My analysis identifies important similarities between Germany and Japan (both seen as prime examples of "coordinated" market economies in the contemporary literature) and between Britain and the United States (as "liberal" market economies). However, I also underscore and explain important differences between these pairs of cases in how training came to be organized, with enormous implications for the type of skill formation that each country institutionalized and for organized labor's role within it.

As I worked out the historical origins of these divergent national trajectories, I became increasingly intrigued with the related but somewhat different question of how institutional arrangements such as these, which are forged in the rather distant past, actually *make it* to the present. This is not an idle question, it seems to me, especially given the massive transformation of the political and economic landscapes in all four countries over the late nineteenth and twentieth centuries. This observation prompted me to undertake, alongside the cross-national dimension, a parallel longitudinal analysis in which I set out to track the evolution of German training institutions over a somewhat longer time frame than the other cases, from the 1870s to the present.

This aspect of the research was organized around a somewhat different, but, I thought and think, even more compelling theoretical puzzle. In the literature on contemporary labor politics, Germany's vocational training system has conventionally (and quite correctly) been seen as a crucial institutional support for the country's high-skill, high-wage, high-value-added manufacturing economy. As such, the vocational training system has been viewed as a key element in a larger institutional complex that actively supports a production regime organized around a kind of "diversified quality production" that reconciles Germany's strong unions with strong performance in world manufacturing markets. As the historical analysis of the genesis of the system had shown, however, the core institutional innovation around which the German system came to be built (in 1897) was inspired by deeply reactionary political motives and was mostly designed to weaken (definitely not strengthen and incorporate) the then-surging organized labor movement.

The longitudinal part of the study traces the evolution of the German system from a core framework aimed mostly at defeating unions one hundred years ago, to a pillar of social partnership between labor and capital today – essentially asking the question, "how did we get from there to here?" I argue against prominent theoretical perspectives based on a strong punctuated equilibrium model that draws a sharp analytical distinction between long periods of institutional "stasis" periodically interrupted by some sort of exogenous shock that opens things up, allowing for more or less radical innovation or reorganization. In the case of the German training regime, I found that institutional arrangements often turn out to be incredibly resilient in the face of huge exogenous shocks of the sort we might well expect to disrupt previous patterns and prompt dramatic institutional innovation. One of the most striking features of this case is the durability of core elements of the original training system through some rather large disruptions over the twentieth century, which in Germany include several regime changes (including into and out of fascism), defeat in two world wars, and foreign occupation.

Conversely, though, and as the German case also shows, more subtle and incremental changes occurring in relatively "settled" rather than "unsettled" times can in fact cumulate into significant institutional transformation. The analytic task, therefore, was to make sense of the incredible stability of some elements of the system through a series of major historic breaks, while also capturing the subtle incremental changes that, over time, had turned the system, in political and especially power-distributional terms, completely on its head. What the German case shows is that institutions do not survive through "stasis" or by standing still but rather precisely through their ongoing adaptation and renegotiation in response to shifts in the political, market, and social environments. By tracking changes in the political coalitions on which institutions are founded, this study illuminates the ways in which the form and functions of these institutions could be radically reconfigured over time.

It is a pleasure now to thank the colleagues and friends on whom I have relied in many different ways over the years in which this book was in the making. Institutional support was provided by the American Institute for Contemporary German Studies, the Kellogg Institute, the Max-Planck-Institut für Gesellschaftsforschung, Northwestern's Institute for Policy Research, and the Wissenschaftszentrum Berlin für Sozialforschung. Separate and special thanks go to the Wissenschaftskolleg zu Berlin, which provided a most congenial setting for the final stages of writing and whose fabulous librarians and staff made the last steps in the process especially easy.

A number of colleagues and friends took time out from their own schedules to comment on various chapters. My thanks go out to Lucio Baccaro, Martin Behrens, Hartmut Berghoff, David Collier, Pepper Culpepper, Gerald Feldman, Jacob Hacker, Hal Hansen, Jeff Haydu, Peter Hayes,

Gary Herrigel, Chris Howell, Peter Katzenstein, Ira Katznelson, Desmond King, Jürgen Kocka, James Mahoney, Philip Manow, Jim Mosher, Jonas Pontusson, Sigrid Quack, Bo Rothstein, Dietrich Rueschemeyer, Theda Skocpol, Steven Vogel, Kozo Yamamura, and John Zysman. The first half of Chapter 4 is a reworked and augmented version of an article I co-authored with my colleague and friend Ikuo Kume, originally published as "The Rise of Nonliberal Training Regimes: Germany and Japan Compared," *Journal of Japanese Studies* 25: 1 (January 1999). I thank the *Journal* for permission to use this material, and I am deeply indebted to Ikuo for opening up to me the world of Japanese labor and political economy.

I had the good fortune to be writing this book at a time when Paul Pierson was puzzling through some of the same theoretical issues explored here, and it would be hard to overestimate the influence our ongoing conversations have had on my own work and thinking about these matters. David Soskice, likewise, has provided ongoing intellectual sustenance and stimulation over the years, and he has always been receptive to my efforts to build on aspects of his work from the slightly different angle from which I approach these things. Jonathan Zeitlin has accompanied this book almost since its inception, and I have benefited tremendously from the expertise and intellectual generosity he brought to bear in reading papers and chapters along the way. I am grateful to my former Northwestern University colleagues Peter Swenson and Michael Wallerstein, with whom I have been discussing these issues for years and whose work has had a deep impact on my own, as anyone reading these pages will surely see.

There are two scholars and friends to whom I owe a special debt of gratitude. Peter Hall sets the standard for collegiality, critical engagement, and support. This particular work was much improved as a result of Peter's extraordinary commentary on the manuscript in the final stages of writing, but his contribution to how I think about politics and political economy goes far beyond this and is hard to capture in a single turn of a phrase. Wolfgang Streeck has provided many different kinds of support for my work over the past several years. He continues to be a source of intellectual inspiration and generally keeps me thinking and learning. Wolfgang is also the one who, in response to an early paper, urged me to delve deeper into the politics of skill formation, which proved to be a very rich vein to mine.

I benefited from exceptionally good research assistance in writing this book. Helen Callaghan and Margitta Mätzke did a superb job with research assignments relating to specific chapters or arguments. Christa van Wijnbergen deserves a separate acknowledgment, as her work on this project and her contributions to improving it went well beyond the usual bounds of research assistance. Sarah Stucky furnished expert help in preparing the index.

I extend special thanks as well to Margaret Levi for her unending and inexhaustible enthusiasm for this project and to Lewis Bateman and Cambridge University Press for all they have done to promote and improve this work. I am grateful to the SK Stiftung in Cologne, Germany, for permission to use the August Sander photograph on the cover and to Steve Krasner and Caroline Jones for pointing me in Sander's direction in the first place.

I have a few personal debts to acknowledge. I begin with three women who immeasurably enrich my life and lives on both sides of the Atlantic – Gisela Kühne, Jessica Ticus, and Sandra Waxman. I doubt they know how incredibly centrally they have figured in sustaining me, not just through this project but generally and every single day – which is why I am writing it down. My family has also accompanied me through this process and each member has contributed in his or her own distinctive way. My wise and wisecracking teenager Andy knew when and how to inject a little levity into the mix, and Amelia's enthusiasm for foreign adventure buoyed me up when things were difficult. My husband Ben Schneider knows exactly and very well all the ways he has contributed to my completing this work. In the unlikely event that he thinks this may have been lost on me, I dedicate the book to him.

1

The Political Economy of Skills in Comparative-Historical Perspective

The past two decades have witnessed an enormous outpouring of literature on the putative effects of "globalization" on the political economies of the advanced industrial countries. A good deal of this literature was inspired by early, sometimes rather breathless predictions of a trend toward convergence in the institutional arrangements governing these political economies. Such convergence, it was argued by some, would result from the pressures imposed by footloose firms engaged in "regime shopping" which would in turn drive competitive deregulation among the advanced countries (see, for example, Kapstein 1996; Kurzer 1993).[1] These prospects were especially worrisome to students of Europe's "corporatist" political economies, which had long been admired as models of economic efficiency *and* social equality.

In the meantime, however, a good deal of evidence has accumulated that calls into question arguments about a convergence among the institutional arrangements that characterize different political economies (Berger and Dore 1996; Brown, Green, and Lauder 2001; Ferner and Hyman 1998; Garrett 1998; Iversen, Pontusson, and Soskice 2000; Kitschelt et al. 1999; Streeck and Yamamura 2002; Vogel 2001; Wallerstein and Golden 1997). Although there are certainly changes afoot in all countries, a number of scholars have pointed to systematic and apparently enduring differences in the organization of capitalism across the advanced industrial countries. Different authors characterize these differences each in his or her own way, but the consensus that has emerged is truly striking. Boyer and Hollingsworth write of distinctive national "production regimes" which are defined by a

[1] Harry Katz and Owen Darbishire make a more nuanced argument about the pace and scope of common trends (Katz and Darbishire 1999; see also Martin and Ross 1999).

set a mutually reinforcing institutional arrangements that together support different types of firm strategies in international markets – situating the United States and the United Kingdom at one end of a continuum and Germany and Japan at the other (Boyer and Hollingsworth 1997; see also King and Wood 1999).[2] This work resonates with Streeck's analysis, which distinguishes between "liberal" market economies such as the United States and Britain and "socially embedded" political economies such as Japan and Germany (Streeck 2001). Michel Albert's popular book draws a distinction between what he calls the "Anglo Saxon" and the "Rhineland" versions of capitalism, which, as Streeck has pointed out, also situates "not just Stockholm but also Tokyo" on the banks of the Rhine (Albert 1993). All this, in turn, maps well onto the analysis of David Soskice, who has characterized cross-national differences in advanced capitalism in terms of a broad distinction between "coordinated" and "non-coordinated" market economies, and more recently, in collaboration with Peter Hall, of "coordinated" versus "liberal" market economies (Hall and Soskice 2001; Soskice 1991).

What all these works share in common is a perspective on national models of capitalism that are characterized by distinctive institutional arrangements which in turn support specific kinds of strategies on the part of firms in international markets. These authors all point to more or less the same set of institutional arrangements that have traditionally been defined as central to the functioning of these political economies – financial institutions, industrial relations institutions, vocational training systems, bank–industry links, and more recently, welfare state institutions and policies (Ebbinghaus and Manow 2001; Estevez-Abe, Iversen, and Soskice 2001). For all their differences, these authors make very similar distinctions across countries, and draw an especially sharp line between "organized" (or "embedded") capitalist economies such as Germany and Japan on the one hand, and "liberal" market economies such as the United States and the United Kingdom on the other.[3] The former are characterized by "patient capital," coordinated

[2] The literature on the political economy of advanced capitalism from the 1970s and 1980s similarly focused on distinctive national models (for example, Hall 1986, Zysman 1983, and corporatism theorists of the 1970s). The newer literature on "varieties of capitalism" is an outgrowth of that earlier work, though with some important theoretical innovations. For an extended discussion, see Thelen (2002b).

[3] In fact, all these various categorization schemes also have trouble sorting the same set of "intermediate" or hard to classify countries, including France and Italy.

employers, and various forms of labor-management cooperation. The latter, by contrast, are defined by short-term financing arrangements, fragmented employers, and more adversarial industrial relations systems.

What these characterizations also share is a view of these systems as more or less integrated wholes, in which the various parts work together in ways that are mutually reinforcing. But what brought these systems into being? And what holds them together today? And, since no one would argue that these systems are not changing in fundamental ways, how should we characterize the dynamics of change and weigh these against the forces of institutional reproduction? These questions are at the top of the agenda in the context of current globalization pressures, and yet on these issues the consensus begins to break down.

Hall and Soskice's characterization of the ideal-typical "organized" and "liberal" market economies emphasizes tight coupling and multiple functional interconnections among the various institutional arrangements that make up a national economic "system" (Hall and Soskice 2001). For these authors, the existence of institutional complementarities across various arenas contributes to the robustness of the system as a whole, for two reasons. One is that institutional frameworks provide the foundation on which (nationally distinctive) competitive advantage rests, so that key actors (especially employers) who have organized their strategies around these institutions will be loath to part with them. The other is that, even if they wanted to change some aspects of the system, shifting rules in one arena would require adjustments in other, neighboring realms, which both increases the costs of change for them and also multiplies the political obstacles to such change. That said, however, and despite the fact that Hall and Soskice overall see the systems as very robust, tight coupling and strong institutional complementarities also seem to suggest that a major disruption in one realm (for example, financial institutions) would immediately "radiate" and translate into significant strains and change in neighboring realms (for example, collective bargaining).

Streeck's historical–sociological account also stresses institutional complementarities but it downplays the functional and economic logic in favor of a more singularly political view. Streeck views national "systems" as the product of past and ongoing political intervention and tinkering, of active maintenance and re-setting. Whatever structural or functional coherence we may now observe in these systems, he argues, "had to be continuously established, restored, redefined and defended against all sorts of disorganizing forces" (Streeck 2001: 31). He emphasizes how national models are not the product of a grand design, and "Ex post accommodation . . . seems to have been at least as important . . . as a priori calculations of the advantages of compatibility and complementarity under conditions of interdependence" (Streeck 2001: 31). Unlike Hall and Soskice's equilibrium-based view of institutions, Streeck sees these arrangements as inherently less coherent and therefore also not at all self-equilibrating, which leads to a picture that is overall less sanguine about the robustness of such systems. At the same time, however, and for many of the same reasons, this alternative view would not necessarily see such systems as vulnerable to the kind of "unraveling" mentioned above in the event of strong perturbations in one realm.

The premise of this book is that in order to understand the likely future of the institutions that make up the different "varieties of capitalism" we need a better sense of where these institutions came from, what has sustained them, and what are the ways in which they have changed over time. This is not the first time these systems have experienced strain, and understanding how they evolved in the past can yield new insights into the modes and mechanisms of change through which they continue to develop today. My analysis focuses on the institutions of skill formation because they constitute a key element in the institutional constellations identified by all the authors cited above. In fact, one recent strand of scholarship sees skills and skill formation systems as causally central to the development and articulation of social policy preferences generally, and thus foundational for the development and maintenance of different systems of social protection across the developed democracies (see, especially, Iversen and Soskice 2001; also Iversen 2003).

I approach the politics of skill formation from two angles, pursuing both a cross-national and a longitudinal dimension. First, the *cross-national component* of the study traces the origins of different skill formation regimes, focusing especially on Britain and Germany, and with only slightly less detailed treatments as well of Japan and the United States. This part of the book asks the questions: Why did different countries pursue such different trajectories in terms of plant-based training? And: how did the evolution of training institutions interact with the development of "collateral" organizations and institutions – especially labor unions and employer associations, and industrial relations institutions?

One of the most widely cited differences between "coordinated" market economies (such as Germany and Japan) and "liberal" market economies (such as the United States and United Kingdom) is that the former support more and better plant-based training.[4] My comparative historical-institutional analysis traces the origins of these contemporary differences back to the nineteenth century. Contemporary differences in skill formation go back to important differences in the character of the settlement between employers in skill-based industries, artisans, and early trade unions. I show how the development of skill formation in the early industrial period interacted with the development of collective bargaining institutions and nascent labor unions and employer organizations in ways that set countries on different national trajectories. The present analysis identifies some similarities between Germany and Japan (both as "coordinated" market economies), and between Britain and the United States (as "liberal" market economies). However, it also underscores the substantial differences between these cases in how training is organized – with enormous implications for the type of skill formation that each country institutionalized and for labor's role within it.[5]

The cross-national component of the analysis draws on an excellent secondary literature on the histories of unions, employer organizations, and skill formation, as well as on primary documents where these were needed to address the specific questions around which this research was organized. The main goal is to situate a number of country experiences

[4] Mine is not the first study to draw attention to these particular cases. As mentioned above, the different literatures on varieties of capitalism tend to focus on the same basic clusters of countries. Likewise, in the literature on skills in particular, it is not uncommon to draw a broad distinction between Germany and Japan on one hand (as "high-skill" economies) and the United States and United Kingdom on the other (as "low-skill" or strongly skill bifurcated economies) (for example, Ashton and Green 1996; Brown, Green, and Lauder 2001). This convention follows pioneering work by Finegold and Soskice (1988), who draw a sharp line between "high-skill" and "low-skill" equilibrium countries, though in the meantime this somewhat simplified distinction has been superseded by a more differentiated view that emphasizes the different types and mixes of skills produced within any one country. This is also why I adopt the somewhat less normatively inflected language of "coordinated" versus "liberal" training regimes, which are characterized by different mixes of strengths and weaknesses in skill formation. See the discussion below.

[5] Ashton and Green (1996) propose an explanation of these outcomes that is broadly compatible with mine. However their historical analysis is very fleeting (five to ten pages per country, and in each case covering both plant-based and school-based training). Their explanation of these outcomes hinges on the behavior of highly aggregated actors ("the ruling class," the "bourgeoisie," the "aristocracy"), and the conclusions – although not wrong – are highly simplified. Many of their assertions (for example, the idea that the Handwerk sector was "undermined" by industrialization or the implication that unions pushed for skill standardization against employer opposition) are not consistent with the results of the historical–empirical research presented here (Ashton and Green 1996: 142–3).

within a theoretical framework that can illuminate causal mechanisms at work across a number of cases. Each of the countries included in the broader study can be – has been – characterized as unique in the literature on political economy and labor development – Britain as the first industrializer; the German "Sonderweg"; American and Japanese "exceptionalism." Without taking away from the fundamental uniqueness of each case, this project attempts to put their experiences with skill formation and labor incorporation side by side to shed light on systematic parallels and differences among them.

Second, the *longitudinal dimension* of the research tracks the development of the German vocational training system over a longer time frame than the other cases – indeed, up to the present. This aspect of the study tackles the question of how institutions evolve and is organized around a somewhat different puzzle. Germany's vocational training system has been held up as an exemplary solution to a number of knotty coordination problems that plague most private sector training regimes. The German system encourages firms to invest in worker skills, and it provides mechanisms to assure that apprentices will receive high quality training. More generally, vocational training institutions in Germany are typically seen as part of a larger institutional package which, along with centralized collective bargaining, strong bank–industry links, and encompassing employer associations and labor unions, are seen as underpinning the country's high skill, high wage, high value-added ("high everything") economy. The vocational training system is viewed as a key element in a larger institutional complex that actively supports a production regime organized around a kind of "diversified quality production" that reconciles Germany's comparatively strong unions with strong performance in world manufacturing markets (Streeck 1991).

Scholars coming out of different theoretical perspectives have offered different views of the German system. From a functional–utilitarian perspective, German vocational training institutions have been seen as part of a complex institutional configuration that, among other things, supports employer coordination around a "high skill equilibrium" (Soskice 1991). From a power–resource perspective, the German vocational training system has been assumed to be a reflection of working class strength (for example, Gillingham 1985). From a sociological–cultural perspective, these institutions have been seen as a prime example of a more general, and distinctively German, mode of self-governance, which operates through the country's social partners and without much direct intervention from the state (see, for example, Lehmbruch 2001).

There is a way in which, looking at these institutions today, all these characterizations contain an element of truth. After an examination of the historical evolution of this system, however, they all seem rather puzzling. The core institutional innovation around which the German system came to be built was legislation passed in 1897 by an authoritarian government motivated politically by a desire to shore up and support a conservative class of independent artisanal or handicraft producers that could serve as a bulwark against the surging and radical working class movement. The 1897 legislation proved to be very important to stabilizing a certain type of plant-based apprenticeship that in other countries was rapidly deteriorating into cheap child labor. Against prominent utilitarian-functionalist characterizations focusing on current effects, however, these institutions were not originally designed with the economic interests of the industrial sector in mind (industry was excluded in fact) and they were certainly not meant to reconcile strong unions with anything. Against perspectives that assume that these institutions must have been the creation of unions, we find that organized labor played no role in promoting the original legislation, and in fact, the Social Democratic party opposed it. Finally, against the cultural–sociological perspective mentioned above, it becomes clear that the particular type of social partnership of which these institutions are (now) seen to be a part was really nowhere on the horizon.

How did we get from there to here? Not through a wholesale breakdown of the old institutions and their replacement with new ones. One of the striking features of the system is the resiliency of core elements even in the face of enormous disruptions over the twentieth century, which of course in Germany include several regime changes, the incorporation of the working class, defeat in not one but two world wars, occupation, and transitions both into and out of fascism. Although changes certainly occurred at these junctures, what is remarkable and in need of explanation are some striking continuities in key features of this system despite these disjunctures. This case, in short, calls for an analysis both of the mechanisms of reproduction that sustained these institutions *and* the mechanisms behind their functional and distributional transformation over time.

An examination of the evolution of German vocational training institutions can provide a window on larger questions of institutional evolution and change. I argue that this case illustrates the way in which institutional reproduction is often inextricably linked to elements of institutional transformation of the sort that brings institutions inherited from the past into synch with changes in the political and economic context. In the case of

German vocational training institutions, I analyze how the emergence and incorporation of new groups whose participation was not anticipated at the time the system was created drove the development of these institutions forward in ways that, over time, produced a system whose political–distributional effects are completely different from those envisioned by the original designers.

While emphasizing and explaining the disjuncture between original intent and ultimate effects, the analysis of the evolution of German vocational training institutions also speaks to the issue of institutional reproduction – a more problematic concept than typically recognized (for a discussion, see Thelen 1999). A point of departure for my analysis is that we need to pay more attention to how institutions created at critical junctures in the sometimes quite distant past actually make it to the present, given the magnitude of some of the intervening events and developments. I argue that it is not sufficient to view institutions as frozen residue of critical junctures, or even as "locked in" in the straightforward sense that path dependence arguments adapted from the economics literature often suggest. In politics, institutional reproduction can be partly understood in terms of the increasing returns effects to which this literature has drawn our attention – but only partly. Only partly because as one observes the development of the German system over a long stretch of time, it becomes clear that institutional survival often involves active political renegotiation and heavy doses of institutional adaptation, in order to bring institutions inherited from the past into line with changes in the social and political context. The question of the mechanisms of institutional reproduction and institutional change is thus the second major theme explored in the pages below.

Skills and Skill Formation

Vocational training institutions occupy a central role in most characterizations of the various political–economic systems cited above – and for good reason. Skills are associated with a variety of outcomes of interest to political economists. The acquisition of skills and investment in human capital are seen by many economists as "an engine of growth" (Acemoglu and Pischke 1999a: F112), and deemed to be "absolutely central to countries' growth performance" (Booth and Snower 1996: 1). Several studies point to a strong link between skills and productivity (Acemoglu 1996; Black and Lynch 1996; Bishop 1994; Lynch 1994: 21–2). In addition, growth and human capital development also figure prominently in "endogenous growth theory," which argues that a country's knowledge base is an important resource for innovation and which has linked cross-national differences in education to persistent disparities in per capita income across national economies (Romer 1990).

Political scientists and sociologists are as interested in the social consequences of various skill development systems as they are in the economic impact (for example, Brown, Green, and Lauder 2001). As mentioned above, analysts have begun pointing to the consequences of different skill formation regimes for broad social and institutional outcomes, including gender inequality and divergent social policy regimes (Estevez-Abe, Iversen, and Soskice 2001; Mares 2000; Iversen and Soskice 2001; Lauder 2001). Different training systems have also been linked to a range of more specific political and social effects. For example, training regimes in what Hall and Soskice call "liberal market economies" tend to be associated with rather wide gaps in the opportunities available to different types of workers, with implications for, among other things, income inequality (also Crouch, Finegold, and Sako 1999: 3). In general, less skilled workers have more opportunities for advancement in what Hall and Soskice call "organized market economies" which are, in turn, also characterized by greater income and wage equality.[6] Wage inequalities based on skill have been rising as a result of changing technology, which increases the skill premium as well as the overall skill intensity of production (Levy and Murnane 1992; Katz and Murphy 1992; Gottschalk and Smeeding 1997).

Sustained attention to vocational training institutions in the literature on the political economy of the advanced industrial countries can be traced back largely to Streeck's pioneering work in this area (Streeck 1992b). Based on an analysis of the German case, Streeck showed how strong private sector training within the context of a standardized and uniform national system for vocational education supported firm strategies based on what he called diversified quality production (Streeck 1991). For Streeck, vocational skills (broad-based and widely available) constitute a crucial competitive advantage for firms operating in "technologically and economically volatile markets" (1992b: 166). But despite the benefits of training, Streeck noted, firms operating according to strict economic rationality will systematically under-invest in the kind of broad and transferable skills necessary

[6] For example, Acemoglu and Pischke note that low education entry-level workers are more likely to get training in Germany than in the United States (Acemoglu and Pischke 1999a: F129).

to compete in these markets. As he puts it: "firms that create only those skills that they need may well end up with less than they need. Cost- and profit-consciousness are more part of the problem than of the solution" (Streeck 1992b: 17). In Streeck's view, cultural or political constraints that bend the logic of individual market incentives – in this case encouraging firms to "over invest" in skills – may turn out "to be more conducive to economic performance under given technological and market conditions than others" (Streeck 1992b: vii).

Given this posing of the problem, Germany was long considered a model of successful vocational training and skill formation for the advanced industrial countries generally. The comparisons to other countries were mostly invidious (see, for example, Berg 1994; Oulton and Steedman 1994; Finegold 1993). In one important contribution, for example, David Finegold and David Soskice examined the institutional bases of Germany's "high skill" and the United Kingdom's "low skill" equilibria (Finegold and Soskice 1988). In particular, they argued that Britain's chronic undersupply of training went back to public good or free rider problems, and the resulting dearth of skills in the economy encouraged firms to pursue product strategies premised on low skills, which in turn discouraged investment in skills, and so on. This dynamic provided the backdrop to their analysis of the inability and/or unwillingness of the British government to take action to break the cycle (Finegold and Soskice 1988: 25ff).

In the meantime, the literature has begun to paint a somewhat more differentiated pattern of strengths and weaknesses (see, for example, Crouch, Finegold, and Sako 1999; Culpepper 2003; Culpepper and Finegold 1999; Hall and Soskice 2001; Green and Sakamoto 2001). Thus, for example, Finegold's more recent work highlights Germany's continued high investment in initial manufacturing skills (apprenticeship) but notes deficits in the commitment of firms to further training – now arguably more important than ever in the context of rapidly changing production technology – (see Pichler 1993), as well as the overall scarcity of certain high-end (information technology and engineering) skills (Crouch, Finegold, and Sako 1999; Atkins 2000). Conversely, the United States, long viewed as a skills "laggard," is now getting more credit for producing an abundance of high-end skills – having become a net exporter of skills in information technologies, for example – despite continued worries about the country's under-investment in traditional manufacturing skills (Hall and Soskice 2001; Smith 2000). In a way, the emphasis in the political economy literature has shifted from an effort to identify overall differences in the *quantity* of training cross-nationally,[7] toward a more fine-grained analysis of cross-national differences in the particular *mix of jobs and qualifications* that characterize different political economies (Estevez-Abe, Iversen, and Soskice 2001; Crouch, Finegold, and Sako 1999).

Economists on Skills

As a first step in situating this literature and in mapping the empirical cases, it is useful to summarize briefly the way in which economists have approached the issue of skill formation. A point of departure for the political economy literature cited above is training market failures going back to poaching externalities, a view which for most of the first half of the twentieth century was widely accepted among economists (see, for example, Pigou 1912; Stevens 1996). The crux of the problem was seen to consist of a collective action dilemma. Specifically, firms that need skills face a choice: whether to provide their own training (at some cost to themselves), or attempt to secure skilled labor on the labor market (in effect, to attract workers from other firms that have invested in training). Since firms are themselves competitors in labor and product markets, each individual company will be tempted to poach workers from other firms, thus avoiding the costs associated with skill formation and in fact making off with the investment of its competitors. The more firms that choose this strategy, the greater will be the costs to those firms that do train; they incur both the costs of training itself and the costs of competing with non-training firms which – free of these costs – can offer these workers a wage premium. If all firms pursue non-training strategies, then of course all are worse off since this would diminish the overall stock of skills on which all rely.

In a widely cited contribution, Gary Becker called into question this posing of the problem (1964). Becker distinguished between general skills and specific skills and argued that poaching externalities would not be a problem in either case. For *general skills* – defined as those skills that are fully transportable and hold value to many employers – it is quite true that firms have no incentive to invest in training. But even if firms do not invest, workers will, or in Becker's words, "it is the trainees, not the firms who would bear the cost of general training and profit from the return" (1993: 34).[8]

[7] The available, mostly OECD, data are anyway notorious for their lack of comparability (for example, OECD 1998: 10–11). For a discussion see also Lynch (1994).

[8] Note that this formulation does not address the question of the *supply* of training, however.

Assuming perfectly competitive labor markets, skilled workers who possess general skills will be paid a wage equal to their marginal product, which means that even though the firm has no incentive to pay for training (being unable to capture returns on that investment), the workers themselves would do so (in the interest of their future higher wages). Becker's argument thus turns the poaching issue on its head: In a completely competitive labor market, poaching is not a cause of under-investment in general skills, but rather a mechanism assuring that a worker's skill is valued at full marginal product, thus providing an incentive for the workers themselves to acquire training.

Specific skills, according to Becker, are completely non-transportable and have value only to the particular firm in which the worker is employed (Becker 1993: 40). Poaching again is not a problem, in this case because firm-specific skills by definition are valuable only to the present employer. Here the equilibrium outcome is for the firm and the worker to share the costs of training. Facing no external competitors for the skills they are imparting, firms can pay workers a wage below marginal product in order to realize a return on the training investment. Workers will be willing to share the costs since the resulting wage will lie above the external market wage but below marginal productivity wage after training (Becker 1993: 42).

The problems that Becker identifies as sources of possible market failure resulting in under investment in skills go back not, as in the previous literature, to poaching externalities, but rather mostly to capital market constraints and especially credit constraints on the trainees. Although willing to invest in their own general training, trainees may find it hard to secure credit to do so because of the high risk of default on a loan and/or the uncertainty of the return on training (Becker 1993: 39–40 fn12). As Stevens (1999: 20) points out, the expected returns on training are the highest for workers at the beginning of their careers, precisely the time at which their accumulated resources are lowest (also Acemoglu 1996; Acemoglu and Pischke 1999a).

Public policies that ease trainees' credit constraints – for example, loans or subsidies for training – could alleviate the sources of market failure identified by Becker. The logic of the argument suggests, however, that any mechanism that effectively helps the worker defer or pay the costs of training will do. In traditional apprenticeship in many countries, for example, fees paid by an apprentice's family to the training firm and/or long periods of apprentice indenture (in which firms continued to pay apprentices very low wages even after they had acquired substantial skills) serve such a function. The logic of the argument points additionally to the benefits of some regulatory framework or system of accreditation that would ensure quality training and therefore reduce the uncertainty of return on the trainee's side. As we will see, the decline of the British system of apprenticeship training (for example) can be traced back to the failure to solve problems of uncertain returns for either employers or trainees.

Beyond Becker

In the meantime a number of studies have emerged which take us "beyond Becker" (Acemoglu and Pischke 1999a) but also, paradoxically, back to some of the training–market problems identified by the earlier literature. This work responds in part to empirical anomalies that point to sources of under investment in skills that appear not to be captured by the logic of Becker's model (Acemoglu and Pischke 1999a; Finegold and Soskice 1988). Most of this more recent scholarship does not take issue directly with Becker's analysis of the two ideal-typical models of training markets characterized by perfect competition (general skills) and non-competitive labor markets (specific skills), but research has focused on the provision of training in the intermediate case of imperfectly competitive labor markets for certain kinds of skills. Specifically, analysts have reacted to two aspects of Becker's argument: (1) the sharp distinction he draws between general and specific skills (Estevez-Abe, Iversen, and Soskice 2001; Stevens 1996; Stevens 1999),[9] and (2) his implicit assumption that the market for general skills will always be perfectly competitive (Acemoglu and Pischke 1998; Acemoglu and Pischke 1999a; Acemoglu and Pischke 1999b).

First, Margaret Stevens attacks the problem by questioning Becker's stark categorization of skills as either general or specific. She focuses on an intermediate category of skills, what she calls transferable skills.[10] Such skills "are of value to more than one firm, and there is competition between firms to employ the worker, but competition is not sufficiently fierce that the wage is driven up to the marginal product" (Stevens 1999: 19). Stevens and others imply that very many skills fall into some kind of intermediate category. In a similar vein, Finegold and Soskice note that a given firm may need a particular mix of skills, and that while each one may be general the mix

[9] Although Becker does recognize that most training is neither purely general nor purely specific (Becker 1993: 40).

[10] This seems similar to the category "industry skills" identified by Estevez-Abe, Iversen, and Soskice (2001).

itself is specific (Finegold and Soskice 1988; Acemoglu and Pischke 1999a: F124). Moreover, Franz and Soskice (1995) argue that the acquisition of general and specific skills is complementary, that is, teaching firm-specific skills reduces the costs of teaching general skills and vice versa.

The introduction of this intermediate category of transferable skills (portable but not really "general" in Becker's sense) re-introduces the problem of poaching externalities since in an imperfectly competitive labor market the value of the skill (= wage) will not necessarily be driven up fully to marginal product, and some of the training accrues to the firm that employs the skilled worker (Stevens 1999: 20). This situation reduces the employee's incentive to acquire skills (since he will not be able to capture the full return on his training investment in the form of wages), but for the very same reason, it also increases the employer's incentive to assume a part of the costs of training. But this, in turn, raises again the possibility that one firm's investment in training might accrue to some other firm – that is, a poaching externality – leading to under investment in skills of this type (Stevens 1999: 27).

Acemoglu and Pischke argue similarly for the possibility of imperfect labor market competition and associated implications for training (Acemoglu and Pischke 1999a: F127). Whereas Stevens and others (for example, Estevez-Abe, Iversen, and Soskice 2001) attack the Becker thesis by drawing out more fine-grained distinctions among types of skills, however, Acemoglu and Pischke focus instead on the structure of the labor market. Against Becker's thesis that firms will never pay for general training, they note empirical examples (German apprenticeship is one) where firms do bear a significant fraction of the cost of general training (Acemoglu and Pischke 1999a: F113–4). By way of explanation they cite labor market imperfections that prevent skilled workers from claiming wages equal to their full marginal productivity and that thus allow employers to earn rents on their training (Acemoglu and Pischke 1999a: F120; Acemoglu and Pischke 1998: 80).

Acemoglu and Pischke consider various sources of labor market imperfections. Institutions or situations that result in low labor turnover, for example, distort the competitiveness of labor markets, making it possible for employers to retain a worker after training at a wage lower than marginal product. One source of low labor turnover is monopsony power exercised by large firms that may dominate a local economy. Firms in such a situation could pay a wage above the local rate but still below the marginal productivity of its trained workers (Acemoglu and Pischke 1998: 80–1). Japanese training is frequently coded as involving "specific" skills in Becker's sense, but as the historical analysis below shows, it may be more properly understood as a case in which imperfectly competitive labor markets stemming from monopsony power (and coordination among monopsonists) allow firms to invest in transferable skills.[11]

Another source of labor market imperfections that figures prominently in Acemoglu's and Pischke's analysis involves labor market institutions that compress wages, thus holding back skilled workers' wages. Wage compression encourages firms to invest in general training, because, by holding wages below marginal productivity, it again allows the firm to capture some of the returns from the investment. This is at odds with a core assumption in Becker's theory, that wages for workers possessing general skills will grow at the same rate as their marginal productivity. Acemoglu and Pischke point out, however, that labor market institutions may prevent this, with implications for firm investment in training: "With competitive labor markets, firms never pay for investments in general training, whereas when labor markets are imperfect, firm-sponsored training arises as an equilibrium phenomenon" (Acemoglu and Pischke 1999a: F112).[12] As we will see below, union policies in Germany that encouraged wage compression in the Weimar years were indeed associated with substantial advances in firm-based training.[13]

Back to Politics

The analytic move made by Acemoglu and Pischke – from the assumption of perfectly competitive labor markets to the observation that the degree

[11] Blinder and Krueger (1996) show that labor turnover in Japan is less than half the U.S. level. Japanese management policies, including seniority-based wages, company-level social policy, and reluctance to recruit experienced workers from other firms, contribute to this outcome.

[12] Acemoglu and Pischke also note other sources of labor market imperfections that have similar effects to low labor turnover and wage compression. These include matching and search frictions, which make it difficult for workers to quit their jobs and find new ones, and asymmetric information about how much training workers have (that is, a firm which trains its workers has an advantage over competitors because it has better information about the workers' skill levels) (Acemoglu and Pischke 1999a).

[13] Additionally, the typical argument about compression is that this creates incentives for employers to replace relatively expensive unskilled workers with machines. Together with the skills argument I am making, this points toward a high-skill, higher technology trajectory (supporting what Streeck has called "diversified quality production") (see also Moene and Wallerstein 1995; Streeck 1991).

of competitiveness in the labor market can vary (with implications for the incentives facing both firms and trainees) – is crucial to the present analysis because, as the case studies elaborated below show, training regimes developed historically in tandem and in interaction with the development of other labor-market institutions and organizations. In Britain, as we will see, union structures and collective bargaining institutions developed in ways that intensified and in some ways distorted competition among employers in both skilled labor and product markets. By contrast, in Germany and Japan, developments with respect to union structures and collective bargaining introduced labor-market imperfections that provided some incentives for firms to train while at the same time (re-)introducing collective action problems associated with poaching.[14]

The point is that the structure and operation of skilled labor markets can be significantly influenced by politics, and historically, the interaction of the development of training regimes and of labor-market institutions had a profound effect on *what kind of skilled labor market* employers (and trainees) faced, as well as the kinds of solutions available for redressing the particular (different) market failures that emerged in different contexts. The problems (and solutions) that emerged historically are what lie behind some of the striking contemporary national differences in training regimes (Acemoglu and Pischke 1999a: F132).

In terms of outcomes, Peter Hall and David Soskice note that in liberal market economies, the incentives are for young people to acquire skills that are generally marketable rather than firm- or even industry-specific. Companies may upgrade this education with some company training but typically attempt to add only non-transferable (firm-specific) skills whose full benefit they and only they can recoup (Hall and Soskice 2001). The U.S. training regime thus does not favor strong firm-based investment in private sector vocational training. It appears, however, to support very well the production of a plentiful supply of "high-end" skills – for example, engineering and programming – that thrive in a context that rewards strong general (especially university) education and where demand for training on the part of young people is driven by intense competition among firms.

[14] Acemoglu and Pischke do not do the historical analysis, but they do stress the complementarities between training systems and labor market regulations (1999a: F136) and suggest that "the more frictional and regulated labor markets [in Europe and Japan] may encourage more firm-sponsored training" (Acemoglu and Pischke 1999b: 567). See also Peter Hall and David Soskice who discuss institutional complementarities between training systems and other political–economic institutions (Hall and Soskice 2001).

In the organized market economies, by contrast, firms are more likely to invest in general training of workers either because labor turnover is low or because other institutions exist which reduce poaching and free riding (see also Acemoglu and Pischke 1998).[15] But labor market imperfections also dampen the demand for training among youth, especially training that involves high investments of their own time and money, since these workers will not be able to capture the full rents on their training investment. This would be consistent with the observation of skill shortages at the high end (for example, information technology [IT] industries) in some such economies (Smith 2000).[16] This book focuses primarily on blue collar training, but I return to these more general observations in the conclusion.

Issues of Credible Commitment in Training: Some Problems and Their Solutions

In a completely competitive labor market, that is, one in which the wages of skilled workers are driven up to their full marginal productivity, firms will not invest in general skills but workers will have incentives to do so. In some cases workers can acquire these skills in public or private vocational schools, or for higher level technical skills, in universities. In terms of firm-based training for blue collar workers, the emphasis of the present study, we have seen that although firms will not be inclined to share the costs of training with workers, they may nonetheless provide training if the costs can be effectively shifted onto the trainee. As mentioned above, traditional apprenticeship in many countries was organized in such a way as to force trainees to pay the costs of training. Long indentures, in which trainees continued to be paid low wages for an extended period, are one example, since near the end of an apprenticeship the training is virtually complete but the trainee wage will be substantially lower than that of a skilled worker. Such provisions serve the dual function of (1) reducing the credit constraints

[15] The present analysis would also stress wage compression, which provides an incentive for firms to invest in training even as it intensifies the poaching problem, the latter being in effect "solved" at least in part by some of the same institutional arrangements that gave rise to it. These institutions are cited by Hall and Soskice, and they include coordinated bargaining (which compresses wages but also dampens poaching), strong employers associations (which punishes free riders), and plant level codetermination (which provides relatively long job tenure).

[16] As Christa van Wijnbergen has emphasized to me.

facing trainees (since they "pay" for their training with low wages over a long period), and (2) at the same time provide incentives for firms to train by allowing them to share in the returns.

As this formulation already suggests, however, a key problem in institutionalizing a stable skill formation regime along these lines lies in the difficulty in establishing a credible commitment between the trainee and the training firm (see especially Hansen 1997: 280). Apprenticeship involves an over-time contract between the trainee and the firm: The firm provides high quality training, but in exchange needs some assurance that the apprentice will in fact stay with the firm through the initial, high-cost period and into the period in which the trainee's contribution to production outpaces the wages he or she is earning. In the absence of such assurances, firms will be tempted to cut corners on training and exploit apprentices as a source of cheap labor. For their part, apprentices will be willing to accept below-market wages so long as they can be guaranteed employment that allows them to reap the benefits of investment in this high-quality training (for example, by putting them at some future date in the market for high-wage skilled labor, or alternatively, by guaranteeing them long-term employment which protects against the skills thus acquired becoming obsolete). However, those apprentices who have reached the final stages of that training (virtually fully trained but still earning below-market wages) will be tempted to break off their apprenticeship in order to enter the regular labor market where the skills they have already acquired can bring much higher wages (Hansen 1997: 13, 280).

The problem is a classic dilemma that revolves around the difficulty of securing mutually credible commitments from both parties to a training contract. Without strong external monitoring and mechanisms for punishing breaches of contract, neither party – neither firms nor trainees – can be sure that the other party will keep up its end of the bargain. Unless some mechanism is found to force firms to train well and to prevent them from exploiting apprentices, at the same time forcing apprentices to stay long enough for the company to recoup its investment, apprenticeship training is likely to deteriorate into cheap unskilled labor.

One solution to these problems is a system of *skill certification*, in which the state, employers, unions, or some combination of these, can devise and enforce procedures for evaluating and certifying skills (Hansen 1997: 380–94). Such procedures hinder firms from exploiting apprentices because firms whose trainees regularly fail standardized certification exams are likely to lose their license to train (and with it, the contribution of low-wage apprentices to production).[17] A system of skill certification also reduces the incentives for apprentices to leave early because trainees have to stay long enough to receive their certificate, which then becomes a widely recognized ticket to better jobs. Nothing guarantees that the relevant actors – employers, trainees, or their collective associations – will actually be able to implement such a system. As we will see, the failure to arrive at a stable solution to these problems contributed to the deterioration of firm-based apprenticeship in Britain, whereas such a skill certification program became a central pillar of the German apprenticeship system.

Issues of Collective Action in Training: Some Problems and Their Solutions

In competitive labor markets the main problems leading to under investment in training are seen to be capital constraints on trainees, and such problems also exist in imperfectly competitive labor markets because firms only share and never bear fully the costs of training. But in addition, and for the reasons sketched out above, poaching externalities will also play a role, since firms can never be sure that they, rather than their competitors, will reap the benefits of their training investment. As Hal Hansen points out, "poaching firms [can] afford to pay a skilled apprentice a premium since they [incur] no training costs to amortize" (Hansen 1997: 282–3).

In ideal typical terms, there are two different types of solutions to these problems. One is a system for the collective provision of a plentiful supply of workers with highly portable skills (to which all firms contribute and then on which all firms can also draw); the other involves the institutionalization of firm-based training in the context of strong internal labor markets.[18] The first, collectivist, solution consists of measures to support the provision of a pool of skills on which all employers can draw. Such a system would have to include provisions that would ensure high portability of skills (for example, through standardized skill certification). But such certification would render skilled labor markets more competitive and intensify poaching problems (since they alleviate information asymmetries that give current employers privileged information about the level and content of a trainee's skills). Thus, such a system would have to incorporate as well

[17] There are also reputational effects. The firms whose trainees do especially poorly on certification exams are unlikely to be able to recruit the best apprentices.

[18] These correspond to Gary Herrigel's distinction between "decentralized" (and collectively coordinated) and "autarkic" production regimes (Herrigel 1996b), and to Peter Swenson's categories of "solidaristic" versus "segmentalist" labor market strategies (Swenson 2002).

strong institutional mechanisms to counteract poaching and avoid costly competition among firms for skilled labor. This could be accomplished through wage coordination – to reduce incentives for workers to engage in "job hopping" – and/or other mechanisms such as strong industry or employers' associations to monitor firm behavior and punish poaching. In addition, since wage coordination is strongly associated with wage compression (Wallerstein 1999), the same institutional mechanisms that create the labor market imperfections that encourage firms to train in the first place can also "solve" some of the resulting poaching problems. As we will see below, Germany's system of vocational training (with its strong corporatist oversight by broad-based employers' associations and unions) approaches the ideal typical collectivist solution to private sector training.

The second solution is in many ways the mirror image of the first. Here employers combine firm-based training with measures to shield themselves from competition over labor in the external market. In such cases, a firm might make a long-term commitment to the apprentice and/or provide a generous package of company-specific benefits that reduces the trainee's interest in leaving the firm. This makes it "safe" for the firm to invest in the worker's skills, knowing that its investment can be amortized over the worker's career in the firm. In such cases training is also associated with complementary personnel policies such as seniority wages and an internal career ladder that reduce workers' incentives to leave. The large firm sector in Japan comes close to the autarkic (Herrigel) or segmentalist (Swenson) ideal type.

The Argument in Brief

To preview the historical argument developed in the pages below: cross-national differences in vocational training regimes can be traced back to differences in the political settlement achieved between independent artisans, skilled industrial workers, and employers in skill-intensive industries in the early industrial period. The kinds of settlements that were possible in individual countries were heavily mediated by state action (or inaction), which frequently tipped the balance in ways that either facilitated coordination, both among firms and between unions and employers, and supported non-liberal (or coordinated) training regimes, or aggravated the conflicts of interest among them in ways that proved fatal to the institutionalization of a stable system of firm-based training.

The Argument in Brief

One broad and consequential divergence among these countries goes back to the fate of the traditional artisanate in the early industrial period. In the United States and Britain, industrialization occurred in a context in which traditional artisanal organizations (the guilds) had either been destroyed (Britain) or never developed (United States) and where early labor organizations faced a less overtly repressive political regime.[19] In both countries, status distinctions between masters and journeymen were more attenuated than in Germany and Japan, and political and market conditions encouraged skilled workers to band together to defend their interests by attempting to control the market in their skills. But union-administered craft labor markets could be stabilized only with substantial support from employers, a rare though not impossible occurrence.[20] More often, the emergence of craft unions in the early industrial period led to a situation in which skill formation was *contested across the class divide*, as unions sought to use apprenticeship to maintain the value of their scarce skills and employers sought to defeat union attempts to control training to get the upper hand in labor conflicts.

Where unions of skilled workers sought to manipulate the supply of skills by imposing restrictions on apprenticeship training, especially on the numbers of workers being trained, employers fought tenaciously (also generally successfully) against these measures. Conflicts between unions and employers over skills and apprenticeship intensified rather than mitigated the credible commitment problems cited above, resulting in an overall decline in apprenticeship and firm-based training. Recurring skill shortages, generated in part by the failure of firms to sponsor training, redounded to the advantage of skilled unions in the short run. However, this dynamic intensified competition for (and poaching of) skilled labor among firms which (à la Becker) further reduced firm incentives to train and pushed them instead toward strategies that minimized their dependence on skill (Finegold and Soskice 1988). Skilled unions responded to these developments by

[19] For a very insightful discussion of Germany with reference to the contrasting British experience, see Kocka (1984) and Kocka (1986b). For other useful comparisons between the two, see Mommsen and Husung (1985) and Crossick and Haupt (1984). Colin Crouch makes a compelling (and much broader) argument about divergent national trajectories that points specifically to the significance of the survival or destruction of traditional corporatist institutions (including guilds) in the course of industrialization (Crouch 1993: especially 316–17).

[20] The construction industry in many countries is an example. Another example, discussed in Chapter 4, can be found in the stove industry in the United States at the turn of the last century. In terms of national patterns, Denmark comes closest to this outcome.

attempting to claim the right to perform particular jobs as their exclusive domain (job control unionism), such that, ironically, craft unions frequently evolved over time into hodge-podge organizations whose membership was increasingly defined more by the jobs they did rather than the skills they commanded (Piore and Sabel 1984).

In Germany and Japan, by contrast, industrialization occurred under authoritarian auspices, and the traditional artisanal sector survived as an important corporate actor in apprenticeship training. In these cases, unions of industrial workers developed in a context in which strategies based on controlling craft-labor markets were not an option, among other reasons because master artisans (self-employed or small employers) monopolized these functions. Here, skill formation was not contested between labor and capital in industry, but rather, between the artisanal sector and the modern industrial sector. For reasons that are elaborated in more detail below, this competition proved constructive rather than destructive to the preservation of firm-sponsored training. Unions were not the constitutive or driving force in the creation of these systems in either case, but union strategies and alliances during and after the 1920s shaped the trajectory of training in both countries nonetheless.

The German and Japanese systems are similar to the extent that both support high levels of investment in private sector training, but the two systems are based on very different principles and sustained by quite different institutional arrangements. I trace these outcomes back to differences in the treatment by the state of the artisanal sector in the early industrial period, which in turn affected the strategies of firms that depended heavily on skills and also powerfully shaped their relations with emerging unions. In Germany, government policy in the late nineteenth century actively organized and modernized the artisanal sector, in the process also endowing it with "parapublic"[21] authority in the area of skill formation. Industries that relied heavily on skills were pushed toward a more coordinated approach to skill formation through their competition with the artisanal sector whose power to certify skills they coveted. And, after their incorporation in the early Weimar years, German unions, which organized significant numbers of workers in these skill-intensive sectors, emerged as potential allies for industry against the Handwerk monopoly and in support of a solidaristic skill formation regime for industry.

[21] The term comes from Katzenstein (1987).

By contrast, government policy in Japan in the late nineteenth century contributed to the destruction and political disorganization of the corporate (organized) artisanal sector, which was viewed as an impediment to modernization and industrialization. Facing severe skilled labor shortages, the state took a more direct hand in promoting skill formation through the importation of foreign workers and the establishment of training programs in state-owned enterprises – in both cases, however, bringing indigenous independent artisans in as important intermediaries in training. Private firms followed the lead of public sector companies in embarking on a more "segmentalist" path, dealing with the problem of skill formation by incorporating traditional craftsmen (*oyakata*) into a system of direct employment and company based training. Early labor unions reinforced such autarkic tendencies in the 1920s to the extent that they defined their goals and strategies within the context of these internal labor markets.

Theories of Institutional Genesis and Change

This analysis of the historical origins of cross-national diversity in training regimes speaks to a broad set of theoretical issues that have become increasingly central in comparative politics. Whereas a first generation of "new" institutionalists focused on comparative statics and mostly asked what impact institutions had on political outcomes, the current literature on institutions has delved more deeply into the questions of institutional evolution and path dependence. The comparisons between Germany, Britain, the United States, and Japan allow us to explore the *origins* of different institutions, but the analysis below also tracks the *development* of the German system over a relatively long stretch of time, from the late nineteenth century through the post-World War II period to the present.

As pointed out above, this is a case characterized by some significant ironies and one that therefore poses a number of interesting empirical puzzles. Germany's vocational training system has been aptly characterized as a central pillar of the country's model of "social partnership" between labor and capital, and a critical support for manufacturing strategies that are compatible with high wages and in some ways actually depend on strong unions (Streeck 1991). As we will see below, however, this was by no means the obvious end point of a trajectory that the authors and proponents of the original 1897 legislation foresaw let alone intended. Second, the German case exhibits an historical trajectory that is characterized (on one hand) by sometimes very surprising continuities through huge historic breakpoints, but that has also (on the other hand) clearly undergone a massive if quieter transformation over the course of the last century. For both these reasons, an examination of the evolution of the German system can provide important insights into the question of how institutions persist and change over time.

Although these are central issues in comparative politics, questions of institutional evolution and change have attracted very little systematic attention. As Pierson has pointed out, one result of this has been a tendency to "fall back" on explanations that attribute the existence and form of institutions to the functions they perform, either for the "system" (or some "collective") or for the (powerful) actors that benefit from the operation of these institutions (Pierson 2000b: 475). Functionalism has a long pedigree in political science, and in the past came in both right-leaning and left-leaning variants (for a discussion see Hall 1986: 5–7). In the structural-functionalism of Easton (Easton 1957) and others, for example, the key functions performed by "the state" were interest articulation and aggregation, whereas Marxist scholarship emphasized accumulation and legitimation. In both versions, however, the existence of specific phenomena was explained with reference to the effects of those phenomena (Hall 1986: 6).

This type of "societal functionalism" has been mostly abandoned, but a somewhat different, more "actor centered" version of the argument is very much alive and current (Pierson 2004: Chapter 4).[22] One relevant literature has its roots in "new institutional economics" (NIE), which has been devoted to explaining how self-interested actors could overcome collective action problems in the market and realize mutual benefits through cooperation, and which in the meantime has been widely applied to politics as well. In international relations, for example, some scholars see institutions as mechanisms through which states can reduce transaction costs and achieve joint gains in an anarchic world (Keohane 1984; Koremenos, Lipson, and Snidal 2001); in American politics, scholars writing on the U.S. Congress see institutional rules as important in eliminating "cycling" and facilitating credible commitments among legislators (Shepsle and Weingast 1981; Weingast and Marshall 1988; Shepsle 1986); in comparative politics, some analysts see electoral rules and other arrangements as providing a stable structure of cooperation for rival elites (Przeworski 2001). That this

[22] This distinction between societal and actor-centered functionalism comes from Pierson, who elaborates the different arguments about institutional choice and institutional development associated with each of these two lines of argument (Pierson 2004: Chapter 4).

viewpoint is pervasive and influential is confirmed in Barry Weingast's recent wide-ranging survey of the rational choice literature on institutions. Summarizing the results of a body of work devoted to explaining "why institutions exist and why they take the specific form they do," Weingast argues, "in brief, the answer is parties often need institutions to help capture gains from cooperation" (Weingast 2002: 670).

Jack Knight (Knight 1992) and Terry Moe (Moe 2003) have criticized this perspective as too sanguine and neglectful of the coercive elements that underlie political institutions. As Moe puts it, in this whole literature "institutions emerge as good things, and it is their goodness that ultimately explains them: they exist and take the forms they do because they make people better off. This is why people choose them and stick with them" (Moe 2003:3). I return to the power aspect below; my point here is to emphasize that analyses resting on a conception of institutions as structures of voluntary cooperation often regularly refer to the functions an institution performs to explain the origins of the institution. Implicitly or explicitly the argument is that institutions are either *designed* or *selected* for the (good, beneficial) effects they generate. The problem, as noted by Pierson, is the strong tendency in this scholarship to "work *backwards* from extant institutional arrangements to develop an account of how these institutions were (or might have been) rationally chosen" (Pierson 2004: 104).[23] Clearly, the benefits of Germany's vocational training system, both for firms that are heavily dependent on skills and for unions whose core constituencies are skilled workers, contribute mightily to the persistence of these institutions. As Robert Bates has cautioned, however, it is crucial not to "confound the analysis of the role of institutions with a theory of their causes" (Bates 1988: 387).[24] Or, as Pierson insists, we cannot assume a connection between current effects and original intentions; instead, "*we have to go back and look*" (Pierson 2000a: 264, italics in original).

The main alternative to functionalist explanations of the form and character of institutions are various approaches traveling under the rubric of "path dependence." Although there are (too) many versions of this

[23] Jon Elster (Elster 2003) makes a much more radical critique of the literature on "rational institutional design," arguing that for a variety of reasons the actors who design institutions will not get institutions that match their objective interests, even in the short run.

[24] Knight puts it even more pointedly: "one of the most significant mistakes made by proponents of rational choice explanations of institutional change is the practice of working back from identifiable institutional effects to determine the initial preferences of the actors involved in the institutionalization process" (Knight 1999: 33–34).

argument, most scholars embracing this idea seriously entertain the possibility of what Stinchcombe has termed an "historicist explanation" of the origins of institutions, which is to say that the "processes responsible for the genesis of an institution are different from the processes responsible for the reproduction of the institution" (Mahoney 2000: 4; Stinchcombe 1968:101–29). This alternative perspective stands in sharp contrast to the theories just described, for the answer it offers to the question of "why institutions take the form they do" is historical not functional. So far this second perspective has been overall more prominent among scholars associated with "historical institutionalism," who tend to emphasize institutions as the product of concrete temporal processes and political struggles (for an extended discussion see Thelen 1999: especially 381–99).

The most influential treatments of path dependence within political science draw significant inspiration and insight from the work of economic historians (especially historians of technology), in particular Paul David and Brian Arthur (see, especially, Pierson 2000a). The whole point of this literature in economics was to refute those perspectives that maintain that "real time and history [can] be safely ignored," since the market will sort out inefficient technologies such that a technological system will gravitate to the same (efficient) equilibrium, no matter where it started (Hodgson 1993: 204). In the alternative historicist versions of technological development, by contrast, timing and sequencing loom large in determining which of several possible equilibria is reached – and whether the most efficient solution is selected. Timing (for example, being "first out of the gate") matters because once a technology is chosen, it is subject to significant increasing returns processes (Pierson 2000c; David 1985; Arthur 1989). Increasing returns effects can translate an early and perhaps idiosyncratically induced advantage into a stable trajectory of development, as firms adapt to the prevailing standard, investing in it in ways that reinforce the initial choice (for example, people invest in mastering the technology, firms make products that fit with the industry standard, and so on). Through these developments, the initial choice can get "locked in," making it hard to shift the standard even if a competing technology is revealed to have been the more efficient one (Arthur 1989; David 1985).[25]

[25] The usual example is the QWERTY keyboard, although I should mention that Liebowitz and Margolis (Liebowitz and Margolis 1990) strongly contest David's famous version of the story. They provide evidence that the QWERTY model is efficient, but they also make some broader arguments about the role of institutions, some of which are broadly compatible with what I argue about politics below.

What political scientists have taken from this is the intuitively attractive idea that politics, like technology, involves some elements of chance (agency, choice), but once a path is taken, previously viable alternatives become increasingly remote, as the relevant actors adjust their strategies to accommodate the prevailing pattern (among others, see North 1990; Zysman 1994). In political science, the concept of path dependence has thus become closely linked to the idea that countries undergo "critical junctures" that set them moving along particular (cross-nationally different) trajectories that are then difficult if not impossible to reverse (Collier and Collier 1991; North 1990; Mahoney 2002). Two large and fruitful literatures have emerged from this, one on "crucial junctures" (mostly about the origins of cross-national variation in important institutional arrangements) and one on "feedback effects" through which institutions, once selected, reproduce themselves and also shape the trajectory of institutional development by constraining subsequent choices (for a more complete discussion, see Thelen 1999). Such analyses provide a powerful refutation of functionalist theories of institutional origins and they do so precisely by showing how the current shape of institutions is deeply conditioned by the historical circumstances surrounding their genesis.

Arguments about increasing returns and positive feedback have also provided powerful alternatives to previous vague formulations that attribute institutional survival to "stickiness" or "inertia." In a widely cited (one might even say path-breaking) contribution, Pierson examined how many of the mechanisms that generate increasing returns in economic systems may, if anything, be more prevalent and intense in political institutions (Pierson 2000a). He argues that many formal political institutions are subject to the same types of large set-up costs, strong learning and coordination effects, and adaptive expectations that Arthur found to be important in economics. Mahoney (Mahoney 2000) moves a step beyond the economics literature, identifying and distinguishing reproduction mechanisms going beyond the utilitarian to include political and normative processes that also operate in a self-reinforcing way to entrench existing political arrangements. The point in this work has been to underscore the role of increasing returns effects on institutional developments to show why, in North's words, although "specific short-run paths are unforeseeable, the overall direction . . . is both more predictable and more difficult to reverse" (North 1990: 104).

As this characterization suggests, however, increasing returns and positive feedback arguments of this variety have been more helpful in understanding the sources of institutional resiliency than in yielding insights into institutional change. When it comes to the latter, the notion of path dependence seems to encourage scholars to think of institutional change in one of two ways: as *either* very minor and more or less continuous (most of the time) *or* major but then abrupt and discontinuous (rarely) (Streeck and Thelen, forthcoming). This has yielded a strangely bifurcated literature that links path dependence as a concept to two completely different (in some ways diametrically opposed) conceptions of change. Some scholars invoke the term rather loosely to support the broad assertion that legacies of the past always weigh on choices and changes in the present (for example, Sewell 1996). Many studies of transitions to democracy and market economy in contemporary Eastern Europe, for example, use "path dependence" in this way, as in: "Path-dependency suggests that the institutional legacies of the past limit the range of current possibilities and/or options in institutional innovation" (Nielson, Jessop, and Hausner 1995: 6). In such cases, the concept of "path dependence" is invoked to emphasize the constraints institutional innovators face, and often presented as a more realistic alternative to accounts that view institution building in a highly voluntaristic way, a matter of "designing" institutions that embody the right incentive structures (for example, Stark 1995).

Others, however, and often those who want to insist on a more precise definition of path dependence, tend toward a very different view of change, one closer to an especially strong version of a punctuated equilibrium model (Krasner 1988). Mahoney, for instance, is critical of loose definitions of path dependence and argues that "path dependence characterizes specifically those historical sequences in which contingent events set in motion institutional patterns or event chains that have deterministic properties" (Mahoney 2000: 1). By emphasizing the very different logic of institutional choice (as contingent) and of institutional reproduction (as deterministic) this definition implies and encourages the analyst to draw a sharp line between the "critical juncture" moments in which institutions are originally formed (or perhaps re-founded) and long periods of stasis characterized by institutional continuity. Any number of examples could be given here but the idea is generally captured in what T. J. Pempel calls "long continuities" periodically interrupted by "radical shifts" (Pempel 1998: 1). In his words: "Path-dependent equilibrium is periodically ruptured by radical change, making for sudden bends in the path of history" (Pempel 1998: 3).

Claims about relative contingency at historic choice points and relative determinism in trajectories once "chosen" are pervasive in the social science literature (also beyond political science) and they are by no means exclusively associated with scholars invoking the concept of path dependence.[26] An example from economic history is the line of argumentation developed by Mancur Olson concerning the way in which war and occupation in Germany and Japan paved the way for subsequent economic miracles in both countries. As Olson put the argument: "In Japan and West Germany, totalitarian governments were followed by Allied occupiers determined to promote institutional change and *to ensure that institutional life would start almost anew*" (Olson 1982: 76, my emphasis). In sociology, Ann Swidler has drawn a distinction between "settled" and "unsettled" times, in which the latter are seen as "periods of social transformation" or "historical junctures where new cultural complexes make possible new or reorganized strategies of action" (Swidler 1986: 278, 283, respectively).

Some scholars have linked such ideas to the age-old debate concerning the balance between agency and structure in political development, arguing that structure figures heavily in the "settled" times, and agency reigns triumphant in the "critical junctures." Ira Katznelson, for example, writes of "multiple possibilities inside unsettled moments of uncommon choice," such moments being defined as times when the "constraints on agency are broken or relaxed and opportunities expand so that purposive action may be especially consequential" (Katznelson 2003: 277, 283). Such views also find expression in Jowitt's work on Eastern Europe, which sees post-Leninist societies as "genesis environments" characterized by new openness and in which "leaders will matter more than institutions, and charisma more than political economy" (quoted in Stark 1995: 68).

Rational choice scholarship also has gravitated mostly to a model of discontinuous institutional change (Weingast 2002: 692), though from a different starting point. In this case, some of the core premises underlying much rational choice theorizing – above all, the view of institutions as self-enforcing equilibria in which behavior is generated endogenously – leads scholars to draw a sharp line between the logic and analysis of institutional reproduction and of institutional change (Greif and Laitin 2003: 2). Similar to the literature just discussed, there is a tendency in this perspective, too, to see change mostly in terms of dynamics unleashed by some exogenous shift or shock, and to elide or ignore the possibility of endogenously generated institutional change (Greif and Laitin 2003: 2). Moreover, beyond the *impetus* to change, the *direction* of change (that is, the reason why a

[26] Nor, conversely, do all path dependence theorists subscribe to a strong punctuated equilibrium model of change, as indicated above.

particular (new) institutional equilibrium prevails over other possible ones) seems also to be a function of factors exogenous to the (old) institutions. As Pierson points out, this perspective has little to say "about what is likely to happen if a particular institutional equilibrium does give way," and in fact the implication often is that "any new equilibrium may be as likely as any other" (Pierson 2004: 143–44). In other words, where the problem of change is posed in terms of breakdown and replacement, there is often no sense of a "path" at all.

Weingast flags the issues of "endogenous emergence, choice and survival of institutions" as an important research frontier (Weingast 2002: 692), and Greif and Laitin are among the first to attempt to tackle the question of endogenously generated change from a rational choice perspective. In a recent contribution (Greif and Laitin 2003), they draw attention to the impact of behaviors within a given institutional framework on the broader (social, political, cultural) parameters within which the institution is embedded, and show how such behaviors can either expand or contract the set of situations within which the institutions are self-enforcing. Although this is an improvement over formulations that see all change as exogenously generated, even Grief and Laitin's version is not really a model of institutional *change*. At the end of the day the outcomes are institutional *reproduction* or institutional *breakdown*, although the latter is not of an abrupt nature, generated by an exogenous shock, but rather the product of endogenously generated behaviors that render the institutions less rather than more stable, and thus "cultivate the seeds of their own demise" (Greif and Laitin 2003: 4).

The present study shares with such work a critique of exclusive reliance on models of change that draw a sharp line between the analysis of institutional stability and institutional innovation, and that sees all change as exogenous. Sometimes institutional change *is* abrupt and sharp (for an example, see Beissinger 2002). It is not at all clear, however, that this exhausts the possibilities, or even that it captures the most typical ways in which institutions evolve over time. The cases examined below mostly do not conform to a model characterized by periods of extreme openness and radical innovation followed by stable, faithful institutional reproduction or "stasis"; rather, they exhibit a pattern of incremental change through periodic political realignment and renegotiation.

The rest of this book, therefore, is devoted to an analysis of the political processes through which institutions emerge, survive, and evolve over time. My analysis is motivated by a sense of the limits to functionalist theories of institutional origins, on the one hand, and to strong punctuated equilibrium theories of institutional change, on the other. Along with some path dependence theorists, I draw attention to positive feedback effects that help explain important institutional continuities over time. I question, however, the determinism of some formulations and the "automaticity" of institutional reproduction that is sometimes implied in the logic of increasing returns, where all the adjustments are one-way (emphasis on how *actors* adapt to the prevailing *institutions*). The cases examined in the pages below show how elements of stability and change are in fact often inextricably intertwined. Once in place, institutions do exert a powerful influence on the strategies and calculations of – and interactions among – the actors that inhabit them. As power-distributional theories suggest, however, institutions are the object of ongoing political contestation, and changes in the political coalitions on which institutions rest are what drive changes in the form institutions take and the functions they perform in politics and society. The present study thus rejects those versions of a path-dependent argument that paint a deterministic picture of institutional "lock in," and elaborates an alternative perspective that underscores the contested nature of institutional development and, in so doing, recovers the political dynamics that drive institutional genesis, reproduction and change.

The Origins and Evolution of Institutions: Lessons from the Present Study

I trace important cross-national differences in vocational training systems back to the turn of the previous (nineteenth) century, and specifically to the strategic interactions among independent artisans, industrial workers, and employers in skill-intensive industries, whose reciprocal dependence was strongly conditioned by state policy and by the political and economic landscape within which they operated. In all cases, institution building involved forging coalitions and thus mobilizing various social and political actors in support of particular institutional configurations. Differences in the alliances that were formed across these four countries account for important early differences in the systems of skill formation that emerged.

Moreover, in all four cases the state played a crucial role in establishing the power of key actors, in influencing the kinds of coalitions that were likely to come together, and thus in shaping the landscape in which institutions were being constructed (see, generally, Skocpol 1985). Among other things, state policy in Germany and Japan directly inhibited the formation of craft-based unions, whereas state policy in Britain and the United States in various ways promoted the emergence of unions organized along skill lines. State policy entrenched and stabilized the artisanate as a corporate actor in Germany, while it actively disorganized traditional craftsmen in Britain, Japan, and the United States. In all cases, the state established broad "regulatory regimes" (liberal in the United States and United Kingdom, state-centered in Japan, corporate-centered in Germany) that became focal points and that influenced how interests were articulated and how debates were framed (Crouch 1993).

When institutions are founded they are not universally embraced or straightforwardly "adapted to," but rather continue to be the object of ongoing conflict, as actors struggle over the form that these institutions should take and the functions they should perform. Rationalist (including functionalist) accounts are quite right to draw attention to what institutions do, because the effects of institutional arrangements is precisely why actors fight about them. My analysis thus shares with Knight the idea that institutional development is "a contest among actors to establish rules which structure outcomes to those equilibria most favorable for them" (Knight 1999: 20). As such it argues against the kind of unspoken consensus that some sociologists associate with institutions (for example, Meyer and Rowan 1991),[27] but it also shares with Knight and Moe a somewhat dim view of the more voluntarist perspective that informs some work in the NIE vein. As Moe has pointed out, the cooperative aspects of institutions need not be neglected, but they must be explicitly linked to the power–political dimension, "for it is cooperation that makes the exercise of power possible, and the prospect of exercising power that motivates cooperation" (Moe 2003: 12).

My characterization of institutional genesis thus emphasizes a strong power-distributional component. It focuses heavily on political coalitions and political conflicts – some fought directly over issues relating to skill formation, others related only obliquely to skills but with implications nonetheless for outcomes in that realm. This analysis differs from some other power-based perspectives in two respects, however. First, and most important, I largely eschew presenting the argument in the language of "power" in favor of identifying the interests and coalitions on which institutions are founded. My reasons are in part purely pragmatic; unlike

[27] I am grateful to Peter Hall for this formulation.

"power," actors and their interests are more tractable empirically. Beyond this, however, an examination of the shifting coalitional basis on which institutions rest is critical to understanding how institutions both survive and change through time. Institutions frequently outlive their founding coalitions, and their endurance and robustness often involves a reconfiguration of their coalitional base in light of shifting social, political, and market conditions. There is nothing automatic or self-enforcing about this, and indeed the political renegotiations that accompany such realignments are crucial to understanding changes over time in how institutions are configured and in what they do.

Second, and related to this, emphasizing interests and alliances allows us to examine intriguing power *reversals* that sometimes flow from changes in the coalitional foundations on which institutions rest. Against power-distributional perspectives that view institutions as straightforward reflections of the interests of the powerful – and thus responding automatically to changes in the balance of power or in the preferences of the powerful – this study suggests a more historicist view of institutional evolution and change. As the cases below demonstrate, institutions are created in a context marked by multiple and simultaneous functional and political demands. As a consequence, institutions designed to serve one set of interests often become "carriers" of others as well. As Schickler (Schickler 2001) notes, the diverse coalitions who can cobble together political support for some institutional innovation are often motivated by disparate, even contradictory, concerns (see also Palier forthcoming; Pierson 2004: Chapter 5). An example from the present analysis is the 1897 legislation that became the cornerstone of Germany's apprenticeship training system, which reflected a remarkable combination of economically progressive and politically reactionary interests and motives.

This and the related fact that institution builders can "never do just one thing" in the sense of creating institutions that have the intended effects and only the intended effects (Pierson 2004: 115) helps explain some of the striking reversals in the power-distributional origins and development of institutions in the country cases examined in this book. The power of German unions, for example, has been very much shored up by a strong system for plant-based training, but the original framing legislation was mostly aimed at weakening unions. Conversely, skilled unions in Britain had a strong interest in a viable apprenticeship system; they were the actors most interested (and most involved) in regulating apprenticeship at the turn of the century. As we will see, however, their strategies in this area inadvertently hastened the demise of firm-sponsored training, which in turn undermined the skill base on which labor power had originally been constructed.

These observations have important implications for how we understand institutional origins and institutional evolution over time. In the cases laid out below, the mechanisms behind path dependence arguments – increasing returns and feedback effects – are certainly part of the story. In Germany, the existence of a system for skill formation dominated by organizations of master artisans in the early industrial period shaped the kind of labor movement that would emerge, among other things by hastening the demise of skill-based unions by denying them any hope of controlling the market in skills. But the operation of the handicraft system generated further feedback effects among industrial workers themselves (many of whom had acquired their own credentials within that system). As a consequence of such connections, Germany's industrial unions developed a strong interest in democratizing and co-managing the system of in-plant training rather than dismantling it, though this goal would elude them until after World War II. Positive feedback, therefore, can tell us a great deal about how key actors got constituted in the first place and also about the strategies they would develop in this area.

If one told this purely as a tale of critical juncture and positive feedback, however, one would miss much of what is in fact interesting and important about the way in which these institutions were *transformed* through political re-alignments and specifically through the incorporation of groups whose role in the system was unanticipated at the time of their creation. As indicated above, institutional reproduction is far from automatic and in some cases "adaptation" on the part of social actors to preceding waves of institutional innovation is as likely to inspire further revision as to entrench existing arrangements. In the case of vocational training, the political incorporation of workers in the early years of the Weimar Republic, and, more directly, the later incorporation of unions into a variety of parapublic "corporatist" institutions after World War II, recast the functions these institutions served in important ways – even as they contributed to institutional reproduction by bringing the system in line with new economic and political conditions. In other words, at critical junctures, old institutions are not necessarily dismantled and replaced, but often either recalibrated or "functionally reconverted" in part or in whole. In the German case, as we will see, institutional survival depended not just on positive feedback, but on a process of institutional adjustment, to accommodate powerful new actors and to adapt the institutions to address new imperatives, both economic and political.

The present analysis thus sheds considerable doubt on what has emerged in the literature as the most common way of thinking about institutional change, through the lens of punctuated equilibrium models that draw a sharp line between the analysis of institutional stability and that of change. For almost any institution that survives major socioeconomic transformation (industrialization, democratization) or political disjuncture (revolution, conquest), the story of institutional reproduction is likely to be strongly laced with elements of institutional transformation. For this reason, organizational forms will often neither accurately reflect the "congealed tastes" of their creators (Riker 1980) nor necessarily mirror the power distribution at their inception (Knight 1992). In contrast to many perspectives that view institutional development in terms of occasional moments of extreme openness followed by long periods of institutional stability if not "stasis," the perspective elaborated in this book suggests a model of institutional change through ongoing political negotiation. Elements of continuity and change are not separated into alternating sequences where one or the other (let alone "agency" or "structure") dominates, but rather are often empirically closely intertwined. Institutional survival in the face of shifts in the social and political environment often involves a renegotiation of the coalitional base on which specific arrangements rest, even as such renegotiations drive important changes in the form these institutions take and in the functions they perform in politics and in markets.

Institutions can be transformed in subtle but very significant ways through a variety of specific mechanisms, among which two figure especially prominently in the pages that follow (Thelen 2002a). One of these is institutional layering, which as Eric Schickler has pointed out, involves the grafting of new elements onto an otherwise stable institutional framework. Such amendments, as we will see, can alter the overall trajectory of an institution's development. In the German case, for example, the original training and certification system covered only the artisanal sector. However, its existence created pressures among key industrial sectors to develop and seek state recognition for their own training institutions. The resulting industrial system ran parallel to the artisanal system (with some points of tangency and also of conflict), mimicking some of its features but not reproducing it precisely. The interactions and linkages between the two in fact altered the trajectory of the German training system as a whole, pulling it away from the decentralized artisanal system toward the centralization, standardization, and uniformity that are now considered its core and defining features.

A second mechanism through which institutions evolve is through conversion, as the adoption of new goals or the incorporation of new groups into the coalitions on which institutions are founded can drive a change in the functions these institutions serve or the role they perform. In the case of Germany, the conversion process took place in two waves, first with the incorporation of the industrial sector and later with the incorporation of organized labor as a full participant in administering the system. Through these moves, the system was not just expanded but also transformed, in functional and distributional terms, and in this way brought into synch with important changes in the societal balance of power.

Thus, by combining elements of path-dependence approaches (emphasizing positive feedback effects) with historical institutionalism's traditional emphasis on sequencing and intersections among different processes and institutional dynamics, we can arrive at insights into when and also how institutions change, develop, and evolve over time. The mechanisms of institutional change identified here are quite different from the more common punctuated equilibrium model, but they are more useful in analyzing the kind of incremental or bounded change that may constitute the more common way that things "work" in politics. The dual notions of layering and conversion open the door for a more nuanced analysis of *which specific elements* of a given institutional arrangement are (or are not) renegotiable, and why some aspects are more amenable to change than others. As such, these conceptualizations provide a way of thinking about institutional reproduction and change that steers a course between deterministic "lock-in" models on the one hand, and overly fluid "one damn thing after another" models on the other hand.

The perspective offered here has several advantages. First, it avoids those varieties of functionalism that read the origins of institutions off the functions they currently perform. The notion of conversion, in fact, provides an analytic point of departure for understanding how institutions created for one set of purposes come, in time, to be turned to wholly new ends. In this sense, the idea provides a framework for a more tractable approach to the issue of "unintended consequences," and thus also addresses concerns raised by Pierson and others for devising a way to think about this problem that "turns on more than a retrospective judgment that particular actors involved 'screwed up'" (Pierson 2000c).

Second, notions of institutional evolution through layering or functional conversion are "genuinely historical" in the sense on which Skocpol rightly insists, looking at social processes as they unfold over time and in relation to other processes (Skocpol 1992). Models of path dependence appropriated from economics tend to focus on a single process in isolation, bringing history in only as bookends, at the critical juncture moment, and then again at the end of a reproduction sequence. By contrast, the model of institutional change suggested by the present study overcomes the distinction that is commonly drawn between the analysis of institutional creation and institutional reproduction, by specifically drawing attention to the ways in which adaptation to *other* ongoing processes (and not just positive feedback generated by the process itself) contribute to institutional and political continuities over very long periods of time.[28]

Third, such a perspective provides some insights into why it is that societies seem to exhibit some cohesion across institutional domains and over time. There is an apparent deep contradiction between the view of societies that institutional sociologists like Dobbin represent (where culturally specific institutions constrain the kinds of organizational forms that emerge, which are then also broadly isomorphic with one another both across organizational domains and over time) (Dobbin 1994), and the highly fluid view of society embraced by other theorists such as Orren and Skowronek (where institutions created at different historical conjunctures embodying very different political settlements coexist and continually collide and abrade) (Orren and Skowronek 1994). I think that there is something to both these views, and perhaps one reason that the kinds of collisions and contradictions that Orren and Skowronek's view predicts are not, in fact, as pervasive and debilitating as one might suppose is that the process of conversion brings organizational forms that are created in the past broadly into synch with currently prevailing power relations and cultural norms.

Outline for the Book

This book is organized around an examination of four countries that vary in ways that illuminate and develop these arguments. In terms of divergent

[28] In a way, the view of institutional evolution elaborated here may provide a more tractable alternative to the highly suggestive but somewhat abstract argument of Orren and Skowronek concerning the way in which "change along one time line affects order along the other" (Orren and Skowronek 1994: 321).

national trajectories with respect to skill formation, I consider cases of both non-liberal systems for skill formation (German and Japan) and liberal ones (Britain and the United States). Although there are some important similarities among the first group (and systematic differences between them and the second group), comparisons across these cases also reveal the forces behind the emergence of these distinctive systems.

Chapters 2 and 3 examine the diverging trajectories of skill formation in the German and British cases. The argument highlights distinctive configurations and interactions among several key actors, specifically the artisanal sector, early labor organizations, employers (particularly in skill-dependent industries), and the state. Chapter 4 extends the argument by considering two further cases – Japan and the United States. These cases represent variations on the themes elaborated for Germany and Britain, and they lend further support for the theoretical claims advanced in the previous chapters. The Japanese case represents a variation on Germany's non-liberal training regime, but one that is organized along more segmentalist lines. The United States shares some similarities with the British case, and illustrates an alternative route to a liberal training regime.

Chapter 5 delves further into the politics of institutional evolution by picking up the German case again to track its continuing development over a longer period of time. In particular, I examine the trajectory of institutional change through three subsequent periods. The first two – the advent of National Socialism and the Occupation and immediate post-World War II period – involve the kinds of historical "break points" in which one would expect substantial institutional reconfiguration. What we find instead, however, are significant continuities, though also important shifts in the role and functions of institutions. The final period, the present, by contrast, is one in which genuinely important changes may in fact be underway. However, these changes have been set in motion not by a clear exogenous "shock" but rather by ongoing, more drawn-out, changes in technology and market competition set in motion in important ways by the very "working out" of the original model. This last period thus allows us to explore the mechanisms of reproduction and change behind these institutions, and to observe how tangencies between the training system and other institutional realms, in this case especially collective bargaining institutions, operate to sustain (or undermine) distinctive national models over time. Chapter 6 summarizes the book's main empirical findings and theoretical implications.

2

The Evolution of Skill Formation in Germany

The German case provides a good point of departure for a study of the politics of skill formation. Germany has long been considered exemplary for its vocational training system, which even despite current strains (discussed in Chapter 5) continues to attract large numbers of German youth and to produce an abundance of high-quality skills (Streeck 1992b; Culpepper and Finegold 1999; Green and Sakamoto 2001: 73). Since the turn of the century, observers from abroad have looked to the German training model as a source of ideas and inspiration (see, for example, Cooley 1912; and, more recently, Reich 1991). This chapter examines the genesis and early evolution of the German system. As we will see, this system was not created "of a piece" but rather, evolved as successive layers were patched on to a rudimentary framework developed at the end of the nineteenth century. The critical legislative innovation around which the whole system was constructed was passed by an authoritarian government, initiated and originally conceived as part of a deeply conservative political strategy aimed mostly against the country's nascent organized labor movement. This chapter begins to track the processes through which this system evolved subsequently into what is now considered a pillar of social partnership between labor and capital in Germany today.

To preview the argument: The crucial starting point in Germany was the survival of an independent artisanal sector, formally (and legally) endowed with rights to regulate training and to certify skills. This outcome was actively promoted by the state, with motives that were as much political as economic. Facing a strong and radical labor movement, conservative political forces in Imperial Germany sought to shore up a viable artisanal sector as a political counterweight to the social democrats. Crucial legislation in 1897 created a framework for apprentice training under the control of the organized handicraft (Handwerk) sector, which was composed of self-employed master craftsmen who were distinguished in legal terms and in social status both from "industry" and from the journeymen and apprentices they employed.[1] Through this legislation the state endowed encompassing and compulsory handicraft chambers with parapublic authority in the area of skill formation; in so doing the law helped to stabilize apprentice training in the artisanal sector, which had previously been sliding toward sheer exploitation. More important still, this framework had enormous implications for actors that formally stood outside the system, above all, emerging labor unions and skill-intensive industrial sectors, especially the machine industry.

Although it is commonplace to view Germany's system of vocational training as a reflection of the strength of organized labor in the postwar period,[2] the history shows that labor's role in the development of this system was mostly reactive and indirect. The 1897 legislation was opposed by the social democrats, who were deeply skeptical of apprenticeship and who had no sympathy whatsoever for the traditional artisanal sector (Hansen 1997: 378). Once the chamber-based system of apprenticeship was in place,

[1] As Kocka notes (Kocka 1984: 96–7), the definition of Handwerk and of Handwerker (craftsman/artisan) has always been somewhat slippery and has shifted over time. The important distinctions are, on the one hand, between "industry" and "Handwerk," and between "Handwerker" and "Arbeiter" (worker) on the other. The difference between the Handwerk (handicraft) sector and industry was traditionally partly a matter of size (handicraft firms typically being smaller) but was linked also to the nature of production, which in the Handwerk sector historically involved "skilled manual work [also by the master-employer himself] without much mechanization" (Kocka 1984: 96). Regarding the line between Handwerker and Arbeiter, Kocka notes that "since the second third of the nineteenth century at least, there has been a tendency towards equating Handwerker with Handwerksmeister (master artisan)" as the term came to be "increasingly reserved for self-employed craftsmen" whereas "Arbeiter" was "increasingly reserved for those who worked with their hands for wages" (Kocka 1984: 96–7). See also Streeck (1992a) for a characterization of Handwerk as a social institution and above all, as a legal concept. As he points out, much – though not all – of what in other countries is coded as small business is organized legally in Germany under the category of Handwerk (Streeck 1992a: 108). Rooted in the history I am about to tell, the German artisanal sector has survived and thrived partly through state regulation but regulation encouraging ongoing adaptation to changes in the technological and market environment.

[2] See, for example, Gillingham (1985: 424) who asserts that historically, "the demand for increased vocational training originated on the political left." Other characterizations of the contemporary system also often seem to imply that organized labor had something to do with the development of various features of the system, for example, skill standardization (Culpepper 1999b: 4, 30) when, in fact, these features had already been well established long before labor's role within the system was institutionalized (1969).

it played a hugely important role in shaping the way that organized labor defined its interests and strategies with respect to skills. Most directly, the existence of this system foreclosed the option of unions organizing around the control of skilled labor markets. Even more important, as the ranks of Germany's social democratic unions filled up with skilled workers who had received their credentials under the system, the unions developed a strong interest not in dismantling, but rather in controlling or co-managing, the system of firm-based training that it represented. Thus, in the Weimar period German unions were already emerging as advocates of in-plant training, and ready allies of those segments of capital that had their own reasons for wanting to break into the system of skill formation that had been created for and was being monopolized by small employer master craftsmen.

The machine industry was the other key player in the early industrial period. This sector was heavily dependent on skills, and therefore was also a major consumer of the skills produced by these small handicraft firms. Around the turn of the century, Germany's premier machine firms sought and tried to pursue an alternative, segmentalist model of skill formation based on training for internal labor markets and relying more heavily on plant-based schools – very similar (as later chapters show) to practices emerging in the United States and Japan around this time. However, for a variety of reasons elaborated below, in Germany these firms could not escape the logic of the pre-existing handicraft system, and the training strategies they developed instead had to accommodate and in a sense work around that system. The result was that industries such as these that relied heavily on skills were pushed toward a more coordinated approach to skill formation through their competition with the artisanal sector whose power to certify skills they coveted. In a case of what Eric Schickler has called institutional layering, the Weimar years therefore saw the creation of a system for industrial training that ran parallel to and alongside the previous Handwerk system. The coexistence of the two created interaction effects that altered the overall trajectory of skill formation in Germany, pulling it in the Weimar years away from the very decentralized, and often unsystematic, training characteristic of the older handicraft model toward a much higher degree of standardization and uniformity – both of which are now considered hallmarks and defining features of the German system as a whole.

In both cases (that is, for labor and for the machine industry), the point is that the handicraft system produced feedback effects that had an important formative impact on the strategies, interests, and identities developed by these other actors. Although neither was part of the original coalition behind the 1897 legislation, both of these actors became invested in the system in important ways, and became crucial "carriers" of the system as it continued to evolve. The fact that these actors defined their interests and strategies within the logic of the existing system stabilized that system in important ways (as debates in the Weimar years revolved entirely around the reform of the system, not its elimination). At the same time, however, these developments set in motion new tensions and political contests, especially over the governance of the system and the content of in-plant training, the results of which also altered the trajectory of training. These conflicts were not resolved in the Weimar years, but the pulling and hauling that occurred in the 1920s established the framework for collective governance into which industry and (later) labor both would ultimately also be incorporated.

The Importance of the Artisanal Economy in the Evolution of Skill Formation in Germany

The construction of the German system of vocational training was premised in part on the defeat of an alternative liberal training regime. The politics through which this was accomplished are tightly bound up with the political weight and fate of the traditional artisanate. In Germany, industrialization occurred under authoritarian auspices and the artisanal sector survived as an important corporate actor in apprenticeship training. In the 1860s, the government's economic policy took a strong liberal turn. Legislation in 1869 liberalized apprentice training, removing all restrictions on who could set up a handicraft shop and take apprentices. Despite this and other laws that were hostile to the survival of traditional guilds, however, voluntary artisanal associations of various sorts in fact lived on.

Meanwhile the social democratic labor movement surged in the 1870s, elevating the "social question" to the top of the German government's agenda. Along with the better known "carrot and stick" policies (labor repression and the precocious introduction of comprehensive social insurance) the Imperial government's policy toward the artisanal sector was a third key response to the social democratic threat (see, for example, Volkov 1978: especially Chapter 7; Winkler 1971).[3] The Conservative and Center

[3] Blackbourn (Blackbourn 1977) describes the way in which policies toward the artisanate in the pre-World War I period fit into a broader conservative Mittelstandspolitik (policies directed at the "lower middle classes" generally). He notes, however, that those who looked

parties in Imperial Germany, in particular, actively cultivated independent artisans as a political counterforce to the surging labor movement (Volkov 1978; Lenger 1988: 154–9). The idea was that a healthy, conservative small business sector could help prevent social disintegration and political polarization, forming a bulwark against rampant liberalism on the one hand and working class radicalism on the other. Initial moves in the 1880s to bolster the powers of the (in Germany, surviving) voluntary guilds *(Innungen)* ultimately gave way to more comprehensive legislation, in 1897, that organized the artisanal sector into compulsory associations, granting them extensive powers in the area of apprentice training (Adelmann 1979: 12–13).

The first legislation of the so-called Reform Period of the 1880s (*Novellierungsperiode*) played to the interests of the existing voluntary guilds (*Innungen*), granting them more authority in regulating apprenticeship and adjudicating conflicts among masters, journeymen, and trainees (see Cooley 1912: Chapter 3; Schriewer 1986: 83; Abel 1963: 35; Volkov 1978: 199–200, 250). A measure passed in 1881, for example, delegated to the guilds a number of privileges and responsibilities, including "the regulation of apprenticeship, provision of ethical and technical training to apprentices, arbitration of conflicts between masters and apprentices . . . and, in general, [looking after] the well-being of the trade" (Hansen 1997: 325). Subsequent amendments to the Industrial Code, in 1884 and 1887, extended these privileges and "granted the voluntary guilds an exclusive right to the employment of apprentices upon a vote of all independent masters within a district, subject to magisterial approval" (Hansen 1997: 326). These measures also gave voluntary guilds the right to force non-member firms to shoulder part of the expenses they incurred in supporting trade schools, providing lodging for journeymen, and maintaining arbitration courts (ibid.). However, the artisanal sector continued to be buffeted by economic crisis, and political pressure for further legislation continued.

The result was a much more comprehensive intervention, the Handicraft Protection Law of 1897. This law created a wholly new structure of *compulsory* handicraft chambers alongside the voluntary guilds *(Innungen)* and other existing (regionally distinctive) institutions.[4] These handicraft

to the Mittelstand as a bulwark against social disintegration by and large ignored the diversity of interests of the groups that fell under this label. Lenger (Lenger 1988: 154–7) similarly stresses the diversity of interests, not just within the Mittelstand but more specifically, among Handwerker.

[4] As discussed below, the handicrafts were organized somewhat differently in different regions, with implications for both their orientation to the market and their political tendencies.

chambers (*Handwerkskammern*; hereafter HWK) were endowed with extensive powers to regulate the content and quality of craft apprenticeship. Under the new law, only persons over 24 years old who had passed a journeyman's examination or had worked independently in the artisanal sector for at least five years would be allowed to take and train apprentices (Hoffmann 1962: 12; Kaiser and Loddenkemper 1980: 12). In addition, the law contained the first regulations to control "*Lehrlingszüchterei*" ("overbreeding," which implies both overproduction of skilled workers in particular trades and exploitation of apprentices through their use as cheap labor). The new law allowed artisanal chambers to set limits on the number of apprentices a firm could take and to regulate the terms of apprentice contracts including length of training (Hoffmann 1962: 11–22; see also Wolsing 1977: 69, 400–2). Another mechanism for monitoring the quality of training was the institutionalization of a system of apprentice examinations administered by the HWK.[5] Finally, to accomplish their enhanced regulatory responsibilities craft chambers were authorized to send representatives to artisanal firms to evaluate their training arrangements, and they possessed the power to revoke a firm's right to train apprentices if its training was not up to their standards (see especially Hoffmann 1962: 11–22; Muth 1985: 21; Kaiser and Loddenkemper 1980: 12; Abel 1963: 36; Wolsing 1977: 400–2).

The 1897 legislation would come to serve as a cornerstone for the German vocational training system. As historians have argued, the impetus behind the original proposals was deeply political and mostly illiberal. As Hansen has emphasized, however, one must distinguish between the political impetus behind the legislative initiatives and the outcome and economic impact of the reforms that ultimately passed.[6] The early amendments to the Industrial Code in the 1880s were clearly "restorative" in design, and targeted the voluntary guilds. By the late 1890s, however, new voices had fundamentally recast the debate. One of the most important such voices was that of "industrial associations" (*Gewerbevereine*) that organized small factory owners and handicraft producers in Germany's southwestern regions,

[5] The law also included provisions for the establishment of journeymen's committees, endowed with rights to participate in the regulation of apprenticeship through the HWK, and to be represented on apprentice exam committees (Stratmann 1990: 40–1; Hansen 1997: 358, 378–9).

[6] On the politics that shaped the actual content of this legislation in important ways, see Hansen's excellent analysis (Hansen 1997: Chapter 5), on which I draw here.

especially Baden, Württemberg, Hesse, Thuringia, and Bavaria (Hansen 1997: 347–8). Although including some handicraft firms, these associations had historical roots different from the traditional voluntary guilds, and unlike the "backward-looking" guilds that dominated in some other regions, they were thoroughly oriented to the market (Hansen 1997: Chapter 5).[7] Rather than seek protection from market forces, the *Gewerbevereine* in Germany's southwestern states "sought to enhance their members' individual competitiveness through mutual support and the systematic promotion of technical and commercial education" (Hansen 1997: 347). Backed up by regional governments, these districts were already promoting the founding and extensive use of public vocational and technical schools in the early to mid-nineteenth century.[8]

Producers in Germany's decentralized industrial districts had looked on the restorative legislation of the 1880s mentioned above with great trepidation. These firms were pursuing strategies that aimed at higher quality market segments, strategies rooted in institutions of regional governance that were completely different from and independent of traditional guild structures. In the 1890s, however, they were confronted with the prospect of further legislation aimed at alleviating the plight of traditional artisans. With justification, more progressive and market-oriented producers (and not just in the southwest) worried that further measures to strengthen the voluntary guilds would impinge on their autonomy and smother their distinctive regional institutions by subordinating these to national institutions that fit the interests of more traditional handicraft producers who mostly sought protection from the market.

[7] Gary Herrigel (1996b: Chapter 2) provides a comprehensive analysis of the role played by these associations in presiding over a very different type of industrialization in Germany's southwestern states. In the pre- and early industrial period, this took the form of an elaborate putting-out system, which evolved into networks of small independent producers linked to one another through a variety of regional institutions (financial institutions, training institutions) that served to manage the high degree of mutual dependence among these producers.

[8] Master craftsmen in these areas founded so-called continuation schools "which required journeymen apprentices to attend school after hours or on the weekend to receive additional technical training" (Herrigel 1996: 52). In some cases (for example, Württemberg and Bavaria) these schools developed out of compulsory religious Sunday schools (Sadler 1908b: 520). In other cases (for example, Baden) the motives appear to have been purely economic (Hansen 1997: 292). Either way, Germany's southwestern states were at the forefront of moves to make attendance at such schools mandatory for youths after elementary school, beginning as early as 1835 when local authorities in Saxony were granted the statutory power to enforce attendance (Sadler 1908b: 521).

In the face of impending national action, the Gewerbevereine and their political allies mobilized to influence the content of legislative proposals in the 1890s, above all to prevent new provisions from undermining their own indigenous institutions. Working through the Federal Council (where regional interests could be articulated and forcefully so) and the imperial bureaucracy, the state governments that were home to these industrial districts sought to shape the legislation in ways that would protect their interests.[9] Their efforts put a decidedly progressive spin on the 1897 law. Thus, the Handicraft Protection Law that ultimately passed was specifically designed "to encourage and force handicraft producers to embrace the market, not [as the law's name suggests and as commonly asserted] to protect them from it" (Hansen 1997: 315). Hansen describes the law as a "felicitous fusion of guild-based handicraft organizational forms on the one hand, and the market-countenancing institutions and self-help practices evolved in regions of dispersed urbanization on the other" (1997: 314).

This legislation was crucial to stabilizing firm-based training in the handicraft sector. The existence of a recognized, parapublic, and, above all, *compulsory* system for certifying skills and for monitoring apprenticeship meant that a fair amount of training would actually take place in artisanal firms.[10] This stands in sharp contrast to other countries, such as Britain, where – in the absence of reliable monitoring capacities (and in the context of ongoing conflicts with unions over skill) – apprenticeship deteriorated at the turn of the century into cheap "boy labour" (see Chapter 3). There were ample signs that at this time in Germany as well; apprenticeship was slipping into child labor in regions dominated by traditional artisans, and it was falling into crisis in the more organized southwestern regions (Hansen 1997: 309–10). Gertrud Tollkühn (1926: 9–12), for example, cites a litany of abuses of apprentice training in Germany in the late nineteenth century, particularly after the liberal Industrial Code (*Gewerbeordnung*) of 1869 eliminated traditional guild restrictions. She cites an increase in the exploitation of apprentices by master artisans and a concomitant decline in the quality of training in that period (see also Dehen 1928: 25; Muth 1985: 18). The initial reforms

[9] The Prussian state dominated the Federal Council of Imperial Germany, commanding 17 out of a total of 58 votes (Herrigel 1996b: 116–17). But while Prussia could veto legislation that it opposed, it did not have the clout to pass new legislation that infringed on the rights of other states, as in this case.

[10] See especially Hansen (1997: 380–5), who provides a very elegant and compelling argument about how certification transformed apprenticeship into a modern training institution (which it had not been, traditionally).

of the 1880s had little effect, as regulation through the voluntary guilds proved weak and ineffectual. However, the *Handwerkergesetz* of 1897 (and subsequent revisions in 1908), which institutionalized certification and monitoring as described above, brought "real progress" (Tollkühn 1926: 13; see also Adelmann 1979: 12–13; Hansen 1997: 310; Kopsch 1928: 18–19).

Skill certification and monitoring, backed up by compulsory organizations endowed with parapublic rights to ensure compliance, provided a powerful mechanism for underwriting credible commitments between trainees and master artisans. The former had strong incentives to accept low wages (in fact, apprentices often still paid a fee to the employer) and relatively long contractual obligations (but a maximum of four years, according to the new Industrial Code) to earn their certification. At the same time, oversight by the artisanal chambers provided a way of evaluating the quality of training and thus acted as a check on blatant abuse and exploitation. Handicraft firms benefited from the apprentices' contributions to production, but in order to avoid losing their training privileges they also had to train their apprentices relatively well. If their trainees consistently failed their exams, the firm's license to train could be revoked (Hansen 1997: especially 382–3).

As Hansen has emphasized, this legislation represents a fascinating amalgam of traditional and progressive elements, as the decentralized industrial regions were able to assert their interests and turn a fundamentally conservative initiative to market-conforming ends. Very similar to developments in social policy around this same time (see especially Manow 2001), deeply illiberal policies were organized not so much around an attempt to preserve the status quo as to modernize and "rationalize the societal order" (Manow 1999: 5). In vocational training as in social policy the results "established an especially modern form of interest intermediation, 'sharing public space'... with organized societal interests and willing to use 'functional organizations as co-opted agents of order'" (Manow 1999: 5). In sum, the 1897 law was absolutely key to the future trajectory of German vocational training, and it fits very neatly into a broader class of legislation in this period which was, as Manow puts it, "modern, but certainly not liberal" (Manow 1999: 5).

Implications for Labor

The existence of a chamber system endowed with parapublic authority to monitor in-plant training and to certify skills had very profound implications for both organized labor and industry. For labor, the most important consequences were (1) effectively to rule out organizational strategies premised on attempts to control the supply of skills in the economy, at the same time (2) setting in motion feedback effects through which Germany's social democratic unions would themselves become invested in strategies premised on maintaining and expanding (but also democratizing) the inherited system of plant-based training.[11] I deal with each of these, briefly, in turn.

First, and especially in the context of the comparison to Britain (Chapter 3), the triumph of industrial unionism in Germany is of crucial importance. German unions were clearly not "born" centralized and there is a longstanding debate on the connections between older handicraft (journeymen's) associations and the unions that ultimately emerged in Germany (see, for example, Engelhardt 1977; Kocka 1986b). In the past, some authors attributed the triumph of industrial organization to the logic of late industrialization (industrial concentration being seen as driving union centralization) or to the influence of working class parties championing socialist ideologies (associated therefore with a critique of traditional "corporate" organizational forms and "narrow" craft identities). However, the late industrialization thesis entirely misses important aspects of German industrial structure, and the arguments about socialist ideology gloss over key features of early working class formation and union organization.

Jürgen Kocka's writings, in particular, have been important in clarifying the way in which early unions in Germany in some ways built on traditional organizational forms (for example, journeymen's brotherhoods) while developing identities and strategies that were *simultaneously* strongly anticapitalist *and* anticorporate (see especially Kocka 1984; Kocka 1986a; Kocka 1986b; also Welskopp 2000).[12] Craft-based journeymen's associations were

[11] This topic merits a more extended treatment than is possible here. It is surprising how most histories of the German union movement have been told separately from (and with little reference to) the history of vocational education and training. As Streeck and colleagues have pointed out, although much has been written about how industrial relations institutions affect training (for example, the way that craft unions have tried to regulate the content and amount of training as part of their strategies) "less is known . . . about the inverse effect of training on industrial relations" (Streeck et al. 1987: 1).

[12] Welskopp's monumental study of the German social democratic labor movement in the late nineteenth century shows (among other things) how German unions were pushed into a different relationship to politics and to the social democratic party by the fact that the regulation of training through the handicraft chambers precluded a stronger emphasis on labor market control (as developed in Britain, for example) (Welskopp 2000).

clearly important in the early German labor movement from the 1840s to the 1860s. By the 1870s class awareness was on the rise, but even then unions were still dominated by skilled workers and fragmented along craft lines (Kocka 1986a: 339–42).[13] As Kocka notes, "most unionized workers belonged to craft- or trade-specific organizations" until the 1890s, though unions like the metalworkers were from quite early on composed of amalgamations of craft organizations (Kocka 1984: 99–100).

In addition, and as Herrigel shows (1993), the organizational landscape in Germany throughout the last decades of the nineteenth century was considerably more differentiated than many accounts of late industrialization premised on the idea of a growing polarization of big industry and proletariat suggest. In Germany in the late nineteenth century a number of "different kinds of organizations – industry associations, trade unions, craft chambers (*Innungen*) – [all] competed for craftsmen's allegiance and membership" (Herrigel 1993: 385). Herrigel puts special emphasis on the *Fachvereine* (associations of skilled outworkers) with strong craft identities as the main competitors for the allegiance of skilled workers in this period. He argues that this organizational competition is what drove the emergence of encompassing industry-based unions, for it forced social democrats to articulate a coherent social ideology that distinguished them from these other organizations. He maintains that the social democratic unions developed by filling "the negative space" that was left by the other groups, which meant embracing an organizational form that appealed to workers on grounds other than their craft identities (Herrigel 1993: 388).

Herrigel is right to note the continuing importance of occupational identities within the German labor movement. But a closer look at the most important industrial union of the time, the Metalworkers (*Deutscher Metallarbeiterverband*, or DMV),[14] reveals that the union sometimes organized *around* the *Fachvereine*, but in the early years especially grew mostly by *absorbing* many of them. At the crucial 1891 congress (at which

[13] Comparing data from strikes in the period 1780–1805 against those between 1871–1878, Kocka shows that craft distinctions had waned over the nineteenth century. Strikes in the earlier period almost never involved cross-craft cooperation, but by the 1870s, about 10% of strikes (20% of factory worker strikes and 6% of journeymen strikes) were waged jointly by different crafts, and support from other crafts was up from 13% to almost one in three. Still, as Kocka also notes, these strike data also show that, although diminishing, there was still a "high degree of fragmentation" along craft lines in the 1870s (Kocka 1984: 110–11).

[14] The DMV was the largest of the social democratic ("free") unions, organizing almost a fifth of their total membership in 1913 (Domansky-Davidsohn 1981: 24).

the principle of industrial unionism prevailed) most of the delegates were themselves representing various associations of skilled workers, both "single craft" and "mixed" (Albrecht 1982: 483). The DMV's strong growth in the years after its founding occurred primarily through the entry of previously independent craft organizations, not through recruiting new union members.[15] In other words, social democratic (industrial) unions such as the DMV only partly grew up in the "negative space" left open around alternative (skill-based) organizations; they also grew right into the space previously occupied by these other pre-existing associations. This is one reason why the union was far less inclusive than its formal organizational form (as an *industrial* union) suggested, dominated instead by skilled workers until after World War I.[16]

Moreover, the skilled workers that made up the core of the early DMV did not leave their skilled identities at the door. On the contrary, and as Domansky-Davidsohn notes: "The trades-based organizations (*Fachorganisationen*) that joined the DMV did not entirely abandon older models of organization. The founding resolution of the DMV explicitly provided for the consolidation of individual occupational groups into local departments (*Sektionen*) under leadership of the DMV" (1981: 28, 35). The DMV also remained very attuned to conditions of the various occupational groupings, undertaking surveys of the wages and working conditions for various trades through the early years of its existence (1891–1914) (Domansky-Davidsohn 1981: 18). The continuing influence of these informal craft groupings may help explain significant features of the DMV's collective bargaining policies in the early years as well. Wage agreements in the Berlin metalworking industry before the war were negotiated individually for separate crafts, that is, separate contracts for separate trades (Mosher 2001: 291). Even in the first postwar contract, in 1919, wages were differentiated by craft (for example, toolmaker) and by the type of work done (for example, machinist, ironworker, and so on) (Mosher 2001: 291).

These observations suggest a different question, why the skilled identities of the various occupational groupings did not prevent them from throwing their lots in with social democratic unions that were explicitly committed to industrial organization. Here a more materialist–institutionalist

[15] The mergers were sometimes voluntary, but by no means always. Sometimes they were the result of pressure by the DMV (Domansky-Davidsohn 1981: 28–9).

[16] In 1913, only about 20% of DMV members were unskilled or semi-skilled workers (Domansky-Davidsohn 1981: 32).

approach can complement Herrigel's identity-based analysis. As Kocka has pointed out, the distinctly anticorporate (in addition to anticapitalist) slant of Germany's early unions must be understood within the context of the broader social and political context in which they emerged and grew. In particular, and in sharp contrast to both Britain and France, "elements of the old corporate order survived much longer in Germany . . . into the midst of the industrial revolution. But they remained in an unbalanced way. The master guilds survived much better than the journeymen brotherhoods, which had been deeply weakened by government policy. From the perspective of the journeymen, the restrictive elements of the old order lasted more successfully than its protective elements did" (Kocka 1986a: 311–12).

In the area of apprenticeship and skill formation specifically (crucial to any strategy organized around craft exclusivity), it is clearly significant that union expansion in Germany took place in a context in which the skill-regulatory functions were effectively occupied by the (master-dominated) voluntary guilds and then (after 1897) authoritatively monopolized by the handicraft chambers (see also Kocka 1986b: 342–3). Thus, as in Britain (see Chapter 3), skilled workers formed the core of the early unions and in many ways held on to their occupational identities. The difference is that in Germany, unions were profoundly discouraged if not blocked entirely from pursuing craft-based *strategies* (for example, based on controlling skilled labor markets) in their dealings with employers.[17] The hold-outs (against industrial organization) would have been those craft workers who for very specific and historically identifiable reasons were in fact able to control the market in their own skill. Within metalworking, the Solingen cutlery workers provide an example of just such a case.[18]

[17] Philip Manow's work has also highlighted the way in which the development of social insurance in Germany cut off strategies premised on controlling skilled labor markets. "Craft unions often offered special insurance benefits to their members. The new social insurance [of the Bismarckian period] increasingly prohibited using these union insurance schemes as 'selective incentives'. Hence, craft unions lost an instrument that was critical for attracting and keeping members, while industrial unions were gaining a new set of selective incentives, including power to allocate numerous jobs in the insurance administration to loyal followers and to have a say over impressive welfare budgets" (Manow 2001b: 117). In addition, though Manow does not stress it, these developments meant that craft unions could not use their friendly benefits in support of trade union goals, as was the case in Britain.

[18] See especially Boch (1985). In the case of the Solingen cutlery workers, the *Fachverein* was itself the direct descendent of the masters guild. The merchants who organized the decentralized production of specialty cutlery actively supported the power of the *Fachverein* to co-manage the market in skilled labor on which production entirely depended.

Beyond blocking unions from pursuing strategies aimed at craft control, the operation of the Handwerk training system and the survival of apprenticeship generally produced feedback effects that were important in shaping union orientations toward skill and skill formation. Certainly in the early industrial period, the vast majority of skilled factory workers were recruited directly from the artisanal sector (Kocka 1986a: 323–44; Lenger 1988: 160–2; Adelmann 1979: 19), and Handwerk continued to train large numbers of workers throughout the late nineteenth and into the twentieth century. Handwerk firms mostly had no intention of keeping the apprentices on after their training was complete, cycling them in and out to keep costs low, taking on new apprentices rather than hiring the journeymen they had just trained. This pattern is quite different from the practices of the large firms in Germany in the late nineteenth and early twentieth centuries, which mostly trained workers that they intended to continue to employ. By contrast, the workers trained in Germany's handicraft sector mostly left that sector, seeking and finding jobs in industry, and also therefore often finding their way into social democratic unions.

The result – both of the role of the handicraft sector in supplying skills to industry and of the survival of meaningful apprenticeship more generally – was that significant numbers of the industrial workers that unions wound up organizing (especially in the pre-World War I period, when the unions were still so dominated by skilled workers) had received their skill credentials in the context of the apprentice system. Schönhoven notes that in 1913, 80% of the DMV's membership consisted of skilled workers who had served an apprenticeship (*gelernte Berufsarbeiter*) (Schönhoven 1979: 411).[19] At the level of leadership as well, the early DMV was composed of "a group of men who all came from apprenticed trades" *(aus gelernten Berufen)* (Domansky-Davidsohn 1981: 30). The point here is to underline the important feedback effects generated by the apprenticeship system in general and the handicraft system in particular. Germany's early social democratic unions contained very significant numbers of skilled workers who had a personal investment in the apprenticeship system, a system through which they themselves had passed and which had conferred their credentials. In

[19] See also Domansky-Davidsohn, who notes that despite an increase in membership among unskilled and semi-skilled workers around 1905, "skilled workers steeped in the handicraft tradition and those trained in industrial trades still set the tone" (Domansky-Davidsohn 1981: 32).

light of this, it is understandable how, despite initial opposition, the unions in a relatively short time came to define their interests not in terms of dismantling apprenticeship, but rather in controlling or co-managing the system of firm-based training that it represented.

Related to this and especially after 1897, unions like the metalworkers (where apprenticed workers figured so prominently) must have recognized the value of the kinds of skill certification functions that the handicraft model represented, not least because certification provided their members with a non-firm-specific way of documenting their skills in the labor market as a whole. It simply mattered a great deal that in Germany not all training took place within the context of large firms seeking to cultivate a loyal core of skilled workers for their own use. From early on German workers benefited from a system of skill certification (allowing them to document their skills) separate from both unions and from large industrial firms. This meant that (as in Britain) labor's strength could be premised substantially on skill, but (unlike Britain) without skill formation itself being contested across the class divide (for example, with unions trying to limit apprenticeship in order to control the supply of skills). Thus, when German unions entered the debates on skill formation (during Weimar in a limited way, later as full participants in the vocational education system) they framed their goals in terms of increasing the availability of training opportunities (rather than regulating the quantity of skills in the economy), and in democratizing and co-managing the system of in-plant training (rather than demolishing it). This is what made Germany's industrial unions powerful potential *allies* of those segments of industry that had their own reasons for wanting to break into the system of skill formation that had been created for and was being monopolized by these small employer master craftsmen.

Implications for Industry

For industry, the implications of the consolidation of a Handwerk-based system for skill formation were no less momentous. In the first place, it meant that industrial firms could rely on a relatively steady stream of certified skilled workers from the artisanal sector. The dependence of German manufacturing firms on Handwerk-based skills was virtually absolute until at least the 1880s (Tollkühn 1926: 4–5; von Behr 1981: 44–5) and diminished only very slowly in subsequent decades. In 1907, 46.5% of all youth in training were still in the smallest artisanal workshops (under five workers)

(Muth 1985: 36).[20] As late as 1925 training was still concentrated in the small firm sector. A national business census in that year showed that 55% of all apprentices were being trained in Handwerk firms, as against 45% in industry (Schütte 1992: 65).[21] In short, many industrial firms in the early industrial period in Germany were able to draw substantially on workers trained in the artisanal sector to cover their skill needs.

Handwerk firms provided a crucial collective good but they too benefited since many of them depended on apprentices as a source of cheap productive labor.[22] Traditionally, firms received a fee from the apprentice, and the handicraft sector lagged behind industry by decades in moving to offer apprentices any stipend at all (Schütte 1992: 137). In small artisanal firms, an extra pair of hands that could be flexibly deployed as needed could make a big difference in terms of overall output, and the training itself could be accomplished mostly during lulls in production (Hansen 1997).[23] Once the apprenticeship was complete, master artisans may well have been perfectly happy to see their freshly trained apprentices disappear (as journeymen) into

[20] Dehen (1928: 25) provides different figures but the message is the same. He notes that in Prussia (excluding the areas of decentralized specialty production described above), in the years before 1871, only 375 apprentices received their training in factories. In 1881, out of 14,616 skilled industrial workers, over eight thousand had received their training in the handicraft sector. In 1891, out of about twenty-seven thousand skilled industrial workers, about one-half had been trained in the handicraft sector. In 1901, it was still well over one-third (approximately fifteen thousand out of a total of about thirty-five thousand).

[21] It must be borne in mind, however, that the line between industrial firms and Handwerk firms is and especially was somewhat fluid. Many industrial firms "grew out" of handicraft firms. To this day, however, Handwerk is still a major training sector (see Wagner 1997: 23; also Streeck 1992b).

[22] The self-interested motives of the Handwerker in apprentices-as-employees is evidenced in the widespread exploitation of apprentices during the Great Depression mentioned above (Muth 1985: 18; Tollkühn 1926: 9–12; Volkov 1978: 73). For this reason, too, some segments of the artisanate resisted the expansion of compulsory continuation schools that required them to release apprentices during working hours for supplementary classroom-based training (Linton 1991: 90–3).

[23] Figures on the net costs of training for the period under analysis here are not available. A recent study shows, however, that even today (when apprentice wages are negotiated by unions as a percent of skilled workers' wages) the net costs of taking apprentices (gross cost of training minus productive output of the trainee) is much smaller for Handwerk firms, where training takes place in the context of production, than for industrial firms (where training is more likely to take place in workshops). Moreover (again, for the 1990s), the variable net cost (variable cost minus fixed costs) was in fact negative for 20% of trainees in industry and for 30% of trainees in the craft sector, which is to say that the contribution of apprentices to production outweighed entirely the cost of training them (Wagner 1999: 44).

large industrial firms; better this than that they set up shop independently and in more direct competition with their erstwhile masters.

Virtually the only complaints against this system before the turn of the century came from Germany's large machine firms – companies such as Maschinenfabrik Augsburg Nürnberg (M.A.N.), Ludwig Loewe and Company, Borsig, and Koenig & Bauer. Like everyone else, these firms benefited from the skills generated by the artisanal sector and they continued to draw on this source to address their skill needs well into the twentieth century. Beginning in the 1890s, however, these large firms had begun to complain that they were pushing up against the limits of the skills provided by the Handwerk sector. First, Handwerk could not produce skilled workers fast enough to keep pace with the needs of this industry, which was expanding exponentially at the turn of the century, and around 1900 overtook all other sectors to become the single biggest employer of post-school-age males.[24] Second, these large firms complained that workers trained in the artisanal sector did not arrive in the factory fully competent in the new technologies being introduced at an accelerated pace in this period (Dehen 1928: 27–8; Tollkühn 1926: 14–16; von Behr 1981: 60–1).

Strategies of the Large Machine and Metalworking Companies

Responding to the perceived inadequacies of craft training these firms embarked on strategies aimed at internalizing skill formation at the firm level and incorporating training into complementary plant social policies and internal labor markets. In contrast to the traditional *Meisterlehre* model (on-the-job training by working alongside a master craftsman), Germany's large machine producers sought to "rationalize" training by instituting firm-based apprenticeship workshops. Apprentices would be trained in somewhat larger groups and, initially at least, separate from the production process (von Behr 1981; Eichberg 1965). M.A.N. established its training workshop in the 1890s, a move accompanied by a steep increase in the number of apprentices at the firm (von Behr 1981: 41, 103). The electrical equipment giant Schuckert & Co. established a training workshop in 1890, the machine producer Borsig set one up in 1898, and other large firms in the machine and electro-mechanical industries followed suit around the same time (von Behr 1981: 41 and passim; Eichberg 1965: 25–34). A number

[24] Together with metal processing, the machine industry accounted for nearly 40% of employment of 14- to 16-year-old (male) factory workers by 1912 (Linton 1991: 28).

of companies also instituted factory schools (*Werkschulen*) that would be responsible for the more theoretical aspects of training (see Dehen 1928: 264–70 for a complete listing, by year of founding up to 1927). Seventeen factory schools were opened in the years before 1900, most of them in companies located in more rural areas in northern and eastern Germany where the educational (and for that matter, industrial) infrastructure was weak (Dehen 1928: 12, 35). A further 55 were founded between 1900 and 1914, increasingly in larger urban centers (Dehen 1928: 65–83).[25]

A number of these firms epitomized the strategies that Herrigel characterizes as "autarkic," designing plant-based training programs to address the specific skills the company needed, and linking these to other plant-based social programs and benefits. The idea was to cultivate an elite core of skilled workers fully versed in the firm's production system and loyal to the company (Dehen 1928: 15–16, 75–7). Especially in the early years, those workers who received firm-sponsored training were explicitly being groomed for leading positions within the firm (von Behr 1981: 188). Heidrun Homburg notes the establishment of company-based and employer-dominated ("yellow") unions in key machine firms including Siemens, Eckert, Loewe, and M.A.N., all of them also leaders in plant-based training (Homburg 1982: 226–8). These companies provided worker housing, established firm-based sickness insurance, improved working conditions, and pursued a policy of recruiting among the families of current workers (von Behr 1981: 93–4; Rupieper 1982: 85).[26] As Anton von Rieppel, the head of M.A.N., put it, in-house training created a "connection between the workers and the plant management . . . so that the workers did not want to leave" (quoted in Ebert 1984: 221, also 166; see also Herrigel 1996b: 105). In short, Germany's large machine producers sought to internalize skill formation and incorporate training into a broader segmentalist production strategy based on labor cooptation and company paternalism.

[25] Of the 145 factory schools founded by the time of Dehen's (1928) study, almost a third (47) were in the machine, tool, and auto industries (Dehen 1928: 7). Writing two years later, the director of the State Technical College for the Iron and Steel Goods Industry in Schmalkalden, Hans Kellner, noted that among the members of the Berlin Association of Metal Employers (*Verband Berliner Metallindustrieller*), ten companies had *Werkschulen* that trained large numbers of apprentices. These included AEG, Bergmann, Borsig, L. Loewe, Mix + Genest, Siemens-Schuckert, Siemens-Halske, Knorrbremse, Stock + Co., and Fritz Werner AG (Kellner 1930: 14).

[26] See also the discussion of company welfare schemes of Krupp, Zeiss, and other companies in Lee (1978: 462–3).

These firms were annoyed, however, by their inability to *certify* the skills their training conferred. After 1897 the only way to become certified as a "skilled worker" in Germany was through the Handwerk chambers (see especially Hansen 1997: 380–91 on the importance of certification). There existed no similar authority or officially recognized framework to certify *industrial* training, which became a source of irritation for those firms engaged in such training. Already in 1902, the association of Berlin Metal Industrialists had sought (unsuccessfully) official recognition and certification for industrial apprenticeship in Berlin, and accreditation for the training workshops of that city's premier industrial training firms – AEG, Borsig, Loewe, and others (Hansen 1997: 510–11).

In the ensuing years the issue of certification and skill testing became an issue of some contention between industry and Handwerk (Schütte 1992: 17–19). In 1907 Handwerk conducted a survey to document industry's heavy reliance on handicraft training as a source of skills, and used this to support a demand that all firms that used artisan-trained apprentices be required to contribute to the costs of such training and to maintaining the handicraft chambers (Schütte 1992: 18; Muth 1985: 35–6). In this period as well, artisans were (still) seeking legislation that would further upgrade and protect the standing of those who had earned "master" status within the handicraft system (Volkov 1978: 143).[27]

Firms like M.A.N. found it preposterous that their own training – more systematic by far than that of the traditional artisanal sector – was not recognized and that they were being asked to contribute to the Handwerk-based system to boot. As they saw it, the existing system of Handwerk-based certification privileged and acknowledged inferior training and perversely supported a system of skill formation they considered outdated. Managers of these firms pointed to the inadequacy of Handwerk training to meet their skill needs and thus the need for a separate system of testing and certification for industry (von Rieppel 1912: 9). They denounced Handwerk's demands for industry to contribute more to its (Handwerk's) system, pointing out that Handwerk training was in fact inadequate to the needs of industry. They went to some lengths to refute the claims of the handicraft sector by

[27] In 1908 artisans got a reduced version of their demands when the government instituted the so-called *kleiner Befähigungsnachweis* which stipulated that only certified master craftsmen (that is, with master certification through the handicraft chambers) could train apprentices (Hansen 1997: 506; Kaiser and Loddenkemper 1980: 12; see also Schütte 1992: 19–20).

documenting industry's increasing self-reliance when it came to training (see, for example, von Rieppel 1912).

The issue of jurisdiction over skill certification and testing generated an important and ongoing contest between handicraft masters and large machine firms. For handicraft firms, a monopoly on skill certification functions was probably most important for enabling competition with larger firms for the most promising young apprentices. In some cases, apprentices (but especially their parents) may have preferred a Handwerk apprenticeship because certification itself had value, opening up avenues that (uncertified) industrial training did not. Hansen emphasizes this point especially: "Thanks to the effects of the Handicraft Law, [handicraft shops] were put in a position to offer their apprentices precisely what industrial firms could not: publicly acknowledged certificates, essential to documenting their training and skills" (Hansen 1997: 512; see also Schütte 1992: 84). Most important, certification was necessary for attaining independent master status (which in turn conferred the right to take apprentices) (Frölich 1919: 108–9). Maintaining a monopoly on admittance to master status was an advantage in competing for bright young workers, and – along with longstanding concerns about overstocking particular trades – was also an important reason why Handwerk defended the special status of the journeyman's examination, a test it alone administered and that was the sole route for a worker to be admitted to the master examination (Pätzold 1989: 275).

Although competition for bright young apprentices may have been an issue for the large machine companies, other factors probably played a larger role.[28] In particular, firms like these, which were pursuing policies based on internal labor markets, had a very strong interest in both lowering the cost of pursuing segmentalist policies aimed at recruiting and retaining top

[28] These firms, as we have seen, were often in a position to offer prospective apprentices other kinds of incentives, including longer term employment prospects – since (in sharp contrast to these companies) Handwerk firms typically did not intend to keep trainees once they had completed their apprenticeships. Hansen has argued that the main value of certification was to underwrite the mutual commitment between apprentices and training firms for the duration of the training contract, to make sure the firm could recoup its training costs through the apprentices' contribution to production. This was certainly one of the main functions performed by certification in the handicraft sector. Unlike in the handicraft sector, however, training in the machine companies was accomplished in workshops where apprentices were not contributing to production, so the "payback" issue was not so salient as the issue of nurturing internal labor markets. I thank an anonymous reviewer for emphasizing the different rationale for larger firms in pursuing certification and testing rights.

skilled workers and in gaining control over the content and definition of skills. As pointed out above, these firms found Handwerk training utterly insufficient. When they recruited from this sector they found they had to invest considerable resources in retraining these workers in the specific skills they needed. Thus, when firms like M.A.N. and Siemens made arrangements with their local craft chambers to examine and certify their apprentices (Hansen 1997: 273–4), these ad hoc arrangements proved unstable, often leading to conflicts over the composition of the examination boards and the types of skills to be tested (Fürer 1927: 32–3; Botsch 1933: 7–8; Mack 1927: 105–7; Kopsch 1928: 14; Frölich 1919: 109–10). M.A.N., for example, had a deal with the local handicraft chamber, but continued to complain that this arrangement was inadequate (Lippart 1919: 7).[29]

Despite the somewhat different motives, contemporary accounts make it very clear that Germany's large machine firms understood the advantages of testing and certification, and perceived their inability to preside over these services as a disadvantage (Frölich 1919; DATSCH 1912: 99, 303; von Rieppel 1912: 9; Lippart 1919: 5–7; Wilden 1926: 1–2; Gesamtverband Deutscher Metallindustrieller 1934: 18–19). As a consequence, large industrial firms that depended heavily on skills organized among themselves to demand the creation of a *parallel* system for promoting and certifying industrial training under the collective control of the Industry and Trade Chambers (and endowed with powers equal to those of the Handicraft Chambers). An important early step in the development of industrial training was undertaken in 1908, with the founding of the German Committee for Technical Education (*Deutscher Ausschuß für Technisches Schulwesen*, or DATSCH). Jointly sponsored by the Association of German Engineers (*Verein Deutscher Ingenieure*, VDI) and the Association of German Machine-Building Firms (*Verband Deutscher Maschinenbauanstalten*, VDMA), the committee demanded from the outset separate testing and certification powers (emphasized, for example, as "urgently desired" in the guidelines the organization set forth for apprentice training; see DATSCH 1912: 99, 303).

DATSCH's broader official goal was to "heighten interest in the promotion of a well educated, skilled labor force" (Abel 1963: 41; Tollkühn

[29] Although there was a gradual expansion of industry examinations under the auspices of employer associations and the chambers of industry and commerce (IHK) in the twenties, these exams were entirely voluntary and had no legal foundation (Kaiser and Loddenkemper 1980: 13).

1926: 38–9).[30] Although the organization made claims to speak on behalf of industry as a whole, in fact its activities and policies in the early years of its existence reflected the interests of the large machine companies who dominated the VDMA in the prewar period. Anton von Rieppel, head of M.A.N., was especially active and served as the organization's first president. By founding DATSCH these companies hoped to increase awareness of the problem of skill formation in industry – partly to garner broader support for their own training efforts but also to spark greater interest on the part of youth in industrial training.[31] Despite the poaching problems that certification would bring (through increased transparency; see Chapter 1), machine producers had a special interest in a large pool of portable skills. Von Rieppel himself emphasized that providing the necessary mechanics, turners, and fitters was part of the package of services that machine makers needed to offer their customers who were not in a position to provide for their own skill needs in this regard (von Rieppel 1912: 6). For firms like his, enhanced organization and joint certification powers would have looked very attractive. They would have established floors and standards for particular skills, as well as offered mechanisms for monitoring training in other companies.

DATSCH's founding corresponded with the onset of rather intense skill shortages in Germany in 1907–08, a situation that hit these firms particularly hard. There is evidence that poaching became an especially serious problem in urban centers such as Berlin, where several large machine companies – among them, A.E.G., Borsig, Loewe, and Eckert – had factories. Companies located in more rural areas were overall less affected since they dominated the local labor market and coupled their training programs with an attractive package of benefits (Dehen 1928: 33). But as labor markets grew tighter, even these firms felt the sting as workers were drawn to higher wages in other regions (Hansen 1997: 511). In this context, DATSCH provided a forum though which these companies sought to coordinate among themselves the management of intensified competition and to discourage firms from cutting back on training, which would only make the problem worse. For example, in 1911, the organization called on all member firms to maintain a commitment to train a number of apprentices equivalent to

[30] See also *DATSCH Abhandlungen* (I 1910: 2–5) on the founding of the organization.

[31] One of the first moves (1909) initiated by von Rieppel was a survey of 18 large machine companies regarding their skill needs and their experiences with handicraft-trained apprentices (Dehen 1928: 27).

10 to 15% of their total workforce (Dehen 1928: 168), though it is not clear how successful this initiative was.

Germany's large machine companies had additional incentives to organize having to do with the developments in the spread of continuation trade schooling for youths over the age of 14. As mentioned above, Germany was, by international standards, a pioneer in developing public trade schools, which in some states had been made compulsory as early as the 1830s. Moreover, in 1891, an Imperial Industrial Law (later amended in 1900) obliged employers to grant their apprentices (and other workers under 18 years of age) time off as necessary to attend continuation schools, in accordance with regulations set down by local authorities (Sadler 1908a: 517; Education 1909a: 147, 156).[32] Over the 1890s and into the first years of the twentieth century, the number of states requiring youth to attend such schools increased so that, by 1908, a large majority of the youth population was covered.[33]

At the turn of the century, questions about compulsion, state financing, and the content of training in continuation schools were subjects of ongoing debate in many regions (notably and perhaps most consequentially, in Prussia). These were issues in which Germany's large, skill-intensive firms had clear and definite interests.[34] In Prussia, small scale artisans were very much opposed to compulsion, and especially compulsory attendance during working hours, as this would make training more expensive for them.[35] Larger firms benefited much more from compulsory attendance in public trade schools, since – especially if they could influence the content – it amounted to a direct subsidy for efforts already underway. The content of continuation schooling was contested, notoriously in Prussia between the Ministry of Education (which sought a more ideological content, that is, as

[32] Backed by sanctions and the threat of fines, but also by possible imprisonment if employers failed to fulfill their obligations (Education 1909a: 147, 156). The Industrial Code of 1869 had given local governments the power to determine local requirements with respect to continuation schooling.

[33] Those states in which attendance at continuation school was still entirely voluntary in 1908 (Hamburg, Lübeck, Reuss, and Schaumburg-Lippe) contained less than 2% of the population (Sadler 1908b: 513–17). Other states mandated it, and still others allowed local authorities to mandate it.

[34] On these debates see especially Hansen (1997: 514–35), on which I draw here.

[35] And if legislation was adopted making attendance compulsory, there was the question of when such classes should be held – also contentious, as Handwerk preferred solutions outside regular working hours. In 1904 the Ministry of Industry and Commerce issued a decree that strongly discouraged holding these classes on Sunday or in the evenings.

a vehicle for socializing youth against social democracy) and the Ministry of Trade (which, under the influence of bureaucrats looking at the southwestern model, favored more technical content and explicit links to the firms in the local economy). The latter prevailed in these conflicts. Although Prussia continued to lag behind the southwest in terms of the quality and the number of trade-oriented continuation schools, the period between 1885 and 1904 saw a significant rise in both the number of schools and attendance at them.[36]

Thus, Germany's large machine companies were expanding their own independent training efforts at exactly the same time that these debates were unfolding, and DATSCH became a vehicle through which they could organize their lobbying efforts. Among other things, companies that had founded factory schools worked with local authorities to get their schools accredited or to shape the curricula of local continuation schools in ways that served their purposes.[37] Through DATSCH, firms lobbied for increased participation by the state to help bear the costs of training, with the argument that since youth training was a social good, the costs should be borne by society as a whole. Premier industrial training firms sought to influence the curricula of public continuation schools by donating models, work plans, work pieces, and materials (Dehen 1928: 80–2). Dehen notes a drop in factory school foundings after 1908 and concludes that this was no coincidence but rather part of a strategy in which these firms were looking for ways to offload some of their training costs onto the state.[38]

We can sum up developments in vocational training to the eve of World War I. The Handwerk-based system of skill formation that came out of the Imperial period began to build some of the scaffolding on which Germany's system of vocational education and training would ultimately be built. It did so first by encouraging the development of unions whose strength derived from organizing skilled workers but which were not wedded to strategies

[36] Hansen's figures indicate that between 1885 and 1904 the number of trade and continuation schools in Prussia rose from 715 to 2,065, and between 1899 and 1904, attendance grew from 83,772 to 175,100 (Hansen 1997: 520). State support was explicitly linked to the adoption of local legislation that made continuation school obligatory for youth up to the age of 18.

[37] Greinert argues generally (also for the Weimar period) that the firms with company schools were always torn between the desire for control and the desire to off-load some of the costs of training onto the state (Greinert 1994: 49). Pätzold notes that in the 1920s many of the large firms with factory schools got their facilities to count as substitutes for the public trade schools (Pätzold 1989: 279).

[38] Between 1910 and 1917 only five such schools were founded (Dehen 1928: 158).

based on limiting the supply of skills. And second, the existence of such a system pushed those industries that were heavily dependent on skills toward strategies based on securing advantage within the logic of the system. The handicraft system was a crucial focal point for the demands of Germany's large machine companies, in two senses. First, it was the foil against which, through DATSCH, they railed in the prewar period. But second, the handicraft system of coordinated training and self-regulation served as a model for industry. Industrial firms engaged in training thus spent the prewar years seeking certification for their trainees through the handicraft chambers, at the same time working collectively to secure separate and parallel certification powers.

Political Coalitions and the Evolution of the System

The Weimar period is less important for what was actually accomplished in terms of formal (legislative) innovation in the area of apprenticeship training for industry than for what was achieved on a voluntary (albeit well organized) basis. These accomplishments laid the political and technical foundations for the system that emerged later. Neither of the two key features of the contemporary German system – a national system for certifying industrial (in addition to artisanal) skills and full union participation in the oversight of plant-based training – was consolidated in the Weimar years. However, most of the groundwork for both was laid in this period.

In the first years of the Weimar Republic, the reform of apprenticeship training was very much on the agenda. War casualties had created an acute shortage of skilled workers alongside a severe shortage of apprenticeship slots for youth (Pätzold 1989: 271–2). The immediate postwar period also revealed growing abuses of apprenticeship training by master artisans in some regions, brought on by the economic crisis after 1918 (Pätzold 1989: 265). Traditional Handwerk firms increasingly relied on apprentices as a source of inexpensive productive labor, and the effectiveness of monitoring by the *Handwerkskammer* was only as good as the willingness of the chambers to punish members who abused their training privileges. These and other problems revealed the fragility of the Handwerk-based system and caught the attention of reform minded bureaucrats, skill-dependent industrialists, and labor leaders who had their own reasons for questioning the sustainability of the old system.

In addition, the years of inflation threw even the producers of Germany's decentralized industrial districts into turmoil. These regions were plunged into intense crisis that unleashed "ruinous competition" in product markets and stretched previous forms of regional collaboration to the breaking point (Herrigel 1996b: 58–66). In this context, these producers asserted their interests and sought solutions to their collective dilemmas through the Association of German Machine Builders (VDMA). With the assistance of the state this organization became a crucial vehicle for facilitating coordination among small- and medium-sized producers in the machine industries in a range of areas including, but not limited to, the area of skills.

As we will see in Chapter 3, training in Britain had by this time deteriorated substantially in the context of fierce competitive struggles among firms and between employers and unions. What prevented training in Germany from suffering a similar fate was not just the oversight rights of the Handwerk chambers, but above all, actions undertaken by unions and the VDMA and DATSCH which attracted the attention of state bureaucrats and kept the reform of vocational training on the agenda. Thus, despite the failure of a coalition for reform to pass legislation in this area in the Weimar years, these organizations presided over important steps forward in rendering plant-based training more systematic and uniform. The efforts of the coalition for reform were vigorously denounced by the artisanal sector. The pressures exerted by reformers, however, enhanced the quality of training, not least by keeping Handwerk-based training in the spotlight and encouraging comparisons of training practices in Handwerk firms with the increasingly systematic training programs developing on a voluntary but collective basis in industry. The *Handwerkskammer* opposed state reform of vocational training, but they could scarcely defend their monopoly to certify skills if they allowed training standards in handicraft firms to slide.

During the war the unions had taken up the issue of vocational training in internal discussions, and they had also floated ideas for reform that in at least certain industrial circles were seen as "quite reasonable" (quoted in Ebert 1984: 264; see also Schütte 1992: 28). In some industries and regions, employers and unions demonstrated a great willingness to work together on this matter (for example, Beil 1921: 8). For example in woodworking, the union and the employers' association convened a joint conference in 1916 and proposed a four-point program for reform that recognized broad participatory rights for labor (Schütte 1992: 31).[39] Within the metalworking industry, similar willingness to collaborate across the class divide was

[39] And there was a similar agreement in 1920 in the book printing industry (Ebert 1984: 270).

evident on a regional level. In Chemnitz, for example, the regional employers association and the local union reached an agreement in 1919 on the regulation of apprenticeship (Ebert 1984: 270).

At the national level, the *Zentralarbeitsgemeinschaft*, or ZAG – formed by organized labor and employers to "institutionalize and organize future collaboration in the formulation of joint economic and social policies" (Feldman and Nocken 1975: 313) – also took up the issue of vocational education reform. By 1921, the social policy committee of the ZAG had produced a set of guidelines for future legislation in this area (Muth 1985: 446–7). These proposals anticipated a uniform framework for the regulation of training, covering both industry and Handwerk. Rather than having the handicraft chambers in charge, the guidelines called for the creation of oversight committees composed of equal numbers of representatives of employers and workers. Such committees were to be endowed with the power to regulate firm-based training (including granting and revoking training privileges) as well as to oversee and administer the examination and certification process for skilled industrial workers. What unions would have gotten out of this was equal representation on the oversight boards, in exchange for which they were prepared to define the apprenticeship contract as involving an educational rather than an employment relationship (and therefore not a subject for collective bargaining).[40] Industry, for its part, would have achieved the independent certification authority that at least the large machine and metalworking companies had long sought (Ebert 1984: 276; Vereinigung der Deutschen Arbeitergeberverbände 1922: 142–3).[41]

Reforms along these lines never materialized, however, and to understand why we need to take a brief look at the interests of the relevant actors and how these interests changed in response to the shifting political and economic climate in Germany in the 1920s. Simplifying greatly, we might characterize the politics of skills during the Weimar Republic in terms of

[40] The issue of whether an apprenticeship contract was an educational contract or an employment contract was the subject of ongoing controversy during the Weimar years. Employers, but especially artisans, were adamant that it be considered an educational contract, for among other things this would allow them to forbid apprentices from taking part in union events (see Stratmann 1990: Chapter 3; Kaps 1930).

[41] See also the discussion of the ZAG guidelines at a conference convened by DATSCH in Cassel in 1921 (especially Beil 1921), and the comment by Dr. Kühne, head of ZAG's social policy committee, who notes with satisfaction the degree of overlap between his committee's proposals and the views of DATSCH (DATSCH 1921: 30).

the early failure of a coalition for the reform of apprenticeship training (including separate industrial certification and with union participation) premised on a core alliance between the machine industry and newly incorporated unions (and with the support of key ministries), and the growing strength of an alternative coalition in defense of employer self-regulation and *against* union participation (with heavy industry and the Handwerk sector at the center).

Organized Labor's Position in the Debates of the 1920s

The most important new voice in the debate on apprenticeship training in the post-World War I period was that of Germany's unions, which now enjoyed full legal recognition. Already in 1919 the unions had called for reforms that involved stripping the artisanal sector of its monopoly (long a goal of the machine industry as we have seen) and for full union participation in overseeing and administering plant-based skill formation.[42] For our purposes the most important point in the unions' role is how they framed their goals in this area. Above all, unions sought to break the artisanal chambers' control over apprenticeship training and replace this with a more "democratic" structure. In line with other demands raised by the ZAG, the unions proposed the creation of oversight committees at the national and regional levels. In the union plan, such committees would be composed of an equal number of representatives of unions and employers (chaired by a neutral public official), and would administer and oversee general legislative regulations in this area (Hoffmann 1962: 96; Schütte 1992: 31–2).

In 1919 the unions called for comprehensive legislation on the issue of vocational training, to replace the system of de facto control through the HWK. In addition to demanding a complete overhaul in the apparatus for overseeing the apprentice system, German unions advocated a massive expansion of such training, a comprehensive guarantee of training to all youth. As Heinrich Abel (1963: 48) notes, what is most interesting is that German unions had no trouble with the idea of firm-based training, but in fact called for more firms to do more of it (see also Herber 1930: 46–7; and

[42] These proposals, though not completely uncontroversial, easily carried the day at the 1919 congress of the central trade union confederation in Nürnberg (Hoffmann 1962: 95–7; also Schütte 1992: 31–3; Ebert 1984: 262). Ebert notes that already in 1918 the unions expressed regret for their relative neglect of the training issue in the past.

especially Kopsch 1928: 43).[43] This stands in contrast to the position of socialist unions in other countries, such as Sweden, who preferred school-based vocational education and were more skeptical of firm-based training as inherently biased toward employer interests (Olofsson 2001; Crouch, Finegold, and Sako 1999: 119). The demands of the German unions in this period are also strikingly different from those of British unions. There, skilled unions were locked in pitched battles, both with employers over deskilling and with other unions over the right to perform certain operations (demarcation disputes). In Germany, the triumph of industrial unions, along with the institutionalization of unitary plant-based representation (in the works council legislation of 1919), largely eliminated the institutional basis for these kinds of disputes.[44]

Many, though not all, of German labor's preferences were accommodated in the guidelines proposed by ZAG's social policy committee. The issue of a comprehensive commitment to training for all youth and the idea of requiring firms that employed skilled workers but did not train apprentices to contribute to the costs of apprenticeship (the whole notion of vocational training as a public duty that implied heavy state oversight and union involvement) were vigorously and successfully opposed by business (Seubert 1977: 71–3; Schütte 1992: 31–2 for union demands). However, the social policy committee did envision a role for organized labor in the oversight of plant-based apprenticeship training, though controversies lingered about whether an entirely new institutional structure was needed (as labor argued) or whether the system ought to be run through existing institutions (specifically the industry and trade chambers, as representatives of industry advocated) (Ebert 1984: 276; DATSCH 1921: 7–34; Stratmann 1990: 40). The more the revolutionary situation that characterized the early Weimar years receded, however, the more the legislative proposals moved

[43] As put in the resolution adopted at the Nürnberg congress, "Theory without practice offers only limited training potential" (Hoffmann 1962: 97); for the union demands, see also Ebert (1984: 269). The unions also favored state support for small- and medium-sized firms to share training facilities (Schütte 1992: 32; Abel 1963: 48).

[44] Kopsch (Kopsch 1928: 75–89) relates the reasons of the free unions for their strongly supportive position, despite the apparent dangers of promoting trade-based identities that could clash with overarching union goals. Among the reasons he cites are the positive effects of training on workers' wages (noting the possibility that unskilled workers could exert downward pressure on wages and/or pose problems in the conduct of strikes), and the positive effect of training on discipline within the union (including as a bulwark against communist influence which was especially strong among unskilled workers at that time).

away from the union's demand for parity representation at the national level (Ebert 1984: 270).

Nonetheless, union collective bargaining policy and evolving industrial relations institutions proved crucial to the evolution of skill formation in industry during the Weimar years. First, sectoral bargaining drove a significant narrowing of wage differentials between skilled and unskilled workers in the immediate post-World War I years.[45] An initial, particularly sharp reduction in wage differentials occurred between 1919 and 1921, by which time unskilled wages in several industries had risen to 85 to 95% of skilled wages (Mosher 2001: graphs 6–5a, 6–5b, 6–5c, 256–8). The trend toward wage compression was partially reversed in the currency stabilization (after 1924), but even in this and the subsequent recovery period, skill differentials remained below their prewar levels. Jim Mosher has traced these effects to three new features of the political–economic context in the Weimar period. First and most important, business finally (grudgingly) accepted collective bargaining with the unions. In the revolutionary situation of the first postwar years this appeared to them the lesser of two evils. Mosher notes that whereas in 1913 only 20% of the German workforce was covered by collective bargaining, by 1924 this figure had increased to 61.2% (Mosher 2001: 280). Second, the Weimar years saw the culmination of the shift from skill-based unions to industrial unions, a process accelerated and in a way completed by state policy that recognized the industrial unions as the main representatives of the working class and shielded them from breakaway craft unions (Mosher 2001: 304–9). Third, there was a shift in the balance of power *within* the unions themselves, as a massive influx of unskilled workers into the unions completely offset the previous predominance of skilled workers (Mosher 2001: 287).

This last point bears emphasis. As Mosher notes (Mosher 2001: 286–7), in 1914 the German metalworkers union overwhelmingly organized skilled workers (only 27% of the members of this industrial union were semi- or unskilled workers). In addition, the strategies of the union continued to reflect the dominance of skilled workers in important ways. The Stinnes-Legien Agreement of 1919 provided a huge boon for union organization – membership jumped from 1.7 million in 1916 to 10.7 million by 1919, most of the new recruits coming from the ranks of unskilled workers. The proportion of skilled workers in the key metalworking union (DMV) dropped from 73% of total membership in 1913 to 59.4% in 1919. Thus, by very

[45] This discussion draws on Mosher (Mosher 2001: 239–44).

early on in the Weimar Republic, skilled workers no longer commanded such an overwhelming majority within the union (Mosher 2001: 286–7).

Conflicts in 1919 in both Berlin and Bavaria (home to a large number of the machine companies I have been discussing, including AEG, Borsig, Loewe, L. Schwartzkopf, H. F. Eckert, Siemens-Schuckert, and M.A.N.) were fought over demands by the metalworkers union to reduce the number of separate wage groups. In the Berlin conflict, for example, the union wanted just three categories – skilled, semi-skilled, and unskilled workers) and lower skill differentials (unskilled workers to receive 86% of a skilled worker's wage). Employers (and although there is no direct evidence of this, perhaps especially those pursuing policies aimed at stabilizing internal labor markets and career ladders for individual workers) wanted to maintain a larger number of wage groups (six, though it should be noted that this was substantially down from the prewar norm of hundreds of separate trades-based classifications) and overall higher differentials (unskilled workers to receive 71% of a skilled wage).[46] In Berlin a compromise was hammered out in arbitration, but across Germany, employers were making some (in comparative perspective) rather substantial compromises on these issues with labor, partly out of fear that intransigence would drive workers into the more radical communist or anarcho-syndicalist unions. Some employers recognized that stabilizing sectoral bargaining with the DMV also had the advantage of preventing bargaining fragmentation and resulting wage competition among firms in a period of relative skilled labor scarcity. In particular, the machine industry faced demands by a craft-based machinist union that sought a separate agreement for its members and machine firms were willing to work together with the DMV to prevent this (Mosher 2001: 306–8).

Skill differentials increased again somewhat after the currency stabilization (1924), a period when unions were weakened by higher unemployment and when the political shift to the right enhanced the role of state arbitrators who were sympathetic to employer demands for greater differentiation (Mosher 2001: 297–301). Skill differentials never returned to pre-World War I levels, however. Some wage compression survived an overall drop in union membership (in 1926, back to 5.9 million workers) despite the fact that losses were heaviest among unskilled workers (in metalworking, for example, the proportion of unskilled and semi-skilled workers fell back to 26.8 percent by 1929) (Mosher 2001: 301). Unions maintained a commitment to reducing skill differentials through these changes, in part

[46] The ultimate settlement in Berlin called for five categories and 76% (Mosher 2001: 292–3).

because union leaders viewed unskilled workers as a core constituency – and after the membership losses, essentially a constituency that had to be won back. In addition, skilled workers had few options in this system, since Weimar legislation and labor market institutions (including works councils) protected the position of the country's industrial unions and shielded them from competition from alternative craft-based organizations (Mosher 2001: 304–9).

The implications of developments in wage bargaining in Germany in the Weimar years for skill formation were significant. In Chapter 1 we saw how labor market imperfections and wage compression provide an inducement for firms to invest in training by allowing the company to capture some of the rents. Wage compression in this period rendered unskilled labor relatively expensive, while holding down the wages of skilled workers. These conditions provided incentives for firms to move up market and to invest in worker training. For the large firms, such training could become part of the "efficiency wage" they offered to attract the best new recruits (Schütte 1992: 137; Swenson 2002). More generally, training would have simply paid off more when skilled workers' wages were held below their marginal productivity (Acemoglu and Pischke 1998: 80–1). Meanwhile, high unemployment provided workers with continuing incentives to acquire training, as joblessness was much lower among skilled workers (Mack 1927: 2).[47] Poaching problems were also mitigated somewhat by loose labor markets for most of the Weimar years, whereas industry-wide bargaining reduced incentives for workers to engage in job hopping.

In short, conditions in the early Weimar years reduced disincentives for firms to engage in training while also providing incentives for youth to invest in skills. Apprentices also bore part of the costs, for as Table 2.1 shows, apprentice wages remained low relative to wages for unskilled youth.

If union wage policy contributed indirectly to maintaining an overall higher level of training, other aspects of union bargaining had a second, more direct impact on the character of that training. In 1919, unions' newly acquired collective bargaining rights were ambiguous on whether they extended to concluding agreements on the terms and conditions applied to apprentices. The extent to which the conditions of apprenticeship could be regulated through collective bargaining was a hotly contested issue

[47] Mack reports that the "latest" government statistics (presumably from 1926) indicated that 24% of unemployed were skilled workers or craftsmen, whereas 76% were unskilled workers (Mack 1927: 2).

Table 2.1. *Weekly wages (in Reichsmark, RM) for youth, by year of apprenticeship*

Year of app'ship	Youth with wage info	No wage (pct)	To 4RM	4–7RM	7–10RM	10–15RM	Over 15
First	44,091	3.0	49.6	36.2	8.2	2.3	0.7
Second	43,452	2.3	26.5	39.2	24.4	5.9	1.7
Third	32,718	2.3	13.1	33.4	29.9	16.4	4.9
Fourth	3,443	1.6	6.9	31.1	36.1	16.9	7.4
Complete	4,546	0.6	0.6	4.8	15.6	43.3	35.1
Unskilled	36,240	3.2	8.2	20.8	22.9	29.8	15.1
TOTAL	164,490	2.6	24.9	32.1	20.8	13.5	6.1

Source: Schütte 1992: 135.

throughout the Weimar years. Traditional artisanal firms were particularly adamant that the apprenticeship relationship be considered an educational not an employment relationship (Kaps 1930: especially 5, 16). Among other things, this allowed them to keep unions out of their affairs, and made it easier for them to continue to use apprentices as a source of flexible and cheap labor without being scrutinized by "outsiders." The issue was not decided formally and definitively until 1928 when – in the context of a case brought by the construction industry – the Labor Court (*Reichsarbeitsgericht*, or RAG) ruled that apprenticeship contracts could indeed be considered a type of employment contract (Kaps 1930: 10–11; Kipp 1990: 224; Stratmann 1990: 37–8).[48]

Even before this, however, where unions were strongest they concluded agreements that included provisions regulating some aspects of apprenticeship. Based on a survey of over three thousand collective bargains from 1922/23, Schütte shows that regulation of apprenticeship was most advanced in the metalworking and machine building industries, where almost 30% of apprentices were covered by contractual regulations at the regional or local level (Schütte 1992: 131). In 1923, 124 of 159 collective bargains negotiated by the DMV had stipulations that "fully regulated" apprenticeship; 35 that "partially regulated" it (Schütte 1992: 133).[49] According to DMV

[48] According to Molitor, court decisions during the 1920s rather consistently held that the apprentice relation was a work relationship (Molitor 1960: 13–16). This opened the door for regulation of apprentice pay and working conditions through collective bargaining in some sectors. However, in the absence of explicit legislation (the ZAG guidelines for vocational training discussed above never having been passed into law), the issue remained contested.

[49] In 1924, 45 of 62 agreements in metalworking regulated apprenticeship "fully"; 17 did so "partially" (Schütte 1992: 133).

statistics, the number of collective bargains that included some regulation of apprenticeship rose from 2.6% in 1920 to 45.7% in 1930 (ibid.). The number of apprentices covered by contractual provisions rose from 61,173 in 1925 to 87,237 by 1929 – which amounted to 66% of the apprentices in the areas covered by the DMV (ibid.). In general, then, it seems that despite ongoing legal ambiguities concerning their right to negotiate on these issues, unions in the Weimar period did win some influence, at least in key "pockets" of industry, over apprenticeship training.

The content of such collective bargains reveals that the interest of unions went beyond securing reasonable pay for apprentices, that to them "social-political aspects were at least as important" (Schütte 1992: 131). Thus, contractual provisions dealt quite centrally with the conditions of work and training, including provisions that limited the number of allowable apprentices, provided for oversight of training and vocational school attendance, laid out the rights and responsibilities of apprentices and firms, and established the length of apprenticeship (Schütte 1992: 132; Mack 1927: 22–4). Since these are all things that in the Handwerk sector would have been overseen by the chambers, union collective bargaining policies in some sense offered "an answer to the questions that had been left unanswered by the industrial code" (quote from Schütte 1992: 131; see also Mack 1927: 23; Kopsch 1928: 88). In addition, unions would have had a strong interest in ensuring that the skills taught by training firms were general rather than firm-specific (Culpepper 1999b: 4). General skills would enhance the market position of their members, but in addition, unions were extremely leery of employer efforts to tie workers to particular companies, part of their ongoing battle against company unionism in this period.

It should be noted, however, that collective bargaining did not produce anything like uniformity in terms of the conditions of apprentice training in industry. Regulation through these means was very spotty, and worked best in the regions that were heavily organized by the unions, for example, industrial centers such as Berlin. From the perspective of the union, regulation of apprenticeship through collective bargaining was mostly seen as a temporary necessity, until more comprehensive legislation could be passed (Schütte 1992: 140–1).

The Position of the Machine and Metalworking Industry

The machine and metalworking industries were in some ways labor's natural allies when it came to initiatives to reform apprenticeship. Large firms in the machine industry had their own reasons for wanting to break the artisanal chambers' monopoly on skill certification. Already in 1918, DATSCH (under M.A.N. Director Gottlieb Lippart) set out an eight-point reform program "to overcome Handwerk's hegemony" in this area through targeted cooperation with the unions (Schütte 1992: 29). DATSCH wanted to forestall direct state control of vocational training and preserve a system of self-administration through economic associations (Pätzold 1989: 273). However, as we saw above, skill-dependent industries like metalworking had longstanding troubles arranging for their apprentices to take exams and have their skills certified (Kopsch 1928: 14; Mack 1927: 105–7; Wilden 1926). "[F]or that reason industry had repeatedly and insistently petitioned the government to modify the legal guidelines pertaining to the apprentice's final examination in the Industrial Code so that they might apply not only to Handwerk but to industry as well" (Mack 1927: 105). Although Handwerk actively opposed the guidelines proposed by the ZAG, and other segments of industry ranged from indifferent to hostile, some members of DATSCH endorsed the proposals as a "worthwhile framework" for reform (Muth 1985: 448; Beil 1921: 8 and passim).

The position of the metalworking industry on the skill issue was rooted in the economic and political realities of the time. First of all, the war itself had brought about intense labor shortages, and heightened competition for skilled workers confounded the strategies of engineering firms attempting to nurture a stable and loyal core of skilled workers. This problem was most intense in Berlin where there was a significant concentration of engineering firms in close proximity to one another. During the war these companies had managed this competition with the assistance of the 1916 Auxiliary Service Law (*Hilfsdienstgesetz*, or HDG), which contained specific restrictions on the movement of skilled workers. But with the end of the hostilities these firms sought an alternative and perhaps more enduring solution.[50] Machine firms in more remote areas faced less intense poaching problems and overall were less enthusiastic about all forms of collective bargaining. Given the political climate, however, they too were willing to tolerate and engage in tactical cooperation with organized labor, not least to keep more radical

[50] As an indication of the poaching problems they faced, it is noteworthy that in the first postwar collective bargaining rounds with unions, in 1919, Berlin metalworking employers sought to impose maximum wage rates within individual wage groups (Mosher 2001: 292, citing *Metallarbeiter Zeitung* 37 (32) August 9, 1919: 125). The union rejected the idea of wage maxima, which it would have been hard put to enforce in any case.

working class currents at bay. Moreover, the formal institutionalization of collective bargaining and works councils rendered previous strategies premised on company paternalism and blatant anti-unionism untenable – or at least more difficult. As Mary Nolan points out, "yellow trade unions were outlawed, collective bargaining was legitimated, and protective legislation and social insurance were expanded, all of which made traditional patriarchal company social policy ineffective" (1994: 181–2). More generally, the shift toward the institutionalization of collective bargaining on a sectoral basis "led to some reorganization of the employers' associations so that the structure better matched the designated fourteen industries" (Mosher 2001: 306–7), which further facilitated coordination.

In addition, wage compression provided a boon to training in these firms, something they were already well set up to do, by introducing just the sorts of labor market imperfections that Acemoglu and Pischke describe (see Chapter 1). This could not have come at a better time, since the political and economic context rendered the skill needs of Germany's machine industry more demanding still. A stagnant domestic market and a tighter and more hostile international market (including the growing success of lower cost producers in the United States and boycotts of German goods by several countries) combined to push German machine producers further up-market, toward the production of more specialized and higher quality machines, intensifying their dependence on a highly skilled workforce (Dehen 1928: 169–70). Even as wages were compressed, training became something that firms could offer as a selective incentive to recruit young workers (or "sold" as insurance against unemployment). This helps to explain why the first round of wage compression (most intense in 1919–21 but continuing until 1924) was accompanied by a flurry of activity in founding new plant-based training schools (Dehen 1928: 158), as seen in Table 2.2. In some regions where legislation had been passed making attendance at vocational schools compulsory for apprentices, large firms were able to have their factory schools count as a substitute, which effectively provided them with a training subsidy (Pätzold 1989: 279; Mack 1927: 100; Kopsch 1928: 17).

In general, representatives of skill-dependent machine and metalworking firms were keen to preserve and expand high quality training in industry. For this reason, they were overall more willing than many other segments of industry to work with unions to achieve joint goals, and in cities like Berlin had achieved "close collaboration" with the unions across a range of training issues (quote from Kantorowicz 1930: 63; see also Beil

Table 2.2. *Number of Factory Schools (*Werkschulen*) founded during and after World War I*

1917–1918	7
1919	10
1920	8
1921	5
1922	4
1923	17
1924	2
1925	2
1926	5
1927	6
1928	3?

Source: Dehen 1928: 158.

1921: 8). Above all, employers in these sectors sought to keep vocational training focused on objective, scientific, and technical training and free from partisan struggles and class politics (see, for example, comments by the head of the Association of Berlin Metal Industrialists in Kantorowicz 1930: 62–3).

The Drive toward Standardization

A more important development in the Weimar years in the evolution of the German system was a significant push toward skill *standardization*. The lead actor in this effort was the Association of German Machine Builders (VDMA), which underwent an enormous and highly consequential shift in composition and orientation during World War I (Feldman and Nocken 1975). Traditionally dominated by large producers, this organization was transformed by the (state-sponsored) incorporation of a large number of small- and medium-sized firms. The government had charged the association with organizing the procurement of wartime machinery and as part of this effort, "a dense internal network of cartels and associations was created within the VDMA itself to organize the machinery industry" that could coordinate the strategies – on wages, training, and other issues – of the firms in the industry as a whole. "This extended the influence of the VDMA into areas of the German economy that it had previously stood outside of" (Herrigel 1996b: 63). As Feldman and Nocken point out, during the

Weimar years the VDMA emerged as "one of the most powerful, best organized, and, in many respects, most modern of trade associations" (Feldman and Nocken 1975: 433).

In particular, the expansion had the effect of drawing into the association increasing numbers of smaller producers, the so-called *industrielle Mittelstand*. By 1923, the VDMA had grown well beyond the dominance of large machine firms, organizing fully 90% of all machine construction firms in Germany (Feldman and Nocken 1975: 422). Herrigel notes, "As the 1920s progressed, the VDMA's former identification with the large autarkic producers gave way to a distinctive small- and medium-sized producer orientation" (Herrigel 1996: 63). A number of these firms had traditionally depended on regional vocational and technical institutions and, because of the high mobility of skilled labor among firms, they also relied heavily on *general* skills (Herrigel 1996b: 52). The VDMA played a key role, not just in promoting coordination on skills but in coordinating the strategies of these firms on a range of issues, including organizing competition and maintaining term-fixing and specialization cartels (Herrigel 1996b: 63).

Enhanced coordination among machine companies through the VDMA had important implications for skill formation and specifically for the drive toward greater skill standardization. Such coordination discouraged firms from engaging in (industry-degrading) cutthroat competition based on lower wage, lower skill strategies and supported increased coordination in training issues. The interests of the *industrielle Mittelstand* in the area of training also dovetailed in very important ways with those of the Berlin machine and metal firms, a key constituency behind training reform and skill standardization. Thus, the new, more inclusive VDMA that emerged from the war became, in the Weimar years, the "reform-oriented vanguard of industry" in the area of vocational training (Schütte 1992: 28). Whereas large firms that could support extensive internal labor markets had long fixed on the goal of developing their own individual (company-based) training programs, the *industrielle Mittelstand* had a greater interest (and also deeper roots) in a collective solution to skill formation.[51]

The large companies that had dominated the VDMA before the war had focused their energies primarily on the issue of *certification*, but the shifting balance within the organization brought the issue of skill *standardization*

[51] These were often also the kinds of firms and regions (and not the large firm sector) where the metalworkers' union was able to achieve a more substantial presence from early on (Schönhoven 1979: especially 416–17).

increasingly to the fore.[52] In this regard, the agenda of the machine industry diverged from the previous trajectory set by the Handwerk-based apprenticeship system. The Handwerk sector had long enjoyed certification powers, but training was not particularly standardized (Wolsing 1977: 423–5). By its nature, Handwerk-based apprenticeship training depended crucially on the specifics of the production process in which an apprentice was engaged. Since an apprentice learned through on-the-job training and working at the side of a master artisan, the training depended heavily on a number of shop-specific factors. Even in the best circumstances, the content and quality of training were extremely sensitive to the pedagogic skills of the employer and the particular kinds of work that came in over the course of an apprentice's tenure (Pätzold 1989: 264). Certification and standardization were not necessarily a tightly integrated package.

The drive toward standardization was led by the VDMA, through DATSCH, whose mission was redefined and redirected somewhat with greater attention to the technical tasks associated with establishing a collective framework for skill development in the industry. The 1920s mark the high point of DATSCH's most intensive efforts toward this goal (Muth 1985: 348–52). DATSCH's pioneering work to systematize and rationalize industry-based training earned it considerable prestige and established the organization as a widely recognized authority in this area.[53] By 1919, the VDMA and the Association of German Metal Industrialists (GDM) had already worked out an apprentice contract for the whole machine industry (*DATSCH Abhandlungen* 1919: 6). In the 1920s, DATSCH produced a standardized inventory of skilled trades for the metalworking industries (including a number of new, specifically industrial trades), with profiles of the skills required for each. The organization also generated and disseminated standardized training materials, including very detailed training courses

[52] Although it should be noted that even some of the large machine companies had begun to question the limits of company-based training policies (Dehen 1928: 166–7; Pätzold 1989: 272). And, as the 1920s progressed, Germany's large machine companies engaged in ongoing internal rationalization efforts that also relied on a higher degree of skill standardization. These companies had previously organized production around rather sprawling networks of very specialized workshops, but by the late 1920s they sought to control costs through rationalization efforts. This involved cutting wasteful duplication of efforts and more interchangeability in deploying resources (including skilled labor) as dictated by changes in the market. This required greater flexibility to rotate engineers and workers around the various production areas as needed (Herrigel 1996: 106–8).

[53] DATSCH received material support from the *Reichskuratorium für Wirtschaftlichkeit* (*DATSCH Abhandlungen* 1926: 11)

(*Lehrgänge*) for the various trades, beginning with the most common – machine builders, fitters, toolmakers, patternmakers, moulders, smiths, and precision mechanics. In this period, DATSCH presided over significant steps forward in the standardization and systematization of skills, making progress on these fronts well before industry enjoyed formal certification powers.

In 1926 DATSCH also began developing skill profiles for a number of semi-skilled occupations. This reflected the organization's effort to prevent companies from misusing the institution of skilled apprenticeship by having apprentices perform tasks that involved a much narrower range of skills than those expected of skilled industrial workers (*Facharbeiter*). An increasing division of labor and accompanying skill specialization in metalworking were underway in many countries, having started at the turn of the century and being well advanced by the 1920s. DATSCH sought to prevent the downgrading of skill by identifying and cataloguing certain occupations as "semi-skilled" and by establishing a maximum two-year training period for such occupations (Rathschlag 1972: 14–15). Stratmann notes that the prestige that DATSCH enjoyed in this period grew to such an extent that in the 1930s, even the handicraft sector allowed DATSCH to formulate technical instructions for its apprentice training (Stratmann 1990: 47).

Although it is difficult to know how widely implemented DATSCH concepts and methods were, there are indications that key industries such as machine building employed them on a relatively broad scale (Schmedes 1931: 12). Referring to the model contract developed by the VDMA to render apprentice contracts more uniform among their member firms, Mack notes that the model contract was "being utilized by firms with or without minor changes made" and that only a few firms had their own contract (Mack 1927: 93). Muth asserts that although the DATSCH guidelines were voluntary, nonetheless, "with the support of the individual trade associations (Fachverbände) they were widely distributed in practice. In this way the mechanical industry became the first sector in Germany to implement a broadly uniform system of vocational training" (Muth 1985: 350). A contemporary observer, Gertrud Tollkühn, similarly asserted that the guidelines and training materials that DATSCH produced and disseminated "were indeed used by most of the firms as a foundation" for their training (Tollkühn 1926: 40). In the absence of regulatory powers like those of the Handwerk sector, the capacity of firms to enforce uniform standards rested on the participation of the unions, and especially, on the efforts of strong trade associations like the VDMA.

Summing up developments to this point: There had been a shift in the market that the German machine industry faced, from generally expanding markets of the pre-World War I period to an absolutely stagnant domestic market and more hostile global markets in the immediate postwar period, forcing machine firms further up-market. At the same time, the VDMA was transformed by a shift from dominance by large machine companies (mostly worried about getting their excellent training facilities equipped with certification powers) to small- and medium-sized firms (which put an emphasis on standardization, since their production networks relied on more flexibility and worker mobility). The work of the VDMA in the Weimar years, organized around stabilizing product market competition through organization and coordination, placed a premium on coordination in training as well. These developments help to explain an overall shift in the work of DATSCH, which along with its continuing lobbying for certification, increasingly promoted skill systematization and standardization.

DATSCH's technical achievements in this period were crucial for the later development of training standards (see below). In the 1920s, however, industrial training was still premised to a very large extent on voluntarism. More precisely, it depended on exhortations but not sanctions by trade associations such as VDMA, but it was supported by the unions' wage policies (which reduced skill differentials) and union efforts (although limited) to regulate apprenticeship through collective bargaining. Some employers associations and some local chambers of industry and trade (IHKs) took the initiative in creating machinery for administering exams for industrial apprentices, but these arrangements still lacked the legal foundations that prevailed in the Handwerk sector (Kaiser and Loddenkemper 1980: 13; Wilden 1926). Separate and reliable certification for industrial apprenticeship and firmly institutionalized union rights in this area were still distant goals. These groups faced formidable political opponents in the Weimar years. I now turn to the topic of the political coalition against reform.

The Political Coalition against Reform

First, the traditional artisanate opposed all reforms from the start, both to preserve its monopoly on skill certification and to keep unions out of the picture. Artisans' opposition to the reforms that were being proposed goes back to this sector's heavy reliance on the productive labor of apprentices (Abel 1963: 45; see also Herber 1930: 49–74 for differences between Handwerk and unions on proposed legislation for vocational training). Without a

Table 2.3. *Weekly wages (in Reichsmark, RM) for young workers in large, medium, and small firms, 1929 (% of firms)*

Firm size	None	To 4RM	4–7RM	7–10RM	10–15RM	Over 15
Large	0.4	11.7	28.0	27.1	22.9	9.9
Medium	1.6	25.0	33.4	21.3	13.6	5.1
Small	7.0	37.1	33.2	14.0	6.3	2.4

Note: Large firm = over 50 employees, middle-sized = 6–50 employees, small firm = 1–5 employees.

Source: Schütte 1992: 136.

monopoly on certification (through the HWK), these firms would have a very hard time competing with industry (which offered higher wages and typically more systematic training). Data from a survey conducted in the late 1920s suggest that the wages of apprentices in small firms (and this would have included most artisanal shops) lagged substantially behind those in larger firms. As late as 1929, 7% of apprentices in the small handicraft firms still received no wage at all (see Table 2.3).

Well into the 1920s, some handicraft masters in small municipalities were still collecting a fee from their apprentices, and sometimes requiring them to work overtime without pay (Schütte 1992: 127).[54]

Handwerk thus had no interest in sharing its special status with industry, for this would squander the one advantage they held over industrial firms when it came to recruiting able young workers. Local handicraft chambers frequently sabotaged efforts to secure the same status for industrial apprentices as enjoyed by their own. For example, although industrial apprentices could in principle be certified through the HWK, local chambers often threw up obstacles, causing problems in the constitution of joint examination boards, failing to recognize the results of tests for industrial apprentices, and refusing to admit those trained in industry to take the master exam (Kipp and Miller-Kipp 1990: 234; Wilden 1926: 1).

But the biggest threat to Handwerk was organized labor, since union participation in regulating apprenticeship would interfere with Handwerk's use of apprentices as a source of flexible and cheap productive labor. Artisans vehemently opposed union influence over training through collective bargaining, which they saw as a direct assault on Handwerk's longstanding

[54] Handicraft firms were also likely to deduct pay from an apprentice for school attendance (Schütte 1992: 127).

system of self-governance (Kaps 1930: especially 5, 16; Pätzold 1989: 268). Until 1918, most matters relating to apprenticeship were governed by the *Reichsgewerbeordnung*, which left it to the handicraft chambers to regulate the length of apprenticeship (but establishing a maximum of four years – paragraph 130), set the terms of the probationary period, regulate the dissolution of apprentice contracts, and establish sanctions for apprentices who broke their indentures (Schütte 1992: 121). Handwerk fought union regulation of these matters as violations of the Reichsgewerbeordnung. They were also, and in some ways most, adamant in their resistance to union wage setting, and struggled with all means available to defend the "wage autonomy" of the handicraft sector (Schütte 1992: 126).

These jurisdictional issues were hotly contested in a series of legal challenges. Conflicts continued despite a number of court decisions and even a ruling by the National Labor Ministry (Reichsarbeitsministerium) that specifically confirmed that the material conditions of apprenticeship could be regulated through collective bargaining, and that limited the role of the guilds and the handicraft chambers to regulating specifically those aspects that bore directly on the training itself – exams, certification, and so on (Schütte 1992: 123–4, 129).[55] It must nonetheless be noted that the handicraft sector as a whole was quite successful in its efforts to keep unions out of its affairs. Union attempts to influence working conditions in the artisanal sector (mostly by trying to have collective bargains declared "generally applicable") were largely unsuccessful. One study covering over three thousand collective bargains from 1922 to 1923 revealed that although unions were able to conclude contracts dealing with apprenticeship matters covering 37% of all industrial apprentices, they could only influence conditions for 3% of Handwerk apprentices (Schütte 1992: 131).

Handwerk opposed almost all the reform efforts undertaken in the Weimar period. Any system that would unify Handwerk and industry under the same framework with union participation would create an impossible situation for Handwerk, which relied on the contributions of apprentices to production but could not compete with wages and conditions in industry.

In addition, other segments of industry had never been that sympathetic to the machine industry's position on certification and industrial training.[56] In particular, heavy industry employed mostly semi-skilled labor and had

[55] On the struggles over whether apprentice relationships should be considered as educational relations or as work relations, see also Molitor (1960).

[56] Hal Hansen emphasized the importance of this to me.

never been as concerned with the supply of skilled labor. In many cases large firms in this industry were more capable of pursuing successful segmentalist strategies (Hansen 1997: Chapter 3; Herrigel 1996b: Chapter 3). Such companies often grew up in remote agricultural areas (that is, without much of an infrastructure for education) so they were forced to create their own skill capacities, but they were also less vulnerable to poaching than firms in areas like Berlin where competition in skilled labor markets was fierce. Where firms dominated their local labor market, they were able to attract and keep good young workers and orient their training very closely to their own internal needs (Kaiser and Loddenkemper 1980: 62).

The lack of a consensus within the larger industrial community was already clear in 1911 and 1914 when – at DATSCH's urging – the "Social Policy Commission" of the Congress of German Industry and Commerce (*Deutsche Industrie und Handelstag*, or DIHT) took up the skill issue. The commission's reports echoed DATSCH's criticisms of the existing Handwerk-based system, as well as of the behavior of the Handwerk chambers in withholding cooperation with industry. On the question of whether industry should administer its own separate exams for apprentices, however, the commission had to conclude that "opinions within industry are still so far apart that the DIHT cannot yet take a position on the issue" (Hoffmann 1962: 43). The commission simply encouraged machine firms to continue to use the craft chambers and advised them to "watch carefully" the composition of the examination boards to make sure that their apprentices were examined against the appropriate standards. As Hansen has pointed out, the opposition of the chambers of commerce (under the strong influence of heavy industry) was decisive, since the chambers were the ones who would have been charged with the task of overseeing skill formation and certification for industry (Hansen 1997: 588).

Heavy industry grew even less accommodating during the Weimar years. The leading firms had seen no alternative but to grudgingly accept accommodation with unions during the revolution, but around 1924 and 1925 many reverted to their previous *Herr-im-Hause* stance.[57] The debate over possible legislative reform of vocational training did not go away, however, and so in the mid-1920s heavy industry began espousing a more ideological alternative to DATSCH's thoroughly technical and collectivist

[57] This turn coincides with the end of inflation, at which point demands with respect to wages became much "harder" constraints in export markets. I thank Hartmut Berghoff for emphasizing the significance of this to me.

approach to skills. Leading Ruhr industrialists took the initiative in 1925 at a meeting of the Association of the German Iron and Steel Industrialists (*Verein Deutscher Eisen- und Stahl Industrieller*, or VDESI). The result was the founding of the German Institute for Technical Training (*Deutsches Institut für Technische Arbeitsschulung*, or Dinta), devoted to the cultivation of a special kind of worker, trained by and for individual firms and instilled with deep loyalty to the company.

Dinta

As the debate on vocational training reform (and possible legislation) continued in the 1920s, and with VDMA and DATSCH representing advocates of a collectivist solution, large industrial producers felt compelled to weigh in in these debates with their own somewhat different interests and perspectives on skills and training. Thus, in 1925, and on the initiative mostly of prominent Ruhr industrialists, Dinta was founded to represent the interests of German heavy industry in the skill debates of this period. Dinta's first director, Robert Carl Arnhold (1884–1970) was originally trained as an engineer, and began his career in training and pedagogy in the steel industry. After a stint in the army during World War I, Arnhold had returned to become head of training for the steel division of Gelsenkirchen Bergwerk AG. Here he developed his ideas on training and presided over the establishment of company-based training workshops (*Lehrwerkstätte*) that were a central pillar of his pedagogy (Kaiser and Loddenkemper 1980: 60–6).

Whereas DATSCH represented a more collectivist approach to skill formation that worked through key trade associations like VDMA and the Berlin machine group, Dinta's conception was more resolutely autarkic. According to Arnhold's vision, "the ideal new skilled worker would be technically well trained, but unlike his predecessor, who had learned his skills from other workers in artisan shops, he would be trained *by* the firm and *for* the firm's particular needs. He would be loyal to the firm and adaptable (*wendig*) to the changing needs of the rationalized production process" (quote from Nolan 1994: 189 and Chapter 9 passim; italics in original; see also Arnhold 1931: 31). Arnhold's training concept shared with DATSCH a critique of the "unsystematic" nature of training by Handwerk, and it recognized and in some ways built on the training materials DATSCH was producing. Thus, the technical/practical component of Dinta training, although firm-centered, was not narrow. Dinta training featured two years of "foundational" instruction – frequently accomplished in a plant-training workshop – followed by two more years of on-the-job training in more specialized skills (see, for example, Nolan 1994: 194). The idea was for trainees to have sufficiently broad training to allow them to adapt to the firm's changing production requirements.

In rather sharp contrast to the work of DATSCH, however, and to the interests of important segments of the machine industry, Arnhold's training concept was specifically *not* limited to the technical and practical (Kaiser and Loddenkemper 1980: 60–6; Arnhold 1931; Kopsch 1928: 53–67). Instead, the technical aspects of Dinta training were closely related to an ideological agenda that can only be described as a particularly virulent strain of anti-unionism. By keeping training closely integrated into the production process at the company, Dinta sought to foster a close association between firm and worker. Arnhold himself argued for the workshop to replace the school, and in his vision, work at "the factory would replace the union as the nucleus of social and political organization, and the employer [would replace] the political leader as moral guide" (Gillingham 1985: 425). In other words, in the Dinta training concept "character-building" was very much part of the program. Much of how Arnhold conceived the project of training for "the whole person" came directly out of his experience in and after the First World War (Seubert 1977: 63–7). Militaristic elements were pervasive in Dinta training. The notions of a strong leader and of camaraderie, for example, were emphasized; trainees were expected to exhibit discipline, obedience, loyalty, and industry.

The plant community was also central to the notion of training in Arnhold's view. Dinta activities went well beyond apprentice training to include other aspects of plant social policy, including but not limited to kindergartens, counseling for mothers, plant insurance policy, activities for senior citizens, plant social clubs, publication of a company newspaper, and the like (Baethge 1970: 52; Pätzold 1989: 277). Since the point of training was to develop a strong bond between the trainee and the firm, the company also took control of much of an apprentice's free time, for example, organizing obligatory hikes and sporting activities. The goal of training was to bind the individual to his work and his company, which meant severing any ties – to "outsiders" (like unions) – that might interfere with this objective or compromise a worker's loyalty to the firm (Seubert 1977: 68). Draconian union-busting methods in heavy industry were thus complemented and supported by policies that employed a softer ideological approach to win over workers. As one Dinta publication put it, company policy – with respect to training but also firm-based social policy more generally – was seen as integral to the "fight for the souls of our workers" (quoted in Kaiser and Loddenkemper 1980: 77). For these reasons, Dinta was opposed at all turns by organized labor, which thought of Dinta as a "breeding ground for yellow unions" (*Zuchtanstalt für Gelbe*) (quote from Seubert 1977: 77; see also Fricke 1930: 95–8).[58]

These autarkic and paternalistic features of the Dinta training concept help to explain why the organization also rejected the idea of working through employer associations and other organized interests to achieve its goals. As Arnhold opined at a conference in 1930, "with this path, we would probably have gotten stuck or organized ourselves to death" (Arnhold 1931: 31). Dinta also opposed all efforts to subordinate firm-based training to any sort of state or parapublic controls. The organization vigorously promoted firm-operated factory schools (*Werkschulen*) using Dinta techniques as substitutes for public trade schools (Nolan 1994: 195; Kellner 1930: 21). Again, this was a move consistent with the cooptative-autarkic goal of transforming apprentices "into a new kind of skilled worker by establishing factory-based alternatives to artisan skill training and to state vocational schools" (quote from Nolan 1994: 193; Seubert 1977: 67).[59]

Dinta originated in, and was particularly strong in, the iron and steel industry of the Ruhr. However, the organization and its concepts appealed to all large producers for whom accommodation with the unions had been purely strategic and who longed for a return to a more autarkic and paternalistic alternative.[60] Dinta's major client firms included a number of Germany's leading industrial giants: Gutehoffnungshütte (GHH, which by this time had purchased M.A.N.), Hoesch, Thyssen, Schalker, and Siemens-Schuckert among them (Nolan 1994: 187). By contrast, however, Dinta had "no influence among technologically advanced and less reactionary firms, such as those in the electro technical and Berlin machinery industries"

[58] Though, as Nolan notes, unions acknowledged that Dinta training was often of quite high quality (Nolan 1994: 201–2). On the skepticism and opposition of even the Christian unions see Kopsch (1928: 67–73; also the remarks by Rütten and Mleinek in Sozialen Museum E. V. 1931: 56–9 and 77–8 respectively).

[59] However, the numbers of apprentices attending such schools always remained rather small (never more than 2% of apprentices) (Pätzold 1989: 280).

[60] This is also how the Dinta Directorate over time came to include some of the founding fathers of DATSCH who came out of large concerns (such as Ernst von Borsig and Gottlieb Lippart), right alongside a number of prominent Ruhr industrialists who had never taken an interest in DATSCH and its concepts (Nolan 1994: 187).

(Nolan 1994: 187). The latter rejected the deeply ideological and partisan slant taken by Dinta as irrelevant to, and possibly even counterproductive to, the task of skill promotion. In explaining why his association did not embrace and support the work of Dinta, Heinz Kantorowicz of the Association of Berlin Metal Industrialists noted that the majority of member firms thought training should be kept free of political and class conflict (Mallmann 1990: 217).[61]

By the late 1920s, however, the backlash against unions and collective bargaining was in full swing, with stepped up efforts to use works councils as vehicles for a company-based and employer-dominated alternative to union bargaining. In these years, Arnhold presided over a significant expansion in Dinta's influence. In just two years (1926–1928) Dinta opened 71 new plant-training workshops (*Lehrwerkstätten*) and 18 factory schools (*Werkschulen*). By 1929, Dinta won over another 50 training plants to its concepts, and Dinta principles were applied in 10 new plant schools (Kaiser and Loddenkemper 1980: 77–8). By the end of the decade, Dinta was running training programs in between 150 and 300 companies in Germany and Austria. It published over 50 company newspapers reaching nearly a half million workers (Nolan 1994: 187).

The Failure of the Reforms

Dinta represented an approach to training different from the existing Handwerk system – more systematic, more autocratic, and more ideological. In the reform debates of the 1920s, however, Dinta's interests dovetailed with those of Handwerk on the issue of unions. Given its orientation, Dinta and its core supporters within heavy industry were adamantly opposed to any legislative initiative that would have given unions a place at the table when it came to vocational training. As we saw above, Handwerk's opposition to reform efforts during the Weimar years were substantially motivated by an attempt to preserve its traditional monopoly position on vocational training (and the many accompanying economic benefits this held for these firms), a goal with which heavy industry was not particularly sympathetic. In their anti-unionism, the interests of Dinta and Handwerk converged

[61] See also the rather friendly tone of the exchanges between union representative Fritz Fricke and Kantorowicz, as compared to the tense exchanges between Fricke and Dinta's Arnhold at a 1930 conference on industrial training (Sozialen Museum E. V. 1931).

and provided sufficient glue to hold them together over the late Weimar years.

The departure of the Social Democratic Party (*Sozialdemokratische Partei*, or SPD) from government in 1923 was clearly contributory to the failure of the reform movement.[62] Under the SPD the Labor Ministry had played a key role in the push for reform and was its strongest institutional advocate. But once the Ministry was no longer in SPD hands, the pressure for a law quickly subsided, and work on reform came to a somewhat abrupt halt. Meanwhile, outside the government sphere, events in the late 1920s continued to promote more intense inter-industry coordination on skills, even as they completely undermined any possibility of state-led reform, particularly any version based on union participation. In 1924, employers began complaining of skill shortages, despite overall still high unemployment (Mosher 1999: 13). Studies also cite worries of a looming skill shortage due to hit Germany in 1929 (a consequence of low birth rates during the war) (Kopsch 1928: 25–6; Mack 1927: 3). Such concerns kept apprenticeship reform on the public policy agenda.

However, by this time, the political and economic climate had shifted considerably. For one thing, unions had been on the defensive since the stabilization crisis, and compulsory arbitration was increasingly filling in where free collective bargaining failed. By 1929, over half of the (nearly ten thousand) industrial conflicts concerning wages and hours were being settled through arbitration, and almost 20% of the time the state mediator's decision was declared binding (Nolan 1994: 161–2). Thus not only was labor much weaker, but also those sectors once most willing to contemplate some form of joint (labor-employer) regulation balked, as it increasingly looked as if "union regulation" in the end meant "state regulation," the one thing most segments of German business – whatever their other differences – wanted to avoid (Feldman 1970; Feldman 1977: especially 146). Combined with the continuing opposition of Handwerk and growing anti-unionism among big industry as a whole, this constellation formed the basis of a coalition against reform, or better, in support of employer-dominated "self-regulation" premised on voluntarism and the promise of greater cooperation between Handwerk and industry (Ebert 1984: 318–20; Herber 1930: 48; Schütte 1992: 84–7).

[62] Jim Mosher has emphasized this point to me in personal communications.

Voluntary Cooperation as an Alternative to Legislative Reform

In 1925, the Association of German Employers' Organizations (*Vereinigung der Deutschen Arbeitgeberverbände* or VDA), the League of German Industry (*Reichsverband der Deutschen Industrie* or RDI), and DATSCH joined together to found the Working Committee for Vocational Training (*Arbeitsausschuß für Berufsbildung*, or AfB) (DATSCH 1926: 11), with Ernst Borsig as president (Mallmann 1990: 215–16; Kopsch 1928: 29–31). The German Congress of Industry and Trade (*Deutscher Industrie und Handelstag*, or DIHT) joined the organization a year later (Muth 1985: 375). Building on DATSCH's work for the machine and metal industries, the AfB drew up the first list of skilled occupations for the metalworking, shipbuilding, and chemical industries and presided over the generation of systematic training materials (Muth 1985: 378). By 1927, the Berlin Association of Metalworking Employers had developed training courses for most of the 58 discrete occupations that the AfB (through the *Gesamtverband Deutscher Metallindustrieller*) had identified for that sector. Even in those cases where training courses (Ausbildungslehrgänge) were not developed, the organization provided occupational profiles that defined the skills required and established boundaries between discrete occupations (Mallmann 1990: 216).

Handwerk was pulled along in the process as training there also became increasingly systematic over the later years of the Weimar Republic. This was partly driven by arguments by progressive elements of the handicraft sector that saw unsystematic training as a threat to Handwerk as a whole. Handwerk representatives themselves began to press for apprenticeship training that was as "systematic, multifaceted and uniform" as that in the big industrial firms (quoted in Pätzold 1989: 266). By the end of the 1920s some regions had begun developing and disseminating training materials for some artisanal trades similar to those being developed for industrial occupations (Pätzold 1989: 266).[63]

Although these developments substantially advanced the cause of collectivism by intensifying employer coordination in apprenticeship training, they also sealed the fate – for the time being at least – of any comprehensive legislative reform, and especially of any reform based on union participation. The evidence suggests that in the late 1920s handicraft chambers in

[63] Although it must be added that this was extremely difficult, since most Handwerker resisted such moves as an infringement on their autonomy. Their chambers therefore had trouble forcing the adoption of these materials (Pätzold 1989: 266–7).

many regions had grown more accommodating, which is to say more willing to strike local deals to test industrial apprentices, including in some cases with "mixed" (industry/handicraft) examination committees (Mack 1927: 106).[64] Finally, the coalition in support of collectivism based on employer domination and self- (as opposed to state) regulation was completed when the key industrial associations reached a national agreement with Handwerk, whose two main associations, the Congress of German Crafts and Trades (*Deutscher Handwerks und Gewerbekammertag* or DHGT) and the League of German Crafts (*Reichsverband des Deutschen Handwerks*), joined the AfB in 1927 (Ebert 1984: 314; Muth 1985: 377).

These developments dealt the *coup de grace* to the by now increasingly languid debate over legislative reform. Instead of a comprehensive new law, industry and Handwerk reached a voluntary accommodation in peak-level negotiations that committed local Handwerk chambers to work together with industry and trade chambers to preside over the examination and certification of industrial apprentices (Schütte 1992: 84–5). This deal had the effect, within industry, of hiving off any support that might have remained or been mustered for reform through any sort of government action by addressing the one issue that had rankled some segments of the business community: certification and testing. The deal thus consolidated industry behind a voluntary solution to the issue, as well as forging an alliance between Handwerk and industry (especially heavy industry) against reform (Schütte 1992: 86–7). Or, as the executive committee of the DIHT put it in 1929, "The DIHT has pointed out several times in the last years that in light of the positive developments in apprenticeship training arrangements on a voluntary basis . . . there is *no urgent need* for comprehensive legislative regulation" (Hoffmann 1962:101, emphasis in original; see also Kopsch 1928: 14).

In the ensuing years it became clear that this was a fairly opportunistic alliance of convenience that was not terribly robust. The solution forged in 1928, which allowed for joint (artisanal–industry) committees in some regional chambers, proved unstable, as some local craft chambers resisted compliance (Kipp and Miller-Kipp 1990: 234; Schütte 1992: 86; Wolsing 1977: 74). Among other regulations, the 1928 deal had called for testing boards composed of representatives of both industry and Handwerk. In

[64] Including (as early as 1924) a deal struck between the HWK Berlin and the Association of Berlin Metal Industrialists providing for joint examinations in industry and Handwerk (Mack 1927: 106).

1932, however, complaints could still be heard about the inability of industrial apprentices to be tested and certified (Kipp and Miller-Kipp 1990: 234). It was up to individual handicraft chambers to decide whether or not to allow industrial apprentices to take the journeyman examination, and problems continued (Pätzold 1989: 276). According to a survey of industry and trade chambers, the difficulties went back to the unwillingness of the handicraft chambers to recognize the results of tests that industrial apprentices took (Kipp and Miller-Kipp 1990: 234).

In any event, the time for reform had come and gone: vocational training was off the agenda for the remainder of the Weimar years. The Depression of 1929 killed any lingering hopes of reform, as vocational training spun into crisis. Firms were engaged in massive layoffs and not in any position to offer apprenticeship positions to youth. The number of company schools "tumbled" after 1929 (Greinert 1994: 49). Between 1929 and 1934, apprenticeship slots fell by a third and did not climb back to 1929 levels until 1936, and then only on the basis of a massive push by the state (Hansen 1997: 603–4). For their part, those young Germans who could find work were under tremendous economic pressure to provide for unemployed family members, and thus opted for unskilled work rather than embark on a long investment in apprenticeship to the skilled trades (Kaiser and Loddenkemper 1980: 13).

The certification that the machine industry sought in the Weimar years was finally granted by the National Socialists, who presided over a massive increase in vocational education and the inauguration of a standardized system for industrial training, with industry and trade chambers – with prerogatives now comparable to those of the handicraft chambers – in charge of the administration and certification of training for skilled industrial workers (Facharbeiter) (see Chapter 5). The system was built on foundations laid down in the Weimar years. Apprenticeship training for industry was explicitly patterned after the Handwerk model of plant-based training and substantially incorporated the technical and organizational innovations developed on a voluntary basis by industry and, above all, by the machine industry through the work of the VDMA and DATSCH.

The final piece of the puzzle, full labor participation in the oversight of in-plant training, was achieved only much later, in the post-World War II period. But here again, important developments were strongly foreshadowed in the Weimar years. Thus, for example, the demands of German unions after 1945 (with respect to apprenticeship training) were virtually the same as those they made after World War I: not a dismantling of in-firm training, but rather an equal role with employers in administering and overseeing it. The comprehensive legislation that unions had sought unsuccessfully in the Weimar years was picked up again as a demand after World War II. The resulting Vocational Training Act of 1969 incorporated many of the important elements of the proposals of the early Weimar years (Chapter 5).

This provides a good juncture to step back from the German case to examine other countries in which the evolution of apprenticeship and skill formation took a very different route. The next chapter examines the deterioration of apprenticeship and plant-based training in Britain in the late nineteenth and early twentieth centuries. The subsequent chapter looks at the Japanese and U.S. cases, which represent variations, respectively, on the German and British themes.

3

The Evolution of Skill Formation in Britain

In the case of Germany, we saw that state policy in the early industrial period was crucial to establishing the trajectory that skill formation there would take. Legislation targeted at the artisanal sector contributed to the survival of a relatively stable system of apprenticeship, and at the same time discouraged unions from pursuing skill-based strategies for labor market control. Firms in industries that depended heavily on skills drew on the artisanal sector as a source of skilled labor but they also competed with Handwerk as a corporate actor, especially over skill certification. This produced a dynamic through which industry was pushed and pulled toward training practices that built on, and in some ways paralleled, those developed in the artisanal sector.

In Britain, state policy worked in the opposite direction, contributing to the deregulation of traditional apprenticeship and indirectly encouraging the development of skill-based unions pursuing strategies premised on craft control. The legal framework in place in the nineteenth century discouraged the formation of unions among unskilled laborers while encouraging skilled workers to organize around the provision of friendly society benefits. Responding to this set of incentives and constraints, early trade unions organized their strategies around the attempt to influence wages and employment by manipulating the supply of skilled labor. This set up a completely different set of dynamics in Britain in which apprenticeship was contested not – as in Germany – between an independent artisanal sector and an emerging industrial sector, but rather between craft unions and employers in skill-dependent industries.

Apprenticeship survived in Britain but what was not achieved was a durable settlement between skilled unions and employers on the regulation of in-plant training capable of punishing opportunism and making credible commitments possible. As Swenson has argued in another context, such cross-class alliances are sometimes the only viable foundation of enduring, effective institutionalized systems for regulating labor markets on a broad basis (Swenson 2002). British apprenticeship was fragile precisely because it rested instead on a balance of power between employers and skilled unions that could be (and was) repeatedly upset by shifting macro-economic and political developments. Thus, despite some notable efforts at reforming training – in the 1910s and 1920s, and again in the post-World War II period – advances achieved under favorable conditions (often periods of skilled labor shortages or strong government support for training) were repeatedly rolled back when the political and/or market context shifted. The kind of trench warfare that skilled unions and employers fought over apprenticeship in Britain repeatedly pushed toward arrangements that far-sighted employers regarded as suboptimal by complicating enormously the achievement of the kind of cross-class settlement on which a more robust and durable system would have had to rest.

State Policy and the Fate of the British Artisanate

As in Germany, the story begins with the guilds, which in Britain, too, traditionally played an important role in regulating apprenticeship. By establishing and enforcing standards for training, British guilds sought to regulate entry to the trade, thus protecting their own position in the market. Where the British experience stands out in international comparisons is not so much in the operation of the guilds in their day as in their fate. Whereas the guilds persisted in other countries until they were abolished through acts of state in the nineteenth century, British guilds faded very early and gradually, beginning centuries before (Unwin 1909: 2). Coleman dates the onset of decay to the Tudor and Stuart periods, when rapid population growth and increasing demand for British goods (especially textiles) abroad encouraged the early and widespread development of the putting out system of production in rural areas (Coleman 1975: 25).[1] As elsewhere,

[1] In contrast to traditional craft production (craftsmen working in their own workshops), the putting out system was based on a new division of labor in which a merchant class (of non-producers) organized and financed production networks of domestic workers who were dependent on the merchants for raw materials and often also the production machinery itself. For a survey of the literature on the development of putting out in Europe as a whole between 1500 and 1800, see Ogilvie and Cerman (1996); for an overview of developments in Britain in the pre- and early-industrial period, see Berg (1985).

these developments exposed urban-based guilds to new competitive pressures from employers who simply ignored guild restrictions and achieved advantage by employing labor at lower rates (Unwin 1909; see also Kellett 1958: 381–2).

In Germany, as we have seen, the state played a critical role in determining the fate of the independent artisanate. In Britain, too, state policy was important in pushing developments forward, though in a very different direction. The centuries-old Statute of Artificers (1563) codified regulations regarding apprenticeship and the practicing of various trades (Ministry of Labour 1928: 10–14; see also Webb and Webb 1920: 48–51). Among other things, the law stipulated that a completed apprenticeship was a prerequisite for practicing a craft, set the length of apprenticeship training at seven years, established apprentice to journeyman ratios (3:1) to ensure proper training, and regulated working conditions, wages, and other matters to prevent exploitation of apprentices (Ministry of Labour 1928; see also Perry 1976: 7; Howell 1877: 834).

In contrast to developments in Germany, however, the British state never provided for institutionalized enforcement mechanisms (leaving enforcement to the voluntary guilds themselves), nor was the traditional legal framework ever adapted to the changing market context. In Britain, therefore, the pattern was one in which the artisanate sought, unsuccessfully, in the face of new market pressures, to defend traditional privileges, invoking the pre-industrial legal framework provided by the Statute of Artificers (Rule 1981: 114–16). As the industrial revolution took hold, however, and the influence of the liberal bourgeoisie grew, British governments grew less and less willing to defend traditional privileges. The guilds could appeal to the British courts in cases of violations, but they found that judges interpreted the law narrowly, applying the rules only to townspeople and also only to those trades that were in existence at the time of the Statute's enactment (Ministry of Labour 1928; Rule 1981: 108; Prothero 1979: Chapter 3). The new occupations that arose with the advance of industry were typically ruled to be beyond the reach of the old law (Perry 1976: 8; also Webb and Webb 1920: 53–5).

Thus, despite the fact that "on paper the whole system of gild privilege remained unimpaired" until the early nineteenth century, in practice it had been rapidly disintegrating for well over a century through lack of enforcement (quote from Kellett 1958: 393; see also Howell 1877; Rule 1981). Even before the official repeal of the Statute of Artificers in 1814, existing protections were explicitly chipped away in the closing decades of the eighteenth century (Webb and Webb 1920: 53; Prothero 1979: Chapter 3). As the Webbs put it,

> The action of the House of Commons [at that time] was not as yet influenced by any conscious theory of freedom of contract. What happened was that, as each trade in turn felt the effect of the new capitalist competition, the journeymen, and often also the smaller employers, would petition for redress, usually demanding the prohibition of the new machines, the enforcement of a seven year's apprenticeship, or the maintenance of the old limitation of the number of boys to be taught by each employer, [whereupon] the large employers would produce such a mass of evidence that these protections were not necessary and indeed injurious of their ability to compete. (Webb and Webb 1920: 53)

In Germany, state policy to protect and modernize the independent artisanal sector helped sustain a relatively large number of self-sufficient, small scale (skilled) entrepreneurs, organized together as employer-producers, while sharpening the differences of interest between this group and skilled journeymen who wound up as employees in industry (Kocka 1986b: 360–3). In Britain, state policy indirectly promoted a very different sort of alliance. Downwardly mobile master artisans found common cause with journeymen-employees, as both fought against abuses of traditional privileges by "illegal" masters and capitalist employers (Prothero 1979: Chapter 2, especially 36–7; Rule 1981: Chapter 4; Rule 1988). Knox, for example, writes of conflicts pitting journeymen and "good" masters against "dishonourable" ones in the textile trades (Knox 1980: 30–1). Such alliances were in evidence in the struggle over the Statute of Artificers in the years before its repeal, and were embodied in a campaign, led by the London-based Committee of Master Manufacturers and Journeymen, to salvage and extend the existing law in the face of pressures to abolish the system altogether. Knox describes this effort as a "tremendous national exercise in inter-class cooperation between the small masters and journeymen against the larger employers" (Knox 1980: 69).

Apprenticed journeymen employed in industry and struggling independent master artisans shared an interest in imposing regulations that would shore up their position in the labor market and prevent them from slipping into the same fate as the unskilled "labouring poor." In vain they advocated extending existing regulations regarding apprenticeship, and proposed legislation that would have restricted the taking of apprentices to those who had themselves served seven years in their trade, set limits on the proportion of apprentices to each master and journeyman, mandated indentures for each apprentice, and required masters to record the number of apprentices and journeymen in their works (Knox 1980: 78–80; see also Prothero 1979: Chapter 3; Rule 1981: 114–16).

The failure of this alliance to protect (or revive) traditional privileges through legislation in some ways cemented the common fate of small masters and journeymen, for it remained for both groups to find other means to defend their position and status in the market. If the political and legal environment was less auspicious than in Germany for defending the corporate autonomy and status of master artisans, it was much more auspicious for the development of trade unions that brought master craftsmen and journeymen together, while also sharpening the distinction between this group and the unskilled (see, for example, Rule 1988). The Combination Acts of 1799 and 1800 banned all forms of trade unions in Britain, but the prohibitions fell far harder on unskilled than on skilled workers. Such laws as existed had to be invoked by employers, and the latter were often reluctant to initiate proceedings against the skilled workers on whom they relied most to keep production going (Clegg, Fox, and Thompson 1964: 46–7; Rule 1988: 4–5). Thus, many of Britain's skilled trades founded very successful organizations even during the period when the Combination Laws were in effect; some of Britain's skilled trades "have never been more completely organized in London than between 1800 and 1820" (Webb and Webb 1920: 83–4).

In addition, and as important, state policy encouraged the growth of associations of workers organized around the provision of mutual aid and insurance, which also provided a site for forging bonds between downwardly mobile artisans and skilled industrial workers (see, for example, Clark 2000; Gosden 1961). So-called friendly societies, or "box clubs" (named after the boxes in which the society's contributions were kept) date back to the seventeenth century in Britain, but they experienced a surge of growth with the advance of the industrial revolution (Gosden 1961; Clark 2000; Thompson 1963: 418).

Friendly societies were voluntary associations to which members made regular contributions and on which they and their families could draw in case of catastrophic losses due to sickness, death of the breadwinner, or unemployment (Hopkins 1995; see also Baernreither 1893: 160–1; Eisenberg 1987: 94; Clark 2000: 356; Thompson 1963: 421). Journeymen were especially prominent members and founders of such organizations, but as Knox points out "a good number of small masters [also] . . . retained membership of a trade club or society as something to fall back on should trade fluctuation prove unfavourable" (Knox 1980: 74). Britain's skilled craftsmen formed the kind of labor aristocracy that could afford the dues and often found it well worth their while to join associations that provided some insurance against impoverishment through sickness or old age (Clark 2000: 360; Hopkins 1995: 23; Prothero 1979: 27–8).

Although government officials were concerned that friendly societies might be used as a front for illegal trade union activity (see, for example, Webb, Webb, and Peddie 1911: 82), they also saw in these insurance clubs an irresistible means for reducing the costs of supporting the poor under the existing Poor Laws (Hopkins 1995; Clark 2000: 370–1). At the close of the eighteenth century, "an upper class consensus emerged, which recognized the need for a statutory framework for benefit societies . . . [which were] seen as an ideal solution for curbing parish expenditure and encouraging self-help among the lower orders" (Clark 2000: 370–1). These sentiments found expression in the 1793 Act for the Encouragement and Relief of Friendly Societies which sought to stabilize the legal and actuarial foundation of the societies, while also subjecting them to some state oversight (Brown and Taylor 1933). The law allowed friendly societies to register with local authorities, thus obtaining a legally recognized status that would allow them to protect their funds against fraud and embezzlement. Societies that chose to register were required to submit their rules to local magistrates who would inspect them to ensure that the society was not involved in "subversive" activities, which would put them in violation of the Act Against Sedition that had been passed a year earlier (Clark 2000: 371). Subsequent legislation (1817) provided further incentives to founding such societies by allowing registered societies to deposit their funds in savings banks at a more favorable rate of interest than that prevailing in the market (Hopkins 1995: 15).

Implications for Labor

In Germany, state policy toward the artisanal sector sharpened the line between independent master artisans and skilled workers in industry, and discouraged early, emerging unions from attempting to control skilled labor markets (Kocka 1986a: 307–16; Kocka 1986b). By contrast, the legislation in Britain promoted a blurring of the line between masters and journeymen,[2]

[2] The term "master" took on an entirely different connotation in Britain from that in Germany (Eisenberg 1987). Whereas in Germany, a "master" referred to an artisan who had completed the course of training and earned a master certificate, in Britain, the "master" did not necessarily work at the trade at all; instead: "he directed it and found the capital" (Howell 1877: 835).

and in many ways drew early unions toward craft control strategies as the obvious means to defend their status and material interests in the market.

The conditions under which craft labor markets can be institutionalized are extremely restrictive (see, especially, Jackson 1984) but that does not keep skilled workers from trying. Unions wishing to establish control over the market in skills must accomplish several things simultaneously. They must secure monopoly control over the pool of skills within the relevant labor market, a task whose success actually depends rather crucially on the structure of the *product* market.[3] Craft control involves establishing organizational boundaries that, ideally, include all workers who compete for the same jobs, while excluding the unskilled (Jackson 1984; Klug 1993: 264). A craft union that successfully organized all eligible craftsmen would then be in a position to establish and enforce a uniform set of conditions under which its members would work, and to ensure compliance on the part of employers by denying offending firms access to a skilled labor force (Klug 1993: 264). Equally important, by controlling access to jobs and benefits, the union could prevent its own members from agreeing to work for an employer on terms that did not meet the "standard rate" set and enforced by the union.

In mid-nineteenth century Britain, state policy and legal and market conditions encouraged artisans to adopt strategies based on craft control. As we have seen above, there was space for skilled workers to organize even when unions were illegal and this space only expanded with the repeal of the Combination Laws in 1824. Early associations of skilled workers often formed around the provision of friendly benefits, whose insurance functions provided a selective incentive for workers to join. The Webbs viewed friendly benefits as "a great consolidating force in Trade Unionism" in Britain (Webb and Webb 1897: 158). Friendly societies commanded strong mechanisms for enforcing discipline internally, through workers' own accumulated contributions: "The member expelled for behaviour 'contrary to the interests of the trade' had no claim on the money he had contributed; and any member who had been paying in for some years was likely to

[3] Craft unions typically strive to organize workers on a local or regional (most ambitiously, national) basis, but the nature of the product is crucial to defining the necessary scope of control. Where products are mobile, localized control of labor markets will fail, for the goods can simply be produced elsewhere. This is why, historically, craft control has proved most stable and prevalent in industries (for example, construction) where the product is by definition not mobile and where therefore local labor market control suffices. I thank Peter Swenson for emphasizing this to me.

feel that he had an investment not lightly to be sacrificed" (Clegg, Fox, and Thompson 1964: 7). In addition, at a time when strikes were illegal and unions' rights were severely restricted, it did not take much for skilled workers to figure out how to exploit the legal protections offered to friendly societies and to use insurance funds in quiet ways to defend worker interests and enforce union controls (Hopkins 1995: 73; Gosden 1961: 9; Clegg, Fox, and Thompson 1964: 6; Baernreither 1893: 162). Certainly until the repeal of the Combination Laws in 1824 and even thereafter, "Mutual Insurance was the only method by which trade Unionists could lawfully attain their end" (Webb and Webb 1897: 166).

In this context, unemployment benefits were especially important tools in support of early unions' trade strategies (Webb and Webb 1897: 153). Worker solidarity was sorely tested in periods of economic downturn when unemployment reduced the willingness of skilled workers to defend the standard rate. "Accident, sickness and superannuation benefits all helped to keep off the labour market men whose quality of work had suffered some temporary or permanent decline which might tempt them to undermine customary wage rates or working conditions; but it was the 'out-of-work' (or 'donation') benefit which offered most protection for the rules" (Clegg, Fox, and Thompson 1964: 6; Prothero 1979: 30). By providing support for members without work, the society kept such workers from being tempted to sell their labor below the standard rate, which would undermine the power of the union to establish and maintain wages, working times, and standards of employment (Webb and Webb 1897: 158–62, 164).

The attempt to establish control over skilled labor markets is what drove union strategies with respect to apprenticeship and training. In order to maintain boundaries around the group and to avoid glutting the market with skilled labor, journeymen's societies sought to insist on certain standards of training (measured, typically, in terms of serving out an apprenticeship or its equivalent in work experience) and to try to restrict the number of apprentices being turned out over time, as well as to prohibit members from working with "illegal" (that is, non-union) men (Clegg, Fox, and Thompson 1964: 7). Requiring workers to document a certain level of skill allowed the societies to restrict their membership and define the occupational boundaries of the group whose position they sought to use their funds to protect. As the main union of skilled workers in the metalworking sector (Amalgamated Society of Engineers, ASE) put it, "if constrained to make restriction against the admission into our trade of those who have not earned a right by a probationary servitude, we do so, knowing such are productive of evil, and when persevered in unchecked, result in reducing the condition of the artisan to that of the unskilled labourer, and confer no permanent advantage on those admitted" (quoted in Knox 1980: 325).

Beyond its role as a signifier of a particular level of skill, apprenticeship was important to the unions as the main point of entry to the trade. Only by controlling the numbers of workers admitted to the trade could unions hope to exercise control over the conditions under which their members would be required to work. This is why most craft societies sought to engage employers in negotiations over the number of apprentices firms would be allowed to take. Employers understood very well that restrictions on apprenticeship were designed to maintain the market power of skilled workers, and union leaders such as William Allan (secretary of the ASE) readily admitted that the object of limiting apprentices was "to keep wages up; no question about it" (quoted in Knox 1980: 325).

In sum, and in sharp contrast to Germany, unions were deeply involved in attempting to regulate apprenticeship. Indeed, as Zeitlin points out, "the most significant attempts to regulate the conditions of apprenticeship in British engineering during the nineteenth century came from the trade unions;" their main interest, however, lay in restricting the quantity of apprenticeships rather than guaranteeing their quality (Zeitlin 1996: 7). Conflicts over this and other "control" issues were bound to be especially intense in industries such as engineering where employers who faced (locally based) efforts by unions to regulate the supply and price of skilled labor were at the same time subject to product market competition that spanned regional and increasingly also national boundaries. In general, the constellation of political interests surrounding apprenticeship in Britain, in contrast to Germany, ensured that plant-based training would become bound up in struggles between employers and unions of skilled workers. As Knox has put it, "apprenticeship became intertwined with trade unionism; an attack on one became an attack on the other" (Knox 1980: 32).

Implications for Industry

Whereas in Germany state policy promoted the organization and modernization of associations of master artisans, which served as key suppliers of skills for industry, in Britain the thrust of state policy was liberal and the effects were therefore quite different. Although skilled artisans would still preside over the training of the next generation, they did so mostly from a very different base, from within the context of unions of skilled workers whose interests, with regard to training, were tied into craft-based strategies of labor market control. Moreover, and again in sharp contrast to Germany, British apprenticeship after the repeal of the Statute of Artificers was a purely private contractual matter unregulated by any public or para-public framework. No collectively defined rules – establishing the length of training, limiting the number of apprentices, setting limits on who could take apprentices, for example – governed the kinds of contracts that might emerge. In some cases, apprentices and employers continued to sign formal indentures, but in the vast majority of cases, indentures gave way over the course of the nineteenth century to individual written contracts or informal verbal agreements.

In the previous chapter we saw how important was certification's role in Germany in mitigating the problems of quality and mutual commitment that typically plague plant-based apprentice training. In Germany, the deal between apprentices and training firms was held in place by the interests of both parties, and stabilized and underwritten by the certification process that institutionalized disincentives for cheating on both sides. Similar mechanisms were not in place in Britain, and this led to several different kinds of problems. First, the structure of the relationship between the apprentice and the training firm made credible commitments on both sides difficult to establish and maintain. In Germany, the master to whom a young worker was apprenticed was directly responsible (and could be held accountable) for the quality of training conferred. In Britain, by contrast, the employers who signed the apprentice contracts were very frequently not directly involved in the training. Rather, the task fell (or was explicitly delegated) to skilled journeymen who were employed in the firm (Perry 1976: 33; More 1980: 44, 79, 142–3; Knox 1980: 118–19). Journeymen in charge of training apprentices often served without additional pay or any explicit agreement about precise responsibilities and therefore had few incentives to use their own work time in training (Howell 1877: 835–6; Fleming and Pearce 1916: 122).[4]

Social reformers at the time railed against the lack of accountability: "The master to whom [the apprentice] was bound no longer taught him his

[4] In addition, journeymen could use their influence over apprentices not just to convey the skills of the craft but also to socialize youth into the secrets and norms of the trade that protected their interests against employers (Eisenberg 1987). Hinton (1983: 95–6) notes that frequently the first job an apprentice was taught was "keeping nix" which "consists in keeping a bright look-out for the approach of managers or foremen, so as to be able to give prompt and timely notice to the men who may be skulking, or having a sly read or smoke, or who are engaged on 'corporation work' – that is, work of their own."

trade; he was, so to speak, pitch forked into the workshop to pick up his trade as best he could, or to learn it from the many journeymen who were there employed" (Howell 1877: 835). Even where foremen or supervisors were charged with responsibility for apprentices, there were problems. In many cases, foremen were under considerable pressure to simply get the product out and were "too much burdened with routine duties to give much attention to apprentices" (Fleming and Pearce 1916: 122).

In addition, Britain lacked any formal certification and examination system to assess the quality of training that apprentices received in a given workplace. There were thus few possibilities for sanctions against firms that trained poorly or narrowly, either formal (revoking a firm's license to train, for example), or informal (for example through comparisons of apprentices' examination scores that would affect a firm's reputation for training). To the contrary, British employers had for some time offered distinct "classes" of apprenticeship. Small numbers of "premium" or "privilege" apprentices were singled out for more systematic and comprehensive training, while "ordinary" apprentices were simply set to work in a specific occupation (Zeitlin 1996: 6; Tawney 1909a: 521).[5] Even in industries such as engineering that relied heavily on skills, "ordinary" apprenticeship became more informal and increasingly narrow over time, although – importantly and paradoxically – without becoming any shorter, remaining at five to seven years well into the twentieth century.

If employers faced fewer sanctions for failing to train their apprentices well (and, given the long length of apprenticeship and the low wages attached to it, enjoyed some incentives to exploit them as cheap laborers), British youth also had fewer incentives to stick with their employers for the full duration of the training period. To become a certified "skilled worker" in Germany, a youth needed to complete an apprenticeship and pass an exam. In Britain, there were many different ways to acquire "skilled" status. It was entirely possible for a young man to "pick up" a trade through an informal "learnership" in a firm or to simply use his ability to move from company to company to acquire different skills. At the turn of the nineteenth century, British firms had youths working for them under radically different sorts of arrangements – from formal indentures to highly informal and fluid employment relationships. And, whereas in Germany the most promising youths were certain to have been heavily recruited for

[5] See Ministry of Labour (1928a: 18) for different "grades" or "classes" of apprenticeship (see also 100–3, 104).

high quality apprenticeships in the premier engineering firms, in Britain these same young people would have found it to their advantage to avoid formal contractual arrangements (which bound them for long periods) and instead to rely on their own resources and the recognition of their talents by employers to piece together their own skill repertoire.[6]

Membership in a trade union was an important signifier of a particular level of skills in Britain. As the structure of apprenticeship became looser over the nineteenth century, however, many trade societies were forced to revise their rules for membership – from the completion of a formal apprenticeship, to several years' work at the trade, and ultimately to the capacity of the worker to earn the current rate for skilled work in the district. By the mid-nineteenth century the Amalgamated Society of Engineers had dropped its requirement of a completed apprenticeship for membership in the union, and accepted "all persons who have worked at the trade for five years successively, and who are nominated by two full members who . . . are able to vouch for him as being able to earn his living at the trade, and to command the current wages of the district in which he is proposed" (Howell 1877: 839; Clegg, Fox, and Thompson 1964: 4). By 1877, one contemporary noted that "scarcely 10 per cent of those now admitted as members of trades unions have been properly apprenticed" (Howell 1877: 854), and the completion of a formal apprenticeship became even more loosely associated with union membership by century's end.[7] Writing in 1904 Booth described an increasingly prominent trend: "It was the ability to command a certain rate – and not a particular level of technical competence per se – that defined the worker as 'skilled'" (Booth 1904: 165).

In sum, British apprenticeship in the late nineteenth century lacked a stable, uniform framework that would have provided incentives for trainees and training firms to commit to each other for a stable period of training in the context of corrosive market forces and countervailing incentives. Contracts could not be enforced since apprentices who broke off their indentures had no resources for employers to try to recover their loss, and

[6] This explains why the firms that developed the country's best training programs (such as Westinghouse) found that the most desirable young apprentices were precisely those who were most reluctant to enter into an indentured relationship, preferring to take the responsibility themselves for acquiring the skills they needed and then move on quickly to the best paying positions. More on this below.

[7] By the turn of the century, the ASE was even allowing some workers, "under certain conditions, to join as probationary members at eighteen, and give them five years from that time in which to obtain full wages, but this limit is not infrequently exceeded" (Booth 1903: 299).

conversely, in the absence of any collectively defined standards of training, apprentices had no legal means to hold accountable employers who did not train well (Zeitlin 1996: 6–7). The entire relationship was, in contrast to Germany at the time, extremely fluid and fragile. As Bray put it, "The master is no longer bound to train the apprentice; the apprentice, even where the name is retained, can usually leave at a week's notice; there is no tie between the two" (Bray 1909: 413).

Union and Employer Strategies in the Metalworking/Engineering Industry

As in Germany, the metalworking industry – as a major consumer of skills – was an important site of struggle and innovation in skill formation. However, whereas in Germany the key political conflicts were played out between large metalworking firms and the organized handicraft sector, in Britain apprenticeship training was contested between employers and unions of skilled workers.

Early unions in the metalworking industries organized skilled workers on a local basis; their strategies were premised on the use of friendly society benefits to press employers to pay a standard rate and to control access for workers to jobs. The most successful such organization in the early nineteenth century, the Journeymen Steam Engine and Machine Makers' Friendly Society, took as a prerequisite for membership either a completed apprenticeship or seven years continuous employment at a trade. The skills thus acquired were seen as the only guarantee of the workers' ability to maintain steady employment and not become a drain on the society or pull wages down (Jeffreys 1945: 24, 59). The "Old Mechanics" (as the Society was nicknamed) did not have an explicit trade policy in the 1830s, "but shorter hours of work and payment for overtime, protests against 'illegal' men working at the trade and objections to 'overburdening the shop with apprentices' appear consistently as issues causing conflicts between the masters and the men" (Jeffreys 1945: 21, 24; Knox 1980: 317–18).[8]

An amalgamation movement among various unions in engineering (led by the Old Mechanics) resulted in the founding, in 1851, of the

[8] Given the ambiguous legal status of strikes, many conflicts were played out informally (resistance to overtime, for example), but the first recorded strike over apprentice limitations in the engineering industry is attributed to the Friendly Union of Mechanics (Knox 1980: 317).

Amalgamated Society of Engineers (ASE). This new society became a premier example of "new model unionism," which combined centralized (national) finances with local strategies for controlling wages and working conditions. Under the forceful leadership of William Newton, the primary goal of the ASE was to "destroy the redundancy in the labour market" and in this way uphold uniformly high wages for its members (Jeffreys 1945: 32–3). Restriction of apprenticeship was one key feature of the overall strategy of craft control that sparked repeated conflicts with employers (Hinton 1983: Chapter 2). In 1852, employers in two of the country's main engineering centers (London and Lancashire) rallied to respond to union attempts to enforce craft controls with a massive lockout that affected three thousand of the ASE's eleven thousand members. In the resulting protracted conflict, employers beat back the union's main control demands but the ASE survived and grew rather dramatically over the next years.[9]

The lockout prompted major changes in the union's tactics, but its goals remained the same. All rules regarding limitations on the number of apprentices in a shop and other such control issues were expunged from the Society's rules, among other reasons to provide legal cover for the organization and its funds. Although the executive council repudiated the use of strikes to achieve its ends, the policy of controlling the market in skills remained (Jeffreys 1945: 68). As Hinton puts it, "Between 1852–1874, the Engineers had no formal trade policy, the original objects of the amalgamation having been formally abandoned in response to the defeat of 1851.... Nevertheless, outside the written rules, the branches conducted the trade policy of the society – resistance to systematic overtime and piecework, limitation of apprentices, establishment of standard rates and hours in each district – and manipulated the friendly benefits in order to achieve this aim" (Hinton 1983: 76).

In other words, after 1852, the ASE's trade policy would be conducted not through noisy formal Executive Council resolutions and open strikes but informally and locally. "Standard rates and hours, bans on illegal men, limitation of apprentices, and monopolies of materials and machines were left to the branches, to be imposed by withdrawing men from illegal shops and supporting them by an unemployment benefit rendered more secure by centralized finance" (Clegg, Fox, and Thompson 1964: 8). The union's

[9] Between 1852 and 1866, membership rose from 9,737 to 33,017, and funds grew from £ 7,103 to £ 138,113. The number of branches affiliated with the Society rose in this period from 128 to 305 (Jeffreys 1945: 75).

strategy hinged not so much on large-scale strikes but rather on the "Strike in Detail" which put pressure on individual employers to conform by depriving them of skilled labor. The advantage for the union was that it minimized costs because only a small number of workers had to be supported at any time (Webb and Webb 1897: 169). In this way, "craft rules were . . . enforced for the most part without large-scale collisions with the employers as a body" (Clegg, Fox, and Thompson 1964: 9).

This strategy worked rather well, not least because the economic context at mid-century was highly auspicious and the fragmented industry structure (overwhelmingly small-scale operations) allowed unions to play firms off against each other (Jeffreys 1945: 54, 102; also Elbaum and Lazonick 1986: 4). When individual employers violated the standard rate or employed excessive numbers of apprentices, the union responded with pressure (sometimes in the form of a delegation from the union) and, where necessary, passive resistance. For example, in the case of too many apprentices, members were instructed not to teach the boys; if the issue was nonpayment of the standard rate, skilled men were withdrawn from the shop. If members were fired for their actions, they would be supported by donation benefits until they found another job (Jeffreys 1945: 69). As the first secretary of the ASE, William Allan, put it in 1867 in testimony to the Royal Commission: "We are very little engaged in regulating" rates of wages, "they regulate themselves, if I may use the expression" (quoted in Webb and Webb 1897: 169).[10]

This strategy of localized labor control was fraught with tension because firms subject to unevenly enforced local union controls were competing in increasingly sprawling interregional and international product markets. By the 1870s, British producers faced more intense competition from other European (especially German) and U.S. engineering firms (Clark 1957). In the 1880s unemployment in the British engineering, shipbuilding, and metal group rose to a level significantly (25%) above that of the rest of industry (Clark 1957: 128, fn3). In this context, the ASE Executive Council (already cautious of large-scale confrontations with employers after the 1852 lockout) became even more conservative – and also more convinced that labor market conditions had rendered obsolete the strategy of

[10] Allan was deliberately exaggerating the non-conflictual orientation of British craft unions. The context, after all, was one in which he was trying to persuade the Commission to support measures that would put unions on sounder legal footing. I thank Jonathan Zeitlin for emphasizing this to me.

controlling wages by attempting to influence the supply of labor (Jeffreys 1945: 93).[11]

A dispute in 1883 over the issue of apprentice limitation is emblematic of the dilemmas faced by the ASE in the late nineteenth century. The conflict began when the union's Sunderland branch took action against companies that were flagrantly exploiting apprentices as low-wage workers. One firm employed 672 men as against 478 apprentices (which worked out to a ratio of 1.39 journeymen per apprentice) (Knox 1980: 327–8). The union local provided evidence of further abuses in other companies, for example, shops with 23 journeymen to 37 apprentices, of 25 men to 54 apprentices, and with 500 apprentices to 700 men (Jeffreys 1945: 102). Employers responded with an offer of concessions on union wage demands but refused to negotiate on apprenticeship restriction (Knox 1980: 328–9). The ensuing strike lasted from June 1883 to May 1885 (in the course of which employers used apprentices as strike breakers) and the result was the "virtual annihilation" of the Sunderland branch. This defeat marked the abandonment by the union as a whole of any large-scale effort to limit apprenticeship (Jeffreys 1945: 102–3), even if it did not signal an end to the skirmishing between unions and employers over training in Britain.

Apprenticeship in Britain before World War I

The decades preceding the First World War underscore crucial differences between the German and British cases. Around the time the Handicraft Protection Law was passed in Germany, and metalworking firms were becoming increasingly obsessed with securing certification powers for their own in-plant training programs, their British counterparts were mobilizing around a quite different project: beating back union controls and reasserting managerial discretion on the shop floor. This development was prompted by the plant-level tensions surrounding the introduction of new machines and work reorganization and it culminated in the so-called Great Lockout of 1897.

[11] This conservatism had been a long-standing source of tension between the executive and the branches. The branches and district committees carried out the trade policies of the Society and had enough funds to get themselves into conflicts but not enough to carry them through to completion. In the 1850s several branches had to be threatened with suspension to force them to comply with executive decisions (Jeffreys 1945: 73). In 1871–72 the rank-and-file had dragged the executive into conflicts over the nine-hour day, the success of which paved the way for the subsequent election of John Burnett (unofficial leader of the strike) as general secretary of the ASE.

The period between 1890 and 1915 witnessed the rapid introduction of new technologies and production techniques, and in the engineering and shipbuilding industries specifically, the widespread introduction of semi-automatic machines that allowed employers to replace skilled workers with semi- or even unskilled labor (Knox 1986: 174; also Clegg, Fox, and Thompson 1964: 139–40; Price 1983). Among ASE members, turners (one of the union's two main constituencies) were particularly affected (Knox 1986: 174). The response of the union was to attempt to maintain control through a policy of "following the work to the new machines," that is, claiming for their members the exclusive right to run new machines, irrespective of the level of skill required. Moreover, and although previous attempts at craft controls – for example, in 1883 – had been roundly defeated by employers, economic recovery in the waning years of the nineteenth century rendered labor markets tighter and emboldened skilled craftsmen to re-assert previous controls (McKinlay and Zeitlin 1989: 35).

The changed technological and market context had, however, altered the strategic calculus of British employers. As Clegg and colleagues point out, before the 1890s employers had seen craft controls as a nuisance but "tolerable . . . so long as conditions were stable or innovations gradual; but they became intolerable when the rate of change increased" (Clegg, Fox, and Thompson 1964: 168). Among other things, the ability of skilled workers to enforce craft controls varied tremendously across different localities and regions, and the market premium that accrued to producers unencumbered by union controls (and therefore able to introduce machines and reorganize production more easily) was substantial. Far from leveling the playing field, the uneven effects of union policy introduced (for the affected employers) maddening distortions in product market competition. The result was to sharpen conflict with unions. The engineering employers struck back in 1897 with a massive mobilization in defense of "managerial prerogative."

The story of the lockout has been told elsewhere, and cannot be dealt with at length here (see, for example, Gray 1976). For present purposes, the two main points concern the impact of the conflict on employers and the outcome of the dispute. On the eve of the conflict, British engineering employers were almost completely unorganized, but in the course of the seven-month conflict, membership in the Engineering Employers Federation (EEF) soared, from 180 to 702 (Clegg, Fox, and Thompson 1964: 165; also Phelps Brown 1959: 162). As Clegg and colleagues note, "for the leaders of the [newly founded] Federation . . . to extend the scope of a lockout, particularly at a time of improving trade, was a difficult if not unique operation. Their success was powerful testimony not only to the strength of their feelings but also to a lack of fastidiousness in their methods" including threats by large firms with extensive supplier networks to do business only with employers who supported the Federation (Clegg, Fox, and Thompson 1964: 166). The outcome of the conflict was a virtually unalloyed victory for the employers and one that struck directly at the decentralized control strategies that the ASE had been pursuing on a range of issues, including apprenticeship. The EEF forced the union to grant broad concessions on managerial prerogatives, including acknowledging the right of employers to hire non-unionists, the power to assign work on new machines unilaterally and at a wage rate satisfactory to the employee and employer, the almost unrestricted right to call overtime, freedom to introduce piece rates, and the abandonment of all restrictions on the employment of apprentices (Clegg, Fox, and Thompson 1964:167; McKinlay and Zeitlin 1989: 36).

It is important, however, that the resolution to the conflict did not obliterate the union.[12] The terms of settlement specifically established collective bargaining and dispute resolution procedures that strengthened the authority of the central union leadership vis-à-vis the union branches, and it institutionalized dispute resolution procedures to enforce that control. The effect of this on craft strategies was aptly summarized in 1914 by an executive of the Engineers: "[p]revious to the 1897 lockout . . . the state of disorganisation amongst the employers enabled us to secure our demands [in shop disputes] with little or no previous negotiation. . . . Individual firms could easily be approached" (quoted in Clegg, Fox, and Thompson 1964: 341). After the 1897 conflict (and under the terms of its settlement) the ASE was expected "to discipline its locals, against threat of another sweeping industrial lockout" (McKinlay and Zeitlin 1989: 36).

Apprenticeship after the Lockout

In Germany, machine and metalworking firms at the turn of the century began organizing and mobilizing around the goal of securing official recognition and certification powers for the training programs they had been developing. The larger producers were spurred on in this endeavor by competition with the handicraft chambers whose powers to certify skills

[12] Nor for that matter did it lead to a complete reorganization of production in most of engineering. This points to important differences from similar-looking struggles around this time in Sweden and the United States. I return to this comparison in Chapter 4.

they coveted. In Britain, engineering firms at century's end had just scored a victory over decentralized craft union controls and were motivated by quite different objectives: institutionalizing a regime with the participation of the national union, but designed above all to preserve managerial prerogatives on the shop floor.

Apprenticeship was if anything less, not more, regulated after 1897. Any notion of joint regulation (with the unions) of apprenticeship was not considered – quite the contrary, as that issue was seen as part of the union "control" package that had been so decisively defeated. Moreover, although engineering employers in Britain had succeeded in banding together to defeat union controls, they did not organize to coordinate among themselves alternative rules regarding in-plant training. Jeffreys argues that in the wake of the 1897 conflict "employers, operating their right 'to select and train' their workers, started flooding the shops with handymen and boys" (Jeffreys 1945: 156). On the union side, "the absence of any other defined policy led the members to adopt isolated shop tactics. The phrase regarding the employers' right to train was taken literally and members refused to assist or instruct newcomers in any way. Training was treated as the employer's responsibility to pursue as best he could" (Jeffreys 1945: 157).[13]

Developments in this period in Britain hastened the decline of systematic apprenticeship through their effects on both *employers' behavior* and the *incentives that youth faced.* First, significant numbers of employers – including some (though by no means all[14]) engineering employers – turned to apprentices as a source of cheap productive labor. Second, and partly in consequence, formal apprenticeship (under either written or verbal agreement) lost the attractiveness it had once held for youths, as fewer young people were willing to forgo the higher wages they could earn for unskilled work and to embark on a long-term commitment to training with uncertain payoffs. Though these two trends overlap and interrelate, the following discussion treats them, to the extent possible, sequentially and in turn.

[13] Even beyond the union's official policy, the disinclination of skilled workers generally to train new recruits was exacerbated by an increase in piecework in engineering in the years following the union's defeat. Any time a skilled worker spent on an apprentice came at the expense of his own earnings (Jeffreys 1945: 206). Knox cites figures indicating that "by 1914, 46 per cent of fitters and 37 per cent of turners were on piece rates, compared to only 5 per cent of all engineering and boilermaking workers in 1886" (Knox 1986: 176).

[14] See below for a discussion of the very different strategies of Britain's largest and most progressive engineering firms.

Boy Labour. Some engineering employers undoubtedly used the defeat of the ASE to extend the use of apprenticeship as a cheap alternative to semi-skilled labor, providing narrow training on particular machines and then using apprentices in place of more expensive skilled craftsmen. In the absence of any overarching regulatory authority governing apprenticeship, broad training and high skill standards could not be enforced. The structure of the British political economy – which as Howell (forthcoming, Chapter 1) has put it, featured a "particularly brutal form of capitalism" built on small producers and low capital requirements – exacerbated collective action problems in training by making it easy for new entrants to the industry to compete on the basis of lower wages (Elbaum and Lazonick 1986; Zeitlin 1990: 412). Many small British engineering firms sought advantage through strategies designed to intensify work but without massive rationalization and work reorganization – that is, "through methods such as the multiplication of apprentices, the manipulation of incentive payment systems, systematic overtime, and the promotion of semiskilled workers onto simpler types of machinery" (Zeitlin 1990: 412).

We saw that in Germany small specialty producers in the country's decentralized industrial districts were able to achieve significant coordination, first through their own regional trade associations and, during the Weimar years, through the VDMA. These organizations – propped up and promoted by the state in various ways – provided a site through which small producers were able to minimize ruinous head-to-head competition in particular product markets. This made it possible for them to invest in training and the same institutions that organized competition in product markets encouraged coordination on training standards. Similar institutions were weak or nonexistent in Britain; it made a huge difference, for example, that the EEF was an employers', not a trade, association. It encompassed firms in widely divergent product markets and therefore with quite different interests with respect to training, not to mention labor relations, which was the association's main brief. The EEF always struggled against centrifugal tendencies and did best when it mobilized its members around lowest-common-denominator demands (for example, defense of managerial autonomy) rather than attempting to subordinate firms to some other (even employer-dominated) authority (see, especially, Zeitlin 1991).

The closing decades of the nineteenth century thus saw a (further) blurring of the line between apprentices and learners on the one hand and boy labourers – that is, those "who are being employed solely with a view to the present utility of their labour" – on the other (Tawney 1909a: 518–19, 524).

The problem of cheap "boy labour" was widely criticized at this time in the business and academic press but a practical reality on the shop floor (Bray 1912; Dunlop and Denman 1912; Tawney 1909a: 519 and passim). The specialization of production processes brought about by technological changes was part of the problem. Tawney quotes one firm as reporting that "Boys are kept as a rule in their own departments. They are not taught, they are made to work" (Tawney 1909a: 522; see also Tawney 1909b: 304). He quotes a Glasgow employer, who bluntly summarized the prevailing logic: "'to put an apprentice on a valuable machine is a waste of money unless he is specialised to it, and in all trades the longer the boy is kept at the process the sooner does he become economically profitable" (Tawney 1909a: 521). The labor of apprentices specialized to particular machines could quickly be turned to profit and the combination of continued long apprentice periods (still five to seven years in Britain) and the low wages they earned made this strategy attractive for some employers (on these developments see especially Knox 1980: v and passim).

Although these practices differed quite a lot across firms and especially across industries,[15] the "proletarianization of apprentices" in Britain at the turn of the century was the subject of a vast literature, one that sparked a broad debate that has no equivalent in Germany at the time (Bray 1909; Bray 1912; Dunlop and Denman 1912; Fleming and Pearce 1916). As one contemporary noted, "inquiry shows that several tendencies are at work to assimilate the position of the boy who is nominally an apprentice or learner to the position of the boy who is employed simply as a labourer" (Tawney 1909a: 519). Another bemoaned the long-term effects of the decline of apprenticeship, as boys were increasingly "set to perform the same operation, and acquire skill and dexterity only in that one direction. . . . As men they are skilled, not in a trade, but in a single operation of that trade" (Bray 1909: 413; Tawney 1909b). Reformers and advocates of strong plant-based training complained that "Even where apprentice agreements are drawn up, too often youths are exploited on repetition work, and no heed is given to the obligations due to the youth or to the community" (Fleming and Pearce 1916: 122).

Another development in this period, related to the technological changes discussed above and the conflicts these provoked with skilled unions, was

[15] More, for example, insists that the exploitation of apprentices was exaggerated, and notes that training did continue to take place in those industries (engineering prime among them) in which production continued to rely heavily on skill (More 1980: passim).

employers' strategic use of apprentices in struggles with organized labor (see, especially Knox 1980: 343; Knox 1986). In the 1897 dispute discussed above, some employers had used apprentices as strike breakers, threatening trainees with prosecution under the Masters and Servants Act of 1875 if they refused to work (Wigham 1973: Chapter 3; Childs 1990: 786–7). In cases in which apprentices did join in the strike, employers often forced them back to work and obliged them to sign a document renouncing any future participation in labor disputes – and to make up for each day out of work with two days labor (Knox 1980: 342).

Knox notes a revival of interest on the part of employers in formal indentures and written contracts between the late 1880s and 1914 (Knox 1980: v, 129–31, 66). Although not the only reason, such interest might be partly understood against the backdrop of the strategic importance of apprentices in conflicts with unions (Knox 1980: 343). The sorts of indentures that emerged in this period support this interpretation. They took the form of private contracts that explicitly "gave the employer all the disciplinary benefits of the traditional indenture," but remained vague or limited in the specification of the reciprocal duties of the firm toward the apprentice (Knox 1986: 180). Such indentures, in other words, were only binding in one direction – and did not necessarily contain any guarantees to the apprentices that the firm would provide high quality training or even continued employment for the full term of the contract. In the wake of a strike by apprentices in 1912 in a number of major engineering and shipbuilding companies in Scotland, Northeast England and Manchester, the EEF issued a model apprentice contract for its member firms that gave strict disciplinary powers to employers, but did nothing to establish standards for training and specifically reserved a firm's right to fire apprentices on the spot for participating in strikes, as well as to lay them off if necessary in an economic downturn (Knox 1980: 134, 226–7; see also Knox 1986 on the strike).

Youth and Apprenticeship. The dynamics sketched out above contributed mightily to a trend in which formal apprenticeship lost a great deal of its attractiveness to many British youths. In a context in which apprenticeship no longer guaranteed comprehensive training and in which there were alternative possible routes to acquiring and documenting skill, many youths began to doubt the value of making a long-term contractual commitment, and came to prefer more flexible arrangements that would allow them to move more freely in response to new opportunities and higher wages.

We saw that by the first decade of the twentieth century in Germany, apprenticeship was an attractive route from the perspective of both promising young boys and their parents, who saw advantages to forgoing higher wages for a well-defined (three- to four-year) period in exchange for the promise of skill certification that enjoyed widespread and growing recognition in the market. The capacity of the handicraft sector to certify the skills they conferred had prompted leading machine firms to seek similar certification powers for themselves in order to exercise greater control over the content of training.

In Britain, formal apprenticeship looked much less attractive. The difference was not in the wages trainees received, for in Germany as in Britain, apprentice wages were well below the rate for skilled workers and even many unskilled jobs. As we saw in Chapter 1, low wages may help stabilize training by shifting the costs, at least partly, onto (credit-constrained) trainees. Rather, the key differences from the German practice were in the length of training and especially in the advantages such training conferred.

British youth were subject to a much longer training period – between five and seven years throughout most of the engineering industry. The length of the apprenticeship had almost nothing to do with the time required to learn a craft. It was determined mostly by the age at which an apprentice began, continuing typically to the age of 21, "since on the attainment of that age it is open to the apprentice to repudiate the contract" (Ministry of Labour 1928a: 83). As Table 3.1 indicates, in 1909 about one-half of engineering apprentices served five years and over a quarter of them served a full seven years.

If this were not enough, trainees were often expected to serve an additional period of "improvership" before they could qualify for full adult skilled wages. Describing conditions in the engineering industry in 1903, Booth notes that "a lad's period of nominal apprenticeship would normally end at age 21" but "must not have been of less than five year's duration, and after that he is usually expected to serve a further period as 'improver'" which amounted to another one to three years with wages ranging "from

Table 3.1. *Length of apprenticeship, percentage, figures from 1909*

	3 years	4 years	5 years	5–7 years	6 years	7 years
Engineering	0.1	0.9	53.5	10.0	8.0	27.5
Shipbuilding	0.2	–	53.0	0.6	18.0	28.2

Source: More 1980: 70.

half to three-quarters of the full men's rate . . . the employers using their discretion quite without let or hindrance in this respect" (Booth 1903: 299). Since the vast majority of apprentices and learners – at least in engineering (according to More, 90% ([More 1980: 73]) – were required to serve such improverships, an engineering apprentice in Britain was looking at a very long-term commitment before he achieved "skilled status" or more precisely, until he would be entitled to the full adult skilled rate.

The second key difference from German practice is the lack of formal certification awarded to an apprentice on completion of his or her training, and, related to that, some guarantee that training would be of relatively high quality. In the absence of regulations and monitoring of training, or any clear standards to which employers could be held accountable, youth in Britain faced a situation in which it often made no sense to them to submit to years of reduced wages with very uncertain returns. As Dunlop and Denman point out, "the boy has no desire to bind himself for a long period of years to serve for low wages when he can easily earn more money in other ways, while his father is unwilling to pay a premium when he can obtain no guarantee that his son will be properly taught the trade" (Dunlop and Denman 1912: 330, fn1). Working class parents, strapped financially, were especially dubious about the advantages of apprenticeship, and "lads [were] drawn to [unskilled] work for the higher wages they [could] earn" (Bray 1909: 414; Bray 1912: 137).

The pull of so-called "blind alley" jobs was overall much greater in Britain than in Germany at this time, not least because boys left school earlier, more typically at 12 against 14 in Germany. Citing statistics gathered by a government-sponsored Education Committee, Reginald Bray painted a bleak picture: Between 11 to 17% of 14- to 17-year-olds were reported to be entering skilled trades, as against 28 to 34% entering low-skill occupations, along with another approximately one-third of 14-year-olds who became errand and shop boys (Bray 1909: 143).[16] Tawney finds the same thing for Glasgow (1909): 53.6% of boys left elementary schools to become milk boys or lorry boys, 24.6% to become unskilled workers, and only 12% to enter into an apprenticeship or learnership (Knox 1980: 42).[17] No wonder contemporaries who bemoaned the decay of indentured

[16] The problem was especially intense in metropolitan labor markets, where the opportunities for low-skill service jobs were greater. Thanks to Jonathan Zeitlin for emphasizing this to me.

[17] Some of this slightly exaggerates the problem, as some youth did take up an apprenticeship after one or two years out. But there was an overall decline between 1901 and 1911 in

apprenticeship worried about the growing reserve of "shiftless, feckless boys" who lacked training and discipline (Bray 1909: 412–13) and the army of "industrial nomads" who were being turned out (Tawney 1909a: 531).[18] The unskilled jobs that young boys performed were by definition without long-term prospects, since as these young workers neared adulthood they would be replaced by new youngsters. Thus, as Tawney complained, "The boy, thrown out at 16, 17, or 18 or 20 years of age, drifts into the low-skilled labour market or the army of unemployables" (Tawney 1909a: 517).

For youth who did decide to invest in training, the flip side of the "boy labour" problem is that youth faced fewer incentives to complete an apprenticeship. In Germany, an apprentice needed to complete his training to collect his certificate, but in Britain youth were not tied to the firm in the same way.[19] Knox documents complaints in this period by employers who were frustrated by the behavior of apprentices who abandoned their training early to take advantage of more lucrative offers (Knox 1986: 177). He also reports that one estimate in the early 1900s indicated that "not more than 50–55 per cent of engineering and shipbuilding apprentices completed their time" (Knox 1986: 177–8).

These problems were well understood by contemporaries, particularly by the firms that had the greatest stake in a well functioning training system. The engineers in charge of training at British Westinghouse (very high quality training, as we will see below) expressed the need for skilled trades to be accorded a "definite status" based on a "practical test" of the apprentice's abilities (Fleming and Pearce 1916: 161, 122, respectively). As representatives of Britain's most progressive training firms, they complained of a lack of a "definite standard regarding what constitutes a skilled workman or

young workers employed in skilled trades (Knox 1980: 54). In key trades such as fitting, turning, and erecting, for example, the number of workers under 21 years old was 33,794 in 1901 and had dropped by over 5,000, to 28,403 by 1911. The story is similar for other trades.

[18] As Childs writes: "A report from Glasgow suggested that most boy labourers and learners (as opposed to bound apprentices) passed through at least six jobs between fourteen and twenty-one; more often the figure was twelve jobs, while figures of twenty to thirty were not unheard of" (Childs 1990: 791).

[19] More argues that the problem of apprenticeship defection has been overstated, and he notes that an apprentice who absconded "risked forfeiting his 'lines' – his certificate at leaving which showed that he had served so many years" (More 1980: 77). My point is that in Britain there were other ways of achieving skilled status and that completing an apprenticeship required a much longer commitment than in Germany.

craftsman" (Fleming and Pearce 1916: 122). Perhaps most tellingly of all, these training experts advocated a *shortening* of the length of apprenticeship to five years maximum (Fleming and Pearce 1916: 162).

As premier training firms such as Westinghouse experienced first-hand, the most promising youth were among the least likely to seek out a formal apprenticeship in Britain, confident as they were that they could achieve skilled status without binding themselves to a particular employer. The engineers who helped develop Westinghouse's training program describe the problem well: "The lack of a definite plan of training is responsible for a great decline in apprenticeship of any kind, because in many works the shop youth who is not 'bound' is able not only to earn more money, but has all the privileges of a formally apprenticed youth, so far as either have any at all. Such a system is, of course, fatal to the success of a sound apprenticeship system, since the most promising boys are unlikely to commit themselves to a long period of service at small wages without any special ultimate advantage to themselves" (Fleming and Pearce 1916: 122–3). Thus, when the British Westinghouse Company began to set up its training program in 1913, they quickly determined that the boys who were working at the company under formal apprenticeship agreements were among the least promising trainees. "It would seem that the system [of apprentice contracts] generally attracted a poor type of youth, who was anxious to possess the security that a period of apprenticeship would give, while the most intelligent youths moved about from shop to shop, and trusted to their experience to enable them to acquire a steadily progressive rate of wages and standard of work" (Fleming and Pearce 1916: 141–2).

The situation in Britain at century's end and up to World War I was aptly summarized by the Webbs: "There are to-day so many opportunities for boys to earn relatively high wages without instruction, that they are not easily induced either to enter upon a term of educational servitude at low rates, or to continue on it if they have begun" (Webb and Webb 1897: 477). They continue: "the system of apprenticeship has lost what was really its main attraction.... What the father and the apprentice were willing to pay for was, not the instruction, but the legal right to exercise a protected trade. When this right to a trade could be obtained without apprenticeship.... father and sons alike have always been eager to forgo its educational advantages" (Webb and Webb 1897: 477–8).

By the first decade of the twentieth century, some similarities but also several key differences had emerged in apprenticeship training in Germany and Britain.[20] Apprentice wages in both countries were low – this being a mechanism through which firms shifted part of the cost of training onto the youth, a practice particularly important to smaller producers. In Germany, however, handicraft producers faced incentives to train well. If they did not, they would lose their license to train and, with it, the cheap extra hand in production. Similar monitoring devices were lacking in Britain, so that there were no real sanctions against British employers who chose to specialize apprentices on particular machines to the detriment of their training.

In addition, there was considerable uncertainty in Britain regarding the quality of training and the value of formal apprenticeship. One of the factors that shored up apprenticeship in Germany was the existence of "clearly defined and formally recognized qualifications [that provided] a 'currency of exchange' between employers and employees and between educational institutions and learners" (Cruz-Castro and Conlong 2001). This type of certification and recognition was lacking in Britain, making it highly uncertain on the employer side exactly what skills even a fully apprenticed worker possessed (hence the need for an additional period of "improvership" in the vast majority of cases), and highly dubious on the side of youth what benefits were associated specifically with apprenticeship as opposed to the other more informal methods available for achieving "skilled" status.

Reform Efforts before World War I

The deterioration of apprenticeship was not looked upon with equanimity in all quarters, by any means. Ever since the Paris Exhibition of Manufacturers in 1867, a growing number of voices could be heard warning that British industry would fall behind its competitors unless something was done to upgrade the country's system of technical education and training (Dunlop and Denman 1912). Educators such as Silvanus P. Thompson (Professor of Experimental Physics at the University of Manchester) spoke for many when he criticized the British system in 1879: "the skilled industries of Great Britain with their irregular bands of workers, trained anyhow, nohow, armed with scraps of empirical knowledge, and swaddled up in the rules of thumb, are doomed before the industries of nations who bring

[20] The categories around which this summary is organized come from Cruz-Castro and Conlong (2001).

into the field ordered legions of trained workers equipped with intellectual weapons, and clothed with sound science. . . . We have, however, one chance left; we must adapt our system to the new social order, and drill and train our workers in a systematic and scientific apprenticeship" (quoted in Knox 1980: 35).

A number of voluntary and philanthropic organizations attempted to redress the problems associated with apprenticeship training in Britain (see especially Knox 1980; Chapter 9). Their efforts are noteworthy because they point to the way that contemporaries understood the problems of youth training and underscore important differences from the institution in Germany. The problems described above – exploitation of trainees by employers, waning interest on the part of youth in apprenticeship – attracted the attention of a number of voluntary societies in Britain in the late nineteenth and early twentieth centuries. In particular, Jewish and Christian organizations became involved in forging connections between training firms and the youth in their communities. This movement began with the formation, in 1868, of the Industrial Committee of the Jewish Board of Guardians, followed in 1886 with the founding of a parallel organization, the East London Apprenticing Fund for Christian Children (Jevons 1908: 455–6).

These organizations took as their goal the initiation and successful completion of training for youth in their communities. They offered a number of services, establishing contacts between firms and apprentices, directing trainees to appropriate firms, and assisting companies in locating suitable apprentices. They also frequently stepped in to pay a premium (or fee) to the company (as a loan to the apprentice), a measure associated with an explicit promise on the part of the firm to offer these apprentices more systematic and comprehensive training than they could expect as regular (non-premium or "trade") apprentices. Such organizations often assigned to each apprentice a "guardian" who would monitor the trainee's progress through periodic workshop visits, and at the same time make sure that the employer was holding up his end of the agreement (Jevons 1908: 455–6; Knox 1980: 299–301).[21]

[21] A secular organization, the National Institute of Apprenticeship, formed in 1898, adopted similar goals and employed similar tools. The institute provided apprentice premiums for boys (and girls as well), aided and advised youth and their parents in negotiating the terms of the apprenticeship, and exercised some oversight over the training process (Knox 1980: 301–2).

A more expansive effort (at least in its aspirations), and one that adopted many of the same practices pioneered by the previous organizations was the Apprenticeship and Skilled Employment Association. This London-based organization began work in the first decade of the twentieth century, and operated as an umbrella for what its organizers hoped would become a national network of local Apprenticeship and Skilled Employment Committees. By 1909, the national association had established 17 committees in London and 10 committees in other cities including Glasgow and Edinburgh (Dunlop and Denman 1912: 326; Knox 1980).[22] This association aimed at "encouraging the entry of children into good trades and occupations with prospects, by offering advice to parents and by finding definite and suitable openings for the children" (quote is from Jevons 1908: 455; see also Bray 1909: 404). Although not associated with any particular religious or cultural organization, this movement, like its predecessors, was a completely voluntary and philanthropic operation. Staffed largely by women officers, the organization reflected middle class concerns about the growing numbers of youth flowing into blind alley jobs (Dunlop and Denman 1912: 326–7). Local committees nurtured strong relations with elementary schools and boys' and girls' clubs within their areas,[23] and they organized their work around finding suitable apprentice positions for youth in firms and establishing the terms of the contract "with a view to securing fair conditions to the employee, and satisfactory workers to the employer" (Dunlop and Denman 1912: 327).

These committees took it upon themselves not just to make the connection between apprentice and employer (and pay the premium for the apprentice, mostly on a loan basis), but also to provide some monitoring of the training process itself. "The work of the Committee does not cease with the placing of the boy or girl. A watch is kept over his progress throughout the time of apprenticeship or period of learning the trade. This is often done through a 'visitor' or 'guardian,' who is asked to take a generally friendly interest in the progress of his charge, and to report on it to the Committee" (Jevons 1908: 457). In some cases, the committee even acted as direct intermediary and contractor between apprentice and employer: "When possible, the Committee uses its own form of indentures, which contains a special clause allowing a representative to act as fourth party with power to cancel the agreement, should it be

[22] Jevons (1908) contains a listing of the committees in operation in 1908.
[23] From a document put out by the umbrella organization, in Jevons (1908: Appendix, 461).

necessary either through the failure of the employer to fulfil his contract to teach the trade, or through the bad behavior of the apprentice" (Jevons 1908: 457).

The efforts of these voluntary and philanthropic societies are noteworthy, especially in comparison to Germany, as an attempt to devise some kind of institutional infrastructure that could underwrite apprentice contracts and monitor compliance on both sides – in effect, to serve some of the functions performed in Germany by certification through compulsory handicraft chambers. From the perspective of the theories outlined in Chapter 1, these committees did serve a number of functions that would have been useful to all parties – facilitating the dissemination of information about employment prospects in various trades, providing information to parents and apprentices about "good" and "bad" employers from the perspective of training, providing oversight mechanisms that would throw a spotlight on both the quality of training offered by employers and the efforts and progress of apprentices themselves (Dunlop and Denman 1912:327). Contemporaries rightly praised the work of these committees for drawing attention to the problems of juvenile labor that were rampant at the time, and for taking measures to ameliorate these problems – at least on a limited basis.

Therein lay the real problem – the limited reach of these programs. Whereas in Germany a very large proportion of apprentice training took place under the auspices of the compulsory handicraft framework, Britain's voluntary system for oversight and monitoring simply never covered a significant number of trainees (see especially Knox 1980: 301–2). The most ambitious efforts by the Apprenticeship and Skilled Employment Committees resulted in the placement of 300 boys and girls in the first year of their existence. This number rose to around 500 by 1907, and in 1909 the committees placed 187 male and 259 female apprentices (along with about double that combined number of male and female learners). The efforts of these voluntary associations were scattered and uncoordinated, however. Although they were acknowledged (for example, in a government report from 1909 on youth education), it was also noted that these initiatives remained very limited in scope and impact (Education 1909a: 63). Moreover, the committees declined after 1909, a consequence in part of the extension of the government labour exchanges instituted in that period. Bray notes that in London (where the Association was most active) not more than 2% of boys who left elementary schools came "under the influence of these associations" (Bray 1912: 91).

Strategies of Large Metalworking Companies

Large engineering companies in Britain also had reasons for viewing the deterioration of apprenticeship with great concern. Like their counterparts in Germany, firms such as Mather and Platt, J & J Colman, Thames Iron Works Company, British Electric, Clayton and Shuttleworth, Hawthorn, and Leslie and Co. relied heavily on skills and stood at the forefront of efforts to improve apprentice training in Britain. Many of these companies saw in German institutions and practices an explicit model to be emulated (Fleming and Pearce 1916). Yet, as this section argues, the context was in many ways hostile to sustaining islands of "best practice" in firm-based training, let alone having these emerge as standard setting for the rest of industry.

Like their German counterparts, Britain's large engineering companies directed considerable energy and resources toward vocational education and training.[24] Mather and Platt, a Manchester engineering firm, was considered a pioneer in the encouragement of technical education. As early as 1873, the company had founded its own workshop-based technical school, to provide more systematic theoretical and practical training for its apprentices (Perry 1976: 31; Education 1909a: 96–7). Another industrial giant, Clayton and Shuttleworth, also developed an elaborate program for apprentice training, designed to combine "with the modern factory system the advantages of the old system of apprenticeship" (Sadler and Beard 1908: 276–7). The program involved a mix of practical and theoretical training, and apprentices were assigned to "superintendents" charged with the responsibility to "supervise, teach, promote, and advise" trainees (Sadler and Beard 1908: 276–7).[25] In addition to requiring the apprentice to take classes in the firm, the company made efforts to move the apprentice around the works to familiarize him with a broader range of trades.

Britain's premier engineering firms strove to recruit the most promising youth into their factories and training programs. This meant avoiding taking apprentices who had only completed the minimal mandatory elementary school, and opting instead for older boys who had continued their education beyond the statutory minimum. This was the policy, for example, of Vickers, which devoted considerable attention to recruitment and among other things "insisted upon a knowledge of algebra and geometry"

[24] For an overview of practices circa 1909 see Education (1909a: 96–100).

[25] This firm's apprentice program, as well as that of many of the other firms discussed below, are summarized in Sadler and Beard (1908).

for the youth into whose further training they intended to pour additional firm resources. Armstrong Whitworth (Manchester) and Barr and Stroud (Glasgow) also took account of the educational achievements and even extracurricular activities in their selection process (More 1980: 67). Cadbury Brothers (Birmingham) required its incoming apprentices to have completed two years of evening school study (Fleming and Pearce 1916: 99).

Once an apprentice had entered the firm, these employers in various ways promoted the continuing participation of trainees in evening technical classes, paying the student's class fees, for example, or relieving trainees of the obligation to perform overtime (or in some cases letting them leave early on the day their evening class was to meet). Such were the policies, for example, of W. H. Allen, Son & Co., Ltd. (Bedford) and Palmers Shipbuilding and Iron Company Ltd. (Jarrow).[26] Palmers instituted an additional system of incentives, raising the wages of apprentices as they progressed through technical classes.[27] Less common was the policy adopted by Mather and Platt, which made attendance at evening technical classes compulsory for all apprentices employed in the firm, and which also paid or reimbursed the students' school fees, contingent on good performance (Education 1909b: 350).

One of the most celebrated training programs in Britain before World War I was that developed by the British Westinghouse Company.[28] The company set up a works school in 1913, and it began operation in 1914 with 100 boys chosen for the program based on interviews. The boys participated in a program of instruction held in the company works school organized into subjects ranging from arithmetic to specific trade classes relating to skills the company required. Although the program enrolled only a very small number of the company's young workers (about 5% of boys under 18 years of age who were employed at the time), the number of apprentices in the works had risen to 272 (or 23%) by a year later (1915) (Fleming and Pearce 1916: 155–6). Significantly, these training initiatives were associated with a revival of bound indentures, and acceptance into the program required

[26] Beyond this, Allen and Son also instituted a smaller program for a select group of premium apprentices who were being groomed for "positions of responsibility." For these apprentices the company arranged additional plant-based theoretical instruction including science lectures during the winter months.

[27] In the case of Palmers, however, the company itself reported, "the scheme has not, up to the present time, been largely taken advantage of."

[28] This discussion draws on the account of Fleming and Pearce, two engineers who played a significant role in developing and running the program there (1916).

the boys' parents to sign a formal agreement committing the youth to stay at the firm until the age of 21 (Fleming and Pearce 1916: 148). Other companies (such as Vickers, Sons and Maxim Ltd. of Sheffield) also used private contracts to bind boys to their training term (Knox 1980: 343).

There are some important similarities between these practices and those developed by the large metalworking firms in Germany before the war – the overall structure and objectives of the best training facilities, and the lack of significant participation by organized labor, for example. One is also struck, however, by some key differences, among them an overall higher degree of stratification of training programs in British engineering firms and a greater emphasis (superfluous in the German context) on measures to facilitate apprentices in attending technical classes outside of working hours. A number of firms took on different "grades" of apprenticeship – so-called premium versus "ordinary" or trade apprentices.[29] Most often, the more elaborate programs described above (providing true all round training) were specifically meant for only a small subset of apprentices who were explicitly being groomed for leadership positions in the firm.

More generally, however, the training a boy could expect to receive was often at least in part a function of the educational background he brought with him to the firm. In the case of Vickers of Sheffield, youths with a high school or grammar school education might qualify for a two-year course at the local Technical Department of Sheffield University, paid for by the company and made possible by the grant of a two-year leave of absence from the apprenticeship (Fleming and Pearce 1916: 99). Similarly, the apprentice program established in 1906 by Cadbury Brothers (Birmingham), took very few apprentices and only those who had completed two years of evening courses were admitted to the company-sponsored trade classes (Fleming and Pearce 1916: 99).

Talented "ordinary" apprentices could work their way up in the ranks by demonstrating exceptional motivation or skill. Certainly the policies of the premier training firms were designed to discover and promote ambitious young workers – for example, by providing various incentives for trainees to enroll themselves in evening technical classes or by rewarding them for

[29] See More (1980: 104–6) on "premium" apprenticeship, which was distinguished from ordinary trade apprenticeship by more comprehensive training and (related to that) payment by the apprentice of a fee to the firm of between fifty to a hundred pounds. More suggests that "premium apprenticeship was widespread in [the engineering] industry . . . before the First World War" and cites evidence that it even continued in some engineering firms in the 1920s and 1930s, though in diminishing numbers (More 1980: 104–5).

good marks they received there. By contrast, it is not clear that the practical in-plant component of training was so different from or so much more systematic than that of other firms. Even in the top engineering firms, such training normally took place not in specialized workshops (as in Germany's top training firms) but rather on the job and under the guidance of skilled journeymen or foremen, with many of the accompanying problems cited above.[30] Firms such as Clayton and Shuttleworth (agricultural machines, in Lincoln) and Elswick Works of Armstrong (armaments) boasted that they provided their apprentices with an all-round training through systematic progression through the works, but even More, who is overall rather optimistic about training in this period, admits that this was "perhaps unusual" and notes other cases where breadth of experience may have been "more by chance than design" – and only "rarely the result of a carefully thought out plan by management" (More 1980: 85–6). Even in the celebrated British Westinghouse case, there were reports that training "was 'quite haphazard'; there was little effective supervision, and although apprentices were meant to be moved in accordance with a plan of training, they could simply ask and be moved" (More 1980: 85).

The policies of Britain's premier training firms must be understood against the backdrop of the quite different (compared to Germany) educational infrastructure they faced. A significant structural problem in Britain, from the perspective of these firms, was the overall lower level of state-sponsored, compulsory education and training for British youth. First and most fundamentally, compulsory elementary education was a more recent phenomenon in Britain than in Germany. The Elementary Education Act of 1870 had created a national system of elementary schools (Perry 1976: 17) but local school boards exercised wide discretion and allowed a variety of exceptions (Sadler and Beard 1908: 320–1). Subsequent legislation raised the compulsory school age and narrowed the discretion of local authorities when it came to younger boys and girls.[31] In 1904 about 32% of British

[30] Fleming and Pearce cite conflicts in some firms between apprentice supervisors and foremen, the former being concerned with training whereas the latter were more interested in output (Fleming and Pearce 1916: 122). More notes that it appears to have been very rare to establish separate training workshops, as most training was in the context of the actual production process. Moreover, very few engineering firms (in 1925, 26 of 1,573) employed separate "apprentice masters" charged specifically with responsibility for training (More 1980: 86).

[31] Legislation in 1880 required local authorities to mandate school attendance up to 10 years of age (Sandiford 1908: 320). Further legislation raised the minimum age step by step, to

children obtained exemptions between the ages of 13 and 14 (Education 1909a: 26). The number of exemptions declined after that, but this occurred slowly, especially in regions like the textile manufacturing districts, where employers had come to depend heavily on child labor (Perry 1976).[32]

Another important factor was that trade-oriented continuation schools of the sort widely compulsory in Germany by the first decade of the twentieth century were neither so widespread nor so well attended in Britain at that time. In Germany these institutions were supported by state or local governments, backed up by laws requiring youth to attend and obligating employers to grant apprentices time off to do so (Chapter 2). In Britain these institutions had a rockier history and received far less support from the state.[33] In the late nineteenth century, some county councils were channeling funds into evening schools offering technical training, but as attendance was entirely voluntary and the schools charged fees, the uptake, especially among working class youth, was very low (Education 1909a: Chapter XI). Despite efforts on the part of some local authorities to prompt employers to encourage attendance by their youth,[34] in 80% of counties, the proportion of youths in evening continuation courses was below 10%; in only 12 counties did it rise above 10% in 1909 (Education 1909a: 127).[35]

In Germany, state support for compulsory continuing education (that is, beyond elementary school) helped to subsidize training for youth with more meager resources, while at the same time imposing more uniform conditions on German employers. Conversely, in Britain, the lack of compulsion contributed to a higher degree of stratification in training (that is, the more education and training a youth arrived with and/or acquired "on his own steam," the more likely he would be rewarded with higher quality training from the firm). The pre-World War I period did see the

11 years of age (1893), 12 years (1899), and 13 years (1902) (Sandiford 1908: 320–1, for 1893 and 1899; Zeitlin 1996: 17, for 1902).

[32] Dunlop and Denman, for example, report that "out of an average number of 47,360 partial exemption scholars given in the returns for 1906–07, 34,306 were employed in factories; 20,302 of these were Lancashire children, the majority of whom probably were working in the cotton mills; 10,517 were returned for Yorkshire, and they, it may be assumed, were for the most part engaged in the worsted manufacture" (Dunlop and Denman 1912: 312).

[33] On the history of trade oriented "mechanics institutes" and continuation schools in Britain, see especially Kelly (1992), Sadler (1908a), Sadler and Beard (1908: 21–31).

[34] For example, the Manchester Education Committee provided monthly reports to firms that were paying for their apprentices to attend classes. The reports contained information on attendance, progress, and conduct in school (Education 1909a: 92–3).

[35] Though the figures were higher in London and the County Boroughs, up to 25 to 30% at the high end.

development of full-time Junior Technical Schools, which provided very high quality training for the small minority of youth who attended them (they too charged fees). The training was of such high quality that the graduates of these schools typically went straight into supervisory or mid-level technical positions – not skilled manual positions (Zeitlin 1996). As Bray put it, "technical education for the minority is successful, but without power to compel attendance and limit the hours of boy-labour it is only the few who can avail themselves of the opportunities offered" (Bray 1912: 150). Or as the engineers in charge of the Westinghouse training programs noted with dismay, "the workers who need industrial training the most fail to take advantage of voluntary facilities that exist at present" (Fleming and Pearce 1916: 163).

In general, then, the kind and quality of training that a British youth might aspire to had a great deal to do with his or her family's ability to allow him to tap into the services available, or to put it in Becker's terms, credit constraints played a much bigger role in Britain in determining which youth received training and of what quality. The premier training firms redressed this problem to an extent, for example, by paying class fees for evening instruction or offering bonuses for good grades in such classes. However, the lack of a comprehensive compulsory system meant that firms that went this route exposed themselves to severe poaching problems (Pollard 1965: 169). A British manufacturer of diesel engines summarized the problem he and other employers faced: "After sending its apprentices to the evening classes, to a technical school or possibly the University . . . [the firm] would find it had expended its money without reaping any harvest because the apprentice would go elsewhere if he were offered better terms" (quoted in Zeitlin 1996: 15–16). A representative of Armstrong, Whitworth and Company pointed to exactly the same problems, and emphasized the need for employers to cooperate on training (Education 1909b: 353).[36]

Even the firms that encouraged attendance at evening classes were reluctant to take the additional step to pay apprentices for hours spent in the classroom. Bray, among others, noted how rare it was for employers to give apprentices permission to attend day classes (Bray 1912: 187). Mather

[36] In an interview published in 1908, Dr. Georg Kerschensteiner, one of the key architects of compulsory continuation schools in Germany, noted that without compulsion "carelessness and greed" on the part of employers would inevitably interfere with attendance (Stockton 1908: 543). As we have seen, Germany was much further along in requiring attendance at this time.

and Platt, for example, required their apprentices to attend continuation classes, but the company was unwilling to reduce their working hours to accommodate this. As an employer witness to the government education committee pointed out, Mather and Platt was of the opinion that since their boys only worked 48 hours a week, they were, "not at all fatigued at the end of the day" and therefore quite capable of attending and getting something out of evening trade school (Education 1909b: 349).[37] A survey of 79 teachers employed in continuation schools in (mostly) northern England confirmed that although instructors knew of instances in which employers promoted attendance in evening courses in various ways – by paying class fees, adjusting working hours, offering prizes and bonuses – most firms were still unwilling to excuse their apprentices from day work in order to attend technical classes (Beard 1908: 247).

The main demand raised in this context by prominent training firms in Britain, therefore – completely understandable in the context described above – was legislation that would raise the general educational requirements for all youth. Such firms were vocal proponents of reforms that would have required youth aged 14 to 18 to attend compulsory technical continuation classes, proposals modeled directly on then-prevailing practices in Germany (Zeitlin 1996: 16; see also Zeitlin 2001). The point was that "statutory compulsion would reinforce employers' ability to insist on young workers' attendance at continuation schools by imposing a similar obligation on their laxer competitors" (Zeitlin 1996: 17). Contemporary social reformers could not have agreed more. As Bray put it, without compulsion "those [employers] who pursue the better methods disappear; those who pursue the worse survive to propagate their kind . . . the bad pushes out and replaces the good" (Bray 1912: 182). R. H. Tawney also argued in favor of increased compulsory training for all youth on the grounds that "the only way of preventing [employers] from recruiting the ranks of low-paid irregularly employed adult workers, is to make their labour scarce and dear by law, and to insist on their obtaining an industrial education in a Trade School" (Education 1909a: 316–17). Along with representatives of firms such as Mather and Platt, such social reformers in Britain argued that compulsion "places all employers on the same level, and enables the best of them to do what was before impossible. It does not thereby interfere with

[37] A conclusion *not* shared by the consultative committee, whose members felt that a substantial number of these youths would be too tired to learn much of anything at all (Education 1909a: 170).

competition; it merely changes the direction of competition by guiding it into less injurious channels" (Bray 1912: 182; see also Sadler 1908b: 125).

A Consultative Committee that reported to the National Board of Education in 1909 also understood very well the problems confronting individual firms in an entirely voluntary system. Reporting on the state of British continuation schools in 1909 they cited a litany of problems, including: apathetic or hostile attitudes among taxpayers and local education authorities in many districts, a lack of cooperation on the part of employers (to make it possible for their young workers and apprentices to attend evening classes), and overstrained youth who could not manage the long hours required to balance work and classes. These were all problems that the Report attributed to the "weakness of a voluntary system in impressing on the public mind the necessity for educational care during adolescence" (Education 1909a: 133, Chapter VII passim). The "disappointing" conclusion reached by the consultative committee, however, was that "so far as can be gathered from the various inquiries that have been made at different times, the majority of employers are quite indifferent to the education of their workpeople," a conclusion that led them to the overall judgment that voluntarism in this area was doomed to fail (Education 1909a: 121).

Based on this report, the Board of Education recommended mandatory attendance at trade classes for all youth under 17. Although the idea was picked up by the Liberal government and formulated as a bill in 1911, lack of employer support prevented passage (Dunlop and Denman 1912; Zeitlin 1996: 17–18). Some industries (for example, cotton, textiles) were utterly opposed, continuing to rely as they did on child labor (Sandiford 1908; Zeitlin 1996: 17). Industries less reliant on skills than engineering were simply completely "indifferent" to the training problem (Dunlop and Denman 1912: 335). Even industries that took apprentices and trained them on the job often did not necessarily see the benefit of classes and were reluctant to adjust apprentices' working hours to facilitate attendance, citing foreign competition and the need to keep labor costs low (Education 1909b: 356–9). In sum, although almost no employers were opposed to their apprentices attending evening classes, the majority were "actively hostile" to the idea of adjusting working hours to make this possible (Knox 1980: 272).

Thus, premier engineering firms in Britain continued to face a dilemma since they relied on skills but had no particular way of ensuring that their investment would pay off in the form of a long-term employment commitment on the part of the apprentice. The relatively strong position of skilled unions (despite strike losses, organization levels were relatively high in engineering) and the multiplicity of unions represented in any given firm made policies based on internal labor markets difficult to implement. In the face of these constraints, and the problems of labor mobility across firms, many employers adapted to the logic of the context and focused significant energy on a relatively small number of apprentices who arrived in the firm with well over the minimum educational qualifications and who could be targeted by the company for leadership positions and long-term employment. For the larger numbers of "ordinary" apprentices, they were more likely to rely on relatively inexpensive measures (relief from overtime, for example) designed to encourage youth to seek additional training outside the firm – but mostly on their own time.

One sees in these strategies an attempt on the part of these firms – perfectly rational given the context – to minimize "irrecoverable" investments in training by privileging youth who arrived with more than the minimum and by insisting in various ways on apprentices themselves (who were, after all, the real beneficiaries of their increasing human capital) bearing a significant share of the costs of their own training – all the while lobbying for the socialization of such costs as well as complementary policies to force other firms to bear their fair share of the costs required to generate the skills on which they all relied.

Union Strategies with Respect to Apprenticeship

The union's position in the debates over apprenticeship and vocational education at the turn of the century was colored by its concern with the overall supply of skilled labor and skilled workers' wages. In general, the ASE was mostly content to blame employers for the sorry state of apprenticeship. The problem, from their perspective, was the abuse of trainees as unskilled workers, associated with a demonstrable overabundance in many firms of apprentices in relation to journeymen. In many instances, the union clearly had a point. But at the end of the day, the ASE also had very little to say about the content or quality of training, and continued to focus mostly on the "numbers" question. As one contemporary noted, the main object of concern for unions was "regulation of the supply of workers rather than the assurance of adequate training" (Booth 1904: 163).

In light of their own mostly failed attempts to limit the number of apprentices, ASE leaders worried that publicly available technical classes would only contribute to overstocking within particular trades. From early on, many unionists were skeptical of the position taken by leading firms on technical education, seeing this as an attempt to use public funds to train enough young skilled workmen to reduce skilled wages (Education 1909a: 143). An official of the Manchester branch put it this way: "Of course, I do not want to speak against technical education, but we find that from technical schools and from boy's institutes and those places, there is a preponderance of lads drafted into our trade more than into any other" (quoted in Knox 1980: 252–3). Unionists also worried that apprentices trained in new methods would pose a challenge to established modes of production and therefore also a challenge to the older generation of skilled workers who had been trained in the traditional way (Booth 1904: 163–4; Knox 1980: 254; Beard 1908: 248).[38]

By the first decade of the twentieth century, however, in light of the restrictive terms of the 1897 settlement, rising unemployment, and widespread abuses of apprenticeship, union attitudes toward technical training began to shift. The ASE came around to strongly endorsing the idea of compulsory continuation schools, very much in line with demands being made at this time by the premier engineering companies. For the unions, the attraction of compulsory technical education with mandatory classroom training was based on different material interests but ultimately on a fundamentally complementary logic. British engineering firms favored compulsion as necessary to punish lax employers, reduce free riding, and mitigate the competitive pressure they faced from firms pursuing lower quality strategies based on cutting labor costs. For unions, the point of compulsory trade schooling was to prevent the abuse of apprenticeship by employers to put pressure on skilled wages. Requiring firms to release youth from work to attend classes would make trainees more expensive for the firms and therefore less attractive as a source of cheap semi-skilled labor (Knox 1980: 262).

[38] In some industries, unions raised concerns about the negative effect of increasing compulsory educational requirements on the incomes of poor families. This is the reason given, for example, by skilled operatives in Britain's textile districts for opposing proposals put forth by the leaders of their own union for an abolition of half time employment for youth under 13 years of age and for raising the age of compulsory school attendance (Education 1909a: 142, 287). Tawney, a leading proponent of technical education, viewed such positions with skepticism, arguing that organized workers, "with left-handed kindness, prevent [poor youth] from overcrowding some trades, and indirectly intensify the struggle in others" (Education 1909a: 316).

Thus, as in Germany, there were possibilities for a coalition between unions of skilled workers and large employers in skill-dependent industries such as engineering with the goal of coordination and regulation of apprentice training. Both sides had an interest in preventing upstart firms from achieving advantage by undercutting high quality, high skill firms on the basis of strategies to reduce labor costs. Agreements on the regulation of apprenticeship were achieved between unions and employers in some industries marked by especially intense product market competition and high reliance on skilled workers.[39] Unions and employers in the printing industry, for instance, were able to reach agreement on a jointly sponsored "Apprentice Training Scheme" in 1912. This agreement was heavily pushed by large printing firms, which sought to curb the practices of smaller firms that relied on the use of cheap labor and price competition. On the labor side, the express goal of the British Federation of Master Printers was to set "a standard of reasonable conditions" and to impose regulations on "those employers . . . who are injuring the workmen by paying sweating wages, and injuring their fellow-employers by unreasonably low prices" (quoted in Knox 1986: 180–1). The point was that "by regulating the ratio of apprentices to journeymen and by improving the training of the former, the 'fair' employer could strike a hammer blow at their unscrupulous competitors by raising the cost of labour" (Knox 1986: 181).[40]

In other sectors, however, including the crucial engineering industry, the years immediately preceding World War I witnessed, if anything, increasing conflict between unions and employers over a range of control issues – apprenticeship among them. In 1912 a new and more aggressive leadership took control of the ASE and proceeded to abrogate the Terms of Settlement signed in 1897, returning the union to an official policy of militant defense of craft control (Zeitlin 1996: 19). The new general secretary of the union, J. T. Brownlie, demanded negotiation of a recognized proportion of apprentices to journeymen, claiming apprentices were not being properly trained. Market conditions were relatively auspicious for resurgent craft

[39] See Knox (1986) and Ministry of Labour (1928a: 135–7) on various agreements between unions and employers discussed here.

[40] In the building industry as well, "leading firms took the initiative on the apprentice question" (Knox 1986: 181). In 1916 an agreement on apprenticeship was worked out between the Institute of Builders, unions, and the Labour ministry; it, unfortunately, was not successfully implemented, partly because of the war (Knox 1986: 181).

militancy; skilled labor shortages in 1911 and 1912, for example, allowed the union in many cases successfully to reimpose on employers previously defunct restrictions in the use of unskilled workers on skilled jobs (Zeitlin 1996: 19).

The Impact of War and Its Aftermath

The onset of World War I only exacerbated ongoing conflicts over shop floor control and managerial prerogatives. As in Germany, intense competition for skilled labor and the power this conferred on unions brought government intervention to keep industrial peace for the sake of military production. In Germany the 1916 Auxiliary Service Act accomplished this end by allowing unions an increased voice in plant decision making (through works councils), a move that set the scene for the postwar incorporation of Germany's industrial unions into a system of unitary plant representation (see also Thelen 1991).

In Britain the government pressured for and then underwrote an agreement between the EEF and major craft unions that imposed a moratorium on industrial action and restrictive work rules in defense-related industries for the duration of the hostilities. This paved the way for widespread "dilution" during the war, freeing employers to introduce new machinery and to put women and semi-skilled operatives on work previously reserved for fully qualified workers (Haydu 1988: 130–1). Although facilitating the reorganization of work in industries producing large runs of standardized parts for the military, these arrangements also caused political friction, particularly between the central union leaders who signed the agreements and the rank-and-file members who were bound and constrained by the provisions they contained.

Despite increasing substitution and dilution, skilled workers enjoyed unprecedented power during the war. Even where significant work reorganization was undertaken, such craftsmen were crucial to setting up and making the tools needed for standardized production. Chronic skilled labor shortages tested employer solidarity and emboldened an emerging shop steward movement that fed on rank-and-file discontent. Legally binding arrangements (backed by sanctions by the state) that limited skilled workers' mobility, prohibited strikes, and allowed employers to proceed against unionists or workers who sought to defend traditional practices became a major irritation for skilled workers who watched as their jobs were redefined and, often, as their wages fell in relation to semi-skilled operatives on piece-rate and premium systems.[41] On the employer side, intense labor shortages and the scramble for military orders fueled competition among firms; the EEF was particularly riven by centrifugal forces in this period (Zeitlin 1991: 62–7).

As in Germany, the war years – and accompanying skill shortages – heightened interest in skill formation and brought forth new initiatives to reform apprentice training.[42] Important impulses in this regard emanated from the British Board of Education, which in 1916 came under the leadership of H. A. L. Fisher, a well-known and determined advocate of significant reform in the area of vocational training. During the war, members of the Board met with engineers and prominent advocates of vocational training reform, including representatives of the premier training firms discussed above.[43] Such deliberations helped pave the way for the passage, in 1918, of the so-called "Fisher Act" that raised the school-leaving age to 14 and provided for a significant expansion of compulsory daytime continuation schooling – 280 hours per year for all youth between 14 and 16 years of age – though continuing opposition from employers in less skill-intensive sectors forced a retreat from more ambitious plans.[44]

The war years also saw significant movement in the area of in-plant training. Meetings between the government and reform-minded employers, for example, resulted in a proposal for a "Central Bureau for Improvement in and Better Co-ordination of Engineering Training" that shared many of the same goals as those articulated by German manufacturing concerns through DATSCH. In addition to supporting compulsory continuation classes, the employers involved in these meetings "reaffirmed the importance of shop training" and saw the Bureau as a means for coordinating regionally based initiatives (Zeitlin 1996: 25–6). In October of 1917, key organizations (including the EEF) and a large number of Britain's most prominent and influential metalworking companies heartily endorsed these proposals

[41] In engineering, the proportion of boys to men also rose between July 1914 and April 1917 from 13.9 to 20.8% (Ministry of Labour 1928a: 13).

[42] On the reform initiatives of this period, see especially Zeitlin (2001).

[43] Sir Arthur Fleming, for example, who served as director of training at British Westinghouse, took part, as did A. E. Berriman, who was chief engineer at Daimler (Zeitlin 1996: 25).

[44] The original plan called for 320 hours of compulsory coursework per year for all youth up to the age of 18. In the law that ultimately passed, the introduction of compulsory classes for 16- to 18-year-olds was to be delayed for seven years after the war, and local authorities could reduce mandatory continuation school hours from 320 to 280 for the interim period as well (Zeitlin 1996: 22). For the provisions of the legislation, as well as some commentary, see Brereton (1919).

(Zeitlin 1996: 26; also Zeitlin 2001). These initiatives were followed up by another meeting, convened by Fisher in London in May 1919, that brought together 49 leading representatives of industry, commerce, and education, and resulted in the founding of an Association for the Advancement of Education in Industry and Commerce (AEIC) (Perry 1976: 46).

Against the backdrop of these developments, one of the most promising and potentially far-reaching initiatives came from the head of the EEF, Allan Smith, who proposed a "bold national strategy aimed at reaching a durable accommodation with official trade unions leaders" that, among other things, would give unions a role in regulating apprenticeship in exchange for greater managerial latitude on craft-control issues (quote from Zeitlin 1990: 415; on the aspects relating to skills specifically, see Zeitlin 1996: 27–9; Zeitlin 2001). Smith told a conference of engineering unions in 1919, "We admit now, or propose to agree, that all questions practically regarding apprentices should be discussed with you" (quoted in Zeitlin 1996: 28).

Smith recognized that a national-level deal was crucial to the success of the project, since divergent rules across regions (based on uneven union influence) was a continuing source of friction in strong interregional product market competition. The idea – similar in some ways to the Terms of Settlement of 1897 – was to draw the national union into a system in which the union leadership would help to enforce greater uniformity. This would involve reining in local activists where necessary. Thus, the offer on the table called for negotiations with the ASE on issues relating to training (including also the proportion of apprentices to journeymen) at the national (specifically not the district) level. In other words, the EEF was prepared to endorse trade union representation and participation in the regulation of apprenticeship as part of a broad agreement to cover a range of issues including wages and working hours and in conjunction with an overall reduction of craft restrictions. In a report issued in 1918 the employers' organization proposed that all apprentices "should henceforth serve under written agreements, whose observance might be secured through cooperation with unions, while a national scheme should be adopted for supplementing workshop training with technical education" (Zeitlin 1996: 27–8).

In short, in Britain as in Germany, wartime skilled labor shortages heightened concerns about training, resulting in both cases in new pressures for reform. In Germany, DATSCH's efforts to secure legislation for a new regulatory framework for training in industry did not bear fruit before or even after World War I. Although the legislative reform process stalled in

Germany, however, in the 1920s, firm-based training continued and grew.[45] In Britain, by contrast, wartime initiatives on training reform quickly fell victim in the early 1920s to renewed conflict between employers and skilled unions.[46] The immediate postwar years brought no relief from skill shortages, and years of centrally imposed restraint produced an upsurge of local labor militancy as shop stewards tried to reclaim ground that had been lost during the war. When government restrictions were lifted, therefore, skilled engineering workers used their power "to press old demands, including restrictions on manning machines, payment of apprentices, and overtime work" (Haydu 1988: 168). The organizations and consortia to promote training that had emerged during the war sputtered when the hostilities ended. As Zeitlin notes, "the 'Engineering Training Organisation' formed at [the 1917] meeting never attracted sufficient funds from individual firms to become self-sustaining and was absorbed by the EEF in the autumn of 1920" (Zeitlin 1996: 26).

This is important because the EEF (unlike the VDMA which emerged as a key actor in Germany) was not an organization through which British firms coordinated in product markets, only in labor markets. It was certainly possible in theory for employers and unions to find common ground through collective bargaining that would assist in stabilizing competition in product markets (for example, Bowman 1985; Swenson 2002).[47] The EEF was notoriously diverse, however, and had always struggled against strong centrifugal forces (Zeitlin 1991). In addition, since its main brief was to negotiate with unions, any agreement the EEF sought on training would have had to be bundled with a broader agreement over a whole range of other control issues – a daunting prospect given the upsurge in militancy in the first postwar years. A core and, it seems, quite fatal problem was that

[45] For the reasons elaborated above, which included the growth of cross-testing and certification for industrial firms, wage compression, and the increasing power of the VDMA which provided a key site for increased coordination among German metalworking firms on training.

[46] Jonathan Zeitlin (Zeitlin 1996; Zeitlin 2001) provides an interpretation slightly different from the one advanced here. He sees the failure of the initiatives of this period, and also subsequent reform efforts in the 1940s and 1960s (discussed briefly below) as much more "contingent" in the sense that the institutional reforms proposed at these junctures might well have taken root had it not been for complicating exogenous events and conditions. My sense is that the differences are in part a matter of emphasis, with my analysis placing more weight on structural conditions and institutional starting points (for example, craft unionism).

[47] And see Chapter 4 for the example of the stove foundry industry in the United States.

the most serious EEF proposals for a *national-level* settlement with labor came at a time when central union control over local shop stewards was at a low point.

Thus, despite the overtures by EEF leaders and even encouraging response from the union leadership, the reform initiatives of the war years did not bring the broad agreement that Smith sought. Instead, rank-and-file militancy in 1919–1921 set the scene for yet another dramatic confrontation between unions and employers over control issues. Employers seized on the economic downturn of 1922 to impose significant cuts in wages and to reassert managerial control over shop floor issues. Once again, the organizational capacities that employers had developed were deployed to defend the autonomy of individual firms (McKinlay and Zeitlin 1989: 42), as the EEF rallied its members again to defeat the Amalgamated Engineering Union (AEU)[48] in a major lockout. In the aftermath, employers moved aggressively to slash skilled worker wages and to reassert their rights to deploy workers as they saw fit, to introduce piece rate systems of payment, and to manipulate working hours to cover production needs.

The AEU suffered huge membership losses both before and especially after the defeat. This was a "rout" from which it took the union over a decade to recover (Tolliday 1992: 46). As McKinlay and Zeitlin put it, in the aftermath of this historic conflict, the AEU "was all but impotent at the national, regional and workshop levels" (McKinlay and Zeitlin 1989: 42). The union's defeat left employers more or less free to organize work and apprentice training as they saw fit. What they did with this autonomy, as before, worked overwhelmingly to the detriment of training in Britain. Over the course of the 1920s and 1930s, apprenticeship by and large deteriorated, as apprentices were put on routine repetitive work and used as a buffer, being laid off in downturns (Zeitlin 1996: 5, 34–6, 49; Zeitlin 1991:72). As one Leicestershire engineering employer reported, "We obtain boys direct from the elementary school as near 14 years as possible. In these days of repetition engineering, we have not, broadly speaking, experienced any great benefit by taking boys at a later age, say 16, from a secondary school" (Ministry of Labour 1928a: 89). McKinlay notes that the response of engineering employers to the recession of 1929 was to engage in the widespread replacement of time-served workers with apprentices, so

[48] In 1920 the ASE merged with several other smaller craft societies to form the AEU, or Amalgamated Engineering Union.

that during the years 1929 to 1932, "apprentices constituted an increasing proportion of the engineering workforce" (McKinlay 1986: 4).

We can pause here to consider – in light of the theoretical arguments presented in Chapter 1– the incentives faced by British firms and also by British youth to invest in training in the post-1922 period. Recall that in Germany, union wage policy in the interwar years was organized around reducing skill differentials. Although frequently forced into somewhat wider differentials by employers (though state intervention often produced compromises between the two positions), skill differentials were significantly reduced in 1919–20 (unskilled workers receiving over 80% of the skilled worker rates), then restored somewhat but never back to prewar levels. Such wage compression– à la Acemoglu and Pischke (Chapter 1) – encouraged firms to invest in worker training (and reduce their reliance on relatively expensive unskilled labor), at the same time prompting technological innovations designed to increase the productivity of skilled workers.

In Britain, too, the interwar years saw a reduction in wage differentials between the highest and lowest skilled workers. The political dynamics and logic were completely different, however. Knowles and Robertson document significant reductions in wage differentials during and immediately after the First World War in Britain; the wage rates of unskilled engineering workers rose from 58.6% of the skilled rate in 1914 to 78.9% in 1920) (Knowles and Robertson 1951: 111). In this case, however, wage compression resulted from increased organization among semi-skilled operators and increased use by employers of payment by results, combined with the union's insistence that anyone (regardless of skill) who performed a "skilled job" be paid at the "skilled rate."[49] As in Germany, the 1920s witnessed a partial restoration of wage differentials but again, not back to prewar levels. Unskilled wage rates hovered around 71% of skilled wage rates from 1924 to 1935, according to Knowles and Robertson (Knowles and Robertson 1951: 111).[50] But in the British case, these effects stemmed

[49] I am grateful to Jonathan Zeitlin for emphasizing this point to me.

[50] Given the increased importance of shop floor bargaining and the expansion of piece rate wage systems in the interwar years, weekly earnings are a better measure of wage differentials than straight wage rates. Hart and MacKay directly address this issue, taking advantage of data collected by the EEF on earnings over the period 1914 to 1968 (Hart and MacKay 1975). The results are more refined but they do not change the overall picture dramatically. For 1926, for example, the wage rate differential is 70.8, whereas the earnings differential is 73.9%; for 1929, it is 71.3 and 74% respectively, and for 1932, it is 71.2 and 71.5% (based on calculations and comparisons between Knowles and Robertson's figures and Hart and MacKay's).

less from an explicit union policy of wage compression than from the decimation and continuing weakness of the AEU combined with the increasing leverage (also later increasing militancy) of semi-skilled workers (Mosher 2001).

In short, whereas wage bargaining in Germany produced outcomes that provided employers with incentives to increase training and hire more skilled workers (at artificially reduced rates), British employers spent the period after 1922 engaged in very different strategies – in the older segments of the industry seeking "cost reductions through the multiplication of apprentices and the downgrading of skilled workers rather than through rationalization and reequipment" and in the newer sectors, through "the manipulation of payment systems . . . to drive production processes that remained flexible and labor intensive" (Zeitlin 1990: 417–18). The resulting wage distortions, as Zeitlin has pointed out, meant that in many cases, semi-skilled workers wound up making more money than skilled time workers (Zeitlin 1996: 48).

These effects had important implications for the incentives facing youth to acquire training. The combination of wage distortions, the declining quality of training, and continuing very long training times, was deadly for apprenticeship in this period (Zeitlin 1996: 5, 39–40).[51] There were no obvious and compelling reasons for youths to subject themselves to long training periods when the payoff was so low and the actual skills they acquired so uncertain. Although many firms were indifferent to the problems this caused, engineering firms concerned about the supply of skilled labor complained that low wages were drawing youth off into unskilled, dead end jobs, and in so doing "diverted suitable recruits from the engineering industry" (Ministry of Labour 1928b: 15).[52]

[51] In 1925–26, 47.7% of engineering apprentices finished in five years, but for 26.1% training dragged on for seven years; only 1.6% of all trainees served four years or less (Ministry of Labour 1928b: 19). In addition, 57% of boy apprentices (across all industries) were still required to serve an additional period of improvership (most commonly, twelve months). In the engineering and allied industries the number of apprentices serving additional improverships was even higher (90 and 62%, respectively) (Ministry of Labour 1928a: 85; Ministry of Labour 1928b: 6, 34). Moreover, training times subsequently increased for many apprentices because of the widespread use of part-time work during the Depression (Zeitlin 1996: 53).

[52] Conversely, relatively higher wages for unskilled work added to the costs of training, as apprentice wages were driven up in certain regions by competition with industries employing youth in unskilled positions. Such was the case, for example, in the textile districts in Britain (Ministry of Labour 1928b: 23).

There was nothing in the structure of firm-based training in Britain at the time to give prospective apprentices confidence that the sacrifices they might make (in wages, for example) during training would produce skills that would be widely recognized on the labor market. Just the opposite: the terms of apprenticeship in engineering were if anything becoming more onerous and costly and the payoff no more certain. In a way, the scenario in Britain in the 1920s was practically the mirror image of that in Germany at the time. In Germany, coordination among firms was steadily increasing the quality of training and establishing ever more widely recognized standards for in-plant training, thus increasing the attractiveness of training to youth. At the same time, narrower skill differentials, imposed first by industrial unions but later upheld and continued through state arbitration (which also inhibited local adjustments) created a "productivity gap" (between the wages of skilled workers and their marginal productivity) that provided employers with an incentive to continue to invest in training.

In Britain, by contrast, very little progress was made in establishing standards, and there was nothing in the structure of bargaining to support and encourage firms to invest in training, even in highly skill-dependent industries like engineering. Skill formation remained virtually unregulated by any overarching set of rules; with the exception of a few highly specialized subsectors, there existed "no agreements between employers and workpeople determining the conditions of employment of apprentices in the engineering industry" (Ministry of Labour 1928b: 42). Certainly the AEU had no say in the matter, union rules on the employment conditions of apprentices having been explicitly ruled out by the 1922 defeat (Ministry of Labour 1928b: 44–5). There was tremendous variety in the types of training arrangements that individual firms might work out with trainees. The EEF did not seek to impose standards either. The rules it offered member firms by way of recommendation were specifically the sort that prioritized the autonomy of the individual firm. Thus, many companies followed EEF recommendations and incorporated into apprentice contracts stipulations that prohibited apprentices from taking part in labor disputes and clauses that explicitly allowed the firm to lay off apprentices in economic downturns (Ministry of Labour 1928b: 46–7).

Thus, as far as training was concerned the legacy of the 1922 struggle was similar to that of 1898 – once again employers had been able to rally around the minimalist goal of managerial autonomy, so that despite a legacy of increased centralization of wage bargaining this was "paralleled by ever greater diversity in other areas, such as training, payment systems and machine manning" (McKinlay and Zeitlin 1989: 42).

British Training on the Eve of World War II

There is no doubt that significant segments of capital saw the need for fundamental reforms in Britain's vocational training system, and in specific regions employers endorsed proposals that, if implemented on a broad basis, would have put skill formation in Britain on an entirely new footing.[53] Such ambitious projects never got off the ground, however. From the perspective of Britain's premier training firms, very little had changed by the mid-1920s, despite the flurry of reform enthusiasm during and after World War I, and what changes had occurred in some ways undermined the more progressive training programs by exposing them to more intense poaching and competitive pressures.

Even the Educational Reforms that had been passed in 1918 (the Fisher Act) that would have raised the school age and imposed compulsory daytime continuation classes for all youth under 18 did not take effect as planned. Some aspects were postponed and the number of mandatory hours was trimmed back. The implementation of the elements that remained in the law also proved problematic. Specifically, and crucially, shortages of teachers forced the Board of Education to delegate authority for implementing the plans to local authorities, producing highly uneven results that redounded to the disadvantage of employers in the more progressive regions (higher production costs) and forced a scale-back in these areas (Zeitlin 1996: 31).[54]

The whole question of compulsory trade classes (at technical institutes) remained highly contested among employers. Based on a questionnaire

[53] Zeitlin notes that the urgency of reform was especially intense in the Northeast where employers confronted severe labor shortages. In 1916 a group of engineers and employers in this region established a "Committee on the Education of Apprentices" to discuss reforms. The committee's proposals called for major reforms, including the establishment by local educational authorities of Junior Day Technical schools that could offer pre-apprentice programs for school-leaving 14-year-olds, legislation that would compel employers to pay for two to three and a half days of attendance in technical classes per week for youths up to the age of 18, and provisions that would allow the most promising youths to become part-time students at local technical colleges. At the height of the war, and in the context of severe labor shortages, all the main engineering and shipbuilding employers in the region approved the report (Zeitlin 1996: 23–5).

[54] For this exact reason, the recommendation of the committee of inquiry that had first made proposals in this area specifically counseled against leaving these matters to the localities (Zeitlin 1996: 21).

circulated among engineering employers in 1922, the Association for Education in Industry and Commerce reported that "compulsory education is advocated by a number of firms" but "some firms are emphatically opposed to compulsion in any form whatever, and several other firms are doubtful of the wisdom of compulsion" (Commerce 1930: 14). The authors note that "one comes to the definite conclusion from the replies that compulsory attendance . . . is inadvisable" (Commerce 1930: 19).

Prevailing practices in the 1920s continued to reflect this situation. A much more comprehensive survey conducted in 1925 by the Ministry of Labour revealed that only a small minority of firms required their apprentices to attend evening trade classes and/or granted trainees time off from work to facilitate this. In the metalworking industries, encouragement by firms for apprentices to attend classes varied widely from very passive (posters advertising evening classes) to more active. Of 1,573 metalworking firms surveyed, only 337 allowed time off to apprentices to attend class (and in some cases this was just permission to leave early on evenings when they had class), 62 made evening classes compulsory, and 19 made day classes obligatory. Works schools remained rare, with only 33 firms maintaining such schools for apprentices (Ministry of Labour 1928b: 40–1). In general, British employers continued to think that "the better method is to offer prizes, bonuses, and wider opportunities as inducements to those concerned to take the utmost advantage of the facilities offered to them to become proficient in their trades" (Commerce 1930: 19).

As for workshop-based training, apprenticeship remained highly informal and unregulated in Britain in the mid-1920s. Of those youth who were in training in 1925, less than one-quarter (23.3%) were serving under some form of written agreement. The rest either were in apprenticeships under more informal, verbal agreements (51.6%) or working as "learners" (25.1%) – the latter frequently confined to more specialized operations (Ministry of Labour 1928b: 10, 40). Skills were still mostly transmitted in the traditional way, by working alongside skilled workers (Ministry of Labour 1928b: 39; Commerce 1930: 11–12). Only 26 of 1,573 surveyed firms had "apprentice masters" and in the vast majority of cases (1,068) apprentices acquired their training from the skilled journeymen with whom they worked (Ministry of Labour 1928b: 39). The (less systematic and comprehensive) survey conducted by the Association of Education in Industry and Commerce confirms this, noting that a number of firms report that they have "no organized training of any description. Apprentices are engaged, placed in the various shops for their trades, and left to pick up information and acquire manipulative skill as best they can from their associating with and assisting the workmen engaged in these trades" (Commerce 1930: 10–11). As contemporaries emphasized, "considerable responsibility for the proper teaching of the apprentice rested upon the skilled worker. Much depended upon his capacity and willingness to impart instruction" (Ministry of Labour 1928b: 39). This arrangement, never ideal, became even more problematic in the 1920s with the increased use of piece rates for skilled journeymen (Ministry of Labour 1928b: 37), since any effort spent in training could easily compromise the worker's own wage (Commerce 1930: 18, 23).[55]

British apprenticeship also remained highly stratified, with distinctions drawn among different "grades" of apprenticeship, depending, among other things, on the prior experience and completed course work a trainee brought with him (Ministry of Labour 1928b: 41, 49–50). Although "trade" apprentices were usually confined to one trade and generally to one department, premium apprentices received more all-round training (Commerce 1930: 14–15).[56] The report of the Association for Education in Industry and Commerce referred to premium apprenticeship as the "method by which the privileged few are allowed wide facilities to obtain training and experience" (Commerce 1930: 14). As before, top training companies still focused heavily on encouraging apprentices to attend classes, paying the class fees, allowing time off to enroll in evening or part time day classes (21% of engineering firms surveyed), facilitating attendance at day classes (though only about 6% of engineering firms with apprentices engaged in this practice), and offering bonuses or prizes for good performance (Ministry of Labour 1928a: 108–9).

Whereas in Germany, firms in the interwar years increasingly coordinated their training through strong trade associations such as the VDMA, British employers still worked, if at all, mostly through the EEF and then coordinated largely on issues such as the length of improverships and on the wages they paid to improvers (Ministry of Labour 1928b: 35, 36). In some regions, the local employers' association recommended wages for apprentices, in some cases setting out maxima and minima (Ministry of Labour 1928b: 43). The content of training, however, was largely unregulated and

[55] Even where firms placed responsibility for apprentices with foremen, there were problems since foremen were not, typically, chosen for their pedagogic skills, and often were most concerned simply to get the product out (Commerce 1930: 23).

[56] Although, as before, there was some possibility for trade apprentices who demonstrated special promise or aptitude to be upgraded.

uncoordinated. The general trend throughout the 1920s was toward a deterioration in both the quality and quantity of training, creating a situation that rendered the efforts of the more progressive firms more vulnerable than ever to poaching and price competition.

There may be no better evidence of the deterioration of apprenticeship in the 1920s and 1930s in British engineering than the uprising of the apprentices themselves in 1937. They demanded not just higher wages but also improvement in the conditions and quality of their training (see especially, McKinlay 1986). The upheaval started in engineering firms on the Clyde, where trainees presented their employers with an "Apprentice Charter" that laid out several demands. Among these, the apprentices demanded paid day release for attendance at technical education classes, so they could get theoretical grounding to go along with their practical workshop experience. "For the boys, trade training was a demand of paramount importance. Not only did apprentices suffer the indignity of being confined to repetitive tasks, but they were intensely aware that circumscribed workshop experience limited their future employment prospects" (McKinlay 1986: 14). The apprentices also sought a "reasonable ratio of apprentices to journeymen," both as a way of improving training and to regulate the industry's skilled labor supply (Zeitlin 1996: 53).

The apprentice strike spread to other parts of England, suggesting that these demands resonated widely. Employers took heed of the strike and immediately sought to bring it under the control of organized labor by granting apprentices union representation. Their speedy reaction reveals the extent to which many employers had come to rely on the labor of apprentices in their shops (McKinlay 1986). From the perspective of the propositions laid out in Chapter 1, however, we can see why the outcome was not altogether supportive of training in Britain. Union representation resulted in an increase in apprentices' real wages, which increased the costs of training for employers (Gospel and Okayama 1991: 24). This move might reduce employers' propensity to exploit apprentices as a source of cheap labor, but it also reduced their incentive to take apprentices in the first place. In addition, as these changes were not accompanied by any agreement providing for enhanced monitoring of the content or quality of training, there still existed considerable disincentives for youth to commit themselves to long training contracts (Zeitlin 1996: 39–40).

The failure to agree on a system to monitor and enforce apprentice contracts left British apprenticeship still subject to the credible commitment and coordination problems cited in Chapter 1. Apprenticeship would rebound again in the 1940s and 1950s in the context of skilled labor shortages and government encouragement and pressure, but in the absence of any enduring settlement – anchored in an alliance between those segments of labor and capital that shared an interest in a strong and durable training system but institutionalized on a broader basis – these later successes were vulnerable to roll-back under less auspicious political and market circumstances.

Comparisons and Conclusions

Several important differences between the British and German cases stand out when it comes to the overall trajectory of apprentice training and skill formation over the nineteenth and early twentieth centuries. First, state policy pushed in a very different direction in Britain. In Germany, state policy established authoritative institutions for monitoring and certifying skills in the artisanal sector, establishing a model that would later be extended to industry as well. The relatively early introduction of compulsory continuing education established a more level playing field for training companies, subsidizing the costs of training for both them and apprentices. By contrast, state policy in Britain did nothing to regulate apprentice training directly, and state encouragement of friendly societies indirectly fostered the formation of unions organized around the control of skilled labor markets.

Second, in Germany, the competition that developed in the pre-World War I and interwar period between the handicraft sector and the industrial sector proved constructive, maintaining high quality training. Industry coveted the powers possessed by the Handicraft chambers to define and certify skills. The leaders in industrial training continuously drew invidious comparisons between their own high quality (and in the Weimar years, increasingly standardized) training, which spurred the handicraft chambers to higher standards as well. Skill certification – originally the domain of the artisanal sector – in this way came to be merged into a system of skill standardization that developed at first on a voluntary basis in industry. In Britain, by contrast, the constellation of interests was such that skill formation was contested first and foremost across the class divide, between unions of skilled workers and employers tenaciously resisting craft controls at all turns. This competition, not surprisingly, proved destructive to apprenticeship when no stable system of joint regulation could be negotiated, and as trainees were frequently dragged into conflicts between unions and employers. Whereas the premier training firms in Germany were preoccupied with certification powers, their British counterparts were obsessed with defeating union-imposed craft controls.

Defeat craft controls they periodically did. But, third, whereas German firms coordinated in the Weimar years through increasingly influential trade associations, to regulate both product market competition and training, in Britain firms organized through their employers associations and were able only to unite around the much more limited agenda of defending firm autonomy. Their victories over skilled unions therefore did not shore up apprentice training and – to the extent that they specifically defended the principle that firms be free to organize apprenticeship (and use apprentices) as they saw fit – contributed to its deterioration. Premier training firms in Britain faced a landscape in which there existed no legal or paralegal sanctions against firms that did not train apprentices well (though there were some negative reputational effects) but plenty of market difficulties for those firms that did train well in the form of labor mobility and cost disadvantages in competitive product markets.

Leading employer representatives such as the EEF's Allan Smith saw all of this clearly at the time, and decried the "short-sightedness" of British employers in their approach to apprenticeship and skill formation. In the depressed economy of the late 1920s Smith correctly predicted that the lack of coordination among employers would have "serious consequences for labour supply and industrial relations when trade eventually improved" (Zeitlin 1991: 71). His prediction came true in the mid-1930s when the economy rebounded and employers experienced intense skilled labor shortages (Zeitlin 1996: 48). Their competition with each other allowed the AEU to emerge from the ashes once again to reassert control on the shop floor.

The apprentice system in Britain rested less on what Swenson would call a cross-class alliance than it did on a tenuous balance of power, which is why apprenticeship experienced ebbs and flows in response to changing market and political conditions. Wigham has pointed to the cyclical nature of industrial relations in the British engineering industry through the late nineteenth and early twentieth centuries, also citing the lockouts of 1852, 1897, and 1922 and their effects. As he points out, after each victory, the employers imposed settlements that reasserted their authority in their own companies, but each time, after the unions recovered, they proceeded again to extend their functions until "once more they intruded painfully into management" (Wigham 1973: 2). Tied up as it was in these conflicts, the trajectory of apprenticeship was similarly cyclical, experiencing periods of rejuvenation and reform initiatives under specific market and political conditions, only to suffer successive setbacks when the context shifted.

This general pattern continued in the post-World War II period. As Zeitlin notes, apprenticeship rebounded in the 1940s and 1950s, a consequence of skilled labor shortages and of government policies that provided firms with incentives to invest in training. But the effects of these trends were contingent on favorable economic and political conditions, and did not prove durable. By the 1960s apprenticeship was floundering again, prompting another round of legislative initiatives to strengthen skill formation in British industry. In 1964, the government imposed a training levy on all firms and created a new tripartite structure for regulating apprenticeship (the Industrial Training Boards), but the effects were partly perverse as increased costs discouraged firms from investing in training.[57] In 1973 the government (under the Conservatives) undertook further reforms, including the introduction of exemptions to the training levy (which reduced overall resources). Whether despite or because of these policies, the 1970s witnessed a virtual collapse in training, as the number of apprentices dropped precipitously from about a hundred twenty thousand in 1970 (mostly in engineering) to about thirty thousand in 1983.[58] As King has argued, all these experiments and innovations "failed decisively to improve training" (King 1997: 383) for lack of a settlement that could break what he calls the country's voluntarist tradition in order to stabilize institutions that could overcome the credible commitment and coordination problems that have long plagued plant-based vocational training in Britain (see also Green and Sakamoto 2001: 138–42).[59]

[57] On these and subsequent developments, see especially King (1997), on which I draw here.

[58] Based on figures provided to me by James Mosher.

[59] Subsequent shifts in policy, inaugurated under Thatcher but ultimately embraced in a different form by New Labour, have brought a retreat from tripartism and state direction in training and a move toward more market-based solutions (King and Wickham-Jones 1997). These moves have the effect – in Becker's (1993) terms – of shifting the costs of training onto youth, while also increasing the incentives for them to acquire at least certain types of skills.

4

The Evolution of Skill Formation in Japan and the United States

This chapter extends the analysis and the line of argumentation developed for Germany and Britain to two further cases, Japan and the United States. Japan provides an important counterpoint to Germany, for there, too, firm-based training rests on institutional arrangements that ameliorate costly competition among firms and mitigate the collective action problems typically associated with private-sector training. Both German and Japanese employers overcame their collective action problems in the area of training, but they did so in radically different ways: in Germany through the construction of a national system that generates a plentiful supply of workers with portable skills, and in Japan, through plant-based training in the context of stronger internal labor markets. Applying the terms introduced in Chapter 1, we note a broad difference between skill formation regimes based on "collectivism" in the German case and "segmentalism" or "autarky" in the Japanese case.

The other case considered in this chapter, the United States, provides a useful counterpoint to that of the British. In both countries, apprenticeship was a source of conflict between employers and craft unions, and therefore, strongly contested across the class divide. As in Britain, so too in the United States only in rare cases (the construction industry is an example) could an accommodation be reached that stabilized coordination across firms and between organized labor and employers in the area of apprentice training. The U.S. case also shares some similarities with Japan, however. Employers in both countries confronted intense skill shortages in the early industrial period and often relied on a system of subcontracting (to independent craftsmen) to handle the recruitment and training of skilled workers. Where these cases diverge is in the political dynamics and the coalitions that took shape, especially in the first decades of the twentieth century. In the United States, these autonomous skilled workmen were coopted into management hierarchies in large firms, and provided a key support for employers who were intent on defeating craft unions. Together they presided over the rationalization of production designed to reduce dependence on skills. In Japan, by contrast, independent craftsmen (*oyakata*) maintained a higher degree of independence and mobility, setting the scene for a different kind of alliance that brought management and emerging unions together around the shared goal of limiting the independent power of the *oyakata*. In the process, large Japanese firms pioneered many policies now associated with strong firm-based training linked to progression within elaborate internal labor markets.

The Evolution of Skill Formation in Japan

Both Germany and Japan developed relatively stable systems for skill formation, but based on very different principles and sustained by quite different institutional arrangements. Both systems have been characterized as embodying a "high skill equilibrium" (Finegold and Soskice 1988) and many analysts have attributed the success of these two countries in world manufacturing markets in the post-World War II period in part to their skill base. Germany's system of vocational training (with its strong "corporatist" oversight by broad-based employers' associations and unions) approaches the ideal-typical "collective" solution to skill formation sketched out in Chapter 1. Japan, by contrast, is best known for its extensive, firm-based system of training strongly associated with complementary personnel policies such as seniority wages and internal career ladders, as well as company unionism. In terms of the analytic categories introduced in Chapter 1, the large-firm sector in Japan comes close to the autarkic or segmentalist ideal type.

These differences in institutional arrangements have important consequences for labor markets and the role of labor. Wolfgang Streeck has argued that where (as in Germany) skills are nationally certified and documented, and therefore portable, the power (and voice) of skilled workers within the firm is enhanced by a credible exit option. Where skill formation is not widely certified and where therefore (as in Japan) the employing firm has privileged information about the quantity and quality of training a worker has received, labor is in a weaker position in the national labor market. Even here, however, employers' substantial investment in skills and the costs of replacement make the threat of a worker's exit carry weight, and this can enhance labor's voice in plant-level decision making (Kume 1998).

The difference is that in Germany, skilled workers' exit options are what give them power on the shop floor, whereas in Japan union influence is based more on labor's indispensable cooperation in production in the context of enterprise unions' "stakeholder" position in the firm (see Streeck 1996: 144–51 for an extended discussion).

This chapter begins by exploring the origins of the Japanese system of strong in-plant training, against the backdrop of the German case as elaborated in Chapter 2. In Japan, as in Germany, a crucial first step involved the suppression of early tendencies toward a liberal solution (freedom of trade in Germany and labor mobility in Japan). In contrast to both Great Britain and the United States, industrialization in Germany and Japan occurred under authoritarian auspices, and in both cases state repression delayed the emergence of stable organizations for labor representation and thwarted attempts by workers to organize around skill. In Japan, as in Germany, traditional artisans played a key role in providing skills for emerging industry. Moreover, in both countries, contests between artisans and large industrial enterprises over skill formation set in motion a competition that proved constructive rather than destructive to the preservation of a shop floor regime premised on significant firm investment in worker training.

Where the two cases diverge – with consequences for the institutionalization of two very different types of training regimes – is in the treatment by the state of the artisanate as a corporate actor in the early industrial period. Such differences affected the strategies of firms that depended heavily on skills and powerfully shaped their relations with emerging unions. In Japan the state confronted an artisanal sector that was both less organized than in Germany and also lacked the progressive element found in Germany in the southwestern states. Moreover, given the weakness of the Japanese labor movement in the late nineteenth century, the political motives that played a role in Germany for promoting artisans' corporate organization and independence were absent in Japan.

In contrast to Germany, where government policy promoted the organization and modernization of the handicraft sector, Japan's developmental state viewed the artisanate as an impediment to modernization, and government policy actively undermined the artisanate as a unified corporate actor. The state itself stepped into the skills void and took a much more direct hand in promoting skill formation, importing foreign engineers and establishing training programs in state-owned enterprises. Private firms tapped into the skills that public-sector companies generated, and both private and public companies dealt with the problem of skill formation by incorporating individual artisans (*oyakata*) into a system of direct employment and company-based training. As in Germany, there were contests between traditional artisans and industry over the content and character of apprenticeship training, but in Japan these were played out at the company (rather than the national–political) level.

My analysis of developments in Japan ends in the 1930s, with only a glance forward. This is not meant to imply that the Japanese system was fully developed at that point – far from it. By this time, however, the divergence between a more collectivist versus a more segmentalist approach to skills that distinguishes the German from the Japanese system is quite evident. As in the German case, subsequent developments would refine a system many of whose main contours were already visible by the onset of World War II.

The Role of the State and the Fate of the Japanese Artisanate

In Germany, as we have seen, the legislation that became the cornerstone of that country's system of skill formation – the Handicraft Protection Law of 1897 – was constructed around indigenous institutions and models. In passing this law, the state embraced a policy that nurtured artisanal organizations as a political bulwark against the radical labor movement, at the same time transforming them into a stable source of skills for emerging industry. In Japan, both the labor movement and the artisanal sector were less organized in the early industrial period. The political motives that inspired government policy in Germany were absent; the kind of strong and surging social democratic labor movement that existed in Germany was not a factor in Japan.

In Japan, state policy in the early industrial period was organized less around preserving social stability than around promoting industrial development. After the Meiji Restoration of 1868 the Japanese government was convinced that destroying feudal institutions was necessary for Japan's industrial development. Eager to abolish all previous barriers to labor mobility, the government embarked on a broad liberalization policy that undermined the traditional privileges of the artisanal sector (Sumiya 1955: 33–6). In a relatively short period of time, the artisanate was confronted with changes – revocation of their traditional privileges coupled with massive state-sponsored industrialization – that completely undermined their corporate identity and organizations (Taira 1978: 188). Apprenticeship training, traditionally the preserve of Japanese craft-masters, was similarly deregulated so that, as in Britain, apprenticeship training continued to exist but not subject to any overarching legal or parapublic framework.[1]

The Meiji government took a strong deregulatory stance with regard to the traditional artisanal sector and it also took a very direct hand in redressing early, acute shortages of skilled labor. As Levine and Kawada point out, "Throughout the first two decades following the Meiji Restoration, the new government and its agencies virtually took sole direction of the training of employees within the newly founded factories, arsenals, and offices – just as it did for the whole initial push to industrialize" (Levine and Kawada 1980: 94). Thus, alongside its efforts to eliminate previous (guild-based) barriers to labor mobility, the government also inserted itself directly into the problem of skill formation by recruiting skills from abroad and by using state resources to found new training institutions within the public sector itself.

The influence of the state in training policy was felt above all in the metalworking and engineering sectors. These were the key industries not just for industrial development but also for military purposes.[2] As elsewhere, the practices developed in these industries were crucial to skill formation overall, but the difference is that in Japan these industries were completely dominated by public enterprises throughout the Meiji era (1868–1912).[3] The strong presence of the state produced an industrial structure very different from the British case. It was dominated by enormous, vertically integrated state enterprises (from foundry operations to machine and shipbuilding) that completely towered over the small, traditional machine shops that had

[1] Although the government issued a decree to regulate apprenticeship in 1872, it simply declared that only master craftsmen could take apprentices for a maximum seven-year term and prohibited human traffic. In some traditional industries, such as brewing and construction, the artisanal organizations still played an important role in skill formation, but they did not have any legal privileges.

[2] As Weiss has emphasized, the state was driven as much by military motives as by the economic exigencies of late development. Japan, she reminds us, was more or less continually at war or preparing for one from 1894 to at least 1912 (Weiss 1993: 332–3; also Taira 1978: 175–9). By 1905, "*more than two thirds* of the work force employed in the nation's engineering works were located in the *state* sector" (Weiss 1993: 333, italics in original), and a good deal of production was directly related to military concerns.

[3] Taira notes that government firms in metalworking and engineering accounted for more workers than private firms throughout this entire period. The balance began to shift somewhat in the 1880s as the private sector took off (in part though privatizations), but the employment ratios did not reverse until World War I. By 1920, however, employment in private enterprises in this sector reached three times the rate in the public sector (Taira 1978: 175–6, 187).

survived the liberalization. These public firms organized production along completely different lines, based on sophisticated imported technologies that required skills altogether different from those the traditional artisanal sector was capable of generating.[4]

The character of industry in Japan, therefore, gave rise to distinctive problems, above all very severe shortages of workers with the skills necessary to operate and maintain borrowed (rather than indigenous) technologies. The availability of government resources, however, and the captive product market (the military) for which these firms produced suggested distinctive solutions to the problems, solutions based among other things on the ability of the firms to pass on the costs of the expensive training methods they developed. In a context of overall severe skilled labor shortages and a deeply interventionist developmental state, the state sector in Japan performed a function for private industry similar to that of the organized artisanal sector in Germany. In Japan, since emerging private-sector firms and factories could draw on workers from state firms as a source of skills, there was much movement of skilled labor from the public to the private sector. Firms like the government-run Yahata steel mill became a major source of skills for other firms and industries (Levine and Kawada 1980: 151).[5]

The Meiji government promoted skill development in two major ways. First, the state aggressively promoted training through "international exchange" – that is, by sending Japanese students to foreign countries to study industrial technology and (especially) by recruiting foreign engineers and craftsmen to come to Japan to work in government-owned factories. This project became a major focus of attention in the late nineteenth century. From 1870 to 1900, the Ministry of Industry spent considerable resources (up to 42% of its total budget, according to some observers) on salaries paid to teachers and consultants brought to Japan to set up imported technologies and to train Japanese workers to use and maintain these technologies (Levine and Kawada 1980: 49, 98).

[4] It is not that the artisanate in Meiji Japan was completely unsophisticated, but more that it had been much more insulated from international markets so that the leap to Western metalworking and machine-making techniques was considerable (see Suzuki 1994). I thank Jonathan Zeitlin for emphasizing this to me.

[5] In the 1880s, many of these firms were privatized but the resulting huge enterprises (some later to become the core of gigantic *zaibatsu* conglomerates such as Mitsubishi and Kawasaki) continued to stand at the forefront of training, and also to occupy a privileged position in the market with the government as a key and very reliable customer. The state sometimes arranged transfers of skilled workers from state enterprises to the private companies on whom they relied for military production (Levine and Kawada 1980: 154).

Importing skills was not an end in itself, however, but a step toward self-sufficiency. Thus, traditional Japanese artisans – now bereft of traditional corporate privileges – were incorporated into the state-sponsored system as individuals and in the role of intermediaries. They were expected to acquire skills from the foreign instructors and pass them on to other Japanese workers (Gordon 1985: 18). Indigenous artisans were meant gradually to take over the role played by the foreign craftsmen, to assist in developing a stock of indigenous skilled workers to run production independently. This strategy was often quite successful, as the case of the Yokosuka Shipyard shows (Yokosuka 1983: 6). Originally constructed in 1865 by the Tokugawa Shogunate, the Yokosuka Shipyard employed 45 French engineers and craftsmen in the late 1860s. Over the next 20 years the number of foreign employees decreased to almost zero, as the skills and technology were acquired by Japanese engineers and workers (Saegusa 1960: 61). The core artisans and regular workers employed at the shipyard were recruited mainly from the pool of traditional Japanese craftsmen.

Second, the government sector pioneered the establishment of factory-based technical schools that included in-class instruction. These schools were not intended to train ordinary workers; the graduates of the technical schools were meant to preside over on-the-job training of others (*minaraikō*). The graduates of the technical schools thus played a role in training next-generation workers.[6] For example, Yahata, a government steel mill, initiated a state-of-the-art in-plant training program in 1898, with the assistance of foreign, especially German, advisors. Nagasaki Shipyard, similarly, had a quite elaborate arrangement that included a vocational school and two main training "tracks." For young workers being groomed for supervisory positions in the firm, training consisted of three years of coursework, after which the trainee would be placed alongside a skilled worker supervisor (*oyakata*) on the shop floor in an assistant supervisory position, followed finally by four more years of class-based vocational training. The other track, for "regular" skilled workers consisted of a combination of on-the-job training and daily classroom instruction at the factory vocational school, for a total training period of five years (Taira 1978: 205–6).

[6] Again, the Yokosuka Shipyard is a good example. The shipyard had two schools, one for engineers and one for technicians. In 1883, the number of students admitted to these two schools was 37 and about 50, respectively, as against a total of 1,505 employees in the factory as a whole (Sumiya 1970: 17).

The State and the Japanese Artisanate

Skill formation outside the public sector (and its private-sector spin-offs) was organized along more traditional lines, and here local artisans played an even more prominent role. In Japan's small firm sector, as in Germany, master craftsmen presided directly over skill formation, taking apprentices in and working alongside them in their workshops. In Japan, such training was often haphazard and exploitative (Taira 1978: 188–9). However, larger factories often integrated traditional artisans into a more effective system for apprentice training through "continuous skill" teaching, adapting traditional skills to new tasks (cf. Sawai 1996: 302; Suzuki 1992). This form of in-plant training increased dramatically at the turn of the century with the expansion of the metalworking sector and the growing role of large private firms in it. In practice it resembled traditional workshop training where young apprentices picked up their skills by working alongside skilled artisans (Taira 1970: 109–10; Taira 1978: 189).

Thus, in spite of the destruction of their corporate organizations, traditional Japanese artisans continued to occupy an important role in skill formation in the early industrial period. In the metalworking industries, as in other "modern" sectors, traditional artisans were absorbed into large companies and served as intermediaries, acquiring new skills either through working with foreign craftsmen or in technical schools and then passing these skills on to younger workers on the job. In the growing and increasingly important private sector, traditional craftsmen were also employed and put in charge of training through an adaptation of traditional skills to new problems and technologies.

Either way, in both the private and public sectors, training in Japanese factories was based on the traditional *oyakata-kokata* (master-apprentice) relationship, and skilled craft masters in Japan (*oyakata*) came to play an important role and to exert wide discretion on the shop floor (Gordon 1985: 38–45; Sumiya 1970: 100). The power of the Japanese *oyakata* derived partly from the structure of the market for skilled metalworkers in Meiji Japan, which was organized around social and economic ties. Labor recruitment by firms, as well as the movement of workers from job to job, was facilitated by the "referencing networks" that developed around well-known *oyakata* (Taira 1978: 190). By relying on master craftsmen as suppliers of skilled labor (through both recruitment and apprentice training), firms could minimize the costs associated with finding appropriate skills and overcome the problem of imperfect information (for example, about a worker's skill level) in the absence of any kind of formal certification or standard.

Subcontracting work to a master craftsman also had the advantage of allowing firms to spread risk in very unstable markets.[7]

In the public sector as well, the *oyakata* craft masters were very powerful, less because of the structure of production and more because of the feudal organization of companies in this period. In most government factories, ex-samurai (the warrior class in the feudal system) assumed management positions. Given their own lack of managerial skills, and in light of the cultural and behavioral gap that separated them from the traditional artisans and ordinary laborers who worked for them, the samurai managers delegated important managerial powers to the *oyakata*.

Implications for Labor

The *oyakata* formed an aristocracy within the working classes in late nineteenth-century Japan. Firms delegated extensive managerial functions (for example, hiring, firing, evaluation) to them. *Oyakata* filled a variety of roles within the emerging industrial sector. Some owned small machine shops and operated as suppliers to larger firms, some contracted their own labor and that of their retinue to large companies, others worked more exclusively as skilled-labor subcontractors in a single firm, and some were directly employed by a company as supervisors, exercising a great deal of discretion over personnel policy (Gordon 1985: 36–7). Similar to German artisans, Japanese *oyakata* were often able to maintain a high degree of individual autonomy. Unlike Germany, however, they did so without any strong corporate or collective organizational base. Japanese *oyakata* in the early industrial period tended to function as independent entrepreneurs, moving around in the industrial sector, taking their skills (and their entire work group in many cases) with them into factories, often returning to their own independent shops in times of slack demand (Taira 1970: 110; Taira 1978: 193).

The situation was also quite different from that in Britain, however. There, political conditions were relatively auspicious for the emergence of organizations of skilled craftsmen with aspirations to collectively control

[7] The nature of the subcontracting relationship varied. In some cases the workers an *oyakata* brought in were not directly employed by the firm at all. But often even craftsmen who belonged to an *oyakata* had formal employment relations with the factory. Therefore, when *oyakata* could not complete the subcontracted work within the budget assigned, individual workers could demand their normal wages from the factory management (Agriculture and Commerce 1903, Vol. 3: 271). In this sense, the employment relationship was not so indirect.

the market in particular trades (see the discussion in Chapter 3). State policy allowed, and in some ways even indirectly encouraged, the forging of links among workers in the same trade but different places of employment. The political context was more restrictive in Japan. Unlike their British counterparts, Japanese artisans were not permitted to form inter-regional links between guilds or journeymen's associations during the Tokugawa Shogunate which preceded the Meiji Restoration (Gordon 1985: 22–5). When the economy was liberalized, skilled artisans in Japan were much more free floating, though they were also able to take advantage of extreme skilled labor shortages as free agents (and employers of others). The huge public or private firms that dominated the metalworking and engineering industry in the early industrial period depended on *oyakata* and their workers for the skills they commanded. Beyond this, the overall lack of managerial expertise (especially in the public sector) meant that large employers also depended on *oyakata* as "the principal method of work-force management in Japanese factories before the First World War" (Taira 1978: 189).

Traditional craftsmen in Japan were thus absorbed, but mostly as individual entrepreneurs, into emerging industry and there often occupied powerful quasi-supervisory positions. As Taira points out (Taira 1978: 187–94), given the early – and growing – bifurcation of the metalworking and engineering industry into a dynamic (mostly state-owned) large firm sector, alongside a less dynamic sector composed of small workshops, the place to make one's career was in the former, because *oyakata* who entered the large-firm sector enjoyed tremendous autonomy, power, and status.[8] The enormous and sprawling factories in which *oyakata* operated were typically run on a very decentralized basis, and workers in this period perceived themselves to be members of a particular *oyakata-kokata* group rather than employees of the company in which the group worked. "Unlike the latter-day workers of Japan, a Meiji craftsman would rarely name the factory as his employer, nor would he derive any particular pride from mentioning its name. His pride was in his trade and in belonging to the circle of a respectable *oyakata*.... The coveted goal for any worker was to establish himself as an *oyakata* with his own workshop and *kokata*" (Taira 1978: 190).

Skill-based unions did not make much headway in Japan for a variety of reasons. One is the legacy of state policy toward the guilds under the

[8] Taira notes that in some cases, *oyakata* commanded very large retinues, of "tens or hundreds" of subordinates that they brought with them (Taira 1978: 193).

Tokugawa Shogunate. More important, after the Meiji Restoration, state repression prevented craft unions from becoming institutionalized. There were a number of attempts in the last years of the nineteenth century to form craft unions along the lines of those in the American Federation of Labor (AFL) in the United States (for example, in printing and iron working) but these efforts were summarily suppressed (see, especially, Garon 1988: 29–33; Gordon 1985). Broader-based organizations of skilled craftsmen met the same fate. The Tekkō Kumiai or Metalworkers Union was formed in 1897 but was moribund by 1907 (Taira 1978: 191–2).

Faced with such political constraints, skilled *oyakata* turned to individual strategies aimed at improving their lot through their own mobility and initiative. Many *oyakata* did not define their futures in terms of employment in industry at all, expecting instead to return to their own independent workshops at some point (Taira 1978: 193; Gordon 1985: 417). And considering the supervisory positions they assumed in the factories of early industrial Japan, these skilled craftsmen in Japan occupied what Erik Olin Wright would call a highly ambiguous class position – enjoying considerable autonomy and authority over other workers on the shop floor. Ordinary workers with grievances about working conditions would more often than not direct these at the *oyakata* labor boss rather than the firm, not unreasonably given the vast powers *oyakata* commanded in the factory in the early industrial period.

Implications for Industry

When it came to skills and skilled workers, the overriding problems that firms faced in Japan in the early industrial period were intense shortages and accompanying high labor mobility and poaching. At the same historical juncture at which machine and metalworking firms in Germany were becoming adamant about achieving rights to certify skills and in Britain were becoming obsessed with reasserting managerial control, their Japanese counterparts were completely consumed with the task of controlling labor mobility.

The *oyakata* system may have fulfilled the minimum need to provide skilled labor in the metal industry in the early industrial period, but labor mobility remained very high and if anything the *oyakata* system promoted it. Although it involved plant-based training, this system did not produce stable "segmentalism," at least in the sense of stable internal labor markets. *Oyakata* felt no particular loyalty to a firm, and "a patron would readily move his retinue from one work site to another in response to the highest bidder," a factor that contributed to extremely high levels of turnover before World War I (Levine and Kawada 1980: 113). Moreover, even if the *oyakata* stayed put, there was nothing binding about his relationship with the craftsmen under him. Since the *oyakata* masters played a key regulatory role in the labor market – controlling well-paid jobs and assigning them to his group members – there were some incentives for craftsmen to stay with the *oyakata*. But there were no formal controls, and an *oyakata*'s workers could and did leave the factory at their own will (Agriculture and Commerce 1903, Vol. 2: 10). The *oyakata* were themselves in some cases important intermediaries, helping craftsmen who were made redundant in one factory to find jobs elsewhere (Yamamoto 1994: 167–8).

In addition, since apprenticeship training was unregulated, there was also nothing to discourage labor mobility even among trainees. The system of training at this time was plant-based, but because it was embedded in highly fluid subcontracting relations, the skills conveyed were highly portable.[9] Moreover, unlike the case in Germany, there were no particular incentives for Japanese apprentices to stay until the end of their formal training period if opportunities arose elsewhere (Labor 1961: 22). Thus, in the metal trades especially, "many apprentices cut short their terms of apprenticeship and took off into the world as independent journeymen" (Taira 1970: 109). A certain amount of mobility was seen as completely consistent with the progress of an apprentice's training. Changing jobs exposed apprentices to new techniques and technologies, so some mobility was seen as useful in helping workers to develop their skills by experiencing various types of work (Sumiya 1970: 162–7).

This type of mobility among skilled workers had always been a factor in Japan, certainly in the public sector where it was a long-standing issue. Public sector enterprises counted on a certain degree of attrition and could maintain high quality and expensive training programs because they were uniquely positioned to pass the costs of training along to the consumer (the military). But because they valued the key skilled workers they had gone to

[9] But with one qualification. Although mobility was a signal of the market power of skilled workers in this period, the lack of "independent standards" for documenting one's skill put some limits on what they could do, since firms could not know what they were getting. One company, Uraga, used a one-week test (employing the worker at a flat rate of 1 yen per day) to determine the worker's wage. If a worker felt that he was being inadequately remunerated, that his real skills merited higher pay, he had not much recourse but to quit again (Gordon 1985: 96–7).

some lengths to train, government factories frequently introduced policies designed to retain a core group of skilled craftsmen, who were expected to preside over the training of others. Therefore, as early as 1868, management at the Yokosuka Shipyard granted 65 core artisans (*kakae shokkō*) "life-time" employment.[10] By 1873, the shipyard had introduced further inducements to retain key skilled craftsmen. In that year, the company selected 110 skilled craftsmen for "salaried" status, which guaranteed them a fixed monthly salary even if they were absent due to illness. The company also added a retirement bonus to keep skilled craftsmen on the job (Hazama 1964: 421). Such plans were seldom effective, however, and they were even less so at the turn of the century as the demand for skills grew, making business very unstable and training extremely costly for firms.

As in Germany, the rapid growth of the metal industry at the end of the nineteenth century generated demands for more and more sophisticated skills.[11] The result was even more intense competition for skilled workers and rampant poaching, both among private companies and, especially, from government-owned firms. Annual turnover rates "often exceeded 100% and occasionally reached 200%" (Weiss 1993: 332). According to a 1901 survey, in the ten major private metalworking factories, more than 50% of workers had been employed there for less than one year.[12] Although firms such as the Mitsubishi Nagasaki Shipyard had attempted to achieve stability by hiring craftsmen on a fixed-term (three-year) basis, neither employers nor workers took this seriously (Hazama 1964: 452). Moreover, as private manufacturing as a whole grew in size, it became difficult for individual companies to recruit a sufficient number of skilled workers from the government-owned firms. In addition, and reminiscent of the problems faced by the large metalworking firms in Germany, the modernization of production technology within the private sector required a larger number of workers with higher skill levels than the traditional *oyakata* system of "continuous skill development" was generating.

[10] At this time, the Yokosuka Shipyard employed 113 regular workers (*jōyatoi*), 397 helpers, and 54 common laborers (Hazama 1964: 403; Taira 1978: 176).

[11] The number of workers in military arsenals rose from about twenty-five thousand in 1899 to just over seventy-five thousand by 1912. Employment in private metal factories rose from just under twenty-one thousand to almost seventy thousand in the same period. See Hazama (1964: 436, 452). On the need for more differentiated and specialized skills, see also Yamamoto (1994: 188), Inoko (1996).

[12] In 1902, the median length of employment was less than one year in private machine companies in Aichi Prefecture (Odaka 1990: 320).

Thus, labor mobility became the overriding concern among Japanese employers in the metalworking industries. We find in the early 1900s a number of attempts to dampen labor mobility – both through attempts to impose restrictions directly on workers and through attempts at collective self-restraint by employers to reduce poaching.[13] For instance, high labor mobility in the closing years of the nineteenth century caused some firms to take punitive steps such as withholding apprentice pay. They also offered inducements such as long-term contracts to a few select workers and/or progressive pay scales to induce workers to stay with the firm, practices that had been pioneered in some large public enterprises (Gordon 1985: Chapter 2).

In some industries, companies attempted to deal with ruinous competition among themselves over scarce skilled labor through collaboration. In these cases, employers organizations brokered and enforced agreements to prevent firms from pirating workers away from each other (Taira 1970: 111–13). In spinning, silk, and coal, the efforts of trade associations to reduce poaching enjoyed some limited success.[14] Smaller scale, bilateral agreements of a similar nature were concluded in the metalworking industries in some regions. For instance, in 1911, at a time when the shipbuilding industry was booming, Mitsubishi Shipbuilding Works in Nagasaki struck a deal with the nearby Naval Arsenal at Kure in which they promised not to bid workers away from each other (though it was possible for the two companies to negotiate transfers) (Taira 1970: 115). These arrangements were unstable, however, in all sectors in which they were tried. In the metalworking industry they were even less successful than elsewhere.[15]

[13] The attempts at collective self-restraint occurred in the context of a proliferation of trade associations in the early twentieth century (Morita 1926: 31–3). Around the same time, business groups also began demanding government regulation of labor mobility (Labor 1961: 22, 36).

[14] For instance, in the spinning industry, in which skilled workers are necessary but on a seasonal basis, employers competed fiercely for workers, resulting in high labor costs. As a solution, the employers organized their local trade association (*kōjō dōmei*) and introduced a worker-registration system. In this system, once a worker was hired by one employer, other employers could not hire that worker (Morita 1926: 107–14). In this industry, the cartel practice worked well in some regions. In the silk industry, the National Confederation of Silk Associations announced in 1920 that workers who were hired by a particular employer in that year were reserved for the same employer in 1921. A similar practice could be found in the coal-mining industry in Hokkaido in the 1920s. Even in these successful cases, however, the practice broke down from time to time (for example, *Jiji shinpō*, March 22, 1926).

[15] In the Tokyo area, the Association of Machine and Iron Works (*Tokyo Kikai Tekkō Dōgyō Kumiai*) was organized and tried to control labor mobility, but it did not work so well as in other sectors (Tekkō Kitai Kyōkai 1974).

In general, such attempts foundered on a number of problems. One was the resistance of the state, which – though often supportive of cartel practices for regulating *product* markets – looked less favorably on restrictions on *labor* market mobility (such as cartelized wage capping and restrictions on the ability of craftsmen to change jobs) (see, for example, the Decree of the Vice Minister of Agriculture and Commerce, June 29, 1916). But collective self-restraint also failed because of conflicts of interest among firms themselves. Traditional firms and sectors wanted greater labor market regulation, but emerging industries often wanted more "liberated" labor (Furusho 1969). Within the metal industry, private companies were less eager to introduce such regulations because they continued to recruit skilled workers from the government-run factories, a practice that had the implicit blessing of the government (Yamamura 1977). In 1904, when naval arsenals established a voluntary rule that none of them should hire craftsmen who quit their jobs at another arsenal, the private sector stayed out of the arrangement, not least because private companies relied rather heavily on poaching from the government-owned factories for skilled labor (Hazama 1964: 454–5).

It did not help matters that apprenticeship training was unregulated, for this did nothing to discourage labor mobility among trainees, contributing to shortages by making training more expensive. Japanese trade associations in the late nineteenth century – concentrated on merchant interests and institutionally separate from traditional guild structures (Miyamoto 1938) – attacked the problem from the demand side but the supply side of skills remained in the hands of the *oyakata* craftsmen whose traditional organizations, as noted above, had been destroyed. Attempts by employers to reduce poaching were hobbled by the lack of any institutional framework to ease their collective action problems by directly generating a steady supply of skilled labor. Thus, time and again their attempts to negotiate collective solutions to the problem of labor mobility broke down in the face of intense competition over scarce skilled workers.[16]

[16] On the development of business and trade associations in Japan in the pre-war period, see the essays by Miyamoto, Kikkawa, and Fujita in Yamazaki and Miyamoto (1988). Prior to World War I, a number of cartels formed in various light industries; only one formed in the iron, steel, and machinery industries in that period (Kikkawa 1988: 65; tables on 62–3). Kikkawa refers to cartels in the silk, paper, and cotton industries that apparently sought to deal with labor shortages. He mentions efforts in those industries to prevent poaching, but there is no mention of any joint endeavors in the area of skill formation (Kikkawa 1988: 65–6).

Strategies of the Large Metalworking Companies

Intense competition among firms for skilled workers redounded to the benefit of *oyakata* craftsmen, whose power derived not (as in Germany) from their institutionalized privileges as an organized social and political group, but rather from the scarcity of their skills and the pivotal position that individual *oyakata* therefore occupied. Whereas in Germany, tensions between the artisanal sector and industry were played out at the national–political level, in Japan they were dealt with at the plant level, as individual employers sought to control labor mobility and to create for themselves a more stable source of skills. In some cases, this involved the creation of wholly new training institutions in the firm (company-based training schools), but in others it involved strategies that sought to institute more direct forms of control over the training provided by *oyakata* bosses, by incorporating the latter more securely into firm hierarchies and establishing direct employment relations with the craftsmen under them. These strategies often blended together in practice. I deal with them in turn.

First, some private firms in metalworking addressed skilled labor scarcities and high mobility by embracing the strategy pioneered in the government sector, instituting their own company-based schools for trainee workers (*minaraikō*). The first company training school in the private sector was the Mitsubishi Preliminary School for Industry (*Mitsubishi Kōgyō Yobi Gakkō*), established in 1900. According to a survey by the Tokyo Advanced School for Industry, more than ten large companies had established such schools by 1911. These schools combined on-the-job training with classroom instruction. The training term was at least three years, and any worker who completed the training was expected to become a core skilled craftsman and commit himself to stay in the factory after finishing for at least as many years as the training term had lasted (Sumiya 1970, Vol. 2: 37).

The more skills the workers acquired, however, the more likely it was that they would be recruited by other companies, and nothing prevented these workers from reneging on the agreement. Gordon quotes a manager who was closely involved in the creation of the training program at a leading engineering firm, Shibaura, speaking in 1908. "Recently . . . the company established a suitable system of education, but workers . . . who have not completed the required number of years are leaving the company in a rush" (Gordon 1985: 74). Nor was Shibaura an isolated case; the same story applied to the school run by Shibaura rival Hitachi. There, too, trainees left either during the training period or soon thereafter, lured away by the prospect of better paying positions in Osaka or Tokyo (Gordon 1985: 75). Mitsubishi's training school enrolled over four hundred students in courses to graduate between 1904 and 1909, but fewer than half stayed to the end of the training term, and only 19% of the total entrants were still employed by the company three years later (Gordon 1985: 75).

Given the expense of such programs (making them out of the question for the vast majority of firms), these efforts often took place alongside other measures designed to draw skilled workers generally into a more dependent relationship with the company. One method was to coopt the *oyakata* and take direct company control over on-the-job training. The early 1900s thus saw an overall shift, a decline in the number of *oyakata* employed as "independent bosses" on a subcontracting basis and a rise in the number of *oyakata* operating as agents within a company. Cooptation involved offering them privileged jobs which combined a high degree of job security with the exercise of significant discretion, though now more in the context of an overarching managerial hierarchy. As Gordon puts it, "The oyakata was to trade his freedom for the security and status offered by the company" (Gordon 1985: 54).

In other cases managers sought to liberate themselves from the "grip" of the *oyakata* by establishing a system for training (in-house) so-called key workers who could substitute for the the *oyakata* bosses. These "key" workers received ongoing broad but company-specific training designed to allow them to be deployed flexibly in response to the company's needs. Firms tried to offset the reluctance of workers to invest in such company-specific training by offering long-term employment commitments, instituting seniority wages and internal career ladders, and introducing company welfare schemes (Levine and Kawada 1980: 114–18).

The transition from indirect to direct control over enterprise-based training was slow and protracted, though overall the declining market position of independent master craftsmen relative to the more dynamic industrial sector helped push the process forward. Taira notes that the first company-trained *oyakata* to emerge from the Mitsubishi vocational school graduated in 1912, emphasizing that due to attrition from the school, it took a very long time to displace traditional *oyakata* (Taira 1978: 206). In many cases, traditional elements and modern innovations were blended together, with young workers who completed training under the patron system being elevated to the status of (low-level) engineer or technician, and put in charge of training the next generation of recruits (Levine and Kawada 1980: 113; Taira 1978: 205–6).

The movement toward company-controlled training was associated with efforts to stabilize internal markets and to encourage long-term employment. Some of the measures that figured most prominently in firm strategies were seniority-based wages, company welfare provisions, and loyalty indoctrination for core skilled workers. For instance, already in 1900 the management of the private Nagasaki Shipyard had introduced a system of regular workers with long-term employment guarantees and temporary workers without secure employment. In that year, there were 5,247 regular workers and 440 temporary workers in the shipyard; this regular worker system resembled the regular craftsmen system of the government-owned Yokosuka Shipyard. Management introduced various inducements, such as a retirement bonus, to keep workers for a longer period. Labor turnover among regular workers in the Nagasaki Shipyard was very high until 1901, but decreased gradually thereafter, an indication that management inducements seemed to be working (Hazama 1964: 454; Odaka 1984: 208).[17] Here we can find a prototype of the management system that proliferated in post-World War II Japan, one of the characteristics of which is company-based skill formation and internal labor markets.

Yahata is another famous early example of this strategy.[18] This leading steel producer founded a company school in 1910. In subsequent years, training here became associated with a "finely graduated promotion ladder and elongated status hierarchy" (Levine and Kawada 1980: 165). Promising young workers who were singled out for special training could rise to a low-level supervisory position (*gochō*), and after three years in this job (and based on examinations to test both their technical and interpersonal skills) they might be moved to the higher position of *kumichō*. As they accumulated additional training and experience, these workers might rise to salaried positions, beginning with promotion to *kochō* (production foreman) and eventually perhaps *shokurō* (managerial assistant), at which point the worker might be deployed as an instructor in the enterprise training program (Levine and Kawada 1980: 165–6).

Despite the relative success of some such efforts, the general problems of labor mobility and poaching remained acute and increased during World War I, fueled by skilled labor shortages (Taira 1970: 129–32). A factory

[17] After the company introduced the regular worker system, the mobility rate (calculated by dividing the number of hired and fired workers in a given year by the total number of workers at the end of that year) dropped substantially, from an average (between 1898 and 1909) of 115% to an average (between 1910 and 1913) of 57%.

[18] My account is based on Levine and Kawada (1980: 158–68).

inspection report from 1919 recorded separation rates for the Japanese machine industry of 75%; a national survey conducted around the same time found that only 11% of the country's three hundred thousand machine industry workers (12% of all industrial workers) had over five years experience with the same employer (Gordon 1985: 87, 89). These conditions promoted company policies designed to stabilize internal labor markets, which strongly foreshadowed practices that would become even more widespread later. "The granting of periodic raises to some of those who remained with a company was one critical practice which became fairly common by the end of World War I" (Gordon 1985: 97), as was the use of promotions (to supervisory or foreman positions) partly on the basis of seniority, plus bonuses and allowances associated with seniority – all used selectively and strategically by management to keep (particular) skilled workers in place (Gordon 1985: 98–101). Wage rates and benefits in the interwar period also came to be associated with length of service although "promotion depended upon successfully passing periodical examinations based on training provided" (Levine and Kawada 1980: 174).

The Evolution of the Japanese Management System

As we have seen for Germany, political realignments in the 1920s were crucial in shaping the fate of vocational training in the Weimar years. There, an increasingly well-organized machine industry (by then representing a growing number of small and medium-sized firms) led efforts to collectivize and standardize vocational training in industry (although the possibility for reform based on a cross-class coalition with labor foundered on political and economic obstacles). In Japan, industrial and political realignments during and after World War I would also be decisive in the evolution of the Japanese training system. As in Germany, labor would play a supportive though not constitutive role, but unlike Germany, the cross-class coalitions that were forged with labor in Japan were at the plant level and not the national-political level. Developments during and after World War I thus pushed the Japanese training regime further along a segmentalist trajectory.

As emphasized above, Japanese firms in the early industrial period had to contend first and foremost with a high degree of workforce instability. The 1920s, however, brought economic conditions that eased the problem of labor mobility considerably. As Levine and Kawada note, an economic downturn in the 1920s rendered skills relatively more abundant and, combined with increased urbanization and better education (including more government support for vocational education), "one reasonably might have expected segmentation to break down and more open labor markets [to] reemerge" (Levine and Kawada 1980: 118). As the context shifted from one of labor shortages to labor surplus, Japanese employers might have abandoned in-plant training and the accompanying generous policies they had instituted to stabilize internal labor markets. But this did not happen.

One important factor in shoring up the system was the consolidation in the post-World War I period of the strongly dualistic industrial structure alluded to above, consisting of (*zaibatsu*-connected) large firms on the one hand, and small and medium-sized firms on the other. Whereas in Germany, small and medium-sized machine firms were becoming more and more organized and adapting to market changes with the aid of their dynamic trade association (VDMA), in Japan the small-firm sector was falling behind. Previously highly independent *oyakata* who may have anticipated a return to their own workshops were more likely than ever to be willing to give up direct management of their own work groups in exchange for "a variety of comforts and inducements such as a status in the management structure [of a firm], permanent tenure, higher pay, and regular increments" (Taira 1978: 205).

The dynamic firms in this period were undergoing significant modernization premised on technology borrowed from the West (Yamamura 1986). A much higher degree of capital intensity increased their concern with retaining skills, especially advanced skills not easily acquired in the labor market. These huge companies (with enormous internal labor markets) commanded considerable market power, which made it possible for them to absorb rather large fixed costs, including permanent employment, to protect their investment in training. These factors, combined with fewer incentives and opportunities for skilled craftsmen to move, meant that the 1920s and 1930s were characterized by greater employment stability than previous decades had known (Taira 1970: 153–4). An extensive review of employment conditions across a number of industries, published in 1929, documents the growing use by large firms of various incentives to increase worker retention rates (Taira 1989: 625).[19]

[19] The interwar period also saw the founding (in 1919) of an organization, the *Kyōchōkai*, (Harmonization Society) which consisted of businessmen, members of the Diet, public interest representatives, and representatives of government, and was designed to promote labor–management cooperation. The organization for a time provided job placement services, conducted research, and acted as a policy advocacy organization. Main strands of activity were to advise employers, promote the introduction of various company-based

Significant wage differentials emerged in Japan in the 1920s as well, with large firms offering higher wages and in general instituting practices meant to keep workers, particularly select skilled workers, in employment (Taira 1989: 623–4). Taira (Taira 1970: 35) reports on a study that tracks wages in two large firms in Northern Kyushu, comparing them to the going (market) rate for the region in these same occupations. At Yahata Iron and Steel Works and Mitsubishi Shipbuilding Yard in Nagasaki, wages rose at the end of World War I and continued to outpace the regional average through the 1920s and 1930s. "The movements of wage differentials between large firms and the labor market in the North Kyushu industrial area were . . . part of what was happening in the whole economy" (Taira 1970: 35).

Another factor that pushed against labor market liberalization and toward continued relatively generous employment packages in the large-firm sector during and after World War I was the rise of the trade union movement. Compared to the German and the British labor movements, Japanese unions were weak, fragmented along ideological lines and organizing fewer than 10% of all workers before the First World War. However, the years between about 1900 and about 1920 had "witnessed the emergence of an energetic working-class movement in the growing industrial centers of Osaka, Kobe, Tokyo, and Yokohama," which posed a strong challenge to direct control and paternalism (Gordon 1985: 421). Moreover, even though overall organization levels remained low through the interwar period, in the crucial engineering and metalworking industries the rate was higher, reaching up to 25% (Taira 1978: 212), so that unions in these skill-dependent sectors possessed significant disruptive potential. Unlike their British counterparts, however, (and as we will see, in the United States as well), Japanese unions did not organize their strategies around establishing craft controls (Lazonick and O'Sullivan 1997: 518), but rather around exercising influence within existing plant employment structures.

This important difference helps explain the particular configuration of interests and alliances that emerged in Japan, as unions and employers – each for their own reasons – banded together to confront the independent

welfare measures, and lobby the government for social policy legislation. The organization also published a report on the state of worker welfare systems in various companies, which may have facilitated a degree of cooperation through information sharing among the segmentalists in this period. Unions rejected the organization as an attempt to co-opt workers but it survived until 1946 when the occupying forces dissolved it because of its role in the war. I am grateful to Ikuo Kume for information on this organization, based on the book, *The Thirty Years of Kyōchōkai.*

power of the *oyakata* bosses. As described above, the *oyakata* craftsmen were in charge of managing as well as training workers. Previous, longstanding skill shortages had enhanced their power within the plant, but these skills were becoming outdated as new (imported, advanced) technology was introduced in factory production. Meanwhile, and parallel to this, young skilled workers who had graduated from company training schools began playing an increasingly important role on the shop floor, posing a threat to the traditional *oyakata*-based shop floor regime. In some cases, union activists organized and mobilized young skilled and semi-skilled workers against the *oyakata* regime.

Important for the present argument is the fact that, in such conflicts, management frequently sided *with the union*. In the large firms in the metal industry the demands of young unionists to curb *oyakata* power dovetailed with the efforts of managers to take direct control of personnel policy. The *oyakata* lost their power, and management began exerting control directly (Sumiya 1970, Vol. 2: 56). In these labor conflicts, management often made concessions to the union in order to incorporate younger skilled workers into the factory regime (Gordon 1985: 421). Many union demands – such as for the introduction of an annual bonus and a retirement bonus system for regular workers – had the effect of further institutionalizing internal labor markets (Gordon 1985, 163–206). Already in the late 1910s a number of firms had confronted and met such demands. These included Shibaura Manufacturing (1916), Nagasaki Shipyard (1917), and Nippon Steel Hiroshima Factory (1919) (Odaka 1995: 153). In addition, in 1919, workers in the Yahata Steel Mill (the largest mill at the time) went on strike demanding not just improvement of working conditions but also equal treatment of regular blue-collar workers and white-collar officials. The young skilled workers also demanded that career paths for managerial positions should be open to them.[20] These demands were met after a long labor conflict (Sumiya 1970, Vol. 2: 86), thus promoting long-term employment and internal labor markets.

In the interwar period, Japanese unions continued to push for stable wage increases based on length of employment (Gordon 1985: Chapter 5), and since management was still concerned about skills, alliances were forged

[20] Such demands make a great deal of sense in the Japanese context where the absence of any legal right to organize and bargain collectively – until 1945 (Taira 1989: 647) – meant that most activism would be localized, and where firm policies organized around efforts to hold on to particularly treasured employees produced a high degree of stratification within a given workforce (Taira 1989: 628).

around policies of continuous skill development linked to increasing wages over the course of a worker's career in the firm. These developments helped to promote the spread (at least among leading firms) of a seniority-based wage system (*nenkō joretsu*, or ranking by years of experience). "The ideal type of the *nenkō joretsu* system required that new hiring was limited to young inexperienced workers and that these workers were trained and moved up to fill various grades of skills over time" (Taira 1970: 157). Engineering firms that opted to implement this system did so as part of their overarching effort to gain direct control over all aspects of personnel policy including "recruitment, training, assignment, promotion, dismissal, and retirement," in other words, stripping the *oyakata* of his power and influence by displacing the traditional practices "based on personal and personalized relations among master craftsmen and between each one of them and his underlings" (Taira 1970: 158). It is no coincidence that precisely in the 1920s a growing number of companies began following the lead of prominent firms (for example, the Kure and Nagasaki shipyards) in recruiting young people directly out of school (in April of each year), and founding company schools for training these new recruits (Dore 1973: 399–400). These developments were especially pronounced in heavy industry, where as Nishinarita notes the seniority-wage system was "firmly established" (Nishinarita 1995: 18).

Thus emerged in Japan the seeds of a system strongly associated with seniority-based wages but which in reality links wages to experience acquired over time in the course of a worker's career in the firm (Thelen and Kume 1999). Clearly managers had to balance considerations of skill against seniority criteria, for if they rewarded workers coming in from the outside too much they would create equity problems for those workers coming up in the ranks within the company (Gordon 1985: 97). The entire process through which firms began exercising direct control of training and linking this to wage developments was accompanied by a parallel shift in which training in a "trade" was gradually broken down into a series of specific tasks (Taira 1978: 189). This development pushed further a process that had already begun in cases where youngsters worked alongside (but not under) patron-craftsmen and where training was increasingly organized around the needs of the firm and in the context of longer employment horizons.

Although unions were in some cases active players in these developments, perhaps the more common pattern was for management to *preempt* labor conflict – and forestall union organizing in the first place (Gordon 1985: 207–35). An official of the Ministry of Interior argued at the time "it is critically important to establish collaborative labor-management relations within the company before class conflict appears" (Ikeda 1982: 9). In the 1920s a number of factory committees were indeed established to facilitate labor-management communication, many of them incorporating management practices begun in the large companies in response to labor conflicts. Taira notes that although collective bargaining and unionization were minimal in Japan in this period, employer-initiated works councils – designed to forestall unionization – were quite widespread (Taira 1970: 144–8).[21]

Policies pursued by the Japanese government of the 1930s and 1940s further encouraged segmentalism and company-based training in the context of strong internal labor markets.[22] In response to a dramatic four-fold increase in strike activity in 1937 (measured in the number of striking workers), the government instituted the so-called Industrial Patriotic Council (*Sangyō Hōkokukai;* IPC) (Okazaki 1993). The IPC was designed to improve communication and avoid conflict between workers and employers, as well as to provide workers with company welfare privileges as part of a war mobilization program (Saguchi 1991: 168).

The war years were very important for solidifying previously emerging patterns (Sakurabayashi 1985). Although the IPC did not achieve its formal purpose (Garon 1988: Chapter 6; see also Gordon 1985: 299–326), it did promote a "managerial revolution" and encouraged deep changes in Japanese corporate governance (Okazaki 1993). Taira argues that this movement (*Sanpō* for short) laid the basis for enterprise unions after the war (Taira 1989). And, although a full-fledged transformation of Japanese corporate governance structure, in which employees' interests were prioritized over those of shareholders, did not occur until after the labor offensive in the post-World War II period (Kume 1998), we can find the roots of such a transformation in this effort (Noguchi 1995).

In addition, the exigencies of war production brought a significant expansion of private-sector training, as in Germany under National Socialism, directly promoted and indeed mandated by the state. In March 1939, two significant pieces of legislation came into effect, requiring many employers to establish worker-training programs (Gordon 1985: 265). Subsequent legislation (between 1939 and 1942) imposed increasingly strict government

[21] Unionization was especially low in large private-sector enterprises; in 1936 there were only 16 collective agreements with firms employing over five hundred workers (Taira 1970, 147).

[22] By contrast, the attempt by the military government to introduce a nationwide system of skill formation (through the so-called "youth schools") failed, largely because the two goals that animated the initiative – skill formation and infantry training – were frequently in conflict and the latter very often overrode the former (Sumiya 1970, Vol. 2: 272).

controls on turnover (Gordon 1985: 266–7), mitigating poaching problems and giving employers the longer time horizons that encourage investment in training. Legislation in this period required employers "to obtain permission from the local Employment Agency office before hiring anyone, and, in the case of experienced people, permission would be granted only if the previous employer agreed" (Gordon 1985: 267).

Although these measures imposed significant restrictions in the labor market, employers did not complain; quite the opposite. Associations like the Kansai Industrial Federation were entirely satisfied with them, and in fact asked the government to expand existing controls (Gordon 1985: 267). Although this legislation – both the laws encouraging training and those limiting labor mobility – fell short of its goals (certainly there was a great deal of illegal movement), it did have an important influence on the training calculus of leading firms. As Weiss points out, this is the period when "company training came into its own" (Weiss 1993: 346), as hundreds of thousands of munitions workers employed throughout the metalworking industry were officially prohibited from leaving their jobs. This in effect made it much more attractive for employers to invest in training. Since the early 1900s the government had repeatedly urged such training, but now exhortations were backed up by the Technical Education Acts of 1939 that "mandated training programs for most *workers* (not simply salaried employees) and for most companies. Thus, by the end of the war, training programs were very widely established within the private sector" (Weiss 1993: 346).

The development of Japanese managerial practices after World War II is well known and need not be rehearsed here (see, for example, Dore 1973; Kume 1998). Clearly training plays a key role in the system. Ongoing skill acquisition is what traditionally has underwritten progressive seniority-based wage increases over a worker's career and lifetime employment guarantees, and helped to reconcile both with firm efficiency and productivity. Perhaps a word should be said, however, about the content of the skills produced by the German and Japanese systems. In Germany, as we have seen, the skills that could be certified were for particular trades or occupations, as a package as it were. In Japan, in the transition away from the *oyakata*-based system and toward direct firm control, trades were unbundled and workers acquired proficiencies in a variety of different tasks valuable to the company. The precise package of skills acquired, in other words, was not so much defined by a commonly understood notion of a particular trade, but rather by the needs of the firm. This does not mean that these skills are entirely non-transferable (in Becker's strict sense), but it does mean that skill acquisition and development are organized around different principles and goals with respect to skill "portability."

The difference becomes clear in the skill accreditation and certification system that emerged in Japan in the postwar period.[23] A 1958 Vocational Training Law established a system for testing and certifying skills under the auspices of the Ministry of Labor. The system is administered with the assistance of the National Vocational Skills Development Association, which recruits representatives of industry and vocational training establishments to set standards, and whose prefecture branches administer the tests themselves. Through this system public and private training institutions are accredited but so too are private sector (company-based) training schemes. The skills tested are narrow but they are not necessarily company specific, and certification makes them more portable by rendering them more transparent to other firms. Unlike the German system, however, the skills that are certified in Japan are "discrete and miscellaneous" and can be mixed and matched.[24] The certification and accreditation system in Japan thus fits and reflects the different (segmentalist) logic of the Japanese training regime (Sako 1995: 6).

Companies may seek accreditation for their own training schemes for a variety of reasons. For many, accreditation helps in recruiting top young workers, by establishing or maintaining a company's reputation as a good firm and a good employer, one that will offer ongoing training and opportunities for advancement (Sako 1995: 25). In many firms a more formalized procedure for worker testing has been folded into the traditional internal promotion schemes. For example, some firms require workers to earn certificates as a prerequisite for advancement or higher pay, thus providing a crucial link between seniority wages and ongoing skill acquisition – necessary to ensure increasing worker productivity across the worker's entire career. Certification also helps organize and facilitate relations between "core" firms and their various "peripheral" partners, for example providing a mechanism for core firms to assess the capabilities of their various dealerships. In other instances, the system provides a means for large firms to assess the performance of their suppliers or to coordinate production with them. Small supplier firms are sometimes required to have workers certified

[23] The following account is based on Sako (1995), Dore and Sako (1989), and Crouch, Finegold, and Sako (1999).

[24] For example, one major car manufacturer had, as of 1995, 219 internal skill tests.

under the buyer's training system. Certification also facilitates corporate transfers – both across firms in horizontally organized corporate groups like Mitsui, Mitsubishi, and Sumitomo, and across vertically linked firms (for example, buyers and suppliers) – practices that are important to many companies in the context of long-term employment policies.

Germany and Japan Compared

In both Germany and Japan employers invest substantial resources in training their workers, but the training efforts of individual firms fit into completely different national political–economic frameworks. The origins of Germany's and Japan's different systems of skill formation, I have argued, can be traced back to differences in the relationship between the artisanal sector and industry in the early industrial period, and particularly the way in which the interaction between these two influenced relations between industry and the emerging labor movement. The argument can be summarized in three steps.

First, state policy toward the artisanal sector was crucial to the subsequent development of the two systems. In Germany, the state actively organized the artisanal sector and granted it monopoly rights to certify skills, whereas in Japan state policy did nothing to regulate traditional apprenticeship training. This difference had a profound impact on the quality and supply of skills available to industry in the two countries. In Japan, craft masters were unregulated and could shirk their training responsibilities and apprentices could abandon their masters – and did so, as we have seen, in large numbers. Thus the first big difference between the two cases is the overall supply of skills available to industry and the fate of the artisanate. Japanese managers faced more severe and chronic skilled labor shortages and became obsessed with *controlling labor mobility*, whereas in Germany the large firms most dependent on skill became intent on *securing the right to define and certify skills*, a right that the Handwerk sector monopolized and that large industrial firms coveted.

Second, in both cases, the emerging metal industries tapped into the traditional artisanate to cover their skill needs, and in both cases frictions and tensions emerged as a result. The difference lies in the level at which such tensions were played out – at the plant level in Japan, at the national–political level in Germany. In Japan, where the *oyakata* craftsmen were not organized, emerging large firms could address their skill needs by contracting with individual *oyakata* to recruit and train skilled workers. This strategy solved some problems but it created others, as independent and mobile *oyakata* could use competition *among* industrial firms over scarce skilled labor to enhance their own power *within* individual companies. After repeated (failed) attempts on the part of industry to find a solution through "collective self control," private firms followed the lead of public-sector firms who had internalized skill formation, setting Japanese firms on a very different trajectory favoring plant-based training.[25] In Germany, where the artisanate was well organized, it could not be absorbed into and subordinated to industry in the same way. Tensions between the artisanate and industry were played out at the national–political rather than the plant level.

It is important to note here that the actual skills possessed by workers in Japan and Germany after the turn of the century were in fact not so different. In Japan, training was plant-based and internal to large firms, but high levels of labor mobility suggest that the skills themselves were very portable. Conversely, in Germany, the existence of skill certificates should not imply that skills were particularly standardized – that development came only later, in the machine and metalworking industries in the 1920s and in other industries in the 1930s and 1940s under the National Socialists.

Third, and finally, the consolidation of segmentalist and solidaristic strategies has to be understood in terms of the way in which these previous developments mediated industry's relationship with the emerging labor unions. In both cases, alignments and realignments among the artisanate, industry, and unions in the 1920s appear to be crucial. In both countries, economic trends in the early 1920s called the existing system into question, and critical realignments (in Japan between the managers of large industrial firms and younger skilled workers at the plant level; in Germany between some segments of industry and labor unions at the industry level) reinforced previous trajectories.

In Japan, segmentalist strategies before World War I were a response to intense skilled labor shortages, and so the slack labor markets of the 1920s might have undermined the strong internal labor markets that had been

[25] In addition, in Germany, the ongoing modernization of "traditional" skills was built into the market-conforming character of the 1897 law, which, as pointed out above, facilitated Handwerk's adaptation to the market (including technological change). This was quite different from Japan, where, if traditional skills were upgraded at all, it was in the internal labor markets of the industrial sector.

developing. What prevented this was the growing complexity of firms' skill needs combined with the increasing threat of trade union influence at the plant level, which produced a critical realignment (management with unions or young company-trained workers against the *oyakata*) that consolidated and deepened segmentalism. In Germany, where skills were more plentiful before World War I, the crisis of the 1920s was different and stemmed from Handwerk's own economic crisis, which severely tested its capacity for "collective self-regulation" and sparked concerns about impending skill shortages. Newly incorporated labor unions emerged as potential allies for industry against the Handwerk monopoly and in support of a solidaristic system of skill formation for industry. In both cases, in other words, there was a critical realignment that brought segments of industry into alliance with labor and against the artisanate, with the difference that in Japan this occurred at the plant level and in Germany at the industry level.

The effect of World War II in both cases was to accelerate developments along these divergent paths. In Japan, as Weiss summarizes, "Before the war, seniority wages, company allowances, and company training programs linked to long-term career structures were practiced in an opportunistic, exclusive, and capricious manner by a small number of core companies. The effect of the war on government policy was to deepen and systematize these tendencies and to extend them to industry as a whole" (Weiss 1993: 346). In Germany, (see Chapter 5) the National Socialist regime during World War II presided over a massive expansion of training and the increasing standardization of apprenticeship through the extension of the collectivist framework that had been evolving in Germany since the nineteenth century.

In neither Germany nor Japan was labor the driving force toward more collectivist versus more segmentalist skill development, but unions formulated their goals within the (different) logics of the two systems, and in so doing helped to push developments further along these distinctive tracks. In Japan, for example, unions defined their goals within the context of strong internal labor markets in ways that helped to consolidate segmentalism and drive skill formation down an increasingly organization-specific path. In Germany, the fact that unions "grew up" in a context in which skill formation was already regulated (by Handwerk) discouraged craft-based control strategies and made unions potential allies of industry in the latter's struggles for separate certification, though labor's relative weakness (especially in Germany's large-firm sector) contributed to the problems of consolidating solidarism in the Weimar years.

The Evolution of Skill Formation in the United States

The U.S. case provides further illuminating comparisons, both to Britain and to Japan. As in Britain, in the United States craft unions emerged among skilled workers in key trades and organized their strategies around the attempt to maintain and regulate craft labor markets. In the United States, unions had an even harder time establishing craft controls due to a number of factors including weaker traditional craft-based organizations of any variety (for example, guilds), higher inter-regional mobility, massive immigration in the early industrial period, a larger and more homogeneous domestic product market, and – related to all these – the late development of craft organizations relative to key technological and organizational changes in industries such as metalworking. As in Britain, apprenticeship would be substantially contested across the class divide, but an important difference is that in the wake of their victories over "control" issues American employers went much further to crush and marginalize unions and to reorganize production so as to reduce their reliance on skilled labor.

As in Japan, skilled workers were incorporated into low-level supervisory positions in large U.S. corporations. The role they performed, however, was very different from that played by traditional *oyakata* in the Japanese system. Rather than serving as intermediaries in skilled labor markets or as trainers of the next generation of skilled workers, salaried foremen in U.S. firms more likely became the "drivers" of (increasingly) semi-skilled labor. To put the U.S. case again in comparative perspective: whereas in Germany, metalworking firms at century's end were concerned to *certify skills*, in Britain to *reassert managerial control*, and in Japan to *dampen labor mobility*, in the United States the goal was above all to rationalize production and *reduce dependence on skilled labor*.

Although some large firms had developed rather impressive and ambitious programs for in-plant training by the turn of the century, the continued ambitions of American craft unions to control skilled labor markets – and a resurgence of union militancy during World War I – set the scene for a rather different set of alliances in the 1910s and 1920s. In the period after the First World War, the premier US training firms largely abandoned earlier programs of broad-based training for manual workers and focused their energies and resources instead on enlisting their foremen in a campaign against resurgent unions, encouraging the introduction of skill-displacing technology. By the time American unions were stabilized and collective bargaining rights were secured (1930s and 1940s), organized labor in the

United States was maneuvering in a more thoroughly rationalized shop floor environment. Union strategies revolved around a narrower form of job control in highly bureaucratized internal labor markets.

Skill Formation in Early Industrial America

The overriding fact about the U.S. case is the lack of guild structures and traditions. Absent this kind of inherited infrastructure, the regulatory framework governing apprenticeship in the colonial period – although directly borrowed from England – took on a quite different character in America (Rorabaugh 1986: 3–16; Douglas 1921; Motley 1907: especially the introduction and Chapter 1). In Britain, apprenticeship regulation as represented in the original Statue of Artificers was closely associated with regulation of the manual trades in the guild tradition. In America, apprenticeship as embraced and enforced (mostly feebly) by colonial authorities was much more tied up in civic education and Christian morality. Under colonial law, "masters were in general required . . . to impart not only trade training, but to give instruction in the liberal arts [reading and writing primarily]" (Douglas 1921: 43), and apprenticeship was part of a broader project to prepare youth (and especially youth from poor families) to be good citizens and to inculcate in them Christian values (Douglas 1921: 45–7; Motley 1907: 12–13).[26]

To the limited extent that oversight was exercised over American apprenticeship, this was accomplished by the officers of colonial towns and counties (Douglas 1921: 50). Given the conditions of "vast distances, shortages of skilled labor, a largely agricultural population and a poorly developed legal system," however, American apprenticeship was even "less vigorously" enforced than its English counterpart (Rorabaugh 1986: 4). U.S. (and colonial) apprenticeship operated in an institutional vacuum, so that virtually anyone could call himself a master artisan and take apprentices (Rorabaugh

[26] Apprenticeship was also used as a disciplinary device for punishment of debt and penalties for idleness (Douglas 1921: 42–3). As Douglas points out, apprentices were thus dealt with more or less as the master's property, so much so that "apprentices were often listed among the assets of bankrupts and were either taken personally by the creditors as payment for debt or sold to satisfy the obligation. Upon the death of the master, the apprentice was often sold with the rest of the estate by the heirs" (Douglas 1921: 48). Motley points out that employers in colonial America had such absolute control over their trainees that some of the laws governing servants and slaves were extended to cover apprentices as well (Motley 1907: 15). As in Britain, an apprentice's term of service, linked to the age at which he started, continued until he reached the age of 21 (for boys; 16 for girls) (Motley 1907: 13).

1986: 4–5; Hansen 1997: 84–5; Motley 1907: 28). As Hansen has summarized: "There were no minimum levels of competence required to practice a craft, no regulation of apprenticeship. Nor were there formal associations of craft brothers to present joint appeals to municipal and state officials, to build and sustain collective identity and interests, or to enforce production standards, labor practices, price floors and the like. What little collective action American mechanics engaged in was voluntary, ad hoc, and ineffective" (Hansen 1997: 95).

Craft identities that in Germany were nurtured by handicraft associations or in Britain by craft unions were, by contrast, difficult to build and maintain in colonial America. Social structures were a great deal more fluid, as vast land resources pulled New Englanders westward and as a very large number of craftsmen worked simultaneously as independent farmers. These farmer artisans – many living in remote areas – of necessity operated with a high degree of self-reliance. Rather than specializing in (and identifying with) a particular craft, these men became proverbial jacks-of-all-trades. The resulting "craft polyvalence," as Hansen notes, "undercut the historic identification of the 'artisan' with a particular craft and its associated traditions, and in the process fashioned an emergent Yankee tradesman, with all the ambiguities that term implies" (Hansen 1997: 89).[27]

Thus, more than in Britain, apprenticeship in the United States was always less regulated and more informal and tenuous. On the side of employers, there is ample evidence of the kinds of abuses we have already seen in Britain (Douglas 1921: 60–2; Motley 1907: 17). The lack of any certification or monitoring left it entirely up to the employer what kind of training, if any, a youth would receive. Employers abused apprenticeship especially in times of labor shortages, making use of "bogus" indentures "as a device to obtain and hold youths to unskilled factory labor" or (later) during the Civil War when apprentices were widely deployed as strike breakers (quote is from Rorabaugh 1986: 202–3; D. Jacoby 1991: 896).[28]

As for apprentices, there were no strong incentives for youth to subject themselves to long years of training with a highly uncertain payoff.

[27] Or, as he pointedly summarizes: "Early American farmer-artisans . . . generally had little time or patience for craftsmanship, possessed strong economic incentives to dispense with it, lacked collective constraints with the capacity to compel them to it, and had virtually nowhere to turn to acquire it" (Hansen 1997: 96).

[28] Contractual obligations of this sort could be fought in the courts but this required time and resources and so enforcement was an enormous problem.

The problem of runaway apprentices was even more acute in the United States than in Britain, and it continued despite legislation passed in twelve states in the closing decades of the eighteenth century to curb the problem (Elbaum 1989: 346–8). There was no stigma for American youth who failed to complete their terms; on the contrary, the popular literature of the day celebrated runaway apprentices such as Benjamin Franklin for their spunk and initiative (Rorabaugh 1986: prologue and Chapter 7). Poor youth were disinclined to pass up higher paying unskilled work to pursue an apprenticeship, and certainly the more ambitious youth and their parents were "discouraged by the uncertainty of the training offered" (Douglas 1921: 83). These were also problems in Britain, but the unattractiveness of traditional apprenticeship would have been greater in the United States, where the prospects for land ownership and independent employment, and the early spread of public education, created avenues for youth, even poor youth, to pursue their own careers.[29]

The skills on which American industries relied in the early industrial period were by and large not generated domestically, as in Germany or Britain, nor through targeted foreign exchange sponsored by the state, as in Japan. Rather, such skills were provided to employers through immigration, beginning in the 1830s and waxing and waning over the next decades in response to business cycles in the United States (Shefter 1986: 200–1). "By the 1850s immigrants were a majority of the skilled craftsmen in most large cities; in New York, for example, they dominated thirty-two trades" (Rorabaugh 1986: 133).[30] This influx of skilled workers – mostly from the industrial districts of northern Europe – continued through most of the 1880s. Artisans from England, Wales, and Germany provided many of the skills on which early American industry was built; in some cases foreign craftsmen were directly recruited through the intervention of state legislatures acting in response to the "urgent appeal of prominent employers" (Brody 1980: 15; Shefter 1986; quote is from Motley 1907: 18–19).

29 In Massachusetts free public schools began to spread from as early as 1700 (Douglas 1921: 44). Certainly by the end of the nineteenth century, the number of youth attending high school was much higher in the United States than in Britain, and that number continued to rise rapidly in the first two decades of the twentieth century (Jacoby 1985: 70).

30 Later, immigration would also provide a huge supply of unskilled workers: "from 1882 to 1900 immigration from Europe to the United States involved some 6.6 million persons" (Klug 1993: 74). The implications of this shift in the kinds of workers entering the United States are explored below.

Implications for Labor

The space left by a lack of traditional guild structures and the comparatively liberal political climate created in the United States, as it had in Britain, the conditions under which organizations of skilled workers in key industries like metalworking could organize to attempt to control craft labor markets. The main immigration streams came from countries with stronger craft traditions and immigrant groups formed the basis for labor organization in many cities. The widespread recruitment of skilled labor from abroad thus provided a direct avenue for the importation of strategies and organizational models (not to mention union organizers and leaders) from Europe, especially Britain (Motley 1907: 18–19). By the 1830s, "the American working classes evidenced striking dispositional and ideological similarities to their English cousins" (Bridges 1986: 158). A number of journeymen's associations were founded in this period similar to those that formed the core of Europe's craft unions (Brody 1980: 15; see also Montgomery 1989: 185).[31]

Important differences in context, however, complicated the consolidation in the United States of substantial craft unions with power to contest skilled labor markets even on a local, let alone a national, basis. Successive waves of immigration introduced a variety of linguistic, cultural, and national differences, complicating the task craft unions faced in forming and maintaining unified and disciplined organizations. As Shefter notes: "When workers did join with others in an effort to improve their lives, ethnicity was at least as likely as social class *per se* to be the basis of association" (Shefter 1986: 221, 229, 231; quote is from 231). Beyond the ethnic cleavages, American unions in the early industrial period also had to contend with a much higher degree of mobility. Particularly after the expansion of the railroads in the late nineteenth century, it became much easier for workers to move. Local trade unions therefore had to contend with relatively large numbers of craftsmen from other areas seeking employment in their district but not feeling themselves obliged to submit to local union rules (Shefter 1986: 215). The overall less auspicious social and market context for union organization was reflected in much lower rates of organization in the United States than in Britain. In the last three decades of the nineteenth century, unionization rates among industrial workers in the United States remained below 10% (Ulman 1955: 19). In metalworking

[31] For a review of the literature on the "artisan origins of the American working class" see Wilentz (1981).

specifically, whereas Britain's ASE and related unions organized around 50% of engineers (mostly skilled fitters and turners) at century's end, only about 11% of American machinists were organized in the main engineering union (International Association of Machinists, IAM) at this time (Haydu 1988: 86–7).

Given the more limited resources of American unions – both financial and organizational – the goal of exercising control over craft labor markets was always daunting and mostly elusive. But if the prospects in the marketplace looked especially bleak in the United States in the mid-nineteenth century, the early enfranchisement of the male working class offered an alternative avenue for pursuing craft control strategies. In the 1870s unions in several states pressed their legislatures for regulation of apprenticeship and in a few cases (Massachusetts, Illinois, and New York) they succeeded in obtaining legislation to regulate in-plant training (Douglas 1921: 67–8). A law passed in New York in 1871, for example, required written indentures signed by both trainee and company. Under the terms of such indentures the period of apprenticeship would have to be set between three years (minimum) and five years (maximum), and employers committed themselves to providing the apprentice with "suitable board, lodging and medical attention" as well as training in "every branch of his or their business" (Douglas 1921: 68). On completion of the apprenticeship, the trainee received a certificate and penalties were established for both apprentices and employers who broke the contract.[32] Such regulations were notoriously hard to apply, however, Enforcement depended on one of the parties bringing suit, but apprentices did not have the resources to take employers to court, nor assets against which a firm would be interested in proceeding if it were the apprentice who broke the contract. Moreover, as was so often the pattern in U.S. labor history, narrow court rulings quickly rendered existing legislation "dead letters" (Douglas 1921: 68–9).[33]

[32] "If the apprentice would not try to learn his trade or serve faithfully, he was to forfeit his back pay and the indenture would be cancelled. If he ran away before his term of service expired, he was liable to a jail sentence.... [For his part] if the employer did not care for the apprentice suitably according to the terms of the indenture and the provisions of the law, he could be sued by the apprentice or by his parents. If it could be shown that the employer had neglected his duty, the court was to cancel the indenture and impose a fine of not less than $100 and not more than $1000, which was to be paid to the apprentice or to his parent or guardian" (Douglas 1921: 67).

[33] On the role of the courts in the United States in undermining pro-union legislation, see also Hattam (1992).

Despite these obstacles, unions of skilled workers in the United States, no less than their counterparts in Britain, continued to recruit (and attempt to restrict membership to) "competent" journeymen and to try to influence the number of apprentices trained and the terms of their employment (Kelly 1920: 55–8; Motley 1907: passim). Thus, the American counterpart to Britain's ASE (the International Association of Machinists, IAM) took advantage of relative skill scarcities in the late nineteenth century to press for agreements with specific employers concerning both working conditions for their members and apprenticeship training.[34] The issue of apprentice regulation figured prominently in the first joint agreement that the IAM was able to reach with an employer (in 1892, with Atchison, Topeka and Santa Fe Railroad Company). The agreement established a ratio of one apprentice to every five machinists (one to every four in the case of boilermakers and blacksmiths) (Perlman 1961: 247).

In those (few) cases where relatively stable joint agreements on apprenticeship could be reached – but also in a more informal way on a somewhat broader scale – unions played an important role in underwriting commitments between training firms and trainees, by ensuring that firms provided apprentices with all-round training and by imposing penalties on apprentices who broke off their training prematurely.[35] The first of these tasks – holding employers to all-round rather than narrow training – could be accomplished directly, since in most cases apprentices acquired their skills from journeymen who were themselves union members. Unions also sought to ensure that the trainee held up his end of the deal, among other things, staying with the firm for the full training period. Craft unions cared deeply about the "runaway" problem, which from their perspective carried the risk of flooding the trade with "half-way" journeymen. The trade journals put out by craft unions often featured a "runaway column" which disseminated information about apprentices who broke off their training prematurely (Motley 1907: 86–7). Through such means unions attempted to prevent apprentices from leaving early and posing as fully skilled workers (to earn the skilled rate) in other districts.

As in Britain, union attempts to regulate apprenticeship were riven with problems of uneven levels of influence across regions, and thus also bound up in broader control strategies that brought the unions into direct conflict

[34] For a comprehensive history of the IAM, see Perlman (1961).

[35] The logic and practice of joint regulation of apprenticeship through unions is spelled out nicely in Motley (1907: Chapter III).

with employers over issues of managerial prerogative. The much later timing of craft union development in the United States (the IAM, for example, was founded in 1888) relative to the drastic expansion of product markets and to technological changes in the metalworking industries in the last two decades of the nineteenth century meant that overall, joint regulation of apprenticeship through collective agreement with unions was always shakier than in Britain (Ulman 1955: 121, 311). Motley reports that of the 70 or so unions that by his reckoning attempted to enforce apprenticeship as a prerequisite to membership in 1904, only 19 actually succeeded (Motley 1907: 58–60). He notes that in the case of the IAM the official rules regarding apprenticeships were "hardly more than the recorded expression of opinion of what should be the rule" (Motley 1907: 70).[36]

Implications for Industry

In Germany, early industrial enterprises were able to draw on the skills of the artisanal sector and adapt these to their needs; in Britain employers could tap into "accumulations of skilled labor supplies in industrial districts" (Lazonick and O'Sullivan 1997: 498). By contrast, in the United States the lack of any skill producing and certifying infrastructure – along with high labor mobility (both inter-regional and inter-occupational) – "rendered skilled labor scarce throughout the nineteenth century" (Lazonick and O'Sullivan 1997: 498). American employers thus faced skill shortages on a scale most similar in many ways to their Japanese counterparts. However, whereas the Japanese state became deeply involved in skill formation and vocational training in the closing years of the nineteenth century, in the United States government efforts to enhance education and training were directed almost exclusively at the college-bound middle classes, not training for manual workers.[37]

If this posed special problems for American employers, it also suggested special solutions to the problems (Ulman 1955: 7–16). The character and especially the size of the domestic market in the United States opened possibilities for employers to innovate in ways that reduced their overall reliance on skill by moving to the mass production of standardized goods

[36] The IAM's British counterpart, ASE, had by this time also long abandoned apprenticeship as an explicit condition of membership, though they required that prospective members should have worked in the trade five years, and be able to command the district rate.

[37] The reasons for this have been analyzed especially thoroughly by Hansen (1997).

(Hansen [1997: 196–212] has an especially good discussion). As Lazonick and O'Sullivan point out, the scarcity of skilled labor provided a powerful motivation for American manufacturers to look to skill-displacing technology from very early on (Lazonick and O'Sullivan 1997: 498).[38] The move toward standardization and skill-displacing technological change picked up more steam over the course of the nineteenth century, spurred forward by the development of a national railroad network that opened new and bigger markets even as it encouraged even greater labor mobility.

The development of an integrated national market had the effect of exposing firms to low-cost strategies elsewhere, at the same time increasing immensely the advantages of scale economies (Hansen 1997: 197–8). These factors became highly salient in the depression of 1873 and led to major shakeouts in a number of industries. In 1869 the average American factory was a family owned firm or partnership, and employed only about eight workers (Shefter 1986: 234). Beginning in the 1870s there was a trend toward "the absorption of small firms by stronger ones during the depressions and recessions of the period, the spread of the corporate form of business organization, and the emergence of a class of professional managers [that] destroyed the organizational base upon which personal relations between employers and employees had been grounded" (Shefter 1986: 235). In consequence and as Jacoby notes, "after 1890, the center of gravity in American industry shifted to giant corporations serving national markets. Between 1904 and 1923, the proportion of the manufacturing work force employed in very large establishments (over 1,000 workers) doubled, rising from 12 to 25 percent" (quote from S. Jacoby 1991: 108; see also Brody 1980: 7–8).

Developments in the labor market reinforced the trend toward the large-scale enterprise in the United States and the associated shift to mass production of standardized goods. One key factor was the changing character of immigration, which after the 1890s brought huge numbers of unskilled workers, mostly peasants from southern and eastern Europe (Brody 1980: 15–17). Thus, whereas skilled labor continued to be extremely dear, unskilled labor in the United States at century's end was relatively "cheap and abundant" (Jacoby 1985: 133). As Hansen notes, it was no coincidence that "mass production reached full flower in its classic Fordist form" when and where it did (Hansen 1997: 196, 214).

38 They note, for example, that the textile industry around Lowell, Massachusetts, was already more highly capitalized than in other countries in the early nineteenth century.

There were significant limits to the process of rationalization, standardization, and task simplification, particularly in some skill-intensive industries such as machine making.[39] The different strategies of various firms are analyzed below. This diversity sustained different approaches to skill formation but the weight and interests of large manufacturers of standardized goods, along with the conflicts with labor across virtually all types of firms, worked strongly against the stabilization and expansion of the more collectivist strategies for skill formation developed (especially in the 1910s) by specialized producers in some cities and regions.

Union and Employer Strategies in the Metalworking Industry before World War I

The evolving strategies of employers in industries such as machine building and metalworking must be understood against these general developments. In Britain, apprenticeship was caught up in ongoing struggles between craft unions and managers who sought to assert managerial control over this and other issues. In the United States, as well, traditional training arrangements relying on skilled craftsmen increasingly ran afoul of employers' efforts to rationalize production and reorganize work on the shop floor. In the United States, however, the move to rationalize production so as to reduce dependence on skill went much further than in Britain, setting the stage for a somewhat different alignment of interests and trajectory of development.

From about 1850 until at least the 1880s skill-intensive industries such as machine building and metalworking relied heavily on immigrant craftsmen and employed quite traditional methods of skill formation. In these industries the "factory was often no more than a congeries of artisanal workshops which had been mechanized and enlarged" and in which skilled workers presided over a highly decentralized production system and could exercise significant autonomy and control (Montgomery 1989: passim; Jacoby 1985: 14). American employers looked to craftsmen not just to organize and manage production but also to serve as intermediaries in the labor market, recruiting skilled workers and presiding over the training of apprentices.

[39] There is a large literature dealing with the diversity of the American political economy and with the role of specialized producers in it. See, for example, Scranton (1997), Sabel and Zeitlin (1997), Hounshell (1984), Nelson (1992), Zeitlin (2000).

What precise form these arrangements took, as Jacoby points out, varied across different firms and segments of the industry, from explicit subcontracting arrangements in which independent craftsmen were contracted to perform specific jobs for which they employed their own workers (similar to Japanese *oyakata*), to a more egalitarian "gang system" in which groups of skilled craftsmen were directly employed by the firm but organized the work among themselves (similar to craft unions in Britain) (Jacoby 1985: 14–15).[40] Both these systems served important functions for employers in the early industrial period, and each was attached to specific training arrangements.

One prominent strategy for securing skills and providing for training embraced by a significant number of firms in the metalworking industries in the early industrial period was internal contracting. As in the *oyakata* system described for Japan, machine and metalworking firms negotiated contracts with highly skilled workers for specific jobs in the plant. These craftsmen then hired and supervised their own skilled work crew, who often themselves employed unskilled helpers (Brody 1980: 9–10; Rorabaugh 1986: 65; Jacoby 1985: Chapter 1 and especially 14–16). Inside contracting was widely practiced as early as the 1820s in the Lowell machinery industry (Rorabaugh 1986: 65), and it was common in the iron, steel, metalworking and machinery industries throughout the late nineteenth century and (in smaller companies) even into the early twentieth century (Clawson 1980: 28, 75–76; Buttrick 1952: 216; Nelson 1975: 37; Patten 1968: 18). Among the companies using this system were such giants as Lowell (one of the 70 largest machine shops), Pratt and Whitney, and Whitin. As Clawson notes, "those establishments which are known to have used inside contracting are among the leaders of the U.S. industry of 1860 or 1880. Not only were they among the largest companies of their time, but they were also the technological leaders of their day" (Clawson 1980: 76–7). In the machine industry generally "inside contracting had spread between 1860 and 1890 to such an extent that a government study found it 'practically universal in New England' and commonplace elsewhere" (Montgomery 1989: 187).

For firms in skill-intensive industries, inside contracting offered a number of advantages. Above all, and in light of the severe skilled labor shortages throughout the nineteenth century, managers found it more efficient

[40] The different models also coexisted and in many cases shaded into each other in practice. For example, skilled workers who served as contractors for one job might later find themselves working for another foreman on the next job (Clawson 1980: 107–8).

and inexpensive to leave the recruitment of labor and even the day-to-day management of production to autonomous (often foreign-speaking) craftsmen (Soffer 1960: 144). Inside contractors performed vital functions in skill formation, since these craftsmen employed and trained their own helper-apprentices. By controlling work organization and job assignments, they were essentially able to determine who acquired skills and of what sort. "At a time when work experience was a far more important qualification than education, the contractor could decide which employees should be trained as skilled workers and which should do routine work" (Clawson 1980: 104; Rorabaugh 1986: 65). Through their role as intermediaries in skilled labor markets, inside contractors also served the function of "certifying" the skills of specific workers. They could directly vouch for the specific job experience and training of the workers they had trained and help connect them to jobs in the industry.

Such were also exactly the functions performed by unions of skilled workers in the early industrial period, and as Soffer has pointed out, in some cases the autonomous craftsmen of the subcontracting system formed the core of early American Federation of Labor (AFL) unions (Soffer 1960). Where skilled workers were well organized, employers sometimes found unions extremely helpful as intermediaries as they navigated tight labor markets. Employers turned to unions to help them recruit skilled labor, and (through their role in apprentice training) vouch for (therefore, "certify") the skills of the workers they organized, thus reducing information costs to employers. Unions also ensured that employers provided apprentices with all-round training in the trade (important to the union to maintain high wage standards). A large number of historical studies have pointed to a high degree of autonomy exercised by skilled workers in many nineteenth century factories (for example, Montgomery 1989; Brody 1980). Even where employers did not formally recognize unions, in some regions and industries they came "to tolerate a high degree of control by unionized skilled workers in the labor process and the labor market" (Klug 1993: 668–70; Haydu 1988: 28).

As in Britain, the stability of such arrangements was highly contingent on local market conditions. Where local differences in the strength of craft controls interfered with competition among firms in product markets employers vigorously resisted. In a way the exceptional case – that proves the rule – was the stove foundry industry where unions and employers reached a relatively enduring settlement in the late nineteenth century because the unusually well organized International Molders Union (IMU) was able to aid employers in escaping a vicious cycle of cutthroat competition and falling profits by enforcing uniform standards across the industry.[41] The conditions that made this accommodation possible, however, and continued to stabilize it for some time, were rather restrictive, including: the lack of major technological innovations in the period, the fact that labor accounted for a large proportion of total production costs, the extremely high degree of organization achieved by the IMU (in 1891, a full 75% of stove plate molders), and a degree of centralization and internal discipline on the union side extraordinary for the time (Klug 1993: 482–501).

Such were not, however, the conditions prevailing through most of the rest of the metalworking and machine industry at century's end. As in Britain so too in the United States, technological and organizational changes in the closing decades of the nineteenth century led to more intense competition in product markets throughout the engineering industry – particularly as technological changes made it possible for companies to increase productivity and reduce labor costs through rationalization. These developments heightened tensions between skilled craftsmen and employers, as the uneven enforcement of craft controls (more pronounced in the United States than in Britain) only increased distortions in product market competition among firms.

In the case of firms relying on subcontracting arrangements, heightened product market competition resulted in intense new strains on autonomous craftsmen that completely undermined their role in training apprentices. Particularly after the depression of the 1890s, managers passed cost pressures directly onto inside contractors; putting "relentless pressure on [them] for cheaper output" (quote from Montgomery 1989: 210; Buttrick 1952: 219–20). The inside contracting system had always (by its very structure and logic) given contractors a "monetary interest in maximizing the output of a group of his workmates" (Montgomery 1989: 187; also Nelson 1975: 37), and they were therefore very receptive to technological and organizational changes that would generate higher profits. At the same time, their participation in such labor-saving (and especially skilled labor-saving) measures undermined the original source of their power as intermediaries in skilled labor markets and trainers of skilled workers.

These new technology- and product market-based pressures had a similarly corrosive effect on skill formation regimes rooted in associations of skilled workers. Skilled unions in many industries traditionally had allowed

[41] The most exhaustive study of this fascinating case can be found in Klug (1993: especially 482–501). But see also Motley (1907: Chapter IV, 42–52) for a contemporary account.

their members to employ apprentices as "helpers." At century's end, however, and particularly with the growth of piecework pay in this period, craftsmen faced incentives to increase their own output and earnings by subdividing the work, cutting corners on training, and using apprentices as cheap extra hands. As Motley put it, "both employers and employing journeymen found it profitable to engage the services of many apprentices" (Motley 1907: 24). The "helper system" (a.k.a. the "Berkshire" or "buck" system, depending on the industry) set in motion dynamics that were self-reinforcing and deeply disruptive to training. The problem – as described by Klug for the molding industry – was that: "so long as even a few tradesmen used helpers, and a company set molding prices in accordance with their rate of production, then all molders (even those opposed to the helper system) were forced to go along in order to make decent earnings" (Klug 1993: 441–2; see also Motley 1907: 22–4). Thus in this period one sees union leaders, with varying degrees of success, appealing for controls on the use of helpers based on the argument that the dynamics this would unleash could only lead to a general deterioration of the position of skilled workers within the trade.[42]

The dominant theme of this period in the United States, as in Britain, however, was heightened tensions between craft unions and employers over the right to manage production. The last two decades of the nineteenth century had seen a sharp increase in unionization among skilled workers, as well as the founding of key unions including the American counterpart to the British ASE, the International Association of Machinists (IAM, founded in 1888). In some industries, employers experimented with collective bargaining as a way to manage relations with their workers and to organize competition among themselves. As Swenson notes, in the period between 1895 and 1905, "about 19 employers' associations and 16 unions had negotiated no fewer than 26 national or large district agreements" including in 1899 and 1900 agreements in the engineering industry "where foundries and machine shops produced metal goods and machinery for America's expanding farming, manufacturing and consuming economy" (Swenson 2002: 49). These agreements spun into crisis, however (as in Britain), in the face of continuing disputes between labor and capital over "control" issues and the apparent inability of union leaders to rein in militant locals (Brody 1980: 24–5).

[42] It is no coincidence that the IMU stands out among organizations of metal craftsmen at century's end in banning the use of bucks (helpers) by its members.

The resulting conflicts (similar in form and also in timing to the Great Lockout in the British engineering industry described in Chapter 3) culminated in the United States in a more concerted and, from management's perspective, overall more successful effort to eliminate union influence in plant decision making – the "open shop" movement.[43] Given their relatively late emergence and weaker presence than in Britain, unions in the United States were mostly deemed by employers to be too unevenly organized and insufficiently disciplined to be of use to them in regulating competition among themselves and were seen as more likely than not to introduce disruptive distortions. In addition, the development of mass markets, combined with technological changes

> made union restrictions more irksome to U.S. employers and simultaneously reduced their reliance on craft unionists to get the work done. [Members of the employers association for the metalworking industries (National Metal Trades Association, or NMTA)] thus had both greater interest and greater resources to attack craft standards. Because the erosion of craft control was under way before the IAM's consolidation, U.S. employers had another advantage: relatively feeble union opposition. The NMTA faced a union much weaker than the ASE. (Haydu 1988: 86; see also Klug 1993: 334)[44]

Employers were most radical in their anti-unionism in precisely those bastions of craft-union strength (for example, Detroit) where unions could impose standards, for these were the employers who found themselves at a competitive disadvantage in national product markets. As a measure of the determinedness of employers and the fragility of unions, even in such "union" cities, it took only a few years for employers to marginalize organized labor and impose the open shop (Klug 1993).

The strategies that firms in skill-dependent industries pursued to consolidate their victory over craft unions varied. One of the most important differences was between large and small firms. Large employers often coopted individual skilled workers into the plant hierarchy, thus transforming them into agents in a so-called "drive" system that relied on increasing output through task simplification (and associated increased reliance on semi-skilled labor), combined with worker intimidation and bullying

[43] On the "open shop" movement in the United States, see, among others, Brody (1980), Montgomery (1989), Klug (1993).

[44] Union presence, it should be noted, was highly uneven. In some localities, for example, Detroit and Philadelphia, the IAM had established a significant presence among machinists (Klug 1993: 668).

(Jacoby 1985). For example, in the aftermath of a crushing defeat of the unions at Carnegie Steel Works, managers devised a new structure in which they "grafted" the top craftsmen (among them, the blowers, melters, and rollers) onto the firm's management structure, making them low-level supervisors (Montgomery 1989: 41). At Winchester Repeating Arms Company, similar policies were pursued; managers eased the transition of formerly independent craftsmen to company foremen through the use of a bonus system (replacing former contract-based profits) and by allowing the foremen to exercise discretion in recruitment of workers (Buttrick 1952: 219–20). The more general pattern was to pay salaried foremen a fixed rate, in effect reversing the previous system of payment and incentives. Where previously independent contractors were paid by the job and in turn paid their own workers by the hour, now the foremen were hired at fixed pay and the workers were put on piece rates (Clawson 1980: 169).

Foremen under the drive system exercised wide discretion within their own departments and performed their newly acquired management functions with gusto. As Jacoby puts it, these were "arrogant, proud, conservative men, mindful of the position to which their skill and knowledge had elevated them. Often they wore white shirts to work and seated themselves at raised desks in the middle of the shop floor. But despite their former status as skilled workers, most foremen were strenuously anti-union. They were well aware that their authority depended on severing ties to their pasts. As one observer noted, 'they spurn the rungs by which they did ascend'" (Jacoby 1985: 16). Important for present purposes, these craftsmen cum foremen were specifically not attached to any new system of skill formation. Very unlike their counterparts in Japan, U.S. managers in many of these companies sought to deal with the "skill problem" through an overall shift toward standardized production based on semi-skilled labor and increased output through "drive" and incentive wages.

Small and medium-sized firms with no or few managerial layers and fewer opportunities to engage in extensive rationalization pursued somewhat different policies. Small machine shops were not in a position to engage in extensive rationalization measures because of the nature of their product, and an internalization of skill formation was not an option because of their size (Hansen 1997: 477; Jacoby 1985: 69). Their continuing higher dependence on skills rendered them more exposed to craft control strategies, which often fueled a strong anti-union sentiment. Such firms were represented in national political debates by the National Association of Manufacturers (NAM) which intensely opposed organized labor. These small skill-dependent firms (through and with NAM) sought to replace their reliance on craft unions through employer coordination (Harris 1991) and lobbied for publicly funded vocational education where the curriculum of local trade schools, it was hoped, would be "geared to the specific needs of local employers" (Jacoby 1985: 69; see also Hansen 1997: 476–8, 630).

A degree of coordination was achieved in certain localities, for example, among metal manufacturers in Philadelphia.[45] After the failure of the national agreement with unions in the metalworking industry, the Metal Manufacturers Association (MMA) of Philadelphia set up its own labor bureau to provide job placement services for local skilled metal craftsmen, aiming to break the union's "stranglehold" on the local labor market (Harris 1991: 125) and also attempting to mitigate poaching among firms through coordination: "To the extent that they hired through the bureau, [association members] were inhibited from hiring skilled men from one another, a practice which, in rush times, gave scarce manpower a real advantage.... [Through coordination among themselves, the firms] were creating an association-wide approximation to an internal labor market for the benefit of members who could not possibly have built their own at the level of the individual firm" (Harris 1991: 126).

To facilitate and encourage such coordination, the MMA published labor market data designed to counteract the ability of workers to whipsaw employers – among other things by exposing member firms who paid above the going rate in times of labor scarcity (Harris 1991: 127–8).[46] In addition,

[45] This account draws on an excellent study by Harris (1991). Philadelphia is not the only case, however; Cincinnati is another (see Haydu in progress), also Minneapolis (Millikan 2001). In general, the smaller, more specialized machinery producers worried a lot about skills and formed the backbone of an NAM campaign to encourage public vocational schools. Anxious commentaries on the decline of apprenticeship that appeared in trade journals like *American Machinist* and *Iron Age* in the late nineteenth and early twentieth centuries reflect the concerns of these small skill-intensive producers. Cincinnati later made significant strides in some aspects of training, working closely with educators such as Herman Schneider who sought to bolster links between technical and practical training. I thank Jeffrey Haydu for emphasizing the fact that there were a variety of local efforts along such lines.

[46] In the 1920s firms that did not belong to the association also began to supply the MMA with data on their own operations, and even large firms joined the small-firm-dominated MMA in order to gain access to this information. It was extremely useful as an orientation point in setting their own (above market) wages, to secure the top workers in the local labor pool.

the employment records the MMA maintained for individual workers served a kind of certification function:

> With the breakdown of traditional apprenticeship, and given the inadequacy of formal training provision, this imperfect labor market for skilled men even served as a way of organizing the process of 'picking up a trade.' . . . A man's employment record with the MMA turned into a sort of certificate of competence, or at least proof of experience. An employer did not have to rely entirely on trying the man out – an expensive, chancy business. (Harris 1991: 126)

Although relatively successful in its day, this type of coordination was ultimately vulnerable to the same kinds of problems as afflicted regionally based craft labor market control through unions. As in Britain, the stimulus for employer organization and the glue that held the association together was the "labor challenge," and as in Britain such coordination was always vulnerable to prevailing conditions in product markets (where the incentives to cheat in times of labor shortages were intense) and the limited "reach" of the association (in this case encompassing only the local labor market), which left it vulnerable to disruption by firms outside the association.

The other strand of the strategy was the movement for publicly funded vocational training. This campaign, spearheaded initially by the NAM, drew inspiration from the apparently highly successful German system (Hansen 1997: 476–8, 630–1). NAM representatives never tired of drawing invidious comparisons between Germany and public schooling in the United States, which – under the influence at the local level of civic minded middle-class activists and at the national level of professional educators – emphasized pre-professional training for middle-class youth to the virtual exclusion of any vocational element (on this subject see especially Hansen 1997: Chapters 6–8). The political lobbying for vocational training did not bear much fruit, however, not least because of lackluster support from larger corporations and the impossibility of any kind of a coalition with the most likely ally, organized labor.

Labor leaders such as Samuel Gompers shared NAM's critique of the American educational system as overly bookish and organized too exclusively around the needs and interests of college bound middle-class children (Hansen 1997: 479–83). Labor unions complained that the system bypassed the needs of blue-collar children. Given NAM's deep and vocal anti-union bias, however, organized labor was justifiably worried that publicly funded trade schools would be dominated by employers and put to use as "scab hatcheries," that is, "merely a method by which the employers could train swarms of boys, inculcate them with anti-union doctrines, and then bring them into factories to undermine wages and deprive union men of employment" (quote from Douglas 1921: 315; see also Kelly 1920: 76; Hansen 1997: 480). Organized labor's experiences with private trade schools in the decades between about 1880 to 1910 did nothing to allay their concerns. Even if "open hostility to the unions was practiced by only a few schools... most of the schools were distinctly unsympathetic towards collective bargaining and their covert influence was anti-union" (Douglas 1921: 316). When push came to shove, organized labor was more inclined to oppose a separate vocational track that was susceptible to employer capture than to stick to the current (albeit middle-class-oriented, overly academic) system of public schooling, convinced as they were that "dedicated trade and industrial schools, whether private or public, posed more of a threat to labor market stability than vocational tracks within educator-dominated public schools" (Hansen 1997: 482).[47]

By about 1910, organized labor had come around to a much more positive attitude toward public vocational schools (Cremin 1964: 50–7), and the AFL wound up endorsing a proposal similar to NAM's, though there was no cooperation between the two.[48] Overall, though, ongoing conflicts between organized labor and employers over control issues subverted any kind of coalition forming around a vocational alternative within the public school realm, despite the fact that both sides saw (different) merits to such a system (Douglas 1921: 328–9; Hansen 1997: 478, 483). The entire discussion over vocational education, therefore, produced only one piece of (mostly ineffectual) national legislation, the 1917 National Vocational Education Act (Smith Hughes Act), which funded some state programs, but which never managed to forge a strong link between school-based training and the economy (for a full analysis, see Hansen 1997: Chapters 6–7). As Kelly noted in 1920: "The chief fault of continuation education is that no plan has been devised for combining civic and general academic studies with technical or shopwork designed to help the pupil to make progress in his employment... For these reasons [lack of a link to the economy and company needs] the teaching is strongly academic and children attend because

[47] See for example, the statement by the president of the United Textile Workers of New York City in 1909, worrying about the extent to which public and private trade schools would be used to produce "half-baked journeymen" (in Kelly 1920: 76).

[48] I thank Jeff Haydu for emphasizing this to me.

they are compelled to, not because they hope to profit by the opportunity" (Kelly 1920: 73).

The Wisconsin Model

An important – and for present purposes instructive – exception to this pattern emerged in Wisconsin in the 1910s, specifically in the area around Milwaukee, which was an important center for the American machine industry.[49] As in Philadelphia, machine firms in the Milwaukee area were looking for ways to replace union-dominated apprenticeship with other organizational forms in order to preserve the supply of skilled labor on which they relied. Facing increased pressures of skilled labor shortages and (related) high labor mobility and wage competition in the first decade of the twentieth century, officers of leading machine makers such as Allis-Chalmers and Kearney & Trecker took the lead in organizing local machine manufacturers around the goal of systematizing apprentice training in the region (Parker 1996: 16–17). But whereas similar efforts in other urban areas (for example, Chicago) foundered on the weaknesses of voluntarism in the face of highly competitive product markets, the Wisconsin system was substantially shored up by active state sponsorship. The victory in 1910 of a socialist mayor set the stage for the founding of a system of jointly (union-employer) administered apprenticeship training that was brokered and sustained by the active intervention of the state (Parker 1996: 19–21). The political turn to the left eliminated the option of employers instituting a system against organized labor and provided unions with the reassurances (elsewhere lacking) that training initiatives would not be used to glut the market with skilled labor and drive down wages (Hansen 1997: 483, 566).

The contours of the "Wisconsin system" can be briefly described as follows (Cooley 1915; Parker 1996). A state law passed in 1911 and amended and extended in 1915 established a framework for the registration, monitoring, and certification of apprentice training. Every apprentice contract was to be made formally, in writing, with a copy filed with the state industrial commission. Employers were required to grant their apprentices

[49] On the Wisconsin "model" see especially Parker (1996) and Hansen (1997: Chapter 6), and for a contemporary characterization see the article by R. L Cooley (superintendent in charge of Milwaukee's continuation schools) in the *Bulletin of the National Association for Corporation Schools*, April 1914 (Cooley 1914).

a minimum of five hours per week of paid time off to attend classes in the local continuation schools, to submit to the regulation of trainees' hours and wages, and to adhere to a specification of the particular processes to be taught the workmen and the approximate time to be spent on each. The entire system was placed under the supervision of a state industrial commission, which was granted powers to classify trades and industries, to construct and supervise apprentice contracts, and to essentially underwrite such contracts by acting as a mediator in the case of violations by, or differences between, apprentices and employers (Douglas 1921: 78–9; Kelly 1920: 141). This commission established a "state apprenticeship board" composed of representatives of employers, unions, and state continuation schools, which was charged with administering the act and given certification and oversight powers.

The system as it was developed in the 1910s in Wisconsin mimicked some aspects of the German model, an outcome closely related to the German roots of a number of prominent machine manufacturers, themselves immigrant skilled craftsmen or their descendants (Hansen 1997: 566). It proved possible – at least for a time – to institutionalize a fairly well-articulated system of apprentice training that established transparent and uniform training standards for firms and instituted the kind of certification process that made investment in training attractive as well for youth. Backed up by legal and parapublic oversight, apprenticeship thrived in the Wisconsin metalworking industries in the pre-World War I period.[50]

The weakness of the Wisconsin experiment – and at the root of its demise which began in the 1920s – was its limited scope. One big problem was poaching externalities that made training increasingly expensive for firms, as employers in neighboring cities (especially in northern Illinois) lured skilled workers away with the prospect of higher wages (sustainable since they were not bearing training costs) (Parker 1996; Hansen 1997: 655). The disincentives to train were made stronger by concurrent trends, especially stagnant employment in the 1920s that relieved some of the pressure in skilled labor markets and made unskilled labor cheaper and more attractive. The most "committed" firms stayed in the Wisconsin system, but the interest in training waned for many other employers (Parker 1996: 24–5), and the 1920s saw Wisconsin's metalworking firms turning increasingly

[50] Douglas (1921: 79) reports an increase in the number of apprentice contracts signed beginning in 1912 after the first legislation was passed (see also Morris 1921: 292).

to the same rationalization strategies that had taken hold in other regions (Hansen 1997: 651–2).[51]

The Corporation School Movement in the United States

If ongoing conflict between craft unions and employers in most regions and industries undermined the prospect for achieving a stable (national) framework for apprentice training, there also existed possibilities, for large firms at least, to turn to a more segmentalist solution to skill formation. As Swenson has noted, the period before the First World War had seen the emergence of an alternative strategy, "a kinder, gentler war against organized labor" than that being waged by the NAM (Swenson 2002: 54). Broadly, the idea behind the alternative approach of "welfare capitalism" was for firms to "inoculate themselves from the disease of radical unionism" through generous company-based social policies (Swenson 2002: 54 and Chapter 3 passim; Montgomery 1989; Jacoby 1985; Brody 1980). To this end, prominent welfare capitalists like Westinghouse, Du Pont, General Electric, Goodyear, National Cash Register, and many others, offered their workers higher wages, more vacation time, and various company-based insurance benefits (Swenson 2002: 55). Such policies were often associated with moves to render company personnel policy more systematic and "rational" through centralization, thus "relieving" foremen of some of their personnel functions (Kelly 1920: 118–19). Welfare capitalists found that the drive system, with its arbitrary and abusive foremen, often contributed to labor unrest and high labor mobility, and they sought to curb these tendencies by bringing foremen under the closer supervision of personnel departments that were attuned to the "human relations" aspects of management (Jacoby 1985: Chapter 2; also Kelly 1920: 74; Buttrick 1952: 218).

Welfare capitalists also often stood at the forefront of innovations in the area of in-plant vocational training. Skill development was seen as crucial

[51] As Parker points out there is some irony in the fact that even as their (coordinated, multi-employer) apprentice system began to thrive, firms in the Wisconsin system (including even leaders such as Falk) were pursuing rationalization policies and introducing mass production techniques designed to reduce their reliance on skilled labor (Parker 1996: 4, 32). Whereas apprentice registrations had risen steadily between 1914 and 1925, from 21 to a peak of 821, they dropped steadily after 1925, to a mere 46 registrants in 1933. The system as a whole was "pushed into oblivion by the economic crisis of the early 1930s" (Hansen 1997: 650–1; Parker 1996).

to the cultivation of a loyal and dedicated workforce.[52] Thus, prominent welfare capitalists were outspoken proponents and practitioners of company-based training as an alternative to union apprenticeship programs (Jacoby 1985: 69). Managers were also motivated by the apparent limits of the drive system, since foremen who were under pressure to increase production were disinclined to devote resources to training young workers. In an essay called "Reasons for the shortage of skilled mechanics and how manufacturers can overcome the deficiency," A. F. Barwell of the Yale and Towne Manufacturing Company (Connecticut) noted that often foremen "had not the time, patience or liking for inexperienced young men" (NACS 1913: 121; see also Park 1914: 13–14). Magnus Alexander of General Electric articulated a similar critique in a 1916 address to the Iron and Steel Electrical Engineers, arguing that foremen were not well suited to training and that in his experience they mostly saw apprentices as an unwanted burden (Alexander 1921: 235, 243).

The firms that founded corporation schools in the United States before World War I included many of the best known manufacturers in the engineering industry, including Brown and Sharpe, Ford, General Electric, and Westinghouse, among others (Parker 1996; Morris 1921). Hoe and Company, manufacturer of printing press equipment, was the first large American company to open a company-based school for training apprentices and workmen (in 1872) (Douglas 1921: 213); Westinghouse Company followed suit in 1888 (Morris 1921: 2–17; Hansen 1997: 267). In 1896 Brown and Sharpe began employing a supervisor dedicated to the task of training the firm's (at that time) 70 apprentices, a measure followed up in 1908 by "the establishment of a formal apprentice school that taught machine drafting, math, business English, and foremanship" for what had by then grown to over 140 apprentices (Hansen 1997: 268). The movement to introduce company training schools picked up steam in the early 1900s, in the immediate aftermath of the control struggles with unions mentioned above and the failure of national collective bargaining in these industries.[53]

[52] See, for example, the article by E. J. Mehren, who characterized corporation schools as "A Factor in Alleviating Industrial Unrest" (Mehren 1914).

[53] The pages of the *Bulletin* for corporation school pioneers hint at how firms were hoping, through new training practices, to redirect the loyalties of young workers away from other workers in their trade, and toward the company. They are full of testimony and tips for employers on how to reduce "unhealthy" influences on young trainees. For example a manager of one machinery company reported on his company's policy: "The policy of the shop school of the Shoe Machinery Company is to keep the boys away from the journeymen

Major companies such as General Electric and International Harvester inaugurated their own programs for in-plant training, in connection with a broader range of company-based welfare measures designed to cultivate a docile and loyal workforce.[54]

The programs of the most prominent companies (detailed in Morris 1921) are similar in some ways to those being inaugurated around the same time in Germany, Japan, and Britain, combining more systematic on-the-job training with significant theoretical instruction. In addition to participating in the in-plant component, some of Westinghouse's "more serious students" attended classes at the local Technical High School, which, although formally independent, received substantial funding (a third of its budget) from the company (Morris 1921: 10–11).[55] These firms also sought to replace ad hoc on-the-job instruction with more systematic and uniform procedures. "Firms like Hoe & Co., Brown & Sharpe, and Pratt & Whitney began to systematize training for all their apprentices, reinstituted formal indentures of four years duration, paid a wage supplemented by a substantial bonus upon completion of the program, and required their apprentices to take formal instruction in mechanical drawing and mathematics, either in a company night school or some other type of formal instruction" (Hansen 1997: 267–8).

In 1913, the leading U.S. firms with company-based training founded the National Association of Corporation Schools (NACS), which shared some superficial similarities to DATSCH, and was designed to be a forum for the exchange of ideas among companies engaged in training, and more generally to promote interest in such training programs (Douglas 1921: 214–15; NACS 1913: 15). Advocates of firm-based training such as Thomas Donnelly (of R. R. Donnelly and Sons of Chicago) hoped "that a school for the training of their own mechanics will be established by every large manufacturing concern in the country, and if the National Association of Corporation Schools can be instrumental in accomplishing this result, the question of vocational training in America is settled" (NACS 1913: 136).

while learning for the first year or two" (NACS 1913: 106). A representative of Yale and Towne Manufacturing Company reported his firm's similar orientation: "Special emphasis is placed on the fact that the students are separated for the first three years from the journeymen while in the shop" (NACS 1913: 114).

[54] Douglas (1921: 214) includes a (non-exhaustive) listing of 23 companies that opened corporation training schools between 1905 and 1913. These include many of the leaders of the metalworking industries, and leaders as well in the corporate welfare movement of the day. See also Alexander (1921), which discusses the GE program in particular.

[55] As in Britain, students paid their own fees, however.

A significant number of NACS member firms sought to stabilize and enhance the quality of their programs by requiring formal, contractual indentures.[56] Leading companies such as GE, Western Electric, Brown and Sharpe, and Westinghouse awarded apprentices bonuses of up to $100 on completion of their programs (Morris 1921: 21 on GE, 40–1 on Western Electric, 135 on Brown and Sharpe; also NACS 1913); a smaller number collected a forfeitable deposit from apprentices or their parents at the start of the program (Morris 1921: 236). In a survey of 31 manufacturers with corporation schools, a full 27 reported that they paid bonuses to their apprentices on graduation, finding such rewards to be "a good stimulus and in reality it is practically a deduction from their wages (in lieu of a bond)" (NACS 1913).

As emphasized in Chapter 1, however, the more effective inducement for an apprentice to complete his term was some sort of certification that held value in the labor market. The importance of certification was not lost on the premier training firms in the United States, and in the absence of any overarching scheme, many firms issued their own company certificates on completion of training. GE issued its certificates in pocket-sized leather cases so that apprentices could carry them around (Commerce 1930: 43). Morris reports that it was general practice to confer certificates on completion of training, but he also notes that there existed no collectively defined, uniform standards for training, so the value of the certificate an apprentice received "depend[ed] much on the standing of the company conferring it" (Morris 1921: 237).

For firms that invested in high-quality apprentice training, such reputational effects were not without weight, and these companies experienced significant problems with poaching by other firms (Morris 1921: 30–1, 217). Jacoby reports widespread raiding of newly trained employees by competitors. "At General Electric's Lynn plant, less than one-fourth of its trade apprenticeship graduates remained with the firm, and other NACS members encountered similar difficulty holding on to their graduates" (Jacoby 1985: 68). Hansen cites findings reported by the NACS itself (1914: 408–9), from a survey of member firms, that only 9.1% of apprentices who started training programs stayed with the firm (Hansen 1997: 280). In short, the premier training companies were the object of intense raiding by other firms, and a prominent advocate of firm-based training, the economist Paul Douglas, noted with some frustration, "Though it

[56] For the practices of the main companies, see Morris (1921).

would be a benefit to the *industry as a whole* to have a supply of well-trained apprentices, to the *individual firm* it usually spells a loss" (Douglas 1921: 81–2; emphasis in the original).

The Politics of Training during and after World War I

These collective action problems were severe but arguably solvable and therefore less decisive to the fate of apprenticeship training in the United States than the class politics that developed during and after World War I. During this time skilled labor shortages and resurgent unions revived cross-class conflict over control issues and, in consequence, reinforced employer strategies of intensified rationalization and union avoidance after the war. Training efforts were redirected away from vocational skills for manual workers and toward training foremen in human relations and "people" skills to make them more effective supervisors of semi-skilled workers. Thus, as in the other countries examined in this book, developments during and immediately after the First World War were crucial to the trajectory of training in the United States.

The exigencies of war production and the resulting labor shortages in the United States led to a revitalization of craft unions and a resurgence of labor militancy.[57] This was nowhere more true than in the engineering industry, which was a key sector for the war effort. Membership in the IAM rose dramatically, from seventy-two thousand in 1915 to more than three hundred and five thousand by 1918 (Haydu 1997: 53). Labor unrest and strikes increased exponentially, again particularly in the metal trades, as unions took advantage of tight labor markets to press for employer concessions – union recognition, but also a range of other material and control issues. Intervening gingerly in highly charged conflicts, government agencies (the War and Labor Departments) often brought union leaders into national discussions aimed at stabilizing industrial relations in key industries. Moreover, even if government policy did not force companies to bargain collectively with unions, it generally made it impossible for managers to continue to openly discriminate against unionists.

What did these rejuvenated craft unions want? They wanted concessions on a range of material benefits – shorter working hours, longer

[57] For an excellent account of developments during the war and their implications for post-war industrial relations, see Haydu (1997). The following paragraphs draw particularly on Chapter 2 of that book.

vacation times, and higher wages – that even open shop employers were prepared to accommodate. But militant unions also used wartime conditions to put forth demands for more thoroughgoing changes. As Haydu notes, "By early 1918 . . . workers were also pressing issues that more seriously challenged the open shop order – above all, demands for classification, union rights, and the recognition of union shop committees" (Haydu 1997: 59).

The call for classifications is especially significant in the context of the present study. From the perspective of workers, the drive system was especially brutal, as it meant all-powerful and capricious foremen who spontaneously meted out highly arbitrary decisions regarding layoffs, promotions, and wages. Workers looked on as foremen passed over qualified colleagues in favor of relatives or friends for jobs and choice work assignments, and as they put untrained workers on machinists' jobs at lower pay. During the war unions voiced demands for more systematic and equitable treatment, and one prominent demand was for the introduction of classification schemes with a small number of standard categories (each associated with a uniform, minimum level of pay) (Jacoby 1985: 151–2). In many cases such demands were limited to skilled jobs, but in crucial centers of war production such as Bridgeport and Newark, local unions took them further and requested "extending proposals for classification to specialists and machine operators" as well (Haydu 1997: 60).

All such demands struck at the heart of managerial control and employers resisted them ferociously – and, one must add, very successfully. Where classification schemes were introduced – through government sponsored awards, for example – they were designed to curb flagrantly unfair policies but they typically did not allow unions a role in setting or administering job standards, nor did they facilitate coordination among workers on a local or regional level (Haydu 1997: 66).[58]

Meanwhile, as skilled labor sources from Europe completely dried up during the war (Commerce 1930: 27) and as pressures for production mounted, firms abandoned their more elaborate training programs in favor of rationalization and work reorganization to reduce reliance on skilled

[58] Government awards usually suggested that classifications be worked out jointly between shop committees and management on a plant-by-plant basis, rather than by craft unions on a local or regional level – which would have established standards and categories that cut across different firms.

workers altogether. The focus of training shifted toward narrower measures aimed at getting newly recruited migrant labor (often, African Americans from the south and women) up to speed quickly. "Faced with an inadequate supply of skilled labor and the supreme need for an unprecedented volume of output, manufacturers and shipbuilders, assisted by government departments, turned to vestibule training and other forms of intensive instruction" (Kelly 1920: 74–5, 134).

"Vestibule training" was designed to accommodate and work around (rather than confront and overcome) skilled labor shortages; it was a system that rested on "principles of production management . . . first enunciated by the leaders of the scientific management movement" (Kelly 1920: 153).[59] Unlike traditional apprenticeship (in any of its many incarnations) there was no pretense of training a worker in a trade, no fixed period of training, and no legal supervision or indentures (Douglas 1921: 220–1). Rather, vestibule training was designed to train workers quickly in single, very specialized operations. One of its practitioners described it as follows:

> The vestibule school is to the industrial organization what the vestibule is to the home. In the home it is a place where the entrant stops, wipes his shoes on the mat, adjusts his garments, and performs those duties that prepare him to enter the house proper. In the factory or office it is a place which detains the incoming employee until he has become adjusted to a new environment and has been prepared to handle the essential elements of his prospective work. (quoted in Douglas 1921: 220)

The training was very short (in some cases three to ten days), typically in a single operation. As workers were shifted to new jobs within the company, they would in some cases be sent back to the vestibule school for additional training on the new operation (Douglas 1921: 221). Companies like the Recording and Computing Machines Company of Dayton, Ohio, started a vestibule school in 1917–1918 in response to skill shortages. In this school, and in many others like it founded at the time,

> no effort was made to train for more than one particular job. The training was not advertised as general mechanical education, but every pupil understood that she was being taught in a very short period and that if she came to have any mechanical skill it would have to be acquired through her work in the shop. In less than ten days the girls were trained to operate hand-turret lathes on work requiring a high

[59] The turn to narrow, specialized training also followed from difficulties firms had during the war to get apprentices to sign on "at reasonable [wage] rates" (in light of tight labor markets and thus the prospect of higher wages for semi-skilled work), and the problems of keeping apprentices in place for the full training term (Kelly 1920: 134).

degree of precision, and it is claimed by the company that these girls when entering the shop attacked the work on their machines with vigor and confidence. (Kelly 1920: 156)[60]

American companies by and large did not abandon such practices when the hostilities ended. On the contrary, the immediate postwar period revealed just how flimsy was the commitment of even the premier training firms to high quality all-round apprentice training.[61] After a brief surge in interest during the war (when membership in the National Association of Corporation Schools rose from 37 members in September 1913 to 146 members by March 1920 [Douglas 1921: 215],[62] the interest of member firms completely collapsed when labor markets slackened after the war ended (Hansen 1997: 570). Even the NACS "began to redirect its attention from formal, broad based training for skilled and supervisory occupations to the promotion of informal training schemes on the job" (Hansen 1997: 634). As explained by a representative of the American Management Association (into which the NACS successor organization was folded in 1923): "Corporation schools as such have pretty much gone out of style. The newer point of view is that of training on the job'" (quoted in Hansen 1997: 635).

The comparison to Germany is probably the most dramatic. Whereas German engineering firms in the 1920s were making a concerted effort (though VDMA and DATSCH) to render in-plant skill development for manual workers more systematic and uniform, their U.S. counterparts were mostly abandoning their more ambitious training efforts and instead increasingly emphasizing "the recruitment, selection, and preferment of personnel, especially of extensively schooled supervisory and white-collar

[60] A representative of C. U. Carpenter Company claimed that "We have demonstrated that strong, healthy women can do work requiring great precision after they are thoroughly trained quite as well as skilled men mechanics" (quoted in Kelly 1920: 158).

[61] Swenson's work (2002: Chapter 3) goes into a fair amount of detail about the motives behind the welfare measures adopted by progressive employers both before and after the First World War. Prominent among the justifications that welfare capitalists cite are the need to increase worker effort and decrease worker unrest. It is striking, particularly compared to the Japanese case, how the issue of training and providing for a healthy supply of skills plays virtually no role in the justifications they cite. There is scarcely a hint that this was of special concern to them. In smaller companies as well, open shop employers specifically pursued a variety of "modern" industrial welfare practices (for example, life insurance policies, group health and accident insurance, paid vacations, loan services, health and safety, rest and recreation) but specifically and overwhelmingly not apprentice training, which was instead "found most extensively in closed shops" (NICB 1929: 22).

[62] Not all members had company-based schools.

employees. To the degree that systematic corporation training persisted, it increasingly became the exclusive preserve of managers, supervisors, and foremen" (Hansen 1997: 634).[63] In short, the trend in the United States was toward narrow, specialized training for manual workers, combined with upgraded training for foremen in "human relations" skills and management techniques (Kelly 1920: 74, Chapter VII passim).

This reorientation must be understood against the backdrop of the developments during the war described above, and can perhaps best be grasped in comparative perspective. In Japan, the 1920s saw the consolidation of an alliance between younger skilled workers and managers in key firms and sectors that presided over the introduction of internal labor markets in which systematic advancement in the firm (and associated wage increases) were specifically linked to the ongoing acquisition of skills. In the United States, personnel departments before the war had been making some progress in rationalizing and centralizing personnel policies (see, for example, Kelly 1920). After the war, however, top managers looked on the kinds of job classifications (the basis for internal career ladders) they had been contemplating with more concern, worried that such a system would encourage unionization and promote collective bargaining (Jacoby 1985: especially 154). The trend after the war, therefore, was if anything toward restoring some of the powers of foremen within the firm – but also subjecting them to more rules and investing more resources in their training as supervisors (Jacoby 1985: especially 193–5).

There continued to be some similarities between the practices implemented in these years by large Japanese firms and American "welfare capitalists." Many of the practices developed in large U.S. corporations before the war – "above-market" wages, company insurance benefits, and the like – continued and in some cases were expanded after the war. From the perspective of individual workers, these were still attractive employers and highly desirable places to work. The key contrast to Japan, however, is that high quality, all-round training, by and large, ceased to be a significant part of the "efficiency wage" these firms paid to recruit and retain the best manual workers. Moreover, although these firms were certainly cultivating worker loyalty and strengthening internal labor markets, in contrast to Japan, American welfare capitalists were not typically institutionalizing a

[63] Such was the case, for example, at GE, where the company had three hundred college graduates as apprentices in 1921 (Douglas 1921: 219).

system in which advancement in company-based job ladders was systematically and transparently linked to ongoing investment in worker skills (Jacoby 1985: 154–7). On the contrary: wages continued to be attached to jobs not workers, and managers shied away from formalized job classification schemes and well-defined seniority-based bidding rights because they worried that these would encourage unionization and collective bargaining, and thus interfere with management's unfettered right to determine advancement on the basis of their own assessments of individual worker merit and effort.

Despite stronger internal labor markets and more concern with reducing turnover, therefore, promotion decisions continued to be quite decentralized (Jacoby 1985). Firms varied in the extent to which they placed limits on foreman discretion in this area, with more progressive firms imposing more rules and subjecting their decisions to more scrutiny. In general, however, promotion decisions were meant to be based on "merit," and as very few firms had formal rating systems in place, the assessment of merit continued to rely heavily on "personal observation" (Gemmill 1924: 240; Jacoby 1985: 194).[64] Practically speaking, the foreman continued to play a crucial role in determining which workers advanced, "since, as a rule, he has first-hand knowledge of the abilities of those working under him" (Gemmill 1924: 244; also Schatz 1977: 134).[65]

The residual powers that foremen continued to command – "to recommend workers for layoff, transfer or firing, the power to distribute opportunities to work overtime, and the power to issue piecework assignments" – were extremely important (Schatz 1977: 134). A worker's earnings in the United States were very much attached to the job. Despite some experimentation with alternative wage systems, firms after the war tended to stick to or revert back to traditional piecework. Based on a 1922 survey

[64] Gemmill (1924) surveyed 150 firms, and found that 81 relied solely on recommendations by foremen and supervisors. Formal procedures for job analysis and eligibility lists were not widespread. A survey conducted in 1929 (cited in Jacoby 1985: 194) found that the vast majority of firms (85%) still "used no formal system to rate workers for promotion but rather relied on 'personal observations', which can be translated to mean that workers were promoted at the foreman's discretion. One semiskilled worker said that the personnel department at his firm was 'a joke' and that workers got their promotions through 'pull' " (Jacoby 1985: 194).

[65] For this reason, too, Gemmill's (1924) study still discusses as a potential problem the practice of "retardation" – where foremen hold back rather than promote their best workers, because these workers are most valuable to the department for output.

of 50 firms who sent representatives to a convention on personnel policy, Gemmill noted the

> continued popularity of the piece work system of wage payment. The newer wage systems, about which so much has been written, and which were originally expected to bring about revolutionary changes in industrial life, have apparently not lived up to expectations, and have yet to prove their superiority, at least as applied to industry as a whole. The present study... tends to show that the older wage systems, and especially straight piece work, are in no immediate danger of being superseded by the more modern and complicated systems. (Gemmill 1922: 208; also Gemmill 1924: 240)

In this system, a foreman's powers with respect to job assignments were absolutely crucial to a worker's wage, because exertion and earnings varied so much from one job to another (Schatz 1977: 68). Workers even in the most progressive firms in the 1920s continued to complain bitterly that foremen used their powers to reward their friends and workers who kowtowed to them; "in many cases, personnel decisions also depended on the workers' race, religion, nationality, lodge membership, and his willingness to bribe his foreman or perform personal favors for him" (Schatz 1977: 116, 135).[66]

As Jacoby in particular has emphasized, despite important changes in personnel policy in the 1920s to ameliorate some of the worst aspects of the pre-war drive system, foremen were by no means completely divested of their powers and if anything there was a move to restore to them some of the powers that personnel departments had previously taken over (Jacoby 1985: 193, passim). Even in progressive firms like GE and Westinghouse, workers in the 1920s in America "lived in a half-way house between arbitrary rule and systematic policy" (Schatz 1977: 69). Promotion decisions in particular were not based on systematic job analysis or eligibility lists, but rather continued to rely a great deal on the seat-of-the-pants judgment of foremen and supervisors. The continuing decentralization of many aspects of personnel policy made it difficult to implement the kinds of internal promotion plans that were emerging in the large-firm sector in Japan (Jacoby 1985: 194). Whatever lines of promotion were operating in these firms, the criteria through which a worker could hope to advance were, by design, not

[66] The same thing applied to layoffs. A survey of large firms published in 1930 found that in two-thirds of firms, the layoff decisions taken in the downturn of 1929 were made by foremen and line managers alone; other studies found that the proportion of firms that involved personnel departments in layoff decisions declined from 36% in 1918 to 24% in 1929 (Jacoby 1985: 193–4).

made transparent to him but based on vague and arbitrary "mental lists" that managers carried around with them, as in "so and so is a good man, and ought to be shoved along" (Gemmill 1924: 241, 247).[67]

What are the implications of this for training? From Chapter 1, we recall that systems of training emphasizing company-specific skills are based on a sharing of the costs between workers and the firm. In Japan in the 1920s, for example, workers' wages began to be tied increasingly to the worker (and specifically associated with seniority). This provided incentives for the firm to continue to invest in a worker's skills, among other reasons to justify ongoing increases in a worker's wage. Such a system also made it "safe" for a worker to invest in company specific skills, knowing that the ongoing acquisition of such skills would lead to ongoing advancement in the firm's internal labor market. In the United States, by contrast, piecework wage systems meant that a worker's earnings were determined mostly by the job he was doing, and not by any characteristic of the worker himself. Moreover, advancement in the firm hierarchy was not transparently linked to ongoing acquisition of skills, and indeed continued to reflect arbitrary assessments on the part of foremen. Despite the fact that many firms reported paying closer attention to a worker's length of tenure in transfer and promotion decisions, seniority was only one consideration among many in the full range of personnel decisions (Schatz 1977: 116). Reporting the results of a survey in 1924, Gemmill reports that "in only two instances [out of 150] can seniority be said to have attained first-rate importance" (Gemmill 1924: 238).[68] The link between advancement and training was especially tenuous, it appears, as evidenced in Gemmill's off-hand remark that an analysis of the training systems that existed in some of the firms he studied was "scarcely essential to a study of industrial promotions" (Gemmill 1924: 244).

The same difference applied not just to movement from production job to production job, but also to promotion to low-level supervisory positions. In Japan, the workers who were likely to be promoted to foremen were the most skilled and experienced of the blue-collar workers. In the United States, by contrast, workers selected for foremen jobs were more likely to be simply the fastest: "Other things being equal, a fast worker is

[67] According to Gemmill, 108 of 150 firms responded "no" to the question of whether they had definite lines of promotion known to employees; one firm said that it did have definite promotion lines but that these were known only to executives and supervisors (Gemmill 1924: 241).

[68] It is interesting that these systems existed "by agreement with employees" in two large railway companies.

usually preferred for a foremanship, since he is likely to try to speed up the productivity of all under him to the high pitch which he himself has attained" (Gemmill 1924: 240). The very different conceptions that Japanese and American employers held of the role of the foreman is clear from these differences. In Japan, by the 1920s internal promotions of manual workers to supervisory and white-collar positions was beginning to lead to a blurring of the line between management and union that subsequently became a distinctive feature of the Japanese shop floor regime (Dore 1973: 169–70, Chapter 9 passim).[69] In the United States, managers in this same period began relying much more heavily on recruitment of supervisory and white-collar personnel from outside the firm, and in particular from among young persons who had opted against a vocational track of any variety and instead stayed on for more academic training in high school and beyond.

This too had important implications for the development of vocational training in the United States. Pre-war lobbying, as noted above, had produced legislation (the Smith Hughes Act) that provided some government support for public vocational schools. These schools remained disconnected from the economy, however, and as firms turned to recruitment from public high schools and colleges for higher level managerial staff, the benefits to youth of attending them was not apparent (see especially Hansen 1997). Again, referring to Becker (1993), any youth who opted to acquire his training in secondary school (whether vocational track or not) was in effect bearing the full cost of such training (in the form of fees, but even in the absence of fees, forgone wages). This being the case, no youth who had a choice would choose vocational schooling over regular high school and a possible college track, since vocational schooling did not lead seamlessly to company jobs and indeed foreclosed options to enter industry in a managerial capacity. U.S. youth responded to these trends and the incentives they brought with them, and increasingly turned their backs on vocational training in favor of completing high school, which they began to do in increasing numbers over the interwar period. The 1920s saw a massive increase in high school enrollments for 14- to 17-year-olds. Outside the south (a special case), the number of youth in this age group enrolled in high school rose dramatically between 1910 and 1935 from 20 to nearly 80% (Hansen 1997: 660).

[69] Although there was some retrogression of Japanese practices as well after the labor scarcity and unrest of World War I had abated. For an analysis that stresses the parallels between Japan and the United States more see Jacoby (1993).

The incentives in the U.S. system led to a kind of negative selection, in which weaker not stronger youth found their way into the vocational track, with the predictable effect that these schools became stigmatized as "lyceums for losers" (Hansen 1997: 538).[70] This being the case, employers became less inclined to tap these schools for recruits, and less inclined generally to support the expansion and improvement of vocationally oriented public schooling. Against the backdrop of Becker's (1993) thesis, it is no coincidence that the collapse of in-plant training and the failure of all efforts, public and private, to rejuvenate vocational training were closely associated with the flourishing of high school education for the masses.

Developments in the 1930s and beyond built on the logic of the system created over the previous decades (see especially Jacoby 1985). Once the Depression had ended and companies again faced labor shortages, it was but a small step for them to figure out how to deal with the problem through further standardization and advancement for workers in increasingly elongated and finely gradated career ladders. As Jacoby points out, a "standard solution" to labor shortages that emerged in 1936 was "a process that combined manpower planning, job simplification, and training by progression from one simplified job to another" (Jacoby 1985: 262–3). These trends were pushed forward by developments in the 1930s affecting unions, in particular the Wagner Act which gave unions collective bargaining rights and a 1937 National Apprentice Law that provided a structure for union participation in the regulation of apprenticeship (U.S. Department of Labor 1991: 16–18).

The continuing inequities of decentralized decision making on a range of key issues including wage and promotions "gave unions a potent organizing issue" in the 1930s (Jacoby 1985: 195). Especially after the Great Depression, "the worker's stake in predictable, rule-bound treatment grew enormously" (Brody 1993: 188) and, under the umbrella of the Wagner Act, workers flocked to unions to provide this. Responding to the continued arbitrariness of many aspects of plant personnel policy, seniority figured very prominently in the demands of American unions. They pushed length of service as a principle in layoffs, transfers, promotions, and so on (Schatz 1977: 116–39). American unions rebuilt themselves, however, in a context

[70] For an excellent account of the process through which this occurred, see Hansen (1997: 537–40).

in which work had been thoroughly bureaucratized and rationalized.[71] When organized labor in the United States sought and achieved control of the internal labor markets of large firms, they found themselves pressing for seniority-based bidding to allow workers to advance within a plant hierarchy defined by simplified, standardized, and rigidly defined jobs, thus embracing demands that as Brody notes arose "out of the logic of the mass-production enterprise itself" (Brody 1993: 188).

Comparisons and Conclusions

The U.S. case offers especially fruitful comparisons to Britain and Japan. As in Britain, issues of apprenticeship and training were deeply implicated in broader conflicts between skilled unions and employers in key industries such as metalworking. As Motley put it in 1907 in the immediate aftermath of the devastating struggles over "managerial control" that had swept across a number of industries and decimated skilled unions in the United States, "the mere fact that the union alone assumed the right to control apprenticeship regulations, especially to limit the number received, caused the employers to oppose them and to prevent their enforcement whenever possible.... Under such circumstances, it was impossible for either side, acting independently, to maintain an adequate apprenticeship system" (Motley 1907: 41).

But if the character of such struggles was broadly similar to Britain, the outcome was different in that U.S. manufacturers went much further than their British counterparts in the pre- and inter-war period to marginalize unions and to reorganize production so as to reduce their dependence on skills. As Brody has pointed out, the battle between the British ASE and the EEF in 1897–98 was "remarkably similar" to struggles in the U.S. machine and metalworking industries at the turn of the century. However, "in England this did not lead to a major reorganization of the workshop. Instead, the victorious British employers chose to exert their power within the existing system of craft production.... In the American metal trades, industrial warfare developed into a life-and-death struggle over control of the shop floor; in England, it took the form of endless skirmishing over the

[71] Government policies in the war encouraged the trend. "In 1940 the WMC [War Manpower Commission] set up the Training Within Industry program, which offered training courses to foremen. One of these courses, Job Methods, taught almost a quarter of a million foremen how to perform job simplification analyses" and assisted employers in setting up job ladders that led from one simple job to another (Jacoby 1985: 263–4).

price of work" (Brody 1993: 185–6). In Britain, shop stewards reemerged in the aftermath of titanic struggles over managerial control and found a role in negotiating collective piece rates with management (Zeitlin 1980). In the United States the reorganization of production and technical rationalization were "unrelenting," and the activities of American unions through most of the 1920s and into the 1930s were confined to "marginal and covert forms" (Brody 1993: 187). Even where a congruence of interests on vocational training could be detected – as, for example, in debates over the reform of public schools in the United States, where organized labor and employers in skill-dependent industries shared a very similar critique of the overly bookish, college-prep orientation of American elementary and secondary education, agreement was rendered impossible because of unsettled struggles over who would control publicly funded vocational training and to which uses it would be put (Hansen 1997: 483).

If ongoing struggles between skilled unions and employers over the organization and control of vocational training interfered with the institutionalization of a national system for skill formation and certification, there still existed the "Japanese" option of ongoing skill formation in strong internal labor markets. This was the more likely path, especially for large companies in skill-intensive industries, who (very much like their Japanese counterparts) strove to deal with skilled labor shortages through the extensive use of subcontracting in the early industrial period and, later, by founding their own corporation schools. But if the overall trajectory toward a "segmentalist" or "autarkic" training regime appeared similar, the political coalitions on which it was based in the two countries were quite different, with important implications for in-plant training. In Japan, the 1920s saw the emergence of a plant-based coalition between firm managers and (non-control seeking) unions against the power of the independent *oyakata* bosses. A system of ongoing training began to coalesce. Spurred on by union demands and the threat of unionization, large Japanese firms specifically linked training to ongoing advancement – up to and including supervisory positions – within the plant hierarchy.

The same period in the United States saw the consolidation of a different approach, in which employers worked hand-in-hand with loyal foremen against (control-seeking) unions. Even progressive firms in the 1920s moved to restore the powers of foremen in order to fill the regulatory vacuum that during World War I unions again had sought to occupy. Pre-war training efforts were redirected away from vocational skills for manual workers and toward "people skills" for foremen who were now expected to act less like drill sergeants and more like human relations specialists – in the interests of forestalling labor unrest and unionization. Although welfare capitalist firms in the United States continued to support various policies that made them attractive places to work, a crucial difference is that continuing decentralization of key aspects of personnel policy – including wage setting, promotions, and layoffs – meant that workers could not be sure that any investment they made in company skills would be rewarded through systematic advancement. Moreover, to the extent that they existed, career ladders often had a rather low and concrete ceiling, since American employers were much more likely than their Japanese colleagues to turn to college graduates to staff even lower level managerial positions. In sharp contrast to Japan, the line between workers and management hardened dramatically in the United States in this period. And for this reason, too, ambitious youth faced strong incentives to avoid vocational training (of all varieties) like the plague in favor of an academically oriented education that opened many more and more diverse opportunities for advancement in the labor market generally.

5

Evolution and Change in the German System of Vocational Training

Previous chapters have focused primarily on explaining variations across the four countries that are the subject of this study, and have traced the roots of important differences in vocational training institutions back to the political dynamics and coalitions that were forged around the turn of the century and into the 1920s. This chapter takes up the German case again and tracks its further development through National Socialism and into the post-World War II period. This involves a shift in focus, away from the origins of cross-national differences to variations over time within a single country. This shift allows us to address a related but distinct set of questions and theoretical issues concerning institutional stability and change.

As discussed in Chapter 1, the most commonly invoked metaphor for institutional change is the punctuated equilibrium model as it was adapted from the work of evolutionary biologists and interpreted for politics by Krasner in 1988 (Krasner 1988). This model emphasizes long stretches of institutional "stasis" periodically punctuated by episodes of relatively rapid innovation. In most treatments, innovation occurs as a result of some kind of exogenous shock that disrupts the stable reproduction of institutions and provides an opening for substantial institutional reconfiguration. This view of political and institutional change is pervasive, finding expression in a good deal of the literature on "critical junctures" as well as some treatments of path dependence.[1] This kind of model captures one important mode of change in political life.

[1] Some but not all. Some of the literature on "institutional choices" in the transitions to democracy and capitalism in Eastern Europe appears to embrace such a view (for example, Crawford and Lijphart 1995). Collier and Collier (1991), however, adopt a definition of "critical juncture" that does not necessarily (or automatically) imply that institutional innovation occurs in short episodes or "moments" of openness. Their definition also does

As we have already seen, however, and as this chapter continues to document, one of the most interesting features of political development is that institutional arrangements often turn out to be incredibly resilient in the face of huge exogenous shocks that we might well expect to disrupt previous patterns and give rise to dramatic institutional innovation. One thinks, for example, of the resiliency of various "statist" institutions and practices in France that can be traced to the absolutist period, and that thus apparently have survived numerous social and political upheavals. In the case at hand, a striking feature of the German story is the resilience of core elements of the vocational training system through a series of rather big "break points" in the twentieth century – defeat in two world wars, foreign occupation, and several regime changes including into and out of fascism.[2]

Conversely and equally intriguing is the effect of ongoing but often very subtle changes in institutional arrangements that, over time, can cumulate into significant institutional transformation. Think of the American Supreme Court or the British House of Lords, neither of which has suffered a "breakdown" but both of which have been substantially reconfigured through the ongoing renegotiation of their roles and functions in political life. In the case of German vocational training institutions, if one took a snapshot of the system in 1897 and again in 1997, one could not help but see the deep irony in how a set of institutions originally designed against labor could have been transformed into a pillar of social partnership between labor and capital today.

For many political–economic institutions that persist over long periods, one is very often struck simultaneously by how little *and* how much they have changed.[3] These observations are unsettling from the perspective of the dominant punctuated equilibrium model of institutional change. Against the idea of alternating periods of stasis and rapid, radical change, there often seems to be too much continuity through putative "breakpoints" in history, but also often too much change beneath the surface of apparently stable formal institutional arrangements.

not imply a primacy of "agency" and "choice" over structure in critical junctures, as other treatments sometimes do.

[2] Space and time do not permit me to go into the separate story that could be told about vocational training in East Germany after the Second World War and after unification (but see Culpepper 2003; Jacoby 2000).

[3] I owe this formulation to comments made by Peter Katzenstein at a conference in Cologne, Germany.

The German System of Vocational Training

This chapter picks up the discussion from Chapter 2, and tracks the further development of vocational training institutions in Germany from the 1930s to the present. The system not only survived but experienced important elements of consolidation and reinforcement in the context of historic "breakpoints." Institutional survival was strongly laced with elements of institutional transformation, however, as the form and functions of these institutions underwent successive waves of renegotiation to bring them in line with changed social, political, and economic conditions. A central message of this chapter is that "stasis" is a particularly misleading notion when it comes to explaining institutional stability, for what we find here is that in order to survive, institutions can rarely just "stand still." Their survival is guaranteed not by their "stickiness" but by their ongoing adaptation to changes in the political and political–economic environment.

This case, therefore, documents how institutions survive *and* change through ongoing political renegotiation. A huge literature has documented the political and political–economic biases of institutions and it is no surprise, therefore, that these institutions are subject to continuous contestation as actors with different goals struggle over their form and especially over the functions they serve. Such political contestation produces frequent revision – sometimes big, sometimes small – as the support coalitions on which the institutions are based (and the relative power of their supporters) shifts.

This case provides illustrations of the general modes of change (discussed in Chapter 1) that ongoing strategic maneuvering and political contestation produce. In the 1920s, industry was unable to "break into" the regulatory structure of the traditional handicraft system, but the machine industry nonetheless succeeded in constructing voluntary institutions and practices alongside, and in interaction with, the existing parapublic system. This "layering" of a new system onto and alongside the old was enormously consequential. The coexistence and interaction of the two altered the trajectory of skill formation in Germany as a whole – pulling it away from the decentralization and lack of systematic and uniform regulations characteristic of the Handwerk model, toward the high degree of standardization and uniformity now considered hallmarks of the system.

The process of standardization and homogenization advanced significantly under the Nazi regime. This was partly a matter of government policy; military interests and war mobilization called for a large number of skilled workers, and the regime pushed skill standardization so that workers could be deployed flexibly according to military needs and exigencies.

However, jurisdictional infighting and political contests over vocational training under the Nazis were also important, as they set the stage for industry to achieve a degree of unity on the question of vocational training structures that had been elusive throughout the Weimar years. Thus, not just the *policies* but also the *politics* of vocational training during the Nazi period were important to the subsequent evolution of the system, and paved the way for the institutionalization (in the postwar period) of an overall more unified system premised on self-governance through the Chambers of Industry and Handwerk. Legislation in 1969 incorporated and anchored organized labor more firmly into the institutions of employer self-governance over apprentice training. The inclusion of unions into the regulatory framework for company-based vocational training completed a long process of institutional development that, by the end, had effectively converted a set of institutions originally designed (in the 1890s) to defeat organized labor into a key pillar of social partnership between labor and capital in the post-World War II period.

Developments over the past several decades demonstrate that institutional survival often involves elements of institutional reconfiguration and adaptations of the sort that bring inherited arrangements in line with changing environmental challenges and political constellations. By extension, the converse is also true. That is, institutions that are not actively updated and fitted to changes in the political and market environment can be subject to a process of erosion through what Jacob Hacker has called "drift" (Hacker 2003). The final section of this chapter turns to an examination of contemporary developments in German vocational training and reveals a growing gap between the political forces that have traditionally shored up the system and the challenges posed by a changing market and technological environment. What we now see is that – after surviving several massive historic breaks – the foundations of the German training system are being undermined through gradual long-term processes affecting both the overall structure of the economy and the character of international competition in manufacturing.

Although it would be premature to announce the demise of the German system of vocational training, its survival and continuing relevance depend a great deal on the way in which political actors respond to the resulting gaps. Hacker argues that drift only brings institutional erosion to the extent that political actors specifically decline to make the adjustments necessary to adapt inherited institutions to new circumstances and challenges. In the case of German vocational training, such adjustment is technically well within the bounds of the possible. What is less clear, however, is the political will and especially the collective capacity to reform, particularly among employers who have historically been the system's most important "carriers." As Baethge has pointed out, we now find a curious role reversal at work, in which unions – long the critics of the system – are now its main defenders, whereas many key employers appear to have lost interest, as a changed competitive environment has brought them to a deep reconsideration of their own interests in maintaining it (Baethge 1999: 12).

The Evolution of the System under National Socialism

Vocational training was an important focal point of attention, and the site of intense interregime bickering, after the Nazi seizure of power.[4] Its importance as well as its contestedness had to do with the fact that vocational training was seen as an important site for ideological indoctrination and as a key institutional support for the Nazi regime's military–economic ambitions (Schneider 1999: 364). The National-Socialist regime strove to institutionalize a system of training that combined the provision of "trade-based competencies and skills with worldview-ideological indoctrination" to promote, foster, and elicit those "'virtues' that served the regime" (Kaiser and Loddenkemper 1980: 76). These two strands – trade skills and ideology – were distinct, however, and this opened the door to furious bickering and intense turf struggles over the aims and above all jurisdictional claims of training under the National Socialists.

The kinds of conflicts and tensions that emerged in the area of training were not unusual, and in some ways fit a broader pattern of politics in the Nazi period, which as Ullmann notes combined monocratic and polycratic structures in a way that frequently resulted in "internal rivalries [and] unclear divisions of competencies" (Ullmann 1988: 184–5). Simplifying greatly,[5] training policy was the object of ongoing contestation between

[4] On the politics of the Nazi regime toward labor, see, especially Schneider (1999); on the relationship between business and the state, see especially Berghoff (2001), Hayes (1987; 2001), Ullmann (1988). On Nazi policies in the area of training and education generally see Heinemann (1980) and on the infighting within the regime over training see Wolsing (1977: 689–739) and Frese (1991: 251–332).

[5] There were many actors making claims in this area, and beyond the main line of cleavage I go into below, there were other conflicts and rivalries, for instance between the German Labor Front and the Hitler Jugend. These conflicts were important but less directly related to the outcomes I am interested in here.

two main opponents. One was the German Labor Front (*Deutscher Arbeitsfront*, or DAF) under the leadership of Robert Ley, a man whom Timothy Mason once described as "Hitler's most slavish follower" (Mason 1966:114). The other was the Economics Ministry, particularly under Hjalmar Schacht, working alongside and mostly very much in the interests of Germany's organized business elite.[6]

Training policy was important to the new regime both as a component of its youth activities and as a means for fighting youth unemployment which had skyrocketed after 1929 (Pätzold 1989: 278). The elimination of the unions in 1933 allowed the old (Weimar) debate over the character of the apprentice contract to be resolved, as apprentice contracts were declared unequivocally to constitute an educational rather than an employment relationship (Wolsing 1977: 245). When implemented under the National Socialists, however, this measure took on a different meaning, and opened the door for the Nazi organizations (and in particular the DAF) to claim for itself a more central role in this area (Hansen 1997: 606).[7] Ley immediately recognized the importance of training policy and became active in this area from the very start.[8] Similar (ironically) to the Social Democratic program of the 1920s, the DAF called for the guaranteed right of all youth to training, and urged every employer to do his part (Seubert 1977: 100).

Vocational training was also extremely important to the Nazi regime on very practical grounds, as a key institutional support for rearmament and later war making. The reality here was that the National Socialist state relied on the expertise and connections of the old business elite, and thus needed to preserve elements of the old social structure to keep the economy going and particularly to gear up for war (Berghoff 2001: 95). The result was a close alliance between the Economics Ministry and organized economic interests, which took on a "Janus-faced" character, serving simultaneously as agents of the state but also as lobbying organizations for business interests within it (Ullmann 1988: 197, 226).[9] What industry mostly lobbied for, and

[6] A number of important works explore the relationship between industry and state in the Nazi era. See, for example, Hayes (1987), Gall and Pohl (1998), Hayes (2001), Ullmann (1988), Berghoff (2001).

[7] On the struggle over the role of politics in education policy, see Kaiser and Loddenkemper (1980: passim).

[8] A comprehensive treatment of labor policy in Nazi Germany, and of the activities of the German Labor Front, can be found in Schneider (1999).

[9] There was, therefore, a great deal of continuity in the economic elite between the Weimar period and the Nazi era. About one-half of the managing directors and about a third of the heads of the *Reichsgruppe Industrie* (RGI) and its various subunits (*Gliederungen*) were people

not unsuccessfully, was to minimize the influence of "outsiders" (in training policy, including and above all DAF) in their affairs. The important effect of these conflicts – never fully resolved during the Nazi period – was that their shared aversion to DAF "interference" in plant-based training helped forge a unity of interests among firms and across industries that broke through the deadlock that had characterized the Weimar years.

The next section begins with a brief overview of the *policies* with regard to training under the Nazi regime, documenting a huge upswing in overall training effort, the upgrading of apprenticeship in the industrial sector, and the massive moves toward standardization and uniformity in training in both the handicraft and the industry sectors. The following section returns to the *politics* under the Nazis that produced these outcomes, as well as the way in which both the policies and the politics set the scene, organizationally speaking, for the post-war period as well.

Training and Skills under National Socialism

The years of National Socialism had a dramatic impact on vocational training in Germany. The Nazi state presided over a massive expansion of training, as well as the development of instruments to render such training more uniform across the economy. Among other innovations, industry and trade chambers acquired prerogatives equivalent to those of the Handwerk chambers to preside over the administration and certification of training for skilled industrial workers *(Facharbeiter)*, and Handwerk training was brought under more centralized control than ever before.

The expansion of training in the first two years of the regime was connected to other measures to combat unemployment but starting in 1935 the goals shifted to rearmament and mobilization for war, which required large numbers of skilled workers who could be deployed flexibly to meet the demands of military production. State policy in this area included various incentives to encourage and also directly subsidize training. In a move that the free unions had once advocated but that no Weimar government had ever seriously considered, the National Socialist state required firms in

who had occupied similar positions before 1933 (Ullmann 1988: 197). Even if they were ambivalent about the National Socialists, many industry leaders (VDMA vice chairman Otto Sack was one) concluded that it was better to get involved in the new corporatist structures being set up, and took up positions in the new order either out of narrow self-interest or because they saw this as a way to protect their associations from domination by state and party (Weber 1991: 122–4).

the iron, metal, and construction industries employing ten or more workers to train apprentices (Hansen 1997: 607; Wolsing 1977: 160; Schneider 1999: 370).

State promotion of apprenticeship training produced a dramatic rise in the overall number of youth in training. "In 1933 about 45 percent of industrial workers were skilled, another 20 percent semi-skilled and 35 percent unskilled. After 1938 about 90 percent of all boys leaving grammar school, together with increasing numbers of those who had left earlier, entered three-year apprenticeships in industry, artisanship (Handwerk), commerce, or agriculture" (Gillingham 1985: 428). The state mandate to train (in some industries) and subsidies (more generally) were important to these outcomes. One should also note, however, that, with unions out of the picture and with wages more or less frozen starting in 1932, the political–economic context during the subsequent economic recovery would have encouraged increased investment in skills even by a strict economic logic (Herrigel 1996b: 139). A large number of firms trained their workers either in production itself, or in "training corners" in close proximity to it. An increasing number of firms created in-house training centers as well. The number of such training workshops increased between 1933 and 1940 from 167 to 3,304. Whereas in 1933, only 16,222 workers had received training in such workshops, the number rose to 244,250 by 1940 (Kipp and Miller-Kipp 1990: 34; Pätzold 1989: 278).

An important focus of attention under the Nazi regime was training *in industry*, which would obviously be of crucial importance to the military. With the economic recovery, skill shortages hampered the regime's military build-up and set in motion disruptive poaching among firms (Mason 1966: 128). Thus, beginning in 1935, a number of measures were undertaken to upgrade and clarify the status of industrial apprenticeship, with the goal of redirecting labor out of Handwerk and into industry (particularly the metalworking industries). The voluntary arrangements developed in the Weimar years allowing industrial apprentices to be examined under the auspices of the Handwerk chambers (with representation by the IHK) were dispensed with and the industry and trade chambers were granted powers equivalent to the HWK to certify training in industry. Against opposition and foot-dragging by Handwerk, the industrial *Facharbeiter* exam was accorded the same recognition and status that the journeyman's exam in the craft sector had long enjoyed, including the right of a certified *Facharbeiter* to be admitted to the Master exam (Pätzold 1989: 276: Greinert, 1994: 45).

Table 5.1. *Numbers of apprentices taking the* Facharbeiter *examination*

Year	Apprentices taking *Facharbeiter* Exam	Percent change
1935	2,801	
1936	7,748	+176.6
1937	23,832	+407.6
1938	46,682	+95.8
1939	110,810	+137.4
1940	85,466	−22.9
1941	99,321	+16.2
1942	121,653	+22.5

Source: Wolsing 1977: 357fn3.

These measures brought about an immediate increase in the number of IHK-based testing offices – from 31 in 1935 to 89 in the spring of 1937 (Wolsing 1977: 346–7; Kipp 1990: 235). They were also accompanied by a dramatic increase in the number of apprentices taking *Facharbeiter* exams, as Table 5.1 shows.

The other aspect of vocational training policy, skill standardization, was similarly designed to facilitate the war effort. Broad-based, standardized training generated a supply of skilled workers who could be deployed flexibly to deal with increased production demands and with continuous changes in production as increasing numbers of men were called up and as production sites were dispersed to shield them from attack. A model "apprentice contract" was introduced in 1935; it laid out conditions governing the terms of both a trainee's employment and his or her training (Wolsing 1977: 254–60). The contract established some baseline minima for apprentices, including a monthly educational stipend (for Handwerk apprentices, sometimes replacing fees that they paid to the master artisan), and minimum vacation time (Pätzold 1989: 270).

Perhaps even more important, training was to be based on skill profiles and regulatory instruments (*Ausbildungsordnungen*) developed by the German Committee for Technical Education (*Deutscher Ausschuß für Technisches Schulwesen*, or DATSCH), which, as we saw in Chapter 2, had been involved in developing training materials for the metal and machine industries throughout the 1920s. The innovation under the Nazi regime was to obligate firms to adopt and employ DATSCH guidelines and methods, thus ensuring that they would be widely diffused throughout the economy (Abel 1963: 58–9; Stratmann 1990: 47–9). The training ordinances DATSCH developed – and that after 1937 were officially recognized through the Reich Minister for Economics (Kipp 1990: 229; Münch 1991: 34; Pätzold 1989: 274–5) – specified the important features of training in a particular trade, including: the occupational title, job description (what specific skills had to be mastered for certification in the trade), the duration of the training program, and the structure of the training (DATSCH 1937).[10] These ordinances established a set of uniform rules as to what was expected both of training firms and of the apprentices.

Apprentices could only be trained in recognized occupations and on the basis of standardized training materials worked out and disseminated nationally. These measures imposed a much higher degree of uniformity across sectors than ever before, ensuring that anyone certified as a "skilled mechanic" (for example) possessed the same technical skills and theoretical knowledge irrespective of the firm or sector in which he received his training. Moreover, and also starting in 1937, apprentices who completed their training programs – whether in Handwerk or in industry – were *required* to take the journeyman (Handwerk) or *Facharbeiter* (industry) examination. "This compelled masters and training firms to present their apprentices for evaluation and served as much to monitor the quality of the training apprentices received as to certify their skills" (Hansen 1997: 608).

Training ordinances were worked out not just for industry but for Handwerk as well. This was important because, as we have seen, in the 1920s the Handwerk sector had lagged behind industry in establishing uniform guidelines for training. After the legislation of 1937, however, Handwerk firms too were forced into greater systematization by an exam system that was "increasingly based, as in industry, on *standardized* occupational definitions, training procedures, and competence benchmarks that masters were not free to ignore" (Hansen 1997: 618, italics mine; Pätzold 1989: 275). Later, DATSCH also began to work out guidelines for semi-skilled occupations as well, which also rendered training for these jobs more systematic and uniform across firms (Rathschlag 1972: 22, 24). By the end of the war DATSCH (by this time subsumed into the state and converted into the National Institute for Vocational Training (or *Reichsinstitut für Berufsausbildung in Handel und Gewerbe*) had developed training materials for

[10] In 1937, 121 industrial trades were officially recognized by the state, a number that increased steadily over the next years (Kipp 1990: 229).

almost a thousand skilled and semi-skilled occupations (Münch 1991: 34; Wolsing 1977: 278–9).

An increase in standardization was reflected as well in changes that made the first year of apprenticeship more uniform across firms, providing a broad "foundational" basis on which apprentices could build and become more specialized in subsequent years (Wolsing 1977: 329–31). DATSCH was also given responsibility for creating stronger links between in-plant and school-based components of vocational training (Pätzold 1989: 274). After years of controversy over the issue, a law was passed in 1938 requiring all school leavers throughout the empire, including young women, to attend at least three years of continuation school beyond the completion of the common school (Pätzold 1989: 283–4).[11] Starting in 1939, uniform (nation-wide) educational plans for trade schools were put into effect (Stratmann 1990: 48–9). The trade school curricula were specifically organized around the trade profiles that DATSCH had worked out for in-plant training (Kipp 1990: 228), thus clearly signaling the primacy of the firm-based component, for which the theoretical school-based component was seen mostly as complementary (Stratmann and Schlösser 1990: Chapter 3).[12]

The capacity to monitor in-plant training was also enhanced in the years of National Socialism. In 1933, the regime introduced a national register of all apprentice contracts. Handwerk had maintained such a register since the turn of the century, but no such instrument had existed for industrial apprentices (Kipp 1990: 227). The 1933 law obliged all firms employing apprentices to register their indentures with the local chamber (either the craft chamber or the chamber of industry and commerce). The chamber was then charged with responsibility for making sure that the contract conformed to

[11] The Weimar constitution had called for compulsory schooling until age 18, but this was never really implemented nationwide, enforcement being left to the states where there was great variety in whether and to what extent trade school attendance was obligatory (Pätzold 1989: 280–1). Moreover, the trade school system experienced a crisis in the late years of the Weimar Republic, due to the depression. Notably and characteristically for the time, budget cuts proposed in 1931 were opposed by DATSCH as well as by the unions, and very much approved by Handwerk and segments of industry that relied less heavily on skills than DATSCH's main constituency among machine firms (Pätzold 1989: 281–2). See Chapter 2, on the coalitions of the Weimar period.

[12] Although the Nazi regime introduced compulsory trade school attendance on a national level, the schools were subsequently left to languish as the war effort geared up and as training came to be more narrowly focused on specific, and highly pragmatic, military needs.

the "recognized" occupations and to the uniform apprenticeship contract guidelines set by the state.

In addition to maintaining a roster of apprentices the chambers were also charged with recording the results of apprentices' certification exams. Such provisions were useful for the National Socialists' policy of vocational guidance (or "steering": *Berufslenkung*), but they also allowed authorities and chambers to keep close tabs on plant-based training, tracking not just which firms were training apprentices and in what occupations, but also the exam scores so they could assess the quality of training (Wolsing 1977: 265–9, especially 268–9; Kipp 1990: 227). Since registration was necessary for apprentices to be admitted to journeymen's exams, the IHK quickly established "considerable influence" over youth guidance (*Nachwuchslenkung*) and especially over the content of training. The IHK collected all sorts of information about firms involved in training, including the number of apprentices they were taking, the types of training facilities they used, and so on (Frese 1991: 271). Companies with repeated bad exam results could bring sanctions on themselves. For example, the chambers might refuse to register more apprentices to them. In general, however, firms sought to achieve good results for the sake of their "image" as well as their ability to recruit promising young workers (Frese 1991: 302).

Monitoring the content and quality of training was also accomplished through complementary institutions and practices. In 1934 DAF organized the first annual skills competition (*Reichsberufswettkampf*) involving hundreds of thousands of apprentices in every craft, trade, and profession (Mason 1966: 124). The competition consisted of a set of tests, in both vocational skills and "political reliability" (Mason 1966: 124). Contests were held at the local, district, and regional level, producing about four hundred winners each year (Gillingham 1985: 425). The number of firms involved in the competition was high, not least because, as Mason points out, it was "difficult not to take part" (Mason 1966: 124).[13] The annual competition created strong incentives for firms to train specifically to national standards, while also giving the DAF and the Hitler Youth some insights into the relative quality of training across various firms and sectors (von Rauschenplat

[13] The number of participants involved in these competitions rose between 1934 and 1939 from five hundred thousand to over three million according to one source (von Rauschenplat 1945: 25), and one million in 1936 to 3.6 million in 1939, according to another (Mason 1966: 124).

1945: 26).[14] As the head of the competition, Artur Axmann, put it, the event operated like an "X-ray for vocational training" which could be used to reveal not just technical but also ideological deficits in training (Kipp 1990: 254; Pätzold 1989: 275).

These measures all served to guide youth into the "appropriate" training slots, which is to say into occupations that served the state and its military interests. A previous (1927) law had put the Imperial Institute for Labor Exchange and Unemployment Insurance (*Reichsanstalt für Arbeitsvermittlung and Arbeitslosenversicherung*) in charge of vocational counseling and matching youths to apprenticeship slots, but these services had not been compulsory on either side. In 1935 the Nazi government gave the *Reichsanstalt* enhanced powers, both as a provider of vocational counseling and as a central clearing house for matching apprentices to training slots (Kipp 1990: 221). The government made all youth subject to obligatory vocational counseling, attempting thus to steer them into the proper vocational channels (Kaiser and Loddenkemper 1980: 79). Whereas in 1926–27, 31% of all 14-year-olds received vocational guidance and in 1931–32 this was up to 67%, the number reached 90% in 1941 (von Rauschenplat 1945: 22). These functions were backed up by the 1938 school law which, in addition to rendering vocational education compulsory for all school leavers, required them to report to their local employment office within two weeks of leaving school (Kipp 1990: 222; Gillingham 1985: 426; Greinert 1994: 56).

The Politics of Vocational Training under National Socialism

The National-Socialist era represented a mixture of consolidation and innovation in vocational training. The consolidation was achieved through measures to institutionalize a national system of skill formation built on components inherited from the pre-World War I period for Handwerk and further developed on a voluntary basis for industry in the 1920s (see Chapter 2). But consolidation came packaged with elements of innovation that overcame some of the political obstacles that had frustrated attempts in the Weimar period to arrive at a unitary and comprehensive national system

[14] As this was a DAF program, there was also a strong ideological component to the competition. DAF directly ran the training program at companies like VW, and held it up as a showcase for its concepts. The Wolfsburg facility came out especially well in the annual skills competition (Kipp 1990: Chapter 12).

for skill formation. Some of the previous political obstacles were swept away through brute repression. The elimination of the unions removed the need to reach an accommodation with organized labor. Other lines of cleavage, for example, between Handwerk and industry and between different segments of industry who advocated radically different models of training (see Chapter 2) were erased or patched over in the Nazi period. This section deals with the politics through which this took place.

The National Socialist regime, redefining private-sector training as an educational relationship, "rendered it a *public* trust and duty" (Hansen 1997: 615, italics in original; Molitor 1960: 16). This settled a long-standing conflict between unions and employers in the Weimar period in favor of the latter. In the Nazi era, however, the reclassification of training became important mostly because it provided the Nazi party and the DAF with justification to insert itself into the organization and administration of skill formation. Employers and their organized representatives resented such intrusions. From their perspective they replaced unwanted meddling by the unions with similarly unwelcome meddling by party functionaries. Business therefore resisted these trends and its interests were represented within the state apparatus by the Reich Ministry of Economics which had its own reasons to oppose party influence (Wolsing 1977: 323). In what follows I return to the main players in the vocational training debates and sketch out the ways in which their interests were represented, re-thought, and partly reconfigured in the Nazi era.

Handwerk. The advent of National Socialism initially produced a series of policies that could only warm the hearts of the Handwerk sector. In addition to suppressing the unions, the Nazis met some important long-standing demands of organized artisans (Pätzold 1989: 268). In 1935, the government signed into law the "major [or comprehensive] certificate of competence" (*großer Befähigungsnachweis*) requiring a master certificate of anyone wishing to open an artisanal shop and/or to pursue an artisanal trade independently (von Rauschenplat 1945; Greinert 1994: 45; Berghoff 2001: 81).[15] The Nazis also made membership in the artisanal organizations

[15] Until this time, a master's certificate was not required, and only about 30% of self-employed artisans had one at this time (Berghoff 2001: 81; Lenger 1988: 197). It turns out that those without the certificate were not actually stripped of their right to practice a handicraft trade. Instead, most of them were given until the end of 1939 to "make up" the exam, and even this was relaxed later (though the regulation did affect anyone seeking master status after this) (Lenger 1988: 197).

compulsory, another long-standing demand. The previous structure was one in which regional Handwerk chambers (endowed with parapublic authority and responsibilities) existed alongside traditional (voluntary) guild associations organized around the various crafts (Weber 1991:112–13). The Nazi regime reorganized the guilds, linking them more closely to the chambers (through staff sharing, for example), and essentially created a single comprehensive and unitary organization, a measure that brought the density ratio of Handwerk associations from 70% to 100% (Weber 1991: 113).

These moves were, however, associated with innovations with which Handwerk was not enthused.[16] The commitment on the part of the party to guarantee all youth a training spot clashed with the goals of important segments of Handwerk, which worried about glutting the market with skilled craftsmen. Some handicraft trades (for example, butchers and bakers) had been using their prerogatives to set limits on training as a way of protecting their trade (Pätzold 1989: 267). DAF's demands with respect to training – promising all youths a right to training and involving the obligation of firms to train – were too radical and intrusive for their tastes (Seubert 1977: 100). Other policies were resented for the higher operating costs they imposed on Handwerk firms. Innovations in the apprentice contract (for example, guaranteeing minimum vacation time and other limitations on apprentice working time) and the introduction of a compulsory trade school component to training weighed on master artisans who were used to relying heavily on apprentices as a source of cheap labor (Pätzold 1989: 270).[17]

One of the most important changes was that Handwerk lost its monopoly position to certify skills (Lenger 1988: 199). After the 1935 legislation discussed above, Handwerk competed with industry for qualified youths, a contest in which artisans mostly lost out (Berghoff 2001: 82; Wolsing 1980; Lenger 1988: 199). Handwerk also suffered major cutbacks in the autonomy it had traditionally enjoyed in the area of apprentice training (Schneider 1999: 371–2). Handwerk chambers had had a great deal of leeway in developing their own local standards and individual masters had had significant autonomy in determining the content and structure of apprenticeship training in their own shops. There were no "legally binding definitions of the craft trades, and no specialized regulations on contents to be taught"

[16] On the effects of Nazi policies on the Handwerk sector, see especially von Saldern (1979), see also Schneider (1999: 370–2), Lenger (1988: 195–202).

[17] Handwerker also complained about mandatory high contributions to compulsory organizations, as well as to the introduction in 1937 of compulsory accounting (Lenger 1988: 197, 200).

(Hansen 1997: 617; Greinert 1994: 50). As we have seen, however, many of the organizational innovations introduced under National Socialism promoted standardization in Handwerk training – something that some but by no means all handicraft firms welcomed.[18]

The certification powers that Handwerk chambers had enjoyed since 1897 were now for the first time explicitly married to increased uniformity in the *content* of training. The handicraft sector had greeted with great suspicion the regime's promotion of DATSCH as its main advisory organ for vocational training, correctly fearing encroachment on Handwerk autonomy through the increased influence of industry (Wolsing 1977: 430). Although a comprehensive rationalization of Handwerk training proved elusive in the Nazi period (because of difficulties in monitoring and enforcement), the overall result was to move training in the Handwerk sector "closer to the organizational principles of industrial vocational training" (Greinert 1994: 50; see also Schneider 1999: 371–2; Pätzold 1989: 270).

In addition, Handwerk firms were increasingly affected by the war economy, as the state, over time, took a stronger hand in directing war materials and skilled labor, with the result that many shops went under for lack of raw materials (Lenger 1988: 199). The most direct state involvement in this regard came through the so-called *Auskämmeaktionen* (or "combing out" operations) in 1939 and 1943, when large numbers of artisans were forced to close their shops, without compensation, to free up labor for the army or for industry (Ullmann 1988: 189; Lenger 1988: 200–1). Lenger reports that in the second half of 1939, almost two hundred thousand artisanal shops (mostly the smallest and most traditional one-person shops) were forcibly closed in this way (Lenger 1988: 200). The Nazi era had widely diverse effects on the Handwerk sector, proving quite lucrative for those firms able to participate in the rearmament boom, whereas others, more marginal politically and economically, were weeded out altogether (Lenger 1988: 198–9).

Industry. Developments in industry were even more complex. Recall that the Weimar period was marked by considerable diversity in the extent to which different segments of industry were committed to training, the extent to which they were open to negotiating with unions on this matter, and

[18] These included the introduction of a uniform apprentice contract, guidelines for master examinations, the development of technical materials for the apprentice and journeymen's examinations, and the introduction in 1938 of a national apprentice roll that subsumed the previous Handwerk rolls (Wolsing 1977: 269–70; Kipp 1990: 224–30; Pätzold 1989: 269–70; Hansen 1997: 594–619, especially 617–19).

in the different models of training they sought to pursue. The legacy of the Weimar period was significant advances in skill standardization in key industries (above all, in machine building and metalworking through the influence of DATSCH and the VDMA). Other organizations, however, sought to promote a very different, more autarkic model that emphasized firm-based and firm-oriented training and company loyalty. This alternative perspective was represented above all in heavy industry and vigorously promoted by their German Institute for Technical Training (*Deutsches Institut für Technische Arbeitsschulung*, or Dinta). In the absence of an overarching legal framework for industrial training such as existed in the Handwerk sector, training in industry in the Weimar years was marked by great diversity across plants, regions, and sectors.

The Nazi seizure of power clearly changed the political–economic parameters within which training policy would be decided and with that, the interests of some of the key actors. The repression of the unions played to the interests of many segments of industry and eliminated any need to compromise with labor on skill formation. In addition, those industries (for example, machine making) that had long sought standardization and separate certification of industrial training on a par with the handicraft training system were much heartened by the National Socialists' bold moves in that direction. But an equally important side effect of the training policies pursued by the Nazis was that it recast the debate entirely. The apparatus for more centralized administration and certification of industrial training became a fact. The question shifted to that of who was going to run it. These developments pushed industry to a more unified position, as business sought to occupy the regulatory space opened up by Nazi training policies, and to defend it, mostly in alliance with the Ministry of Economics (RWM) and mostly against the ambitions of the German Labor Front (DAF) (Pätzold 1989: 278; Seubert 1977: Chapters 10, 11; see especially Frese 1991: 251–332 passim; Wolsing 1977: 234–396, and especially 689–739).[19]

The conflicts over training between the DAF and the Ministry of Economics involved some familiar players, among them Dinta and DATSCH, each of which was subsumed into a different part of the regime (Seubert 1977: Chapters 10, 11). Dinta was incorporated into the DAF, a key party organ, whereas DATSCH was associated (at first loosely then more closely)

[19] The split between the Economic Ministry and the DAF, and the animosity between the leaders of the two – Hjalmar Schacht and Robert Ley – were legendary and by no means confined to issues of vocational training (see, for example, Hayes 1987: Chapter 4).

with the Ministry of Economics. The conflict that unfolded was partly a pure jurisdictional turf war, but overlaid on this were questions about the balance between the ideological and the technical aspects of training and above all the balance between direct state regulation on one hand, and managerial autonomy and employer self-regulation on the other (Wolsing 1980: 306–8).

Dinta was the creation of heavy industry in the Weimar period and its longtime leader Carl (later Karl[20]) Arnhold promoted a view of vocational training explicitly designed to provide a more autarkic alternative to DATSCH's collectivist ideas. Dinta's concept since its inception in 1925 was to encourage the development of systems of training that would be under the exclusive control of the individual firms and that would simultaneously promote systematic training and strong company loyalties.[21] Dinta's mission underwent a significant transformation, however, through its affiliation in the Nazi era with the German Labor Front (DAF), first (in 1933) as an independent but associated institute known as the German Institute for National-Socialist Technical Trade Research and Education (*Deutsches Institut für Nationalsozialistische Technische Arbeitsforschung und –schulung*) (Seubert 1977: 96; Kaiser and Loddenkemper 1980: 78; Greinert 1994: 46). A year later it was completely absorbed when Arnhold was named head of DAF's Office for Vocational Training and Works Management (*Amt für Berufserziehung und Betriebsführung*, AfBB) (Seubert 1977: 98; Greinert 1994: 46; Schneider 1999: 209–10).

DAF's interest in Dinta emanated from Ley's ambitions to lay claim to a large role in training policy. Dinta brought with it years of experience and expertise in this area (Wolsing 1980: 305). There were also some obvious affinities between Dinta's ideology and that of DAF (von Rauschenplat 1945: 14–18).[22] Anti-communism, anti-unionism, and the idea of a plant community resonated strongly with National Socialist ideology; both DAF and Dinta thought of training not in the narrow sense of technical skills,

[20] After 1933, he adopted the more Germanic spelling of his first name (Gillingham 1985: 424).

[21] Different, therefore, from DATSCH, which unlike Dinta worked through trade and business associations in the interests of skill standardization (therefore also interchangeable skills and with no particular ambitions to generate company loyalty).

[22] Hitler had admired Dinta's work in the area of training for some time. Arnhold met Hitler in 1931 and worked discreetly with the National-Socialist Party (*Nationalsozialistische Deutsche Arbeiterpartei*, NSDAP) before it took power, though it was only after Dinta was brought into the German Labor Front that the organization publicly embraced National Socialism (Seubert 1977: 92; Kipp and Miller-Kipp 1990: 28; Gillingham 1985: 425).

but as a vehicle for indoctrination or, as they put it, "training for the 'whole person'" (Kaiser and Loddenkemper 1980: 84; Seubert 1977: 90). For Dinta and Arnhold, the association with DAF also had its attractions. The most obvious advantage was that it gave Dinta access to the resources of a major player in the new regime, and Dinta did not want for financial support for its concepts: "By late 1936 Dinta had vast sums of money at its disposal and was running 400 apprenticeship training workshops while another 150 were in preparation. The various Dinta training schools and programs employed 25,000 teachers and had taught 2.5 million workers" (Nolan 1994: 234).

DATSCH, meanwhile, had been incorporated into the state, although on quite different terms. DATSCH had a longer history of involvement in vocational training than Dinta, and the work it did on behalf of systematic training in the 1920s had earned it widespread recognition and respect in business and government circles. Even before 1933, the National Economics Ministry as well as state ministries referred to DATSCH materials in their decrees on vocational training (Seubert 1977: 99). In the first years of National Socialism, DATSCH remained a purely private economic institute, with a loose affiliation to the Economics ministry, but by 1935 it had been officially designated as the Ministry's main advisory organ (Wolsing 1977: 278; Greinert 1994: 46; see also DATSCH 1937). Later (1939), it was converted into a governmental agency in its own right, the National Institute for Vocational Training in Trade and Industry (*Reichsinstitut für Berufsausbildung in Handel und Gewerbe*), and its jurisdiction expanded to cover not just industry but Handwerk as well (Wolsing 1977: 278–9; Pätzold 1989: 273).

DATSCH's approach to vocational training continued to stress the technical and functional aspects, and the organization remained strongly connected to industrial interests in general and to employers' chambers in particular.[23] With these economic interests and backed up by the Reich Ministry of Economics, DATSCH represented a perspective on training at odds with DAF's more ideological approach. In the National Socialist period DATSCH worked in a de facto alliance with the Ministry of Economics in the interests of industry and economy, as both sought to keep the technical and functional aspects of training from being subordinated to the DAF's ideological agenda and, more important and more generally, to

[23] By contrast, as we have seen, in the Weimar period, Dinta had not fostered close relations with organized business associations, preferring to organize its work around individual companies.

protect firms to the extent possible from direct state or party intrusion into managerial affairs.

Political Struggles over the Control of Vocational Training

At first, heavy industry looked favorably on Dinta's absorption by the DAF, thinking this would anchor their training concept within a key National Socialist mass organization (Frese 1991: 255). It soon became clear, however, that Ley's ambition to claim "complete authority" to decide on all aspects of training policy would represent significant encroachments on managerial autonomy. Developments very early on led industrial giants like Krupp and GHH to resist these developments, vowing to work to maintain employer discretion in this area (Frese 1991: 252, 255). Even those firms that had adopted Dinta training methods before 1933 and continued working with them after, were more skeptical and distant toward Dinta after its incorporation into DAF (as the AfBB) in 1935 (Frese 1991: 256). Arnhold watched as his former clients distanced themselves, unsure as to what extent Arnhold was operating on their behalf and to what extent as the "long arm of Ley" (Frese 1991: 257).[24] Firms that had traditionally worked closely with Dinta engineers were now "hesitant" to let them into their plants to advise them (Frese 1991: 258).

These firms now saw their affairs as better represented by DAF's main opponent in the state, the Economics Ministry, which especially under Hjalmar Schacht was closely allied with organized business interests (Ullmann 1988: 198). The conflict over vocational training was not the only area of tension between party and state apparatus, but it was an important one. DAF jousted with the Economics Ministry over these issues throughout the 1930s (Kaiser and Loddenkemper 1980: 82; also Greinert 1994: 45–7; see especially Seubert 1977: Chapter 11; Wolsing 1977, part VI: 689–739).[25] Ley based his claims to "total authority" in this area on an October 24, 1934, ordinance issued directly by Hitler on the "nature and goals of the German Labor Front" (Schneider 1999: 364–5; Frese 1991: 258–64). His efforts to have the AfBB assume the role of *Brennlinse* (focus

[24] Arnhold was in an overall ambiguous position; Ley remained suspicious of Dinta because of its links to industry, and sometimes accused the organization of putting its ties to industry above its ties to the DAF (Frese 1991: 253–4).

[25] This was part of a general conflict over power and influence within the National Socialist regime, between the Economics Ministry and DAF (Wolsing 1977: Part VI; Hayes 1987: Chapter 4).

or focal point) (Frese 1991: 261) for all aspects of training policy created immediate jurisdictional problems in light of the RWM's competing claims (exercised mostly through delegation to DATSCH and administered through organized business interests themselves).

A meeting between DAF and the Economics Ministry in March 1935 produced a vague agreement (the so-called Leipzig Agreement) that presumably obligated DAF to seek the "prior approval of the Organization of Industry for any measure affecting the economy" (Seubert 1977: 103–4; Mason 1966: 124). Specifically, in the area of training, Schacht had apparently been willing to accept a certain division of labor: The DAF would be responsible for ideological–political training and employers and their associations would be responsible for technical qualification (Seubert 1977: 107). Ley soon found this too constraining, however, and – invoking a number of decrees by Hitler – continued to claim competency in the whole area of vocational training and continuing education. He considered the private-sector organizations of self-government (for example, chambers) to be "relics of the old system," and sought to subordinate them to the party (quote is from Seubert 1977: 105; see also Wolsing 1977: 241; Mason 1966: 124; Greinert 1994: 45–7).

In the ensuing years, Ley sought to reinforce his claim to authority in the training area with policies that directly contradicted government policy, therefore deeply irritating Schacht (Wolsing 1977: 309), but Schacht's protests "followed one another into the waste-paper baskets of the Labour Front [DAF]" (Mason 1966: 124). In 1935, in flat contradiction of the Leipzig Agreement, Ley's lieutenants began to set up DAF training courses, also claiming the exclusive right to award industrial qualifications. Schacht and industry representatives viewed this as a direct assault on the rights of the chambers and economic groups (Seubert 1977: 104). The *Reichsgruppe Industrie* (RGI) advised firms to stay away from AfBB (as Dinta was by now called) and DAF, and to work instead to implement the policies of the Economics Ministry (Frese 1991: 261, 298 fn143). For his own sake, but also at the urging of "influential firms" who wanted the situation clarified in their interest, Schacht issued an official decree that plant-based vocational training should be based on DATSCH materials, and not the materials produced by the Office of Vocational Training within DAF (Frese 1991: 297–8; Kipp 1990: 229; Schneider 1999: 365; Seubert 1977: 110).[26]

[26] A further conflict centered on the notebooks in which apprentices were meant to record their progress in training. DATSCH had originally introduced these materials, but soon

A number of other such conflicts arose, with actors cleaving along the same lines. DAF opposed the Economic Ministry's (1938) introduction of uniform nationwide apprentice lists (*reichseinheitliche gewerbliche Lehrlingsrolle*), preferring instead to maintain its own "lists of occupational cadres" (*Berufsstammrolle*), which were more comprehensive and provided an instrument of control even beyond the exam for skilled industrial workers (*Facharbeiterprüfung*). This bid was rejected by the Economics Ministry which forbade the use of DAF's rolls, a move that was largely successful, as the vast majority of *Facharbeiter* did wind up registered with the IHK (Wolsing 1977: 269–271). In the end, the DAF's alternative apprentice lists, as well as their model apprentice contract, were superseded by a single uniform list and apprentice contract worked out through the national economic chambers (*Reichswirtschaftskammer*) and underwritten by the Economics Ministry (Wolsing 1977: 270–1; Kipp 1990: 225–8).

There were also furious conflicts over testing procedures. DAF and AfBB attempted to require that the chambers place DAF representatives on their examination boards, and DAF at one point even developed its own testing system. Industry resisted these moves, and was backed up by the Economics Ministry, which insisted on the sole right to testing through the industry and trade chambers and which also instructed the chambers not to test apprentices who had not registered with them but rather with the competing DAF (Frese 1991: 272, 301–2; Schneider 1999: 364–5). Organized business (through the *Reichsgruppe Industrie*, or RGI) offered Schacht "massive support" and warned its members not to put their own role in testing in jeopardy by adopting DAF materials (Frese 1991: 272–3).

Through all these jurisdictional conflicts, industry rallied behind the Economics Ministry under Schacht, which consistently represented the interests of organized business and sought to protect the rights of the chambers to administer key aspects of the training system (Frese 1991: 259, 262). These conflicts were never fully resolved with a clear and unambiguous delegation of authority (Wolsing 1980: 308). Moreover, industry lost its most reliable ally when Schacht left at the end of 1937. In any case, his position had been weakened by the establishment of a separate "Four Year Plan" Office under Hermann Göring (Ullmann 1988: 187). Schacht's

after, Dinta introduced its own version. The DAF intervened on the side of Dinta, attempting to force firms to adopt its materials with the argument that DATSCH's behavior was interfering with DAF's ability to pursue the mission assigned to it by order of the Führer (Wolsing 1977: 308–9).

successor adopted the same general policies, however, and over time the DAF's position in training policy was weakened by the firms themselves (which engaged in a great deal of shirking and foot-dragging) and the onset of war, which encouraged the regime to adopt an increasingly pragmatic and very instrumental approach to training. As the war economy geared up, "'duplication of work' in the area of vocational training was increasingly dismantled to the benefit of the Reich Ministry of Economics" (Greinert 1994: 46; see also Kipp and Miller-Kipp 1990: 34). In May 1941, the DAF's Office for Vocational Training and Plant Management was merged into the (DATSCH successor) *Reichsinstitut für Berufsausbildung*, thus becoming formally subordinate to the Economics Ministry (Stratmann and Schlösser 1990: 47–9; Greinert 1994: 47).

Especially important in the present context was the effect these ongoing conflicts had in promoting among business interests greater unity on the issue of training than had prevailed before the war. Heavy industry – having always embraced a more autarkic and resolutely firm-centered approach to training – had not been enthusiastic about registering their apprentices with the IHK, with the imposition of a model apprentice contract, or with the review of apprentice contracts through the IHK. Over time, however, and in light of the threat posed by DAF to sideline organized business interests altogether, these firms came around. As Frese puts it, "the activities of the DAF [in this area]... strongly encouraged firms to change their attitude" (Frese 1991: 272).

The Impact of National Socialism on Vocational Training

What was the net impact of National Socialism on vocational training in Germany?[27] The balance sheet is mixed, and a lot depends on what dimension one is looking at. Undeniably, the years of National Socialism forged a unified and much more standardized system for vocational training in Handwerk and industry, albeit one, as Hansen has emphasized, constructed largely out of pieces inherited from the Weimar period (Hansen 1997: 603). Industry had achieved some uniformity in training in the Weimar years but lacked certification powers; Handwerk had certification powers but no particular provision for strong standardization in training. What

[27] There is a long-standing debate in German historiography on whether the Nazi period had an overall modernizing or reactionary impact on German society and economic institutions. (For a very useful review and argument, see Berghoff 2001.)

the National Socialist regime did was to bring these two strands decisively together. The regime granted industrial training the same rights and status as Handwerk training, backed up by state recognition of uniform industrial profiles and strong promotion of standardized training. Handwerk training became more systematic as a result of the application (under state auspices) of uniform occupational profiles and standardized training ordinances of the sort pioneered in industry (Hansen 1997: 617). Taken together, these measures gave a tremendous boost to both the *numbers* of apprentices trained in Germany and *standardization* in the training they received.

Over time, however, the exigencies of war and the chaotic administrative apparatus often produced stopgaps and shortcuts that were very detrimental to training. As the war continued, training times were shortened in some trades, against the protests of some segments of industry, worried about declining quality in skills and not happy about the prospect of paying 17-year-olds skilled worker wages (Frese 1991: 285–7). The regime also frequently had to reverse course in ways that produced confusion and conflict. For example, the policies put in place in 1935 to draw youth into skilled occupations were overall rather too successful, and led to serious shortages of semi-skilled operators in many industries (Frese 1991: 279–80; Gillingham 1985: 424, 427; Hansen 1997: 609–10; Rathschlag 1972: 17). A great many of the jobs involved in mobilizing for war could easily be learned in less than two years and some employers (particularly in the iron and steel industry) complained about the discrepancy between the training policies they were required to pursue and their actual production needs. Having elevated the status and attractiveness of industrial training, however, and having committed itself to the right to training for every youth, the National Socialist state had to search for ways to attract youth to the "correct" (in this case, increasingly, semi-skilled) occupations. This is the background to the efforts to upgrade semi-skilled training by having DATSCH work out training materials and secure official state recognition for these occupations as well (Rathschlag 1972: 17, 24; Gillingham 1985: 429).[28]

[28] Semi-skilled occupations had been an issue in the Weimar years as well. In the earlier period the point was to draw sharper distinctions between skilled trades and semi-skilled occupations (to prevent abuse by firms of skilled apprenticeship), but now the idea was to upgrade the training of semi-skilled occupations to increase their attractiveness, making their training *more not less* like that of the skilled trades (Rathschlag 1972: 17, 29–31, 42). In addition, as Rathschlag points out, there were somewhat different types of occupations at stake. It was not so much, as in the 1920s, a matter of traditionally semi-skilled occupations so defined when an increase in the division of labor split skilled work categories. At stake

More generally, the strains of war production led to the deterioration of apprenticeship training in the regime's waning years. The school-based component had never been strong, partly as result of a shortage of teachers – something the National Socialists had brought on themselves with massive firings of left-leaning teachers. The result was the relative (and over time, growing) neglect of the school-based component in favor of training in plants, administered by the party and its affiliated organizations (Kipp and Miller-Kipp 1990: 44; Stratmann and Schlösser 1990: Chapter 3). The number of plant-based trade schools (in companies but under government school supervision) rose from 95 at the end of World War I to 126 in 1929 but declined from 1929 to 1938, first as a result of the depression but also as more and more resources were poured into rearmament and then war (Kipp 1990: 240–1). Once the war broke out, vocational school training was "cut back significantly" (Pätzold 1989: 284). In-plant training, too, suffered under the relentless demands of war, as apprentices found themselves more and more doing production work in the regime's final years.

In sum, the National Socialists presided over the institutionalization of a more unified national system for apprenticeship training with roots in the handicraft system but also incorporating the technical/organizational innovations developed in the 1920s on a voluntary basis by industry, above all by the machine industry. Nazi training policy can be seen as an instance of a broader class of events in which the "dictatorship parasitically made use of existing social structures" but redirecting them to somewhat different ends (Berghoff 2001: 99).[29] This consolidation involved an element of innovation to the extent that the effect was only possible through the forced extension of a model that had by no means emerged as hegemonic in the Weimar years. The Nazi legacy that was produced through the "generalization of preferred solutions" and the "homogenization of sectoral arrangements" (Streeck 2001: 22, 26) was partly a matter of direct design. Its stabilization, however, was a consequence of political realignments (in this case, especially, a new-found unity of business interests on training) that were, as Berghoff has argued in another context, only "indirectly and unwittingly caused by Nazism" (Berghoff 2001: 100). The conflicts described above,

were quite specialized "niche" occupations that were simply not able to recruit sufficient numbers of apprentices (Rathschlag 1972: 28–9).

[29] At least in the case of Handwerk, it seems plausible to argue that Nazi policies resulted in its overall modernization, eliminating the marginal producers and imposing new conditions (for example, accounting, more standardized training) on those artisanal firms that remained.

played out between DAF and RWM, ultimately spoke to broader issues concerning business autonomy and self-governance. The balance between these two principles – corporate self-governance and state control – again became an issue, though in a completely different form, in the post-World War II period, to which I now turn.

Vocational Training in Postwar Germany

The West German vocational training system was reconstructed after the Second World War along lines that built directly on pre-war institutions and practices (Crusius 1982: 89).[30] As Pätzold notes, there were no dramatic departures from the pre-existing system, either during the occupation or in the 1950s.[31] This continuity can be partly explained by the more or less spontaneous re-emergence of previous practices under conditions of high uncertainty about the future of the German economy in the immediate postwar years, and in a context in which the plant-based component of apprentice training was not a major focal point of public debate (Pätzold 1991: 1; Taylor 1981: 103). Against the backdrop of a strong punctuated equilibrium model, the lack of change seems surprising. What this case clearly demonstrates, however, is that actors, when faced with great turbulence and uncertainty, do not necessarily seize this as an opportunity for creative experimentation, but rather, hold tight (to the extent possible) to familiar institutional forms and routines.

The role of foreign occupation was similarly less decisive than one might think. The occupying governments did seek changes in the German education system, but the Allies were interested above all in the *school-based* component of training, the main goal being to expose German youth to a curriculum that included heavier doses of civic responsibility and democratic values. With respect to the *plant-based* component of training a relative legal vacuum existed, in which traditional structures and practices re-emerged largely on the initiative of employers and with the implicit or explicit approval of the Allies. War casualties had produced a highly skewed age profile among the working population and employers had a double interest in apprenticeship, both to replenish the stock of skills lost in the war and as

[30] East Germany is another story, one that cannot be told here; but see Jacoby (2000), Culpepper (2003).

[31] As he put it, "a new beginning was not attempted" (*ein Neubeginn wurde nicht versucht*) (Pätzold 1991: 1).

a source of productive labor. For the occupying powers, apprenticeship offered a welcome solution to the problem of high youth unemployment and thus addressed worries about political volatility if German youth were left to drift. Thus, by the time the Federal Republic was founded in 1949, many of the previous elements of the system of self-government through the handicraft and industry and trade chambers were, de facto if not yet entirely de jure, back in place.

The reconstruction period (1950s) mostly saw the consolidation and legalization of developments in vocational education that had emerged on an informal basis under the occupation. In particular, legislation of 1953 and 1956 extended formal recognition to the chambers of Handwerk and of industry and commerce, and authorized them to exercise parapublic functions in the administration and oversight of plant-based vocational training under a modified form of self-governance. The tasks of producing training materials and ordinances, updating occupational profiles, and disseminating standardized training guidelines and materials – previously performed by DATSCH and its Nazi-era successor – were taken over by the reconstituted chambers. National-level coordination was achieved for industry through the founding (1947) by the chambers of industry and commerce of an overarching office for vocational training (*Arbeitsstelle für Berufserziehung des Deutschen Industrie- und Handelstages*), and for the craft sector through the national organization of Handicraft chambers in collaboration with the Crafts Institute at the University of Cologne (Pätzold 1991: 5).

Germany's unions objected to locating these important regulatory and oversight functions in the (employer-dominated) chambers but political developments placed important constraints on the more significant changes organized labor was proposing. The Federal Republic's first election, in 1949, brought to power a conservative government skeptical of the need for deep reform and particularly unreceptive to union calls for greater state involvement. Instead of more dramatic change, the laws of 1953 and 1956 required the employer chambers to allow union representatives (or elected representatives of workers) to participate in their internal deliberations on training (Streeck et al. 1987: 9, 18). This gave unions a voice in these issues but within the context of the system of employer self-government.

Unions continued to press for more democratic accountability in the area of vocational training (through state oversight and expanded codetermination rights), and in 1969 a Grand Coalition government of Social Democrats and the conservative Christian Democratic party finally passed the overarching national legislation that unions had been calling for since 1919. This law created a new oversight structure for plant-based vocational training consisting of tripartite boards at the national and state levels. This was a significant innovation in that it created a comprehensive public framework "above" the chamber system in which unions are full (parity) participants. There are also strong continuities, however, above all in that the most important aspects of administration and supervision of plant-based training are still accomplished in the chambers. As Faulstich puts it, the 1969 law for the first time unified the rules governing apprentice training, but did so "only in a way that legalized and therefore reinforced the previously prevailing practice" (Faulstich 1977: 171).

The next three sections analyze the most important developments – during the occupation, in the reconstruction period, and finally surrounding the 1969 Vocational Training Act – that, overall, exhibit a pattern of reinforcement through bounded innovation. A final section considers the extent to which contemporary changes in the political and market context are undermining the deeper foundations on which the system has traditionally rested.

The Occupation

Education policy in the three Western zones differed in the extent to which the French, American, and British occupying forces tried to impose reforms. In all three zones, however, the military governments were above all concerned with basic education, so that in the area of vocational training, the attention was mostly on vocational schools rather than in-plant training. All the occupying powers moved swiftly to reopen public schools in Germany after the surrender of May 1945, a move hampered by a lack of suitable space and a dearth of (politically acceptable) teachers (Taylor 1981: 39–40). It is quite striking how soon vocational schools were back in operation. In the British zone, for example, by June 1946, 1,071 part-time vocational schools were operating for 356,179 of an eligible total of 481,703 young men and women (Taylor 1981: 43). The time frame was broadly similar in the other zones, though the reopening of vocational schools in more remote rural areas in the U.S. zone lagged somewhat behind (Taylor 1981: 56).

The policies of the French, British, and Americans shared some features, above all, an almost exclusive emphasis on the school-based portion of training, and within this emphasis, on denazification and civic reeducation. There was variation in the extent to which the occupying forces sought to shape the structure and content of school-based education, with the French and the Americans taking an overall more active stand than the British.[32] As Taylor points out (Taylor 1981: 85, 101), however, most of the major structural reforms discussed at that time did not lead to real changes. Adjustments were made, for example, to enhance the civic component of the school-based part of vocational training, but deeper structural reforms that would have revised the German "dual" system in more significant ways were subtly but effectively resisted by the German authorities who took charge of education policy in 1947 and 1949 (Taylor 1981: 64–5, 105–8).

Employers were singularly unenthusiastic about any initiative that pointed toward greater reliance on school-based vocational training, since firms at this time relied heavily on the productive labor of apprentices. A 1952 report by an American advisor to the U.S. High Commissioner on Germany (George W. Ware in the so-called Ware report) noted that "in a very real sense the three-year apprenticeship system, particularly the productive work in the last year, is one of low-cost labor and in toto constitutes a substantial part (more than 10%) of the whole German labor force" (quoted in Taylor 1981: 132; Ware 1952). For this reason, as Ware remarked, "strong economic pressures persist against decreasing the working hours and increasing the schooling for apprentices" (Ware 1952; see also Stratmann 1999; quoted in Taylor 1981: 132), even though the defense of the traditional system was framed in terms of the proven value of "praxis-oriented" vocational training (Pätzold 1991: 3; Taylor 1981: 103). Spokesmen for Handwerk would later note with undisguised satisfaction that all efforts on the part of occupying forces to implement "alien political–economic experiments" (*wesensfremde wirtschaftspolitische Experimente*) in vocational training had failed (Walle 1963: 216).

The most important single innovation in the structure of German education was that responsibility for public education – including vocational

[32] For a comprehensive account of the policies of the three Western occupying powers, see Taylor (1981: Chapters 2–5). The French retained direct control over the education system for the longest period (until 1949, with the founding of the Federal Republic of Germany). The British and Americans handed responsibility over to German authorities earlier, at the beginning of 1947 (Taylor 1981: 44–5, 101–2). The British were inclined to encourage the Germans to take on responsibility themselves as early as possible, whereas the French and Americans submitted rather detailed reform proposals, in the American case to merge secondary and full-time vocational schools, and in the French case to revamp the curriculum, especially in German and European history.

schools – was vested in the state governments rather than the national government (see, for example, Faulstich 1977: 147–8). This reform reflected an interest among all the occupying powers in promoting a dispersion of power.[33] The German version of federalism, however, allowed for significant coordination among the states, and in the area of education such coordination was institutionalized through the formation in 1948 of a Standing Conference of the [state-level] Ministries of Culture (*Kultusministerkonferenz*, or KMK) across the three Western zones (Faulstich 1977: 152–3). In 1950 the KMK turned its attention to the question of possible reforms of the vocational school system, and appointed a committee to review this issue. The committee – on which employer interests were especially well represented[34] – issued a report that mostly endorsed the basic structure of the existing "dual" system, and did not see vocational schools as any kind of acceptable substitute for enterprise-based training (Engel and Rosenthal 1970: 11; Abel 1968: 26; Bundesrepublik 1952: 264–6; Taylor 1981: 105–6, 141, 146–8; Stratmann and Schlösser 1990: 64).

Less attention was devoted to a serious consideration of reforms to the system of firm-based training during the occupation period. Plant-based apprenticeship more or less spontaneously re-surfaced after the war, recommencing most quickly and thoroughly in the craft sector, as early as 1945 (Taylor 1981: 131). Given the widespread destruction of major industrial areas, apprentices who had been employed there were advised to figure out for themselves how to finish their training. In many cases this meant turning to the craft sector, since handicraft firms were flush with orders connected with reconstruction work of all varieties (Pätzold 1991: 2–3). Industry, too, contributed to the revival of enterprise-based training as soon as feasible, and plant-based training was re-instituted more or less "automatically," under the auspices of individual firms and their employer organizations and chambers (Crusius 1982: 90).

One important reason why in-plant training was swiftly reopened without much fundamental debate stemmed from widespread concerns about youth unemployment in the immediate post-war years. The working population in Germany just after the war was overall on the older side due to

[33] For the same reasons, state governments were also put in charge of radio and television, as well as police (Katzenstein 1987).

[34] The committee included six employer representatives, three education specialists, one representative from the Ministry of Labor, one from the union confederation DGB, and one member of the KMK, along with an academic chairperson (Taylor 1981: 141).

war casualties. Very soon after the war, however, large numbers of youth (the fruits of the Nazi population policy) were entering the labor markets.[35] Apprenticeship provided a structure for German youth, and thus addressed concerns on the part of the Western Allies, especially as the Cold War began, that hopelessness and disillusionment would make them susceptible to the influence of political movements not just on the right but on the left as well (Taylor 1981: 30).

German business, in this period always looking for ways to rehabilitate its tarnished reputation, could bill itself as making efforts to deal with this problem by re-establishing apprentice training programs quickly and unbureaucratically (BDI 1950; Crusius 1982: 90–1; Pätzold 1991: 2; Rohlfing 1949: 3–4).[36] In October 1950 the Ministry of Labor reported 1,011,805 registered apprentices (in industry and Handwerk) (Arbeit 1950: 30). At end of 1954, the *Deutscher Industrie- und Handelskammertag* (DIHT) reported that about 660,000 apprentices were in training for various skilled and semi-skilled occupations in industry, and that in the five years between 1949 and 1954, about 870,000 had already completed their training and taken their exams (Stemme 1955: 7).

Apprenticeship brought with it the issue of regulation and oversight, and here again employer and handicraft associations re-emerged and assumed their traditional roles somewhat organically, as Abel puts it, "in the absence of the state" (Abel 1968: 32; Crusius 1982: 89–91). All three occupying powers had their doubts about the separation of technical and vocational education from general education, and also about having the former under the control and dominance of employers. The Allies were also united, however, in their desire to break up concentrated powers of the state and to establish decentralized nodes of authority. The re-establishment of business self-government looked like a viable alternative. As Herrigel has pointed out, employer representatives emphasized wherever possible the ways in

[35] In 1948 the number of school leavers was six hundred thousand; a year later this was up to seven hundred fifty thousand. The trend was expected to continue for the next several years, and to peak in 1955 at eight hundred eighty thousand (Taylor 1981: 126). See also the assessment of the system by the state governments in Bundesrepublik (1952: 259).

[36] The rhetoric – if not the reality – was altruistic bordering on selfless. For example, in an appeal to firms, the President of the *Bundesverband der Deutschen Industrie*, Fritz Berg, asserted that "only serious and meaningful work can save people from despair and political agitation [*Verhetzung*]" (BDI 1950: 144), and "[German youth] can and must be helped through training and work. Firms and managers feel a deep moral responsibility toward the next generation" (BDI 1950: 145).

which their interests resonated with the values of the occupying powers (particularly the Americans), underscoring the role that private capital and employer self-government could play in limiting state power and guarding against a return of authoritarianism (Herrigel 2000: 377). The head of the DIHT department for vocational training, Adolf Kieslinger (who had occupied basically the same position in the Weimar and the Nazi periods) never tired of insisting that "vocational training is not the task of the state" (*die Berufsausbildung ist nicht Staatsaufgabe*) (Kieslinger 1950: 146).[37]

The occupying forces did not stand in the way of the chambers resuming a leading role in these areas; in many ways they promoted this development (Greinert 1994: 50). The National Socialist regime had folded together chambers of industry and commerce and the handicraft chambers, to form more encompassing national economic chambers (*Reichswirtschaftkammer*). After 1945 the Allies undid this forced integration, so that separate chambers for the handicraft and industrial sectors were reconstituted. The main questions under the occupation concerned official recognition of the chambers and compulsory membership, as well as their precise responsibilities with respect to training. In the British and French zones, the chambers were reconstituted as institutions under public law, but the Americans – less enthusiastic about compulsory membership – allowed them to be reconstituted as voluntary associations under private law (Kieslinger 1966: 12; Walle 1963: 206–7).[38]

Handwerk faced the interesting challenge of wanting very much to preserve some of the gains (for example, the major certificate of competency) that they had sought for decades but only achieved under the Nazis (Ullmann 1988: 255–6). This involved convincing the occupying powers

[37] Kieslinger had been active in vocational training issues through three regimes. In 1929 he was employed in the Weimar labor department offices dealing with vocational training and labor market politics. In 1937 he became head of the vocational training department of the *Arbeitsgemeinschaft der Industrie- und Handelskammern in der Reichswirtschaftskammer* (the Nazi era successor to the DIHT). After the war he became the head of the department for vocational training at the IHK in Munich, before taking up the position (in 1950) of head of the Department of Vocational Training and Labor Supply Questions [*Berufsausbildung und Arbeitskräftefragen*] of the re-founded DIHT, a job he held until his retirement in 1965. I am grateful to the DIHT for providing this biographic information.

[38] An exception is Berlin, where the chambers were forbidden entirely, and where the state itself stepped in – though in consultation with economic organizations – to administer vocational training. This is one reason why Berlin was the first to have explicit legislation on vocational education (in 1951) of a scope and form (with significant union representation, for example) that was not achieved elsewhere in Germany until 1969 (see, for example, Crusius 1982: 91).

that these practices were based on a long Handwerk tradition rather than National Socialist principles, an argument that proved mostly successful. Thus, in the fall of 1945 the HWK were still working in accordance with National Socialist Handwerk law, and by November 1946 (French zone) and December 1946 (British), the military governments passed decrees for the Handwerk sector that put the chambers back in charge of regulating apprentice training, under essentially the same terms as the Handwerk laws of 1934 and 1935 (Rohlfing 1949: 4; Richter 1950: 53; Ullmann 1988: 256–7).[39] The same was true in practice for the American zone, though without the explicit legal basis (Ullmann 1988: 256–7). There, a 1948 ordinance stripped the guilds and Handwerk chambers of their official responsibilities, but it allowed them to continue their previous functions as private voluntary associations. As Richter notes, this was of no practical consequence and was "hardly noticeable," since the functions of the chambers were recognized and followed anyway (Richter 1950: 53).

In industry, as well, the Allies generally did not interfere with the rather rapid reconstitution of the chambers and indeed they had an interest in their "quick reactivation" since they needed them to act as intermediaries between the military administration and companies in rationing measures (Ullmann 1988: 238). In the British and French zones the industry and trade chambers were up and running in 1945 and officially reconstituted along old lines (that is, along the lines of pre-1933 law) in 1946 and 1947 (Ullmann 1988: 238). In the American zone the chambers were civil private institutions with voluntary membership and without any official parapublic responsibilities; the latter provision was almost immediately modified, however, to allow the chambers to resume traditional functions in the area of apprentice training (Richter 1950: 55–6; Ullmann 1988: 238).

[39] Thus, the chambers were again charged with promoting apprenticeship, regulating apprenticeship according to the terms of the HWK, monitoring in-plant training, conducting journeymen exams, and so on. Anyone wishing to take an apprentice needed the approval of the Labor Office (*Arbeitsamt*) but the handicraft guilds played a key role in vetting such applications, making judgments about the quality of particular firms as training institutions (based on rankings from "very good" to "good" to "satisfactory" to "not satisfactory"). No application from a firm designated as unsatisfactory would be accepted by the Labor Office (Rohlfing 1949: 5). The right to revoke a Handwerker's right to train (on the basis of infractions against rules, exploitation of apprentices, and so on) was also delegated to the handicraft chambers, either de jure (British zone) or de facto (French and American zones) (Rohlfing 1949: 12). See also, Richter (1950: 45) on the more or less spontaneous re-establishment of apprentice examinations through the Handwerk chambers.

As summarized by a contemporary observer, as soon as the chambers were reconstituted

> they immediately took up again their functions – even if under a different set of legal conditions in the American zone, and among other things began conducting apprentice exams in the previously common way without any problem and with the tacit tolerance (stillschweigende Duldung) of the military and state governments – and this despite the fact that the chambers had no legal authority to actually do this. (Richter 1950: 45)

The lack of specific legal grounding for chamber activities in the area of vocational training reflected the ambiguities of the immediate post-war legal environment. In 1949 and 1950, publications sponsored by chambers and individual firms appeared that summarized and attempted to clarify for employers the legal status on which apprenticeship now rested. These documents invoked a wide range of ordinances stretching back to the *Gewerbeordnung* of 1869 and the *Handelsgesetzbuch* of 1897, but complemented and revised by subsequent legislation of other periods including under the Nazis, to produce a mosaic obviously not entirely transparent to contemporaries (see, for example, Rohlfing 1949; Richter 1950). These legal ambiguities did not stop chambers from resuming their previous functions. As early as 1945, the Düsseldorf IHK began again to register and examine apprentices, using the materials previously developed by DATSCH. This chamber's leaders wrote to all other IHKs in the British zone encouraging them to work together to counteract tendencies introduced under the Nazis (for example, shortening of apprentice training time) to rejuvenate apprenticeship (Düsseldorf 1945: 129). Beginning in 1949 the chambers of industry and commerce began publishing data on the number of apprentices being trained in particular trades, as well as the aggregate results of apprentice examinations (Stemme 1955: 5).[40]

Employer initiative in the absence of clear and uniform legal foundations became an important part of the employer rhetoric in subsequent conflicts with unions over regulation of firm-based training. The DIHT would later (1955) refer back to post-war initiatives and stress that these first years after the war showed "how even without a sufficient legal foundation, valuable work can be accomplished not just for the country and the economy, but also for individual citizens" (quote is from Stemme 1955: 7; see also Richter

[40] The results were also published in yearly reports, 1947–49 together, then each year through 1954; the publication cited here (Stemme 1955) is a compilation of all of these.

1950: 45). For the DIHT, the events of this period were taken as evidence of the viability and value of employer self-governance (through the chamber system) in the area of apprentice training (Stemme 1955: 7).[41]

Equally important, the first chambers of industry and commerce to become operational after the war took the initiative to found overarching offices for *coordinating* vocational training at the national level, one for industry (in operation starting July 1, 1947, in Dortmund) the other for commerce (commencing operations a few months later, from a base in Munich). After the formal refounding of the German Congress of Industry and Trade (*Deutscher Industrie- und Handelskammertag*, or DIHT)[42] these two offices were combined (in 1951), to form a unified Office for Vocational Training of the Association of German Chambers of Industry and Commerce (*Arbeitsstelle für Berufserziehung des Deutschen Industrie- und Handelstages*) with headquarters in the capital city of Bonn. This entire structure was subsequently (1953) put under the joint sponsorship of all three of the principal employer associations (that is, incorporating the *Bundesverband der Deutschen Industrie* (BDI) and *Bundesvereinigung der Deutschen Arbeitgeberverbände* (BDA), although the day-to-day administration and legal oversight stayed with DIHT), at which point it was renamed the Office for Enterprise-Based Vocational Training (*Arbeitsstelle für betriebliche Berufsausbildung* or ABB) (Berufsausbildung 1958: 7–8; Greinert 1994: 50).

From its inception, and in its earliest post-war incarnations the ABB saw its role as a direct continuation of the work of DATSCH and its successor, the *Reichsinstitut für Berufsausbildung*. Pre-existing training profiles and guidelines continued to be used, and the chambers only accepted apprentice contracts based on such "recognized" skilled and semi-skilled occupations (Pätzold 1991: 7–8).[43] As early as 1947 the *Arbeitsstelle* resumed the work of defining and updating occupational profiles for industry, establishing guidelines for training for the various trades, providing materials regarding

[41] Employers would continue through the 1950s to appeal to the principle of subsidiarity in this area, pointing out (misleadingly, as the present analysis shows) that the strong and highly successful system of enterprise-based training was something that employers historically had created without the help of the state (*ohne dass der Staat mitgewirkt hat*) (Kieslinger 1950: 146).

[42] In 1949, after the founding of the Federal Republic.

[43] In Handwerk, too, a 1949 publication notes that the *Fachlichen Vorschriften zur Regelung des Lehrlingswesens* are the "authoritative" materials governing the conduct of training (Rohlfing 1949: 27).

how training should be structured, and the like (Berufsausbildung 1958, passim). A 1955 ABB publication provides a complete index of all recognized occupations in industry (ABB 1955); and the DIHT was also active in publishing training ordinances and materials for use by firms (six volumes covering a total of 674 occupations) (DIHT 1955). In 1954 (with authorization from the Economics Ministry) the ABB struck 137 occupations from the list of "recognized" trades. The vast majority of these (all but 34) were semi-skilled occupations, so this action was partly designed to move back to the status quo ante, counteracting the big build-up of recognized semi-skilled occupations that had occurred in the Nazi period (Stemme 1955: 163–6).

The level of national coordination was much higher after the war than it had been during the Weimar years, when DATSCH's influence was less well established and the organization lacked the explicit backing of the DIHT and AfB (see Chapter 2). Thus, "the development of the regulations for in-plant training proceeded on a more uniform basis" after the war than it had been before, and was more standardized even than the curriculum for vocational schooling, which was a matter for regulation at the state level (Bunk 1979: 102; Greinert 1994: 50). The activities of the chambers throughout this period were guided by foundational principles that hark back to the goals traditionally articulated by DATSCH, including (1) homogeneous training for all apprentices in the same vocation regardless of which firm or sector trained them, (2) uniformity in training and education conditions across and within enterprises, (3) equivalence of certificates with the same qualification, and (4) adaptation of apprentice training (both occupational profiles and the content of training) to ongoing market and technological developments (Kieslinger 1960: 52–3).

Enhanced coordination and centralization were legacies of the Nazi period, with the difference after the war that the chambers rather than the state assumed the key coordinating role.[44] After 1945, the chambers exercised

[44] See also Kieslinger (1960: 45–56) for a complete elaboration of the precise role of the chambers in all aspects of apprentice training, which includes among others (a) developing new training professions as these are made necessary by market or technological changes, (b) imposing uniform conditions on the terms of apprentice contract for particular occupations, (c) keeping apprentice rolls and monitoring firm training (including denying apprentice registration to firms deemed unqualified or unsuited to such training), (d) assisting and promoting enterprise-based training through the supply of training materials and other supports, and (e) presiding over examination of apprentices by appointing the relevant committees and monitoring results.

all the important regulatory functions, even though official recognition for the ordinances they produced required approval by the Federal minister in charge of the economic area in question – for industry, commerce, and the crafts this was the Ministry of Economics and for occupations in agriculture, it was the Federal Minister of Food, Agriculture, and Forestry (Münch 1991: 35). Union representatives were for the first time explicitly and formally allowed to participate in the review of training ordinances prior to their official adoption through the Ministry.[45] It should be noted however, that the role of both state and union in this process was largely pro forma, and there is really no particular evidence that the influence of either mattered significantly with respect to the substance of these ordinances.

Reconstruction

By the time of the founding of the Federal Republic (1949) and the installation of its first government under the conservative Chancellor Konrad Adenauer, the enterprise-based part of the dual system had been re-established on the basis of employer self-governance, with distant supporting roles assigned to both the state and the unions. Occupational profiles and training materials developed before the war were picked up again as the basis for in-plant training, and the chambers took up the role traditionally played by DATSCH and the *Reichsinstitut für Berufsausbildung* in updating, rationalizing, and disseminating training materials and guidelines. With good reason, Pätzold refers to developments in the reconstruction period as a "re-anchoring of traditional training structures" (*Neubefestigung traditioneller Ausbildungsstrukturen*) (Pätzold 1991: 2).

The main debates of the 1950s and 1960s regarding plant-based training all turned on the same basic line of cleavage. Employers and their political allies defended the principle of employer self-governance (and the

[45] This innovation goes back to policies introduced by the British military government. In 1946, the British representative for vocational training in the Central Office for the Economy (*Zentralamt für Wirtschaft*) issued a directive for the "necessary uniformity in vocational training for youth in industry." According to this decree, recognition, changes, or elimination of skilled and semi-skilled occupations, as well as approval of occupational profiles, training establishments, and plants, had to be submitted for review to the legal representatives of the trades (this would have been the ABB or the craft chambers) and the unions. These rules were transferred to the unified (British-American) economic zone in 1948 and adopted and applied generally after the founding of the Federal Republic of Germany (FRG) (Pätzold 1991: 7).

subsidiarity principle[46]) as the only viable way to prevent bureaucratization and to preserve the "elasticity" of the system in the face of changing market and technical conditions (see especially Kieslinger 1966: 57–61; also Baethge 1970: 178–83). They also pointed out that since firms themselves bore the costs of training and would be the ones held responsible for the quality of such training, it was both practical and justified to vest the important regulatory powers in the chambers which were "in constant active collaboration" with their member firms (Richter 1950: 49). Unions and their political allies, by contrast, defined vocational training as a "public task" which therefore required more democratic control and increased participation rights for employee representatives.[47] The unions questioned the appropriateness of putting private industry in charge of the education of a large number of 16- to 18-year-olds, and criticized the class biases involved in such a strict separation of general and vocational training tracks (Crusius 1970: 115, 127; Baethge 1970: 98–100).

Other debates revolved around the nature of the training contract – whether defined more as an educational relationship or as a work relationship, a long-standing issue as we have seen (see especially Molitor 1960: passim).[48] As in the past, the unions lobbied for considering apprentice contracts to be work contracts so they could represent trainees' material interests. Employers, and particularly craft employers, were adamant about having training contracts defined as educational relationships and preventing the "training allowance" from being considered a wage (Kieslinger 1966: 23–5; Rohlfing 1949: 20). Industrial employers were overall less worried than craft masters about the costs, but they too resisted having the training contract "dragged into the conflictual realm of wage disputes" (quote is from Kieslinger 1966: 23; see also Molitor 1960).

These conflicts overlapped and intersected with ongoing jurisdictional disputes (again, nothing new), this time between the Ministries of Economics and Labor, with business strongly supporting the continued jurisdiction of the Economics Ministry and unions siding with the more

[46] The idea being that the state could only intervene when business and its self-government institutions were not fulfilling their tasks satisfactorily (Lipsmeier 1998: 450).

[47] For a discussion of the positions taken by employers and unions in debates on vocational training, see Faulstich (1977: 108–43), Taylor (1981: 130–40), Kell (1970).

[48] As seen in Chapter 2, this is something never fully clarified in the Weimar years, though in the late 1920s court decisions specifically allowed apprentice compensation to be dealt with in collective bargaining – without, however, really mandating this. Under the Nazi regime, apprenticeship was defined as a pure educational relationship.

reform-oriented Labor Ministry (see, for example, Taylor 1981: 134–7).[49] In 1955 the latter made a bid to have the portfolio for vocational training shifted from the Economics to the Labor Ministry (Kieslinger 1966: 54). The proposal was vigorously resisted by the DIHT, however, and completely quashed by the Economics Ministry, at the time under the forceful leadership of Ludwig Erhard, who very much supported the status quo (Taylor 1981: 133, 137).[50] Erhard defended his Ministry's jurisdiction and warned against any legal initiatives that would "hamper the flexibility, adaptability, and humanity which characterised the present system and which were indispensable to vocational education in a constantly changing and developing economy" (Taylor 1981: 140).

What is in many ways as striking as the areas of conflict are the many areas of agreement, noticeable above all in what was *not* controversial. One feature that stands out, for example, is organized labor's continued support for the basic framework of the dual system, including the continuing strong plant-based component. Such consensus should not be taken for granted. The 1952 Ware report, for example, specifically criticized the German training system as overly grounded in an economic rather than an educational logic, noting that German business appeared to rely rather heavily on the "cheap" productive labor of apprentices and pointing out that "apprentices are really substantially workers and not pupils" (quote in Stratmann and Schlösser 1990: 64; Ware 1952: 45–47). Far from picking up on such critiques, however, German unions if anything joined with industry and Handwerk representatives in the rather spirited defense of the value of plant-based training, warning against an overly "bookish" approach to vocational education (*Verschulung*) (Stratmann and Schlösser 1990: Chapter 4; Abel 1968: 21–3, 33; Baethge 1970: 170–3; Crusius 1982: 91–3).[51]

To the limited extent that the Ware report was discussed at all, the discussion took place in an informal circle of experts convened initially by a Free Democratic MP, Dr. Paul Luchtenberg, that included educationalists,

[49] The Labor Ministry had jurisdiction over occupational counseling for youth and labor exchange functions including matching apprentices to apprentice slots, but responsibility for enterprise-based training lay with the Economics Ministry (Taylor 1981: 134).

[50] For the DIHT position, see Kieslinger (1950: 146–7).

[51] The unions were calling for changes, but their demands for a vocational training law and increased state oversight were pitched at the level of governance and regulation, not the core framework of plant-based training itself. As Crusius notes, unions may have held back from demands for more significant changes in the 1940s and early 1950s due to acute apprenticeship gaps. They only began pressing these points later when full employment was restored (Crusius 1982: 115).

entrepreneurs, union representatives, politicians, and others involved in vocational training.[52] This so-called Central Office for Research and Promotion of Vocational Education (*Zentralstelle zur Erforschung und Förderung der Berufserziehung*) – which met irregularly between 1951 and 1960 – provided a forum for a "non-binding" exchange of opinions among experts on vocational training from a wide range of organizations involved in this area (Abel 1968: 23, 27). At its second meeting (1953) the group considered the question "Is the system of vocational training grounded in the firm the appropriate form for Germany?" The two key speeches, by Herbert Studders of the National Confederation of German Industry (*Bundesverband der Deutschen Industrie*) and by Josef Leimig from the German Trade Union Confederation (*Deutscher Gewerkschaftsbund*, DGB), both answered in the affirmative. Speaking on behalf of the unions, Leimig underscored the importance of trade school classes and advocated an overall increase in compulsory attendance from eight to ten hours. However, he also, in no uncertain terms, embraced the strong plant orientation of German vocational training with the argument that this system was in line with the "mentality of Germans" (Stratmann and Schlösser 1990: 61–2).

Crusius explains organized labor's acceptance of many aspects of the German training system in part with reference to the background of the unions' post-war leadership. Leimig (and most other union functionaries having responsibilities in the area of vocational training) had a "traditional understanding" of the concept of a skilled vocation (*Beruf*) and of vocational training, in many cases having earned their own skill credentials within this system (Crusius 1982: 89). Leimig was active in the British zone during the occupation, working hand-in-hand with employers on an informal basis in the interests of re-activating plant-based apprenticeship training (Crusius 1982: 90). Thus, although the unions sought significant reforms in the regulatory structure of the vocational training system, they continued to support key aspects of the dual system – including and above all, the merits of in-plant training (Abel 1968: 33; Crusius 1982: 91–5; Baethge 1970: 170–3). As Leimig put it at a 1953 union conference on the subject, "After the war, the unions were actively engaged in rebuilding the system of vocational education. They have a very positive attitude toward vocational training.

[52] The managing director was Erwin Krause, head of the Office for Vocational Education of the German Industry and Trade Congress (*Arbeitsstelle für Berufserziehung des Deutschen Industrie- und Handelstages*). The number of members in the group grew over time from 16 to 40. On this whole episode, see especially Abel (1968: 23–4) and Stratmann and Schlösser (1990: 61–2), on which I draw here.

That is independent, however, of their often pointed criticism of how such training is carried out" (quoted in Crusius 1982: 92).[53]

Germany's unions did not seek a complete overhaul of the country's training system, and instead returned to demands they had first articulated in 1919, fixing their hopes on legislation to guarantee organized labor full parity rights within the system (Crusius 1982: 90). In the case of Handwerk, this position did not interfere with, and in some ways promoted, the reassignment of regulatory functions to the reconstituted Handwerk chambers. This is where unions saw more of a chance to exercise codetermination rights (Crusius 1982: 110). Beyond Handwerk, unions were very much oriented toward large firms, and – in the early 1950s – were deeply involved with an effort to secure codetermination rights in the coal and steel industries (1951) and with the debates surrounding the Works Constitution Act of 1952. The unions placed their bets on national legislation that would guarantee them full codetermination rights in vocational training as well, and while they waited and lobbied for such overarching legislation, the system of in-plant training under chamber auspices was simply rebuilt.

Even if the unions had been mobilized around this issue – which they were not[54] – the political climate in the 1950s was not auspicious for the chances of full codetermination rights for labor in vocational training at the national level. The conservative government was singularly unreceptive to the idea of significant change in training policy. Adenauer was not inclined to undertake any major reforms and certainly not in the direction of increased government involvement. In his first government statement of September 1949 the new chancellor commented on the decline in technical training under the Nazis and asserted that the traditional strength of the German economy was due to the skills of the German worker (Crusius 1982: 117).

Thus, the policies of the conservative government of the 1950s endorsed, consolidated, and confirmed the principle of employer self-governance

[53] A 1961 statement by the Handwerk committee of the metalworkers union (*IG Metall*) similarly makes a number of suggestions for improving Handwerk training, but all are completely within the logic of the existing system – calling, for example, for greater cooperation between the Handwerk chambers, the unions, the trade schools and other parties, and arguing against Handwerk's proposals to increase the training periods for apprentices to make up for time lost because of the compliance of firms with the new Youth Protection Law (Pätzold 1991: 106).

[54] As Crusius emphasizes, vocational training in particular was not a major focal point for the unions in the early postwar years. The subject did not come up at all at the DGB's founding congress in 1949 (Crusius 1982: 90, 95).

in vocational training, assigning responsibility for oversight and administration of apprenticeship to the employer chambers. It amended this, however, to mandate employee representation and participation in chamber deliberations and decision making on these issues. The legislation of this period defined the activities of the chambers in vocational training as "public" and official and therefore subject to some state supervision, to the extent that training ordinances were given the force of law when recognized by the relevant minister (Richter 1968: 29; Engel and Rosenthal 1970: 4).[55] Key legislation of this period included the 1953 Handicraft Law (*Handwerksordnung*, or HwO, amended 1965) and the 1956 Law for the Provisional Regulation of the Rights of the Industry and Trade Chambers (*Gesetz zur vorläufigen Regelung des Rechts der Industrie- und Handelskammern*, IHKG). In both cases, the chambers were defined as the "competent authorities" in the area of vocational training, though operating under some state supervision and with a mandate to allow employee participation.

The HwO of 1953 re-established explicit legal foundations for the existence of the handicraft chambers and their role in administering and overseeing training in the handicraft sector.[56] The law recognized regional chambers of artisans (spanning all handicraft trades in a region) as public law institutions with compulsory membership, in addition to 65 trade-specific guild associations (also public law institutions, and subject to legal control by the chambers) (Streeck 1992a: 116–20).[57] The chambers fulfilled the full range of responsibilities with respect to training – establishing occupational profiles and training guidelines for handicraft trades, monitoring training in handicraft firms, and overseeing the examination and certification of journeymen and master craftsmen.[58] Handwerk chambers also assumed responsibility for keeping training lists and registering apprentice contracts, important roles in monitoring firm-based training.

[55] On certification procedures see Walle (1963: 220–2), *Berufsausbildung* (1958: 11–13).

[56] The most important excerpts can be found in Pätzold (1991: 42–52).

[57] Membership in the latter, however, is voluntary rather than compulsory, a fact made necessary by the country's constitution (Basic Law) in order that they be able to negotiate with unions.

[58] As noted above, training regulations were made official through a ministerial decree and national-level coordination was accomplished through the German Association of Chambers of Artisans (*Deutscher Handwerkskammertag*, or DHKT) (Engel and Rosenthal 1970: 74).

On the issue of employee participation, the HwO stipulated that one-third of the members of the general assembly, the executive board, and the committees of a chamber must be elected delegates of journeymen (Walle 1963: 212).[59] In the case of the vocational training committee, the requirements for employee representation were higher, calling for an equal number of representatives of employers and journeymen. Seats were also assigned to vocational school teachers appointed by the government (Streeck 1992a: 122). Guilds were required to institutionalize employee participation through the establishment of a separate committee for journeymen whose members "participate in deliberations of the executive board on subjects related to training," and whose approval was required for any action in this area (quote from Streeck 1992a: 122; Walle 1963: 210–13; Engel and Rosenthal 1970: 98; Abel 1968: 33). These provisions fell substantially short of union demands – state supervision being minimal and employee participation rights very limited – but Crusius argues that the unions did not push very hard for codetermination in this sector in part in exchange for Handwerk's acceptance of the unions' campaigns (in 1951 and 1952) for codetermination in the coal and steel industries and for legislation on works councils (Crusius 1982: 110).

The HwO was amended in 1965, when concerns about the quality of Handwerk training were brought to public attention through a series of reports published in the magazine *Stern* in 1963 and 1964. These reports were deeply unflattering to Handwerk, exposing cases of poor training and exploitation of youth as cheap laborers (Taylor 1981: 195–6). The amended law strengthened state oversight, making it possible for supervisory authorities to revoke a firm's right to train if an inspection of conditions in the plant revealed inadequacies. The new law also required a pedagogic component in the *Meister* exam (for advancement to the status of master craftsman). The idea was to ensure that those achieving the master certificate commanded not just technical expertise, but also basic pedagogic skills before being allowed to take apprentices (Engel and Rosenthal 1970: 98–9). However, the basic structure of chamber-based administration and oversight was left in place.

In 1956 the chambers of industry and commerce officially regained their status as institutions under public law and were also accorded explicit

[59] The terms under which artisanal organizations (HWK and *Innungen*) perform their duties in the area of vocational training, including journeyman representation, as of 1960, are laid out in Raspe (1960).

recognition and legal grounding for the administration and supervision of vocational training in industry (Hoffmann 1962: 152; Walle 1963: 208–10). The 1956 *Gesetz zur vorläufigen Regelung des Rechts der Industrie- und Handelskammern* (IHKG) put the industry and trade chambers in charge of keeping the apprentice rolls (an important control instrument) (Engel and Rosenthal 1970: 97), and the chambers assumed responsibility for working out training ordinances and regulations governing the various industrial trades, which were given the force of law through the Ministry of Economics (Engel and Rosenthal 1970: 74).[60] The chambers were also charged with monitoring plant-based training and making decisions about the suitability of particular firms to train apprentices.

As regards employee participation, the IHKG called for the establishment of a special committee for vocational training to be set up within the chambers with 50-50 representation for employers and employees (plus an employer representative as chair), and endowed with advisory functions on matters pertaining to enterprise training (Ipsen 1967: 80; Walle 1963: 209–10). As this was the only committee required by the IHKG, it is also the only place where employee participation rights were required by law within the system of business self-government (Walle 1963: 210–13; Engel and Rosenthal 1970: 98; Abel 1968: 33). Exam committees in chambers of industry and commerce were to be composed of two employer representatives, one representative of vocational teachers, and one employee representative (Engel and Rosenthal 1970: 98).[61]

In short, the reconstruction period saw some, but really very minimal, revisions to the system. What was not accomplished was the comprehensive vocational training law that unions sought, nor did unions achieve the codetermination rights they demanded. The two key pieces of legislation in this period mandated employee representation (but not codetermination) and within the context of the associations of employer self-governance (rather than under the auspices of an overarching national legislative framework).[62]

[60] The law appears in Pätzold (1991: 172–4).

[61] In the crafts, it was a committee head, one staff member of a vocational school, one independent craftsman, and one journeyman (Engel and Rosenthal 1970: 98).

[62] On the issue of whether apprentice contracts would be considered primarily as educational or as work contracts, there were mixed results (Molitor 1960: 31–48). The HwO was vague on this point, an omission that the Handwerk sector sought to exploit by continuing to deal with the question of pay at the level of the chambers – to the chagrin of some contemporary observers (Molitor 1960: 36). The IHKG, by contrast, was clear on this point and specifically denied the chambers of industry and trade the right to represent the political interests of apprentices or to directly regulate their material interests (Molitor 1960: 34, 48).

The 1969 Vocational Training Act

The legal framework for vocational training remained a point of contention after the 1953 and 1956 legislation on chambers, and an issue that the Trade Union Confederation (DGB) pursued in 1959, producing and circulating its own proposal for a new vocational training law. The main motives were familiar – to provide a unified legal basis and enhanced oversight by the state, and to ensure full codetermination rights to the trade unions (Taylor 1981: 183). The organizations of business self-governance were not mentioned at all in the draft; rather, all of the relevant administrative, regulatory, and supervisory functions were to be put under the auspices of a federal committee for vocational training, supported by state-level and local committees in charge of implementation. In the DGB proposal the entire system was to be put under the jurisdiction of the Labor Ministry (Walle 1963: 287–92; 336–43).

These proposals were met with skepticism and opposition. Handwerk insisted that the codetermination rights that the unions sought were already covered through the participation of journeymen in both the chambers and guilds. In defending a system of self-governance against DGB demands for greater state and union involvement, Handwerk representatives invoked invidious comparisons to the state-dominated systems of training under the Nazis, and the ones in place in East Germany (Rohlfing 1949: 26; Walle 1963: 259, 261).[63] Handwerk denounced the idea of increased state involvement in vocational training as "questionable and dangerous" (Walle 1963: 376).

Industrial employers and their chambers also argued that the provisions in the IHKG for an employee voice in vocational training issues were already sufficient. DIHT and its affiliates worried less than craft employers about the sheer costs of training but were adamant about protecting their managerial autonomy. Defense of employer self-government was couched mostly in terms of minimizing stifling bureaucratic procedures that would interfere with the system's proven flexibility and adaptability (Adam 1979: 163, 170). Employer representatives repeatedly pointed out how many workers had been trained in both the industrial and handicraft sectors at absolutely no cost to taxpayers, and that German business was training more apprentices on a voluntary basis than companies in any other

[63] This argument, at least in the version elaborated by Walle, includes repeated references to bureaucratization and increased rigidity through *Gleichschaltung* – a highly charged term in Germany if there ever was one (Walle 1963: 377).

country (Walle 1963: 376–7).[64] Despite slightly different motives, industry and Handwerk were unified in their opposition to greater state involvement, and in 1958 the Chambers of Industry and of Handwerk issued a joint declaration insisting that there be "no experiments in vocational training" (Abel 1968: 32).

What kept the issue alive in the 1960s, despite the unreceptiveness of the conservative government, was partly pressure from the SPD and perhaps also the *Stern* reports that continued to keep a spotlight (still dim in this period, however) on the deficits of the vocational training system. The window for reform opened in 1966 when the SPD joined the government for the first time in the postwar period, as part of a "Grand Coalition" with the Christian Democratic Union (CDU). The SPD made its own formal proposal for a vocational training law, which forced the CDU to respond in kind (Lipsmeier 1998: 449) and set in motion a legislative process that would culminate in a new framing law, the 1969 Vocational Training Law (*Berufsbildungsgesetz*. BBiG). This was a compromise that gave the unions the unified national framing legislation they sought[65] but left a great deal of the previous framework for vocational training intact.

Specifically,[66] the 1969 Vocational Training Law provided for *national* regulation and oversight through the governing board of a newly created Federal Institute for Vocational Training Research (*Bundesinstitut für Berufsbildungsforschung* or BBF).[67] This board was to be composed of six representatives each from the unions and from the employers' associations, five representatives of states (*Länder*), three vocational education specialists and one representative from the institute itself, and was charged with advising the federal government on all issues relating to vocational training. The BBF took over the overarching regulatory functions previously handled by the chambers – the definition of training standards and the preparation of

[64] The claims about costs were somewhat exaggerated, since the state subsidizes vocational training through its support of the mandatory public vocational schools.

[65] In this sense and as Stratmann points out, many elements of the unions' demands from the 1919 Nürnberg congress ultimately made their way into the legislation of 1969 (Stratmann 1990: 40).

[66] This is drawn from Ralf and Schlösser (1994: 112–13). But see also Faulstich (1977: 171–4), Helfert (1970b), or Taylor (1981: 210–13) for a summary of the structure of control and oversight over vocational training after the 1969 law.

[67] Subsequent legislation in 1976 converted this into the current Federal Institute for Vocational Training (*Bundesinstitut für Berufsbildung*, or BIBB).

official regulations and curricula (establishing the skill content and length of apprenticeship for particular occupations) – and made recommendations to the relevant ministries which officially issue the directives that govern training (Bildungsforschung 1979: 245; Streeck et al. 1987: 13).[68] At the *state* level, the law provides for the establishment of vocational training committees composed of equal numbers of representatives from employers, unions, and the state government. These committees are charged with coordinating between the school and in-plant components of training, and collaborating with the other states to ensure uniformity nationwide.

Even under this new regulatory framework, however, some of the most important functions in the supervision and monitoring of firm-based training are still accomplished through the chambers. Thus, at the *district* level, the law calls for the regulation of vocational training – for example, supervision of training and administration of exams – through special committees within the relevant chambers (HWK, IHK). The new law set the composition of the committees at six each for employers and employees. Six representatives of vocational schools sit on these committees, but in an advisory role only. The committees have to be consulted on regulations concerning all aspects of in-plant training, although any policy changes that affect the costs of training have to be ratified by the general assembly of the chamber (where, in industry, unions are not represented).[69] In addition, the chambers (alone) continue to perform many key monitoring functions, including deciding on the suitability of particular firms to provide training and considering applications from firms to extend or reduce training times for particular apprentices (Streeck et al. 1987: 28).

Regarding the issue of portfolios and ministerial jurisdiction, a complicated inter-ministerial compromise was worked out in which the Economics Ministry remained in charge of approving training ordinances, but its work

[68] The ABB was formally disbanded in 1971, after its functions had been assumed by the BBF under the terms of the 1969 law. Subsequent legislation (in 1976) transferred all these responsibilities to the current Federal Institute for Vocational Training (*Bundesinstitut für Berufsbildung*, or BIBB) (Bunk 1979: 103; Pätzold 1991: 8; Berufsausbildung 1958).

[69] In the IHK there is no labor representation at all in the general assembly, in handicraft chambers a third of the seats are still reserved for journeymen. Craft training remained under the jurisdiction of the HWK. By last minute intervention by the CDU/CSU, Handwerk training was regulated a bit differently (Adam 1979: 174) and basically the relevant sections of the HwO were carried over and adapted to the third part of the law (Engel and Rosenthal 1970: 101; Taylor 1981: 295).

relied on cooperation with the Labor Ministry.[70] Further training (that is, beyond initial apprenticeship) was put under the Labor Ministry but relying on the Economics Ministry's consent. The Labor Ministry was given responsibility for coordinating vocational training matters across ministries and it also acts as the monitoring agency for the new Federal Institute for Vocational Education Research (Engel and Rosenthal 1970: 100–3). A few years later (1972), all these responsibilities were put under the jurisdiction of the Federal Ministry for Science and Research (*Bundesministerium für Wissenschaft und Forschung*).

The 1969 BBiG clearly represented some important changes. Before the law was passed, training was solely the province of the chambers (IHK and HWK) and therefore governed through chamber ordinances (*Kammerrecht*). An essential element of the reform was to take exclusive control out of the hands of the chambers and vest it instead in the supervisory committees described above (with parity representation for unions). The 1969 law thus brought greater unity to the previously disparate legal framework governing apprentice training, and gave unions a stronger voice in the overarching regulatory functions surrounding the definition and elaboration of training regulations and occupational certifications.[71]

Significant as these changes were, they should not obscure the high degree of continuity in the apparatus for the day-to-day regulation and monitoring of firm-based training. Crucial administrative and supervisory functions are still performed by the chambers, which continue to be the key interface between the federally established guidelines and the training firms themselves. Although unions enjoy representation rights in the chamber committees on vocational training, there are limits to the role they play there – through the provisions that require policy changes affecting financing to come before the chambers' full assembly (effectively, an employer veto point since unions have no representation there), and through the chambers' sole and autonomous rights to monitor in-plant training and to approve as competent firms that wish to train. As Crouch, Finegold, and

[70] The sharing of responsibilities worked out between the Economics and Labor Ministries is extremely complicated. It is explicated in Engel and Rosenthal (1970: 101, fn. 168).

[71] The role of the unions in the new system is by far more important than that of the state, with the latter operating more as a rubber stamp. As Streeck and colleagues point out, the "federal government makes the overwhelming majority of decisions on vocational training only after the union and employer representatives in the committees of the BIBB have given their consent" (Streeck et al. 1987: 13; see also Engel and Rosenthal 1970: 13).

Sako point out, trade unions in Germany continue to have a rather "limited formal role," and to the extent that they can exercise influence, it is informally and through works councils who can "maintain their own watch on the quality of training being provided by a firm" (Crouch, Finegold, and Sako 1999: 144).[72]

The 1969 legislation introduced important innovations – above all in the national-level regulatory superstructure for vocational training. As Taylor points out, however, "by locating the most crucial of all functions in an employer organisation, the chamber of trade . . . the Federal Parliament had confirmed its faith in the Wirtschaft's ability successfully to control vocational training for the benefit of the nation in the future" (Taylor 1981: 213; see also Helfert 1970a: 153; Lipsmeier 1998: 450–1). In light of the significant retained powers of the chambers, it comes as little surprise that the DIHT – despite expressed regrets over the "complicated" ministerial arrangements and the new layers of bureaucracy and committees – was nonetheless able to see in this legislation a codification of "the structure and the order of the [existing] system, both of which are the result of decades of responsible and flexible work on the part of business and its chambers, and both developed in the law-free space [*gesetzesfreien Raum*] of business self-governance" (DIHT 1970: 96).

Organized labor regretted and protested loudly against their limited codetermination rights (especially at the chamber level), blaming the particular coalition (CDU/SPD) that presided over the passage of the law. However, the outcome at some level also reflected the fact that the unions had consistently articulated their goals in a way that confirmed and built around (rather than called into question) many of the foundational features of the existing system, not least the continued clear subordination of school-based to plant-based vocational training. Baethge emphasizes the deeply "pragmatic" nature of union goals in the area of vocational training. He wonders, even if the unions achieved more of their goals, if this would do anything more than "minimize the crassest excesses" of the existing system – a contribution, clearly, but hardly a radical alternative to it (Baethge 1970: 170–2; see also Helfert 1970a: 154).

[72] Some of this was covered in the 1972 Works Constitution Act, and the new (2001) Works Constitution Act provides additional levers (see discussion below). As Schömann points out, however, works councils have only information and consultative rights, and the extent to which this translates into real influence depends very much on the initiative and strength of the plant labor representatives (Schömann 2001: 17).

Developments after 1969

The debates over vocational training did not end with the 1969 legislation. When the Social Democrats took office in 1969 as senior coalition partner with the Free Democratic Party (F.D.P.) new discussions ensued.[73] The government of Willy Brandt focused on a number of education issues. Among the goals was a concern to integrate vocational and general education in order to equalize opportunities for working class youth. Many proposals had to do with relaxing the barriers among the three primary school tracks in Germany that had long operated to reinforce socio-economic and class cleavages.[74]

Other proposals returned directly to issues dealt with in the 1969 Vocational Education Act, addressing again the control issues that continued to preoccupy the unions. These issues were of interest to a Social Democratic government concerned with democratic accountability and equality of opportunity. In the early 1970s a highly activist and reform-oriented Minister of Science and Education, Klaus von Dohnanyi, was floating proposals that represented a very significant threat to chamber self-governance and would have increased substantially the role of the state.[75] These proposals were furiously resisted by representatives of employers' associations and their member firms, the latter threatening to cease training entirely (Taylor 1981: 281–2; see also Stratmann 1999: 419; Crusius 1982: 285). Such threats carried a great deal of weight, particularly as the debate unfolded in the context of the first oil crisis and ensuing recession, when apprenticeship slots were hard to come by and youth unemployment was on the rise. The business community rallied against all changes that interfered with managerial prerogative and employer self-governance, and the opposition CDU/CSU provided political backing. The latter argued that "in times of economic growth and full employment we can talk about all sorts of reforms" but a period of economic crisis was no time for experimentation (Görs 1976: 353, quoting from *Frankfurter Rundschau*).

73 This account of the reform initiatives (and their fate) under the Social Democratic governments of the 1970s relies on Taylor (1981: Chapters 10 and especially 11).

74 For example, many proposals in this period sought to reform the three separate tracks of Hauptschule, Realschule, and Gymnasium, either to eliminate the tracks entirely or to build bridges across them (*zweiter Bildungsweg*, for example).

75 Dohnanyi was Minister from 1972–1974. The idea was for state governments to assume jurisdiction over all aspects of vocational education, including the control and administration of in-plant training, accreditation and control of training premises, preparation of training curricula, and administration of exams (Taylor 1981: 255).

The combination of economic turmoil and employer opposition was sufficient to put the entire debate on hold, and the prospect for significant structural reform was subsequently brought to an end in 1974. Along with continued economic turbulence, that year brought a change of government, and both the new Social Democratic chancellor (the pragmatic Helmut Schmidt) and his liberal (F.D.P.) economics minister Hans Friderichs (1972–1977) opposed any reforms that might interfere with economic recovery. Dohnanyi apparently saw the handwriting on the wall and when he tendered his resignation (only two years after having taken office) Schmidt "showed little regret" (Taylor 1981: 265). Dohnanyi's successor in the Science Ministry, Helmut Rhode (1974–1978), specifically distanced himself from any significant reform agenda, promising instead to pursue more modest goals ('*kleinere Brötchen backen*') (Crusius 1982: 284–5).

More modest indeed, and mostly within the structure and logic of the traditional system. The economic crisis had not only quashed all prospects of significant structural reform; the problem of youth unemployment shifted the focus of the debate completely – toward measures aimed at *extending* the system by increasing the number of training slots. The Apprenticeship Promotion Act of 1976 (*Ausbildungsplatzförderungsgesetz*) was mainly concerned with the problem of an insufficient number of apprentice slots in the face of rising demand due to demographic trends. Among other things, the law established a National Institute for Vocational Education (*Bundesinstitut für Berufsbildung*, BIBB, replacing the BBF), which was charged with producing an annual "Vocational Training Report" (*Berufsbildungsbericht*) with statistics on national trends in apprenticeship and apprentice training.[76]

What is significant is that the control issues and conflicts over chamber-based administration and supervision that had dominated previous debates were now completely eclipsed. The late 1970s and the 1980s turned out to be years in which tensions in the vocational training system (mostly precipitated by economic and demographic trends) were effectively regulated within the existing institutions of corporatist self-regulation. Probably the most controversial feature of the 1976 law was a provision that would allow the government to impose a training levy on firms if the supply of apprentice slots (nationwide) did not exceed the number of applicants by at least 12.5% (Baethge 1999: 4; see also Taylor 1981: 271, 274–5).[77] These financing

[76] The BIBB has a number of other functions; it was charged, for example, with improving coordination between in-plant training schedules and vocational school curricula.

[77] An overhang was deemed necessary to ensure apprentices a choice of trades.

provisions were strongly opposed by business and the law was struck down by the Supreme Court in 1980 (on grounds that the *Bundesrat* also needed to pass on the legislation (see Taylor 1981: 269–74). The 1981 law that replaced it no longer contained the controversial financing provision.

More important and more telling than the public debates, after 1975 employers undertook strong efforts on their own initiative to keep the levy issue at bay.[78] In an act of supreme coordination and power on the part of firms and especially their employers' associations, industry orchestrated a *voluntary* increase in the number of apprentice slots offered.[79] As Baethge notes, "All training areas increased the number of training spots offered (measured in the number of training contracts signed) continuously and significantly" in the decade between 1976 and 1986, with industry alone increasing its apprentice slots by 62%, from 81,734 (in 1975) to 132,560 (in 1985) (Baethge 1999: 4). Clearly employers opposed the idea of levies, but as Baethge notes, labor leaders, too, were very sensitive to arguments that levies might be counterproductive and could bring perverse effects – for example, if training firms reduced apprentice slots in anticipation (Baethge 1999: 6).[80]

The 1980s saw continued adaptation of the *content* of vocational training to changing economic conditions based on a high degree of cooperation between unions and employers. A good example of this is the complete revamping of the occupational profiles of the entire metalworking industry by the union and employers, accomplished in 1984 in a completely consensual manner despite the fact that this took place against the backdrop of the biggest strike in that industry in the postwar period (Streeck et al.

[78] The exception that proves the rule is the construction industry (see Streeck 1983: 46–53, on which this is based). In this case, the employers' association – together with the union – responded to a particularly serious training crisis in the early 1970s by negotiating a collective agreement (later declared universally binding for the industry as a whole by the government) that imposed a training levy on all firms in the sector. This solution was specifically embraced and sold politically as an alternative to the state levy being deliberated at that time. Both union and employers devised and defended the collectively bargained levy as a sign of continuing "joint responsibility" and as fully in line with the subsidiarity principle traditionally invoked to keep the state out (Streeck 1983: 57; also Soskice 1994: 35).

[79] My account here draws on Baethge (1999).

[80] The prospect of a levy has been raised several times since then, and in fact the current Red-Green coalition is considering such a measure again. The idea is controversial within the S.P.D., however, and even its advocates (including Chancellor Schröder) would still prefer a private-sector solution if possible (*Der Spiegel*, May 5, 2003: especially 105–6; *Welt am Sonntag*, February 15, 2004: 1; *Süddeutsche Zeitung*, February 14–15, 2004: 1).

1987: 3–4).[81] As Streeck and his colleagues note, the sometimes conflictual rhetoric should not obscure the deep commitment of both employers and unions to the vocational training system at that time:

> trade unions and employers are far apart when it comes to the question of how training should be financed and to what extent individual employers providing training should be subject to external supervision.... But the public debate hides the fact that neither side doubts the principle that each school leaver should have access to high quality vocational training, and that training profiles should be continually upgraded and modernized. While both sides find the existing system wanting in important respects, neither finds it wanting enough to be willing to let it fall into disuse or decay. (Streeck et al. 1987: 4)

Since the 1970s, corporatist self-regulation and collaborative social partnership have helped to shore up the German system of in-plant training even (and especially) in periods of economic turmoil and recession. Economic trends might bring problems but at such points several stabilizing mechanisms traditionally kick in. The following paragraphs consider how a number of such mechanisms have operated in the past. This discussion serves as the backdrop for a subsequent consideration – in the final section of this chapter – of the extent to which contemporary trends pose new challenges that make previous forms of adaptation more difficult.

One important stabilizing mechanism in the German vocational training system has been the division of labor between large and small firms. As we saw in Chapter 2, small firms (especially Handwerk firms) traditionally had very different reasons to train than large firms, and this remains the case today. Large firms can justify significant training expenditures because they expect to continue to employ a large number of the apprentices they train. Small firms do not necessarily keep their trainees on after the apprenticeship. Because of the very different structure of training, however, especially

[81] The reorganization reduced the number of recognized trades dramatically, to produce overall more multifaceted occupations of the sort increasingly called for to deal with new production methods. These developments are just one example of a more overarching pattern of ongoing incremental changes, mostly negotiated by the social partners, to adapt the system to ongoing changes in the technological and market environment. As Crouch, Finegold, and Sako note, "In the 1950s a total of 900 occupations had formal VET [vocational education and training] preparations. By 1970 this had been reduced to 500.... By 1992 it was down to 377, including the addition of new occupations in services and high-tech sectors" (Crouch, Finegold, and Sako 1999: 144). As they also note, most such revisions and combinations of previously separate trades were undertaken in the interests of overall broader and more "polyvalent" skills, so that workers could be deployed more flexibly in new production arrangements, group work, and the like.

in Handwerk firms (being accomplished on the job and mostly during production lulls), the costs of training have in the past been very small, and often negative, since these firms benefit from the availability of a flexible extra hand in production (Wagner 1997; see also Soskice 1994; Bellmann and Neubäumer 2001: 191–2; Alewell and Richter 2001; Wagner 1999).[82] For these reasons, as Crouch and colleagues point out, even if large firms cut back on apprenticeship in periods of economic downturn, Handwerk firms have traditionally been able to pick up the slack (Crouch, Finegold, and Sako 1999: 142).

A second mechanism that has traditionally stabilized apprenticeship is the system for cost sharing in which apprentices bear some of the costs of training with training firms (see the theoretical discussion in Chapter 1).[83] Although unions in Germany negotiate for apprentices they accept that such wages must be kept low in order to encourage continuing training (Crouch, Finegold, and Sako 1999: 142; Soskice 1991; Streeck et al. 1987: 23). Soskice notes that the wages of unskilled workers in Germany are three to four times higher than apprentice wages (Soskice 1994: 35, 41). Apprentices agree to defer gratification with respect to income during the apprentice period so long as such training continues to serve as a ticket to success in the labor market generally, as an entry point to higher-paid and more secure employment (Soskice 1994: 35, 41, 53–5). Such has traditionally been the case for apprentices, and especially for apprenticeships served in large and dynamic firms. Drawing on a 1985 sample, Soskice found that large firms retained a very high proportion of the apprentices they trained, between 80 and 90% (and for firms employing more than a thousand workers, 87%) (Soskice 1994: 35, 37). This sets in motion a healthy, virtuous cycle of competition among firms for the most attractive apprentices, which encourages young people to do their best in school (Soskice 1994: 54–5).

Finally, and not least, the system of corporatism and strong associations, compulsory chambers and also voluntary trade and employer associations, has traditionally served as a crucial stabilizing mechanism. As the example

[82] The *Bundesinstitut für Berufsbildung* occasionally conducts surveys to determine the costs of training, including differences in net training costs in Handwerk and industry and by firm size and other variables (see, for example Noll et al. 1983: iv–v). Soskice argues that these statistical analyses are likely to overstate the costs of training for small firms. The calculations on which the statistics are based are accurate for larger companies, but for small ones they systematically overestimate the costs and underestimate the returns of apprenticeship (Soskice 1994: 52; see also Richter 2000: 236–7).

[83] As does the state, through its funding of public vocational schools.

by Baethge noted above vividly demonstrates, Germany's strong employer associations have traditionally played a very important role in overcoming collective action problems and allowing German employers as a whole to achieve joint gains through coordination rather than pursuit of narrow individual interest (see especially Culpepper 2003; Culpepper 2002). The system of employers associations has had an enormously important function in counteracting tendencies by individual firms to deal with recession by cutting back on training (Streeck 1988: 22, 30; Streeck 1989). Employers' associations accomplish this end by educating, admonishing, and cajoling member firms. As Streeck and colleagues point out, however, beyond pressure and persuasion, self-monitoring through employer associations has helped stabilize the system by adjusting standards and treating training firms with a degree of leniency in periods of economic turbulence. Unions complain but chamber oversight and monitoring is important because "particularly in times when apprenticeships are in short supply, it may be prudent in some firms not to enforce training regulations to the letter" (Streeck et al. 1987: 31). More generally, and as Soskice has noted, firms are more willing to submit to monitoring by employer chambers than by the state (Soskice 1994: 42).

Contemporary Developments in the German Training System: Erosion through Drift?

Since the 1990s, the situation has shifted somewhat and in ways that pose new challenges that previous regulatory mechanisms so far have been unable to counteract, at least not entirely.[84] A number of the problems plaguing the system today can be traced back to long-term trends, many related to the intensified competitive pressures German firms face in the high-end markets they long dominated. It used to be that German firms could charge a price premium because of their reputation for high quality, but this is no longer true and as a result German firms have had to become more cost-conscious (Finegold and Wagner 1997: 213; Wagner 1999). This problem is related to technological changes that involve ongoing rapid innovation both in products and production methods (Finegold and Wagner 1997;

[84] For a very useful and comprehensive analysis of the current situation see especially Culpepper (2003; 1999; also Green and Sakamoto 2001: 80–5). Culpepper's analyses paint a guardedly optimistic picture (on balance, perhaps, more optimistic than mine), also acknowledging, however, the problematic trends cited below. See also Brown, Green, and Lauder (2001: 148–51) for a discussion of contemporary problems.

Herrigel 1996a; Pichler 1993), and has been accompanied by a continuing shift away from manufacturing toward the growing importance of the service sector (Culpepper 1999). The effects of these long-term trends have also been greatly exacerbated in Germany by the "unification shock" (Schluchter and Quink 2001) that generated a huge set of problems for the traditional vocational training system (Brown, Green, and Lauder 2001: 80–5; also, especially Culpepper 2003).

Some of these developments – for instance, accelerated technological change and production reorganization – play into longstanding "gaps" in the German vocational training system. Herrigel and others have argued that the German system produces skilled workers whose qualifications and identities are rooted in traditional and rigid occupational categories that have prevented German manufacturing from embracing and adapting to new innovations and new, more flexible, manufacturing techniques (Herrigel and Sabel 1999). This, they argue, accounts for Germany's new vulnerability to high quality Japanese competitors (Herrigel 1996a). Finegold and Wagner's comparative research (pump manufacturers) provides some support for this thesis, finding that in Germany "the lower the proportion of skilled workers, the more likely the organization was to adopt a team-based structure," and noting that skilled workers in some cases resisted the introduction of multifunctional teams that clashed with a skill system organized around individual (not group-based) skill acquisition (Finegold and Wagner 1997: especially 221–2).[85]

A second, longstanding weakness in the German system is the relative underdevelopment of *continuing* vocational education and training, a weakness that contrasts sharply with the very elaborate and highly articulated framework for supervision, oversight, and certification of *initial* training (Crouch, Finegold, and Sako 1999: 145–7; Backes-Gellner 1995; Crouch 1998; Soskice 2003: 12–13). Not only do German firms overall do less continuing training,[86] the system for ongoing skill acquisition is

[85] However, Finegold and Wagner draw a conclusion different from that of Herrigel, with Herrigel arguing that Germany needs to move away from the traditional apprentice system and Finegold and Wagner arguing that adjustment will require building on the system's traditional strengths and "making greater use of the broad base of skills" it provides (Finegold and Wagner 1997: 229–30).

[86] A comparative study of training in Britain, France, and Germany (focusing on the metalworking industry, conducted in 1992) found that German firms were more heavily involved in initial apprentice training than French and British firms, but lagged behind the other two in continuing training (Backes-Gellner 1995: 15).

mostly laissez faire and very much up to the individual firms to construct and manage as they like. Most of it is firm-specific (Crouch, Finegold, and Sako 1999: 146), and when certificates are devised and awarded it is not clear what they mean (Sauter 1996: 126). The relative underdevelopment of continuing vocational training is not a new problem, but the effects of this deficit may be magnified in the current period. Particularly in rapidly evolving sectors such as information technologies and related industries, ongoing skill development is simply essential to keep pace with production technologies. "Initial vocational training alone is no longer a guarantee of job security, of remaining qualified in one's occupation or profession, or of developing one's abilities. Initial vocational training is becoming the prerequisite for successful continuing training" (Sauter 1996: 113).

Exacerbating these problems is increased international competition and long-term economic stagnation in Germany. A growing number of firms have become extremely cost conscious, leading to an overall reduction in training (Crouch, Finegold, and Sako 1999: 143; Wagner 1999). Since the mid-1980s the supply of apprentice slots in Western Germany has slumped (with the exception of 1989 and 1990). The high point (in 1984) was 726,786, dropping to a low (in 1996) of 483,165, before recovering slightly by 1998 to 506,499. Overall, the period between 1980 and 1998 saw a net reduction of apprentice slots by 27% (Alewell and Richter 2001: 144–5, 172 contain the relevant figures and tables). Although many authors emphasize that there is still an overall balance in the supply of apprentice slots and demand for them,[87] the new equilibrium has settled at a decidedly lower level. Leaving aside Eastern Germany (where the situation is much more critical), West German firms are offering a hundred thousand fewer apprentice places than they did 20 years ago, and two hundred thousand fewer than they did a decade ago (Culpepper 1999: 49).

Large firms traditionally trained because they expected to keep the great majority of the apprentices they took, making it economically rational for them to make the investment in the first place (Soskice 1994). Now, however, large firms are if anything looking to shrink their workforces, with implications for both their overall training effort and their record for retention. Longitudinal data are needed here, but if we compare Soskice's retention

[87] Alewell and Richter (2001) and Culpepper (1999) both emphasize this point. A part of my argument is that apprenticeship may be becoming less attractive to youth (see below), and thus a decline in both supply and demand would be relevant to the argument I am constructing here.

figures based on 1985 data with more recent (1998) data, we find that the retention rate of large firms, although still high, is significantly lower than before. Whereas Soskice's 1985 data suggest an average retention rate of 87% among large (over a thousand employees) firms (Soskice 1994: 37), Bellmann and Neubäumer's 1998 survey data reveal an average retention rate for firms with over two thousand employees of 77.5%, and for firms with a thousand to two thousand employees of just 71.3% (Bellmann and Neubäumer 2001: 198). Maybe more tellingly, Bellmann and Neubäumer record an increase in the propensity of firms to hire former apprentices on a limited-contract (*befristete*) basis (Bellmann and Neubäumer 2001: 200). This is probably related to some recent collective bargains that require firms to continue to employ apprentices after completion of their training (see, especially, Bispinck et al.). But even if so, the short-term nature of the contracts and the motives (collective contracts and union pressure) may be as much an indication of a breakdown of traditional self-regulatory mechanisms as their continued healthy functioning.

Reductions in the number of apprentices taken by large firms in the face of economic downturn is perfectly in line with past patterns. The difference is, however, that previous regulatory mechanisms are not "kicking in." Wagner (1999) has argued that the German system was "finely balanced" until 1991, with smaller firms at around the break-even point on the cost of apprenticeship, and larger firms having other reasons to think that the costs of training were equal to or outweighed by the benefits. She documents a number of trends that have led to overall higher costs and therefore threaten to upset that balance, not only increased costs due to reduced working times and increased apprentice wages, but also costs associated with upgrading and broadening apprenticeship training in recent years.[88] Cost considerations have arguably become more important than ever to small and medium-sized industrial producers in key industries such as metalworking, where recent collective bargains have produced wage deals that large firms can tolerate but that small and medium-sized firms are finding they cannot afford.[89]

[88] For instance, the reorganization of the metalworking occupations means that companies have to devote one and a half years to general training, which cuts into the contribution of apprentices to production in smaller firms. In addition, there has been an overall increase in vocational school attendance since 1980, fully in line with the increased need for more theoretical training but also involving additional costs for firms who have to pay the release time (Wagner 1999).

[89] The problem is that large firms, which have traditionally shouldered the burden of industrial conflict that is sometimes necessary to secure a moderate wage deal, have become conflict

This phenomenon is related to a crisis within key employers' associations, above all, the association of metalworking employers (*Gesamtmetall*) which has experienced a hemorrhaging in membership as a growing number of firms are leaving the association to avoid inclusion in contracts negotiated with the union (Thelen and Kume 1999; Thelen and van Wijnbergen 2003). This declining membership has huge consequences for the viability of the training system to which business coordination and employer organizations are by all accounts crucial – in advising, monitoring, persuading, and pressuring members to shore up solidarity and coherent collective action (Soskice 1994; Culpepper 2003; Streeck et al. 1987). Germany's employer associations now organize a smaller proportion of German firms than ever before, and their authority (moral and other) is deeply compromised.

The problems are particularly acute in collective bargaining, where small and medium-sized firms in key industries are more or less fed up with the dominance of large firms and sometimes just going their own way. A breakdown of employer coordination in wage formation would have deleterious downstream consequences for vocational training. To the extent that these developments lead to greater wage differentials across firms, the incentives for companies to continue to invest in general skills should decline. Wage coordination through encompassing national bargaining is one of the key mechanisms for reducing poaching among firms and for establishing and sustaining the labor market imperfections that make it safe and attractive for firms to invest in general worker skills (Acemoglu and Pischke 1998).[90]

Another factor that may have a strongly destabilizing effect is the impact of rising standards of training.[91] New technologies and new production requirements demand ongoing upgrading of training, mostly in the

averse in the extreme. Large firms have off-shored a great deal of production to lower wage countries abroad and decreased employment domestically. The resulting lower labor costs have allowed large firms to agree to relatively generous contracts (in the interests of preserving labor peace), but this has produced a situation in which contracts come closer than ever before to exhausting the ability of the larger firms to pay – thus squeezing small and medium-sized producers (Thelen and Kume 1999; Thelen and van Wijnbergen 2003).

[90] A viable and perhaps increasingly attractive alternative could be a more segmentalist approach (see Chapter 1). Although Germany still lags behind other countries in continuing firm-based training, the number of workers involved in such programs has "soared" over the last decade (Sauter 1996: 116). German firms appear less inclined than before to take apprentices on within the context of the traditional system (which requires them to train in particular ways and to uniform standards), and more inclined to invest in continuing training, which is not regulated in the same way or to anywhere near the same extent. See also Crouch, Finegold, and Sako (1999: 146).

[91] I am indebted to Wolfgang Streeck for emphasizing the importance of this.

direction of more general skills and more theoretical training (Soskice 2003; Brown, Green, and Lauder 2001: 83–4). Some such adaptations have been undertaken, for example, the trend toward more general occupational profiles and the increase in vocational school attendance (see footnotes 81 and 88). In some sectors, the need for more general and more theoretical skills has also been accompanied by a softening of the line between traditional apprenticeship and higher education (Brown, Green, and Lauder 2001: 82–4). In the banking sector, for example, Quack and colleagues note a trend among German banks toward "developing stronger links between the system of higher education and the banks, as well as between the universities and the dual system" (Quack, O'Reilly, and Hildebrandt 1995: 781, 782, figure 3).

These developments are in some ways powerful testimony to the adaptability of the German system, and there are many good reasons to promote them further (Culpepper 1999; Brown, Green, and Lauder 2001: 82–5). It should be clear, however, that this route is fraught with dilemmas and possible unanticipated and unwanted consequences. At the most basic level, rising standards and more general occupational profiles, although clearly necessary, have not come free but have come bundled with increased costs to firms (Wagner 1999). But more generally, the broader and especially the more theoretical the educational requirements for new skills become, the less well suited firms are to do the training. Companies may well, and understandably, prefer to offload their problems and costs onto the state or onto apprentices themselves (that is, pointing toward an overall more "liberal" model very much in line with much of the current rhetoric in German business circles).

It already appears that firms (even small, medium-sized, and handicraft firms) are increasingly inclined to recruit new workers from among applicants holding university degrees (Berger, Brandes, and Walden 2000: 79–91). This is a general trend, especially pronounced in the service sector, which accounts for an ever-increasing proportion of employment.[92] Berger and colleagues write of increasing competition between job applicants from the traditional vocational training track and those with technical-college and university degrees. Although they note that one cannot yet talk of a

[92] The service sector has always been a weak spot in the traditional system, since fewer certificates were offered in services and because it is not clear that training in that sector produces the same kind of comparative advantage associated with diversified quality production in manufacturing (Culpepper 1999: 56; Soskice 2003).

"displacement of workers with plant-based vocational training credentials by those with degrees from polytechnics," almost one-third of the large firms in which they conducted research are considering such substitution (Berger, Brandes, and Walden 2000: 91). As Baethge notes, one incentive for firms to look to graduates of technical colleges and universities is that, in the current context of high unemployment, the costs of recruiting from among this pool of applicants is not so high as in the past (Baethge 1999: 12).

The downstream implications of this should be obvious. Once it is clear to young people that there are other avenues to rising in the ranks within top businesses, they are more likely to be drawn to alternative sources of skill acquisition. If it appears that apprenticeship is not the only or even the most direct route to good jobs, then youth will be drawn to other venues (for example, technical colleges, *Fachhochschulen*) to acquire training. The old formula for success (broadly speaking) was apprenticeship plus further qualification to rise in the ranks. Now a higher-level school certificate allows young people to enter at a higher level and to climb higher, thus circumventing the traditional system. The more this occurs the more this breaks the virtuous circle described by Soskice, and turns into a vicious circle in which those youth left in apprenticeship are overall of lower quality, which fuels a reluctance by firms to use apprentices, which draws the best youth away from the traditional system, and so on (Crouch, Finegold, and Sako 1999: 143).

Finally, there is the challenge of unification (Culpepper 2003; Jacoby 2000). Culpepper quite rightly suggests that when talking about German training, one must really distinguish two very different systems, one in the East and one in the West (Culpepper 1999). The state has played a huge role in directly supporting training in the East (see also Crouch, Finegold, and Sako 1999: 143; Konietzka and Lempert 1998: 322; Dobischat, Lipsmeier, and Drexel 1996). In the first years after unification, for reasons easy to understand there was massive use of provisions in the Work Promotion Act to provide training slots to unemployed persons (Sauter 1996: 122 has figures). As of 1997, 79% of all apprentice slots in the East were wholly or partly subsidized by the state, 10% of such apprenticeships outside of firms (in training centers, for example) (Culpepper 1999: 50–1). These state-based solutions are obviously well intentioned and some see them as serving a bridging function. These things cut both ways, however, and there are important interaction effects between developments in the East and West. In particular, just as Western firms learned from the East that life outside the collective bargaining system was entirely possible, so too could they question (and resent) their investment in worker skills that are quite portable. In light of heavy subsidies to Eastern firms, Western firms may well begin to ask themselves why they should continue to bear these costs (Jacoby 2000).[93]

As Baethge notes, the situation since the 1990s shares only a superficial similarity with previous crises. Whereas the problem of a shortage of apprenticeships in the 1970s was mostly a problem of an imbalance in the market for apprenticeship, the problems now may be more structural than cyclical (Baethge 1999). More important, Baethge makes the point that politically, things have been turned on their head. Whereas in the past unions were more likely than employers to criticize some aspects of the system, today they are ardent defenders. Meanwhile, a growing number of employers have become more skeptical, and significant numbers of them are simply walking away.

Long-time observers of the system have begun to talk of a "serious threat to the vocational training system" as employers' interest in it is declining (Stratmann 1994: 25). As the analysis in this book should have made clear, employers are absolutely central actors in the history, and therefore also vital to the future of the German vocational training system – a system which after all rests on their *voluntarily* taking apprentices. Since no one can force German firms to train, there can be no plant-based apprentice system if employers defect in large numbers. Therefore, when faced with the prospect of a serious shortfall in apprentice slots, Chancellor Gerhard Schröder began by exhorting firms to fulfill their "elementary obligation" to give youth a chance to acquire skills (*Der Spiegel*, May 5, 2003: 105). His subsequent resort to the idea of a government-imposed training levy is a signal of how serious the training problem has become (*Welt am Sonntag*, February 15, 2004: 1; *Süddeutsche Zeitung*, February 14–15, 2004: 1).

It would be premature to announce the demise of Germany's dual system of apprentice training; many authors have done so in the past only to see the system survive and thrive (Konietzka and Lempert 1998). The point here is not so much its imminent demise or continuing function; it is, rather, that for institutions to survive they cannot stand still. They must be constantly adapted to changes in the social, market, and political environment.[94] The staying power of the German system therefore hinges

[93] With thanks to Martin Behrens and Wolfgang Streeck for this insight.

[94] As this book goes to press, the Schröder government has just pushed through a significant reform in the handicraft sector. The reform is part of a broader set of measures, authored

very much on whether or not the problems and trends identified above are taken up by the relevant actors, particularly employers, and whether they can muster the collective capacities to undertake the reforms necessary to keep individual firms invested (and investing) in the system.

by the Minister of Labor and Economics, Wolfgang Clement, aimed at easing employment relations to counter continuing high unemployment. The new legislation makes it possible for skilled journeymen in certain Handwerk trades to open independent businesses without having achieved "master" status – the latter traditionally requiring not just training and experience beyond the apprenticeship, but also successful completion of the master exam. Advocates of the reform saw this as an overdue adaptation of the traditional system that could bolster training by responding to the decline in the number of master exams being taken (and the associated decline in training slots for apprentices). Opponents (representatives of Handwerk, but also opposition CDU/CSU politicians), by contrast, argued that the reform would have a deleterious effect on training by reducing incentives for individuals to acquire additional skills (*Hamburger Abendblatt*, May 30, 2003; *Frankfurter Allgemeine Zeitung*, November 28, 2003). The law passed in a compromise form (fewer trades affected than originally envisioned) and it remains to be seen what impact any of this will have on training in the handicraft sector.

6

Conclusions, Empirical and Theoretical

This chapter summarizes the main empirical findings of the analysis, both the cross-national and the longitudinal dimensions, and relates these findings to several major theoretical debates in the literature. The analysis of cross-national differences in the institutions governing in-plant training and the over-time analysis tracking the evolution of the German system over a longer period speak to debates in the political–economic literature on "varieties of capitalism" concerning institutional origins and institutional complementarities. Moreover, the analysis here provides insights into a broader literature in political science concerning issues of institutional reproduction, institutional change, and path dependence in politics.

Cross-National Comparisons: The Origins of Divergent Skill Regimes

The single variable that mattered most crucially to the divergent trajectories of skill formation documented here was the behavior and strategies of leading firms in skill-intensive industries, particularly the machine and metalworking industries.[1] Around the turn of the century, large machine and metalworking firms across all four countries shared similar interests and were pursuing roughly similar strategies with respect to skill formation. Circa 1895 firms like M.A.N., Mather and Platt, Yokosuka, and General

[1] Note well that these firms by no means always got what they initially wanted. As we have seen, they mostly could not achieve their goals on their own steam. The extent to which their preferred options prevailed was a matter of the coalitions they did (or did not) forge with other groups with complementary interests. In many cases, the strategies to which I refer here are compensatory strategies to deal with failure to achieve a first preferred option.

Electric were all engaged in efforts to develop their own in-plant capacities for skill formation and combining these with various policies designed to co-opt workers and exclude unions. From then on, however, trajectories diverged as these firms adapted their strategies to the particular constellation of incentives and constraints they faced in their separate countries.

They looked out on very different political and economic landscapes. Of crucial importance to "modern" industry, it turns out, was the fate of "traditional" associations of skilled craftsmen, customary guardians of apprenticeship and holders of the skills these firms needed. In Germany and Japan, state policy toward the artisanal sector sharpened the line between independent master artisans and skilled workers in industry. Economic and political conditions in Britain and the United States, by contrast, if anything contributed to blurring the boundaries between these two groups (Kocka 1986a: 307–16; Kocka 1986b). These differences were important in determining whether early unions were drawn to or prevented from organizing around craft-control strategies – and by extension affecting whether apprenticeship would be contested across the class divide in industry. The fate of the traditional artisanal sector determined what sorts of problems (and opportunities) the leading firms in skill-dependent industries faced, influencing the strategies they developed to deal with them.

In Germany, the state actively organized the artisanal sector and granted it monopoly rights to certify skills. This framework for certification and monitoring stabilized a system of in-plant training that had been sliding toward exploitation of cheap child labor. The stabilization of apprenticeship in the artisanal sector meant that dominant producers in skill-intensive industries like machine building could count on a relatively steady stream of certified skilled workers, since small artisanal shops were not necessarily interested in holding on to the workers they had trained. Over time, however, and as the deficits of a system not under their own control became apparent, the large firms most dependent on skill became obsessed with *securing the right to certify skills*, a right that the Handwerk sector monopolized.

The situation in Britain was wholly different because here traditional corporate artisanal associations had been destroyed through liberalization. Skilled craftsmen still presided over the training of the next generation, but they did so from a very different base and vantage point – from within craft unions whose goals with respect to apprenticeship were bound up in broader strategies to control the market in their trade. In Britain, apprenticeship was contested not – as in Germany – between an independent artisanal sector and emerging industrial sector, but rather between craft unions and employers in skill-dependent industries. Thus, as metalworking firms in Germany were mobilizing to fight for certification powers for their own in-plant training programs, their British counterparts were mobilizing around a quite different project, *beating back union controls and reasserting managerial discretion* on the shop floor.

In Japan, state policy in the early industrial period liberalized labor markets by actively disbanding traditional corporate artisanal associations and repressing nascent craft unions. Thus neither organized artisans nor craft unions were in a position to (attempt to) regulate apprenticeship at a corporate level. Here too traditional artisans played a key role in providing skills for industry, but in a very different way, as individual entrepreneurs. Firms in skill-dependent industries used them as subcontractors who brought their own retinue of skilled workers and trained their own apprentices. This so-called *oyakata* system was useful to industry because these independent craftsmen performed similar training and certification functions as the handicraft chambers (Germany) and unions of skilled workers (Britain). *Oyakata* were highly mobile, however, so the system was associated with very high levels of job hopping and poaching. Thus, at the same historical juncture in which machine and metalworking firms in Germany were becoming adamant about achieving rights to certify skills and in Britain were becoming obsessed with reasserting managerial control, their Japanese counterparts were completely consumed with the task of *controlling labor mobility* by stabilizing internal labor markets.

In the United States, as in Britain, craft unions emerged among skilled workers in key trades, which meant that here too apprenticeship would be substantially contested across the class divide. Craft unions in key industries like metalworking were, however, much weaker, having emerged much later than in Britain, and at a time when craft controls had already been substantially eroded through the introduction of standardized production and new technologies. As in Britain, so too in the United States, there were pitched battles between employers and craft unions at the end of the nineteenth century, but with the difference that in the wake of their victories American employers went much further than the British to crush and marginalize unions and reorganize production. To put the U.S. case in comparative perspective: Whereas in Germany, metalworking firms at century's end were concerned to certify skills, in Britain to reassert managerial control, and in Japan to dampen labor mobility, in the United States the goal was above all to rationalize production and *reduce dependence on skilled labor altogether* through technological change, work reorganization, and product standardization.

Coalitions and the Further Evolution of the System

In each case, the strategic choices of machine and metalworking firms around the turn of the century set the scene for coalitions and dynamics in the 1920s that would begin to consolidate different trajectories. In Germany, social democratic unions organized significant numbers of skilled workers who had received their credentials in the traditional handicraft system, so despite the Social Democrats' opposition to the original 1897 legislation, unions came around to strategies aimed at democratizing and co-managing, rather than demolishing, that system. In the Weimar years newly incorporated labor unions thus emerged as potential allies for industry against the Handwerk monopoly and in support of a more expansive (covering industry) collectivist system for plant-based skill formation. Although a national-level consensus behind reforms along these lines did not materialize in the 1920s, significant progress was achieved on a voluntary basis, spearheaded above all by the efforts of key trade associations that tirelessly advanced the cause of uniform, standardized skills. Collectivism competed with alternative segmentalist models of skill formation until the Nazi era, but the development of a solidaristic approach to skill formation pioneered in the Weimar period preserved a model of plant-based training with overarching oversight and supervision into which organized labor could later (1969) be incorporated.

The possibility of a cross-class coalition for some form of collectivist skill formation also appeared possible in Britain in the early interwar years. Segments of capital that relied heavily on skill were if anything more willing to work with unions on this than were their counterparts in Germany. However, unlike in Germany, the policies of Britain's craft unions toward apprenticeship were bound up in broader shop floor control strategies. A durable accommodation would therefore have required a much broader settlement across a whole range of knotty control issues. British apprenticeship survived because British industry remained dependent on skills, but apprenticeship training was fragile because it rested less on a stable cross-class alliance than it did on a precarious balance of power between employers and skilled unions that could be (and was) repeatedly upset by shifting macro-economic and political developments. Notable advances in training achieved under favorable conditions (periods of skilled labor shortages or strong government support for training) were thus repeatedly rolled back when the political and/or market context shifted.

In Japan, the *oyakata* system involved massive contradictions from the perspective of firms in skill-intensive industries, providing necessary skills but also generating disruptive labor mobility. Firms responded with intensified efforts to reduce their dependence on independent *oyakata* bosses and to link internal training to a series of complementary measures (seniority wages, elaborate internal career ladders, and long-term employment guarantees) to stabilize the situation. The growing complexity of the skill needs of firms in the 1920s, along with the increasing threat of trade union influence at the plant level, produced a critical realignment (management with young, company-trained workers against the *oyakata*) that consolidated and deepened a segmentalist model of skill formation. Emerging unions, which had their own reasons to oppose the arbitrary *oyakata* system, formulated their goals and strategies within the logic of the system that employers were constructing, and in so doing helped to consolidate a segmentalist system for skill formation.

In the United States, industry went further than in Britain to rationalize production and to marginalize (control-seeking) craft unions around the turn of the century. However, key branches (especially, metals, machines, and electrical machinery) still relied on a fair amount of skill. This they dealt with in much the same way as their Japanese counterparts, through a system of subcontracting (to independent craftsmen) to handle the recruitment and training of skilled workers. Unlike the system in Japan, however, these salaried skilled workmen were enlisted in the continuing fight against organized labor, and together with management presided over the rationalization of production designed to reduce dependence on skills. Rather than serving as intermediaries in skilled labor markets or as trainers of the next generation of skilled workers, salaried foremen in American firms served as the "drivers" and supervisors of (increasingly) semi-skilled labor (Jacoby 1985). By the time American unions were stabilized and collective bargaining rights were secured (1930s and 1940s), organized labor in the United States was maneuvering in a more thoroughly rationalized shop floor environment, and as a result their strategies revolved around a narrower form of job control in highly bureaucratized internal labor markets (Brody 1993).

Cross-National Comparisons

Youth and Apprenticeship

All these developments shaped the landscape that youth faced as they made choices about training. The behavior and strategies of prospective apprentices was also decisive to the trajectory of vocational training institutions in these countries. In Germany, where certification and monitoring were established early on, apprenticeship was a more transparent and attractive option for youth. The motives of handicraft producers in taking apprentices were clearly not altruistic; they paid them very little (in the early years, as we have seen, actually received a fee from them), and they used apprentices as a source of cheap labor. Artisanal producers in Germany, however, faced incentives to train well because if they did not, they would lose their license to train and, with it, the cheap extra hand in production. Going back to the theoretical discussion in the first chapter, certification helped shore up apprenticeship by mitigating credible commitment problems between learners and training firms. Apprentices contributed to the costs of their training through reduced wages, but after three or four years earned a certificate that had real value in the labor market at large. The extension of this system of certification to industry stabilized it further, rendering the content of skills (through standardization) increasingly transparent and because training became a portal to promising careers in top industrial firms.

Apprenticeship in Britain, by contrast, was entangled in conflicts between employers and craft unions, and their failure to reach a settlement left in-plant training utterly lacking in comparable monitoring devices. Nothing prevented British employers from using apprentices as cheap laborers and/or specializing them on particular machines to the detriment of their training. This generated rampant credible commitment problems, since training was extremely uncertain in quality and its duration very long (five to seven years for most). From the perspective of British youth, the value of formal apprenticeship was dubious to say the least, and even less attractive since the absence of certification meant that there were many other avenues through which ambitious youth could advance and achieve "skilled" status. Firms that trained well subjected themselves to massive poaching problems, and beyond (mostly unsuccessful) lobbying to socialize the costs of training through increases in compulsory public school attendance, they quite rationally sought to minimize "irrecoverable" investments by focusing their efforts on a relatively small number of youth who came to them with above-average (public) educational backgrounds. We thus see the beginning of the consolidation of a liberal regime in which (à la Becker 1993) the costs were shifted increasingly to youth, with firms playing a decidedly secondary role.

In Japan, training was central to the consolidation of managerial practices based on strong internal labor markets, complementary personnel policies, seniority wages, and so-called lifetime employment guarantees. Contrary to some popular conceptions, however, the logic of advancement in firm-based career ladders (as early as in the 1920s) was based on the steady acquisition of skills, not on job tenure per se (Levine and Kawada 1980: 174). Since the best (among other things, most secure) jobs were to be had in the large firms of the industrial sector, Japanese youth had an incentive to work hard in school to do well in the initial selection process. Once in the firm, they found that the structure of incentives encouraged ongoing investment in skills. The embedding of training in a broader network of complementary social policies provided incentives for firms to train and for workers to submit to training that was heavily biased toward the needs of the company. Firms could count on workers staying on after training (and on increasing productivity as well, due to ongoing skill acquisition), and trainees could count on their investment in skills being rewarded through ongoing advancement in the internal labor markets of the country's premier firms.

In the United States, prominent welfare capitalists similarly pursued strategies to internalize training and stabilize firm-based labor markets even as they continued to rationalize production and introduce skilled-labor-saving technologies. But after the First World War, these firms mostly abandoned the more ambitious broad-based training programs they had developed for blue collar workers, shifting attention to training for supervisory staff in "human relations management." Firms continued to offer all manner of company-based benefits in order to cultivate worker loyalty and reduce turnover, but (unlike Japan) wages continued to be attached to jobs not workers and managers resisted the introduction of transparent company-wide job classification schemes (and associated career ladders), concerned that these would encourage unionization and collective bargaining (Jacoby 1985). Moreover, and again in contrast to Japan, the route to supervisory positions within the firm was mostly not by rising in the ranks, since U.S. managers were much more likely to privilege college graduates for such positions. The incentives facing ambitious young workers were clear, and led them to avoid vocational training (of all varieties) like the plague in favor of an academically oriented education that opened many more diverse opportunities for advancement in the labor market (Hansen 1997).

Institutional Complementarities

As pointed out in Chapter 1, the literature on the political economy of the developed democracies features a view of distinctive "varieties of capitalism" that sees political economies as more or less integrated systems in which various institutional arenas (industrial relations systems, financial systems, vocational education and training systems, and systems of corporate governance) cohere in important ways, characterized as they are by what political economists call "institutional complementarities." Peter Hall and Daniel Gingerich have provided very compelling evidence of the existence of such complementarities among a number of realms based on quantitative data drawn from across the developed democracies (Hall and Gingerich 2001, 2004).

Other authors have documented synergies and mutually supportive interactions between specific institutional realms, for example, industrial relations and key financial arrangements (Hall 1994; Iversen, Pontusson, and Soskice 2000). Such studies show that systems that give labor a strong voice in plant decision making are underwritten by complementary financial arrangements that provide the "patient capital" necessary for firms to take a longer perspective on personnel policy. Others have drawn attention to the ways in which the institutions governing industrial relations and/or skill formation have "elective affinities" to specific social policy regimes (Mares 2000; Estevez-Abe, Iversen, and Soskice 2001; Iversen and Soskice 2001; Manow 2001; Iversen 2003). So, for instance, skill formation regimes that encourage long-term investment in skills seem to "go with" systems of unemployment insurance that support unemployed workers at higher levels (thus preserving skills by removing the pressure for skilled workers to take jobs that do not tap and sustain their training) (Mares 2000).

The existence of these kinds of complementarities must be seen as an historic achievement of considerable significance, since it is clear that the various institutional arrangements that comprise any national polity or political economy were not created in a single "big bang." Individual components were forged at different historical junctures, brought into being through the actions of different political actors and coalitions. There is no reason to think that the various "pieces" will necessarily fit together into a coherent, self-reinforcing, let alone functional, whole. Indeed, Karen Orren and Stephen Skowronek have argued forcefully that the divergent "temporal underpinnings" of various institutional arrangements should generate contradictions and tensions as institutions representing different political "logics" clash, or as they put it, "collide and abrade" (Orren and Skowronek 2002: 747). These arguments raise important questions about the sources of apparent complementarities or why it is that the kinds of collisions and contradictions Orren and Skowronek's view predicts are not so pervasive and debilitating as one might suppose.

Historically speaking it would be somewhat empty to argue that the existence of a particular set of institutions in one realm "increases the returns" to the existence of a compatible or complementary set of institutions in neighboring realms. Although in some cases, such formulations provide a very apt characterization of the current functioning of particular constellations, as causal claims they leave much to be desired. Since typically there is no real "market" for political institutions, agent-less versions of the argument that rely on the logic of selection through market competition are unpersuasive.[2] Such arguments can be made compelling, however, when one embeds them in an historical account that attaches the outcomes to agents pursuing specific interests. In this more political version, "powerful actors" (and these must be specified) may be influential in, perhaps even decisive to, the genesis of particular institutional arrangements (say, industrial relations) and may therefore also have a strong interest and role in creating complementary institutions in neighboring realms (say, social policy).

This is the gist of Peter Swenson's account of the construction and elaboration of the "Swedish model," which features highly centralized industrial relations institutions and a universalistic welfare state – institutional arrangements that turn out to be mutually supportive in important ways. Swenson (1991, 2002) traced the centralization of collective bargaining institutions back to a cross-class alliance forged in the 1930s between employers in industries exposed to international competition and workers in low-pay sectors. Centralization served the interests of these particular employers because it brought under control disruptive behavior of employers and unions in high-pay sectors (for example, construction) that were sheltered from international competition. The success with which centralized bargaining operated in institutionalizing wage restraint had some nasty side effects, however, above all chronic labor market scarcity, which became

[2] Some economists (for example, Aoki 2001) therefore invoke culture as a unifying causal variable.

especially severe in times of buoyant demand and growth. Labor scarcity created new problems – unleashing "disloyal" competition among firms that existing institutions (governing wages) were unable to control. By the 1950s, therefore, important segments of Swedish capital were quietly rallying behind initiatives for the introduction of comprehensive health insurance, generous sick pay, and an active labor market policy since these provided solutions to the specific pathologies that had developed in the Swedish labor market.

This kind of interest-based account is important, and it is certainly congruent with the conventional wisdom that institutions are designed by strategic actors with their own interests very much in mind. The actions of "powerful agents" would produce strong complementarities across various realms if there were a high degree of continuity in who these powerful agents are, both across various institutional arenas and over time. One question, therefore, would be whether we can, a priori, identify a set of actors whose interests will systematically prevail over time.

Since we are dealing in this literature with capitalist countries, a prime suspect would be employers and one of the points that Swenson's analysis persuasively makes is that political–economic institutions with any kind of staying power are precisely those achieved not against capital but in collaboration with some segments of capital.[3] Swenson's account of the "fit" between industrial relations institutions created in the 1930s and social policy in the 1950s hinges on an argument about how capitalist interests evolved over time. In the case just discussed, for example, he shows how previous rounds of institutional innovation (centralization of wage bargaining) produced effects (labor scarcity) that interacted with changes in the broader market context in ways that, over time, re-shaped capitalist interests in other, neighboring realms (social policy) (Swenson 2002 and forthcoming).

Other authors, by contrast, have been more inclined to emphasize the structural constraints within which capitalists are maneuvering. Hacker and Pierson, for instance, do not deny the importance of employer interests, but they insist that in order to understand outcomes it is important to analyze the structural conditions that establish the *menu of options* from which actors (including employers) are forced to choose (Hacker and Pierson 2002). Invoking insights from studies of agenda setting, they point out that the crucial issue in most situations is not the final choice between the two or

[3] A finding, by the way, confirmed in this study as well (see especially the concluding discussion in Chapter 5).

three (or x) specific policy options on the table at any given moment, but rather the prior question of whose preferred range of options forms the "choice set" from which the actors are allowed to select (Hacker 2002; Hacker and Pierson 2002). Hacker and Pierson attach their critique to an analysis of the genesis of the Social Security Act in the United States, highlighting the way in which the broader political context had already removed certain previously viable options (options earlier embraced by very powerful business interests) from the agenda (Hacker and Pierson 2002: 12).[4]

Huber and Stephens (Huber and Stephens 2001) also draw attention to structural and political constraints, emphasizing how previous policies have powerfully reshaped the *distribution of preferences*, by which they mean the universe of actors who are around to express their interests in particular (later) policy debates. So, for example, while acknowledging (with Swenson) that some Swedish employers supported universalistic welfare policies in the 1950s, Huber and Stephens put a different spin on this observation by drawing attention to the fact that twenty years of uninterrupted Social Democratic rule had largely eliminated low-wage producers and in so doing eliminated as well an important source of potential opposition to policy initiatives at that time. Huber and Stephens argue that analyses emphasizing capitalist interests need to make sure they do not "lose sight" of the way in which the preferences and strategies of these actors have been shaped by the prevailing structural and political context (Huber and Stephens 2001: 33).

Whether emphasizing especially the evolving interests of capital (Swenson) or the structural and political constraints within which employers define and defend their interests (Hacker and Pierson, Huber and Stephens), these analyses all highlight the need to situate the interpretation of specific choice points within a broader temporal framework that takes account of the feedback effects that have defined the conditions within which specific policy and institutional choices are being made. They highlight the way that policies initiated at one point affect which actors are around to fight the next battle, how they define their interests, and how and

[4] Dobbin (Dobbin 1994) has made a similar point from a more sociological perspective. He argues that in order to understand cross-national differences in outcomes, it is necessary to consider not just a particular decision node (even the final one) but rather the range of options entertained in the first place, often completely different cross-nationally.

with whom they are likely to ally themselves subsequently (Skocpol 1992; Pierson 2003a; Weir 2003). Attention to such feedback effects is crucial for understanding how institutional complementarities are forged historically because they alone provide the necessary *causal links* between the specific episodes – across different periods and often involving different political actors and coalitions – in which successive rounds of institutional innovation occur. Such feedback effects establish the raw materials (constellation of players, definitions of interests) with which policy entrepreneurs, as well as defenders and challengers of existing institutions have to work.

How do such feedback effects operate? The present analysis confirms some of the insights from previous scholarship, but also contains new leads and insights. In some cases, and in line with contemporary theorizing on "path dependence" in politics, we can observe a traditional logic of "increasing returns to power" – that is, situations in which the victors at one stage impose institutional solutions that reflect and entrench their interests, thus biasing outcomes in the next round. An example from the present study is the case of the United States, where employers – already less dependent on skilled labor than their counterparts elsewhere – were in a position to decisively defeat the control strategies of organized labor (and crush craft unions) at the end of the nineteenth century. This set the scene for more innovations in production technology and personnel management that further reduced their dependence on skilled labor – which in turn rendered the possibility (indeed the necessity) of joint (union-employer) regulation of training, and of skilled labor markets generally, more remote over time. This line of argument mirrors Huber and Stephens's account of Sweden sketched out above, in which the victory of the proponents of centralization in struggles over industrial relations institutions in the 1930s created an environment (a wage environment, above all) in which low-wage producers could not survive. This tilted the playing field for subsequent institutional and policy choices, in their case, discussions in the 1950s over social policy.

Beyond arguments based on a logic of increasing returns to power, however, the present analysis highlights the way in which institutions created by one set of actors and for one set of purposes can sometimes be embraced and "carried forward" on the shoulders of another coalition altogether. As we saw in the German case, for example, neither organized labor nor the machine industry was part of the original coalition behind the crucial legislation of 1897, yet both would eventually become hugely important carriers of the system that evolved subsequently. The existence of this handicraft-based system of training had important feedback effects – crucial above all in shaping the way that unions defined their interests with respect to skill formation. As the ranks of Germany's social democratic unions filled up with skilled workers who had received their credentials under the system, the unions developed a strong interest not in dismantling the system but rather in controlling or co-managing (codetermining) the system of firm-based training that it represented.[5] The important point is that from quite early on German unions were themselves invested in a system of plant-based training, and therefore pursuing strategies that were very different from those of social democratic unions elsewhere (for example, Swedish unions), which were more skeptical of all forms of firm-based training and spent their time pushing instead for publicly managed, school-based vocational education for blue collar workers.

The machine industry was the other key actor in Germany in the early industrial period, not part of the original coalition but one whose strategies with respect to the handicraft system were also vitally important to its evolution. The machine industry, heavily dependent on skills, was therefore a major consumer of the skills generated by these small handicraft producers. As elaborated in Chapter 2, large machine companies tried to pursue a completely different model of skill formation based on training for internal labor markets – very similar to practices emerging in the United States and Japan at around the same time. But these firms could not escape the logic of the pre-existing handicraft system altogether. Skill-intensive industries in Germany were pushed toward a more coordinated approach to training through their competition with the artisanal sector whose methods they abhorred and whose power to certify skills they coveted.

Saying that labor unions and the machine industry framed their interests in relation to the existing handicraft system, however, is not the same as saying that these groups were invested in those institutions *as originally constituted*. Here I part ways with some path-dependence theorizing that emphasizes "lock in" as actors adapt their strategies to conform to the logic of prevailing institutions. Once in place, institutions do indeed affect the interests and strategic options available to various groups. Against the determinism of some lines of argument, however, institutions continue to

[5] Employing Greif and Laitin's terms (Greif and Laitin 2003), this could be characterized as a situation in which the operation of these institutions produced behavioral effects that expanded the "quasi parameters" within which the institution was self-enforcing.

be the object of ongoing political contestation, and changes in the political coalitions on which they rest hold the key to understanding significant shifts over time in the form the institutions take and the functions they perform in politics and society.

The issue becomes the extent to which institutions generate only self-enforcing feedback or whether their operation also generates dynamics that complicate rather than contribute to the "*reliable* reproduction" of these arrangements (Clemens and Cook 1999: 449; on this point, see also Orren and Skowronek 1994). The increasing interest of both the machine industry and organized labor in the system of training if anything unleashed new conflicts, particularly over the governance of that system. The resulting renegotiation of the governance structures over time drove changes in the content of training toward greater standardization and uniformity, and culminated in the political-distributional transformation of the system as a whole.

This case can be seen as an instance of institutional development and change that combines elements of positive feedback with new developments that did not necessarily always push in the same direction but altered the overall trajectory. It thus takes us beyond increasing returns and positive feedback arguments (associated with the path-dependence literature) by demonstrating how actors on the periphery ("losers" in one round) can become invested in prevailing institutions in certain ways, such that shifts in the balance of power that go their way may result in institutional conversion rather than either straight reproduction or breakdown (see also Thelen 2002).

The key to understanding institutional complementarities is to think in terms of institutional co-evolution and feedback effects as processes through which coherence does not emerge so much as it is constructed, as institutions inherited from the past get adapted – in this case through political incorporation and associated renegotiation – to changes in the political, market, and social context. To the extent that things "fit" together, it may be partly because one group or coalition is always winning, or because new institutions are selected for their compatibility with those that already exist. However, it may well also be due to processes through which inherited institutions are actively "fitted" or adapted to new circumstances, new interests, and new power constellations. These considerations bring me to the broad question of institutional origins, evolution, and change to which the foregoing analysis speaks.

Institutional Evolution and Change

The analysis above thus also provides insights into general processes of institutional reproduction and change. Whereas earlier generations of institutional analysis focused primarily on the effects of different institutional configurations on policies and other outcomes, a growing number of studies have turned their attention to the question of how institutions themselves originate and evolve over time (for example, among others, Clemens and Cook 1999; Pierson 2004; Greif and Laitin 2003). Current work in this area has been largely driven by dissatisfaction with existing treatments of the subject, particularly those that draw a sharp line between the analysis of institutional reproduction and that of institutional change. As pointed out in Chapter 1, a common understanding in the literature sees institutional change in highly discontinuous terms, as the consequence of exogenous shocks that wipe the slate clean (Mancur Olson's [1982] theory of postwar economic growth) or that open new possibilities for agency and innovation (Katznelson's "unsettled moments of uncommon choice" [2003: 277, 282–3]).

Without denying that such critical junctures are possible, the present analysis offers a somewhat different angle on institutional reproduction and change. Contrary to strong punctuated equilibrium models that lead us to expect big changes in the context of big historic breaks, we often find significant continuities through historically "unsettled" times, and ongoing contestation and renegotiation in "settled" periods that nonetheless over time add up to significant change. As the case of Germany vividly demonstrates, institutional arrangements often turn out to be incredibly resilient in the face of huge exogenous shocks of the sort we might well expect to disrupt previous patterns and prompt dramatic institutional innovation. As events in the immediate post-World War II period (Chapter 5) make clear, in times of crisis or deep uncertainty, political actors often specifically eschew experimentation and instead fall back on familiar formulas – resulting in institutional reproduction not change.

As the German case has also shown, however, more subtle and smaller scale changes in "settled" rather than "unsettled" times are also worthy of our attention, as, over time, they can cumulate into significant institutional transformation (see also Djelic and Quack 2003: 309). Chapters 2 and 5 of this book traced the evolution of the German system from a core framework aimed mostly at defeating unions to a pillar of social partnership between labor and capital one hundred years later. This process was defined not so much by massive renegotiations at historic "breakpoints" (of which in Germany over the twentieth century there were certainly plenty), but rather through processes of layering and conversion (Chapter 1), as the incorporation of new groups into pre-existing institutions resulted in the *addition* of new elements that altered the overall trajectory and *renegotiations* based on changing coalitional foundations that redirected the institutions toward goals and functions completely unanticipated by the original founders.

Much of the early literature on diverse national trajectories tended to obscure these issues by conceiving of institutions as the "frozen" residue of critical junctures, or as the "sticky" legacies of previous political battles (see, for example, Lipset and Rokkan 1968: 3, 50, 54, which employs the language of "freezing"). More recent literature on path dependence and increasing returns effects has, however, pushed the debate forward by specifying the *dynamic* processes that sustain institutions over long periods of time (Pierson 2000a). Increasing returns arguments tell an important part of the story, but they are mostly designed to capture the logic of institutional reproduction, not institutional change. Moreover, in many cases, explaining institutional persistence will require that we go beyond positive feedback arguments. As we scan the political and political–economic landscapes, we find that institutional survival is often strongly laced with elements of institutional adaptation and even sometimes transformation of the sort that brings inherited institutions in line with changing social, political, and economic conditions.

The general argument I have made is that institutional reproduction and institutional change, which are often treated as completely distinct analytic problems, have to be studied together and are in some important ways quite closely linked (see also Thelen 1999). Formal institutions do not survive long stretches of time by standing still. The language of stasis and inertia is particularly unhappy because as the world around institutions is changing their survival will not necessarily rest on the faithful reproduction of those institutions as originally constituted, but rather on their ongoing active adaptation to changes in the political and economic environment in which they are embedded.

An obvious and general lesson that emerges from the foregoing analysis is to underscore Robert Bates's cautionary note not to "confound the analysis of the role of institutions with a theory of their causes" (Bates 1988; see also Knight 1999:33–4). The present study serves as a strong warning against varieties of what Pierson calls actor-centered functionalism that engage in a kind of backward deduction and in which "the effects of the institutions [are taken to] explain the presence of those institutions" (Pierson 2000b: 475). Looking at German vocational training institutions from today's vantage point, analysts quite reasonably portray this system as part of a high-wage, high-quality production regime that reconciles the existence of strong unions with strong performance in export markets. As the history shows, however, this was not the obvious endpoint of a trajectory that could have been foreseen in the late nineteenth century.

As Pierson notes, the point is not that institutions are not designed by purposive actors with particular interests; clearly they are.[6] The point is that "changes in the broader social environment and/or in the character of the actors themselves" (among other things) can, over time, produce a significant and unintended "gap" between the goals of the designers and the way institutions operate (Pierson 2004: 108–9). Cases where such "gaps" can be observed may be particularly fruitful ones to mine for insights into the way in which institutions evolve over time. The perspective on institutional development elaborated in this book has emphasized the political contestedness of institutions, and argued that shifts in the coalitions on which institutions rest are what drive changes in the form they take and the functions they serve in politics and society.

In line with some current theorizing about path dependence in politics, the present analysis shows that we need to be sensitive to the possibility of what Stinchcombe has termed "historicist explanations," that is, the idea that the "processes responsible for the genesis of an institution are different from the processes responsible for the reproduction of the institution" (Mahoney 2000: 4; Stinchcombe 1968; Pierson 2000a). Against functionalist accounts that read the origins of institutions off their current functions, a somewhat longer time frame will often be necessary for us to see how institutions created for one set of purposes can be redirected to serve quite different ends. Alongside power-distributional accounts that stress how powerful actors design institutions to anchor their position, we often need a longer time frame to see how institutions created by one configuration of power or coalition of interests can be "carried forward" on the shoulders of some other coalition entirely. And beyond some

[6] Although as Schickler (Schickler 2001), Palier (Palier forthcoming), Pierson (Pierson 2004), and others have pointed out, institutions also often represent compromises among groups with very different and even contradictory interests. In the present study, the 1897 Handicraft Protection Law is a perfect example of this (see the analysis in Chapter 2).

cultural accounts that see institutions as faithfully reflecting shared cultural scripts, a longer time frame may allow us to see more clearly how institutions created at one juncture can be constitutive and not just reflective of a particular social or cultural orientation. The point in each case is that the creation and existence of the institution at one juncture can have a formative impact on actor strategies, interests, identities, and orientations subsequently.

Positive feedback is clearly part of the story but what also emerges from the present analysis is the way in which such feedback effects are not necessarily associated with the faithful reproduction of the system as originally conceived. In terms of the sources of (or pressures for) change, the present study underscores the insight of Clemens and others that analyses of institutional development need to be attuned to processes unfolding on the periphery (Clemens 1993; Orren and Skowronek 1994; Weir 1992). This is because institutions do not just generate positive feedback, they also "generate grievance... [and] actors who are aggrieved but not co-opted are an important source of pressure for institutional change" (Schneiberg and Clemens forthcoming: 35). Here it is important to remember that, in politics, unlike the marketplace, the "losers" at one juncture do not necessarily disappear and their "adaptation" can mean something very different from "embracing and reproducing" the institution, as in increasing returns arguments from economics. Where the institutions that prevail do not generate significant positive feedback effects among the aggrieved, their later empowerment is likely to spell institutional breakdown. This is the case for Britain, where union-enforced apprenticeship was actively destroyed by employers when changing market conditions shifted the balance of power sharply away from skilled unions.

As the German case highlights, however, it is also important to look at whether actors who are on the periphery themselves become invested in the prevailing institutions and if so, in what ways. In the present analysis the most important initiators of change were those that were "outside" the vocational training system as originally constituted (that is, for the handicraft sector), above all, the organized machine industry and organized labor. In both cases, the strategies these groups pursued in some ways adapted to the logic of the existing system while in other ways putting intense pressure on those institutions to accommodate their different agendas. In cases such as this, shifts in the balance of power between "insiders" and previous "outsiders" may result in institutional conversion rather than breakdown. Such cases combine elements of increasing returns and positive feedback with new developments that do not necessarily always push in the same direction but rather can alter the overall trajectory.

The kind of analysis articulated here helps us get beyond blunt models of discontinuous change based on a strong juxtaposition of periods of institutional "stasis" versus "innovation." It does so not just by identifying modes and mechanisms of gradual change, but also – this is important – by forcing us to specify *which aspects* of the system are getting stably reproduced over time and which are subject to renegotiation and why. What is incredibly stable through the many truly massive breakpoints in Germany (from 1897 to the present) has been the idea of a collectively managed system for monitoring how firms train their workers (a quite unusual historical achievement). On the other hand, what was not at all stable, and subject to intense contestation and periodic renegotiation was the governance structure through which this system would be administered. That is what was periodically renegotiated in ways that on the one hand allowed the system to survive – by bringing it into line with changes in the societal balance of power – while at the same time putting on these institutions an entirely different and unanticipated spin compared with the political and functional logic of the system created in 1897. This case makes clear that one can often make sense of the form and functions that institutions have assumed only by viewing them, as Pierson and Skocpol (2002) recommend, in the context of a larger temporal framework that includes the sequences of events and processes that shaped their development over time.

Bibliography

ABB. 1955. *Verzeichnis der anerkannten Lehr und Anlernberufe in Industrie, Handel und Verkehr*. Bielefeld: W. Bertelsmann.

Abel, Heinrich. 1963. *Das Berufsproblem im gewerblichen Ausbildungs- und Schulwesen Deutschlands (BRD)*. Braunschweig: Georg Westermann Verlag.

Abel, Heinrich. 1968. *Berufserziehung und beruflicher Bildungsweg*. Edited by K. Stratmann. Braunschweig: Georg Westermann Verlag.

Acemoglu, Daron. 1996. Credit Constraints, Investment Externalities and Growth. In *Acquiring Skills*, edited by A. L. Booth and D. J. Snower. London: Centre for Economic Policy Research.

Acemoglu, Daron, and Jörn-Steffen Pischke. 1998. Why Do Firms Train? Theory and Evidence. *Quarterly Journal of Economics* 113 (1): 79–119.

Acemoglu, Daron, and Jörn-Steffen Pischke. 1999a. Beyond Becker: Training in Imperfect Labour Markets. *Economic Journal* 109: F112–F142.

Acemoglu, Daron, and Jörn-Steffen Pischke. 1999b. The Structure of Wages and Investment in General Training. *Journal of Political Economy* 107 (3): 539–72.

Adam, Hermann. 1979. *Der Einfluss der Industrie- und Handelskammern auf politische Entscheidungsprozesse*. Frankfurt: Campus Verlag.

Adelmann, Gerhard. 1979. Die berufliche Aus- und Weiterbildung in der deutschen Wirtschaft 1871–1918. In *Berufliche Aus- und Weiterbildung in der deutschen Wirtschaft seit dem 19. Jahrhundert*, edited by H. Pohl. Wiesbaden: Franz Steiner Verlag.

Agriculture and Commerce, Ministry of. 1903. *Shokkō jijō*. Tokyo: Ministry of Agriculture and Commerce.

Albert, Michel. 1993. *Capitalism versus Capitalism*. New York: Four Walls Eight Windows.

Albrecht, Willy. 1982. *Fachverein, Berufsgewerkschaft, Zentralverband: Organisationsprobleme der deutschen Gewerkschaften 1870–1890*. Bonn: Neue Gesellschaft.

Alewell, Dorothea, and Julia F. Richter. 2001. Die Ausbildungsplatzabgabe als Instrument zur Internalisierung externer Effekte. In *Bildung und Beschäftigung*, edited by R. K. von Weizsäcker. Berlin: Duncker & Humblot.

Alexander, Magnus. 1921. Apprenticeship in the Metal Trades. In *Trade Unionism and Labor Problems*, edited by J. R. Commons. Boston: Ginn and Company.

Aoki, Masahiko. 2001. *Toward a Comparative Institutional Analysis*. Cambridge, MA: MIT Press.

Arbeit, Bundesministerium für, ed. 1950. *Die Arbeiter und Angestellten nach Beruf und Alter sowie die Lehrlingshaltung in der Bundesrepublik Deutschland am 31. Oktober 1950. Ergebnisse einer Sondererhebung der Arbeitsämter*. Bonn: Bundesministerium für Arbeit (Statistik).

Arnhold, Carl. 1931. Arbeitsschulung im Rahmen des Betriebes, gemäss den Grundsatzen des Dinta. In *Industrielle Arbeitsschulung als Problem: Fünf Beiträge über ihre Aufgaben und Grenzen*, edited by S. M. E. V. Frankfurt/Main: Industrieverlag Späth + Linde.

Arthur, W. Brian. 1989. Competing Technologies, Increasing Returns, and Lock-In by Historical Events. *Economic Journal* 99: 116–31.

Ashton, David, and Francis Green. 1996. *Education, Training, and the Global Economy*. Cheltenham, UK: Edward Elgar.

Atkins, Ralph. 2000. Germany's Greens watch as their support withers. *Financial Times*, March 17, 2.

Backes-Gellner, Uschi. 1995. Duale Ausbildung und/oder betriebliche Weiterbildung? *Berufsbildung* 49 (33): 15–16.

Baernreither, J. M. 1893. *English Associations of Working Men*. Translated by A. Taylor. London: S. Sonnenschein & Co.

Baethge, Martin. 1970. *Ausbildung und Herrschaft: Unternehmerinteressen in der Bildungspolitik*. Frankfurt/Main: Europäische Verlagsanstalt.

Baethge, Martin. 1999. Glanz und Elend des deutschen Korporatismus in der Berufsbildung. *Die Mitbestimmung online* 4: 15.

Bates, Robert H. 1988. Contra Contractarianism: Some Reflections on the New Institutionalism. *Politics & Society* 16 (2): 387–401.

BDI, Bundesverband der Deutschen Industrie. 1950. Der Präsident: An die industriellen Unternehmer und Betriebsleiter. In *Quellen und Dokumente zur Geschichte der Berufsbildung in Deutschland*, edited by G. Pätzold. Köln: Böhlau Verlag.

Beard, Mary S. 1908. Results of an Inquiry into the Working of Continuation Schools in England. In *Continuation Schools in England & Elsewhere*, edited by M. E. Sadler. Manchester, UK: University of Manchester.

Becker, Gary S. 1993. *Human Capital*. 3rd ed. Chicago: The University of Chicago Press.

Beil, E. 1921. Die Ausbildung der Industrielehrlinge in Werkstatt und Schule. In *Lehrlings-Ausbildung und technisches Berufschulwesen (Abhandlungen und Berichte über Technisches Schulwesen)*, edited by DATSCH. Berlin: DATSCH.

Beissinger, Mark R. 2002. *Nationalist Mobilization and the Collapse of the Soviet State*. New York: Cambridge University Press.

Bellmann, Lutz, and Renate Neubäumer. 2001. Die Übernahme betrieblich Ausgebildeter: Theoretische Überlegungen und empirische Ergebnisse auf der Basis des IAB-Betriebspanels. 1998. In *Bildung und Beschäftigung*, edited by R. K. von Weizsäcker. Berlin: Duncker & Humblot.

Bibliography

Berg, Maxine. 1985. *The Age of Manufactures, 1700–1820*. London: Fontana Press.

Berg, Peter B. 1994. Strategic Adjustments in Training: A Comparative Analysis of the U.S. and German Automobile Industries. In *Training and the Private Sector: International Comparisons*, edited by L. M. Lynch. Chicago: Univeristy of Chicago Press.

Berger, Klaus, Harald Brandes, and Günter Walden. 2000. *Chancen der dualen Berufsausbildung*. Bonn: Bundesinstitut für Berufsbildung.

Berger, Suzanne, and Ronald Dore, eds. 1996. *National Diversity and Global Capitalism*. Ithaca, NY: Cornell University Press.

Berghoff, Hartmut. 2001. Did Hitler Create a New Society? Continuity and Change in German Social History Before and After 1933. In *Weimar and Nazi Germany: Continuities and Discontinuities*, edited by P. Panayi. New York: Longman.

Berufsausbildung, ABB Arbeitsstelle für Betriebliche. 1958. *10 Jahre Arbeitsstelle für Betriebliche Berufsausbildung*. Bonn: W. Bertelsmann Verlag.

Bildungsforschung, Max-Planck-Institut für. 1979. *Between Elite and Mass Education*. Translated by R. Meyer and A. Heinrichs-Goodwin. Albany, NY: State University of New York Press.

Bishop, John. 1994. The Impact of Previous Training on Productivity and Wages. In *Training and the Private Sector: International Comparisons*, edited by L. M. Lynch. Chicago: University of Chicago Press.

Black, Sandra E., and Lisa M. Lynch. 1996. Human Capital Investments and Productivity. *American Economic Review. Papers and Proceedings* 86 (2): 263–7.

Blackbourn, David. 1977. The Mittelstand in German Society and Politics, 1871–1914. *Social History* 4: 409–33.

Blinder, Alan S., and Alan B. Krueger. 1996. Labor Turnover in the USA and Japan: A Tale of Two Countries. *Pacific Economic Review* 1 (1): 27–57.

Boch, Rudolf. 1985. *Handwerker-Sozialisten gegen Fabrikgesellschaft*. Göttingen: Vandenhoeck & Ruprecht.

Booth, Alison L., and Dennis J. Snower, eds. 1996. *Acquiring Skills: Market Failures, Their Symptoms and Policy Responses*. London: Centre for Economic Policy Research.

Booth, Charles. 1903. *Life and Labour of the People in London*. Vol. 1. New York: Macmillan.

Booth, Charles. 1904. *Life and Labour of the People in London*. 1903 Edition. Vol. 5, *Industry*. New York: Macmillan.

Botsch, R. 1933. *Lehrlingsausbildung und Gesellenprüfung in der metallverarbeitenden Industrie*. Berlin: Julius Beltz.

Bowman, John R. 1985. The Politics of the Market: Economic Competition and the Organization of Capitalists. *Political Power and Social Theory* 5: 35–88.

Boyer, Robert, and J. Rogers Hollingsworth, eds. 1997. *Contemporary Capitalism: The Embeddedness of Institutions*. New York: Cambridge University Press.

Bray, Reginald A. 1909. The Apprenticeship Question. *The Economic Journal* XIX: 404–15.

Bray, Reginald A. 1912. *Boy Labour and Apprenticeship*. Second Impression ed. London: Constable & Co.

Brereton, M. A. Cloudesley. 1919. Continuative Education under the Fisher Act. Points for Employers. Westminster, UK: Knapp, Drewett and Sons.

Bridges, Amy. 1986. Becoming American: The Working Classes in the United States before the Civil War. In *Working-Class Formation: Nineteenth-Century Patterns in Western Europe and the United States*, edited by I. Katznelson and A. R. Zolberg. Princeton, NJ: Princeton University Press.

Brody, David. 1980. *Workers in Industrial America: Essays on the Twentieth Century Struggle*. New York: Oxford University Press.

Brody, David. 1993. Workplace Contractualism in Comparative Perspective. In *Industrial Democracy in America: The Ambiguous Promise*, edited by N. Lichtenstein and H. J. Harris. New York: Cambridge University Press.

Brown, C. H. L., and J. A. G. Taylor. 1933. *Friendly Societies*. Cambridge, UK: Cambridge University Press.

Brown, Phillip, Andy Green, and Hugh Lauder. 2001. *High Skills: Globalization, Competitiveness, and Skill Formation*. Oxford: Oxford University Press.

Bundesrepublik, Ausschuss für Berufserziehung im Auftrage der Ständigen Konferenz der Kultusminister in der Deutschen. 1952. Gutachten zur Berufsausbildung der deutschen Jugend. In *Quellen und Dokumente zur betrieblichen Berufsbildung, 1945–1990*, edited by G. Pätzold. Köln: Böhlau Verlag.

Bunk, Gerhard P. 1979. Aus- und Weiterbildung in der deutschen Wirtschaft in der Bundesrepublik Deutschland vom Ende des Zweiten Weltkriegs bis zur Gegenwart. In *Berufliche Aus- und Weiterbildung in der deutshen Wirtschaft seit dem 19. Jahrhundert*, edited by H. Pohl. Weisbaden: Franz Steiner Verlag.

Buttrick, John. 1952. The Inside Contract System. *The Journal of Economic History* XII (3): 205–21.

Childs, Michael J. 1990. Boy Labour in Late Victorian and Edwardian England and the Remaking of the Working Class. *Journal of Social History* 23 (4): 783–802.

Clark, Peter. 2000. *British Clubs and Societies, 1580–1800*. Oxford: Clarendon Press.

Clark, R. O. 1957. The Dispute in the British Engineering Industry 1897–98: An Evaluation. *Economica* 24 (94): 128–37.

Clawson, Dan. 1980. *Bureaucracy and the Labor Process: The Transformation of U.S. Industry, 1860–1920*. New York: Monthly Review Press.

Clegg, Hugh A., Alan Fox, and A. F. Thompson. 1964. *A History of British Trade Unions since 1889*. Vol. I. Oxford: Clarendon Press.

Clemens, Elisabeth. 1993. Organizational Repertoires and Institutional Change: Women's Groups and the Transformation of U.S. Politics, 1890–1920. *American Journal of Sociology* 98 (4): 755–98.

Clemens, Elisabeth S., and James M. Cook. 1999. Politics and Institutionalism: Explaining Durability and Change. *Annual Review of Sociology* 25: 441–66.

Cole, G. D. H. 1924. *Organised Labour: An Introduction to Trade Unionism*. London: George Allen and Unwin.

Coleman, Donald C. 1975. *Industry in Tudor and Stuart England*. London: Macmillan.

Collier, Ruth B., and David Collier. 1991. *Shaping the Political Arena*. Princeton, NJ: Princeton University Press.

Commerce, Association for Education in Industry and. 1930. *Report on the Training of Manual Workers in the Engineering Industry*. Birmingham, UK: Association for Education in Industry and Commerce.
Cooley, Edwin G. 1912. *Vocational Education in Europe*. Chicago: Commercial Club of Chicago.
Cooley, R. L. 1914. Schools and Continuation Schools. *Management Review (National Association of Corporation Schools Bulletin)* 1 (April): 11–21.
Cooley, Robert L. 1915. Continuation School Work in Wisconsin. Journal of Proceedings and Addresses of the Fifty-Third Annual Meeting and International Congress on Education, August 16–27, at Oakland, CA.
Crawford, Beverly, and Arend Lijphart. 1995. Explaining Political and Economic Change in Post-Communist Eastern Europe: Old Legacies, New Institutions, Hegemonic Norms and International Pressures. *Comparative Political Studies* 28 (2): 171–99.
Cremin, Lawrence A. 1964. *The Transformation of the School*. New York: Random House.
Crossick, Geoffrey, and Heinz-Gerhard Haupt, eds. 1984. *Shopkeepers and Master Artisans in Nineteenth-Century Europe*. London: Methuen.
Crouch, Colin. 1993. *Industrial Relations and European State Traditions*. Oxford: Clarendon Press.
Crouch, Colin. 1998. Public Policy in a Private Arena: The Case of Vocational Education and Training. In *Estudios Working Papers, Centro de Estudios Avanzados en Ciencias Sociales*. Madrid.
Crouch, Colin, David Finegold, and Mari Sako. 1999. *Are Skills the Answer?* Oxford: Oxford University Press.
Crusius, Reinhard. 1982. *Berufsbildungs- und Jugendpolitik der Gewerkschaft: Struktur und Verlauf bei DGB und einigen Einzelgewerkschaften 1945–1981*. Frankfurt: Campus.
Crusius, Werner. 1970. Kritik der Berufsbildungsgesetzes. In *Zur Situation der Berufsbildung*, edited by Deutscher Gewerkschaftsbund. Düsseldorf: DGB.
Cruz-Castro, Laura, and Gavan P. P. Conlong. 2001. Initial Training Policies and Transferability of Skills in Britain and Spain. In *Working Papers of the Centro de Estudios Avanzados en Ciencias Sociales, Instituto Juan March de Estudios e Investigaciones*. Madrid.
Culpepper, Pepper D. 1999a. The Future of the High-Skill Equilibrium in Germany. *Oxford Review of Economic Policy* 15 (1): 43–59.
Culpepper, Pepper D. 1999b. Introduction: Still a Model for the Industrialized Countries? In *The German Skills Machine: Sustaining Comparative Advantage in a Global Economy*, edited by P. D. Culpepper and D. Finegold. New York: Berghahn Books.
Culpepper, Pepper D. 2002. Associations and Non-Market Coordination in Banking: France and East Germany Compared. *European Journal of Industrial Relations* 8 (2): 217–35.
Culpepper, Pepper D. 2003. *Creating Cooperation: How States Develop Human Capital in Europe*. Ithaca, NY: Cornell University Press.

Culpepper, Pepper D., and David Finegold, eds. 1999. *The German Skills Machine: Sustaining Comparative Advantage in a Global Economy*. New York: Berghahn Books.
DATSCH. 1912. *Arbeiten auf dem Gebiete des Technischen niederen Schulwesens*. Edited by DATSCH. Vol. III, *Abhandlungen und Berichte über Technisches Schulwesen*. Berlin: DATSCH.
DATSCH, ed. 1921. *Lehrlingsausbildung und technisches Berufschulwesen*. Edited by DATSCH. Vol. VII, *Abhandlungen und Berichte über Technisches Schulwesen*. Berlin: DATSCH.
DATSCH. 1926. Abhandlungen und Berichte. Berlin: DATSCH.
DATSCH. 1937. *Die Arbeiten des DATSCH: Eine Übersicht*. Berlin: DATSCH.
David, Paul. 1985. Clio and the Economics of QWERTY. *American Economic Review* 75 (2): 332–7.
Dehen, Peter. 1928. *Die deutschen Industriewerkschulen*. München: A. Huber.
DIHT. 1955. *Ordnungsmittel für die Berufsausbildung*. Vols. I–VI. Bielefeld: W. Bertelsmann.
DIHT. 1970. Bericht 1969 Deutscher Industrie- und Handelstag. Berlin: DIHT.
Djelic, Marie-Laure and Sigrid Quack, eds. 2003. *Globalization and Institutions*. London: Edward Elgar.
Dobbin, Frank. 1994. *Forging Industrial Policy: The United States, Britain and France in the Railway Age*. New York: Cambridge University Press.
Dobischat, Rolf, Antonius Lipsmeier, and Ingrid Drexel. 1996. *Der Umbruch des Weiterbildungssystems in den neuen Bundesländern*. New York: Waxmann.
Domansky-Davidsohn, Elisabeth. 1981. Arbeitskämpfe und Arbeitskampfstrategien des Deutschen Metallarbeiterverbandes, 1891–1914. Ph.D. dissertation, Department of History, Ruhr-Universität, Bochum.
Dore, Ronald. 1973. *British Factory Japanese Factory: The Origins of National Diversity in Industrial Relations*. London: Allen & Unwin.
Dore, Ronald, and Mari Sako. 1989. *How the Japanese Learn to Work*. New York: Routledge.
Douglas, Paul H. 1921. *American Apprenticeship and Industrial Education*. Vol. XCV, *Studies in History, Economics, and Public Law*. New York: Longmans Agents.
Dunlop, O. Jocelyn, and Richard D. Denman. 1912. *English Apprenticeship and Child Labour*. New York: Macmillan.
Düsseldorf, IHK. 1945. Erziehung besserer Ausbildung und Prüfungsergebnisse. In *Quellen und Dokumente zur betrieblichen Berufsbildung 1945–1990*, edited by G. Pätzold. Köln: Böhlau Verlag.
Easton, David. 1957. An Approach to the Analysis of Political Systems. *World Politics* 11: 383–400.
Ebbinghaus, Bernhard, and Philip Manow, eds. 2001. *Comparing Welfare Capitalism: Social Policy and Political Economy in Europe, Japan and the USA*. London: Routledge.
Ebert, Roland. 1984. *Zur Entstehung der Kategorie Facharbeiter als Problem der Erziehungswissenschaft*. Bielefeld: Kleine.
Education, Board of. 1909a. Report of the Consultative Committee on Attendance, Compulsory or Otherwise, at Continuation Schools, Vol. 1: Report and Apprentices. London: His Majesty's Stationery Office.

Education, Board of. 1909b. Report of the Consultative Committee on Attendance, Compulsory or Otherwise, at Continuation Schools. Vol. II: Summaries of Evidence. London: His Majesty's Stationery Office.

Eichberg, Ekkehard. 1965. *Die Lehrwerkstatt im Industriebetrieb*. Weinheim/Bergstr.: Julius Beltz.

Eisenberg, Christiane. 1987. Handwerkstradition und Gewerkschaftsentwicklung im 18. und frühen 19. Jahrhundert. Deutschland und England im Vergleich. *Tel'Aviver Jahrbuch für deutsche Geschichte* XVI: 177–99.

Elbaum, Bernard. 1989. Why Apprenticeship Persisted in Britain but Not in the United States. *The Journal of Economic History* XLIX (2): 337–49.

Elbaum, Bernard, and William Lazonick. 1986. An Institutional Perspective on British Decline. In *The Decline of the British Economy*, edited by B. Elbaum and W. Lazonick. Oxford: Clarendon.

Elster, Jon. 2003. Authors and Actors. Paper presented at a conference on "Crafting and Operating Institutions," April 11–13, 2003, at Yale University, New Haven, CT.

Engel, Dieter, and Hans-Joachim Rosenthal. 1970. *Berufliche Bildung und Berufsbildungspolitik in der Bundesrepublik Deutschland 1960–1970*. Wiesbaden: Franz Steiner Verlag.

Engelhardt, Ulrich. 1977. *'Nur vereinigt sind wir stark': Die Anfänge der deutschen Gewerkschaftsbewegung*. Vol. II. Stuttgart: Klett-Cotta.

Estevez-Abe, Margarita, Torben Iversen, and David Soskice. 2001. Social Protection and the Formation of Skills: A Reinterpretation of the Welfare State. In *Varieties of Capitalism: The Institutional Foundations of Comparative Advantage*, edited by P. A. Hall and D. Soskice. New York: Oxford University Press.

Faulstich, Peter. 1977. *Interessenkonflikte um die Berufsbildung: Das Verhältnis von gesellschaftlichen Interessenstrukturen und staatlicher Bildungspolitik*. Weinheim: Beltz Verlag.

Feldman, Gerald. 1970. German Business between War and Revolution: The Origins of the Stinnes-Legien Agreement. In *Entstehung und Wandel der modernen Gesellschaft: Festschrift für Hans Rosenberg zum 65. Geburtstag*, edited by G. A. Ritter. Berlin: Walter de Gruyter & Co.

Feldman, Gerald. 1977. *Iron and Steel in the German Inflation*. Princeton, NJ: Princeton University Press.

Feldman, Gerald, and Ulrich Nocken. 1975. Trade Associations and Economic Power: Interest Group Development in the German Iron and Steel and Machine Building Industries, 1900–1933. *Business History Review* XLIX (4): 413–45.

Ferner, Anthony, and Richard Hyman, eds. 1998. *Changing Industrial Relations in Europe*. Malden, MA: Blackwell.

Finegold, David. 1993. Making Apprenticeships Work. *Rand Issue Papers* March 1993 (1): 6.

Finegold, David, and David Soskice. 1988. The Failure of Training in Britain: Analysis and Prescription. *Oxford Review of Economic Policy* 4 (3): 21–53.

Finegold, David, and Karin Wagner. 1997. When Lean Production Meets the "German Model." *Industry and Innovation* 4 (2): 207–32.

Fleming, A. P. M., and J. G. Pearce. 1916. *The Principles of Apprentice Training*. London: Longmans.

Franz, Wolfgang, and David Soskice. 1995. The German Apprenticeship System. In *Institutional Frameworks and Labor Market Performance*, edited by F. Buttler et al. London: Routledge.

Frese, Matthias. 1991. *Betriebspolitik im "Dritten Reich": Deutsche Arbeitsfront, Unternehmer und Staatsbürokratie in der westdeutschen Grossindustrie 1933–1939*. Paderborn: Ferdinand Schöningh.

Fricke, Fritz. 1930. Aufgaben und Grenzen technischer Arbeitsschulung, beurteilt vom Standpunkt des Arbeitnehmers. *Industrielle Arbeitsschulung als Problem: Bericht über die "Siebente Tagung für Werkspolitik,"* at Frankfurt/ Main.

Frölich, Fr. 1919. Die Gesellenprüfung der Industrielehrlinge. In *Abhandlungen und Berichte über Technisches Schulwesen*, edited by DATSCH. Berlin: DATSCH.

Fürer. Dr. 1927. Förderung der Facharbeiter – Ausbildung durch Industrieverbände. *Der Arbeitgeber: Zeitschrift der Vereinigung der Deutschen Arbeitgeberverbände*, No. 2: 30–6.

Furusho, Tadashi. 1969. Shoki rōdōrippō no tenkai to keizai dantai. *Komazawa Daigaku keizaigaku ronshū* 1 (1–2).

Gall, Lothar, and Manfred Pohl, eds. 1998. *Unternehmen im Nationalsozialismus*. München: Verlag C. H. Beck.

Garon, Sheldon. 1988. *Labor and the State in Modern Japan*. Palo Alto, CA: Stanford University Press.

Garrett, Geoffrey. 1998. *Partisan Politics in the Global Economy*. New York: Cambridge University Press.

Garrett, Geoffrey, and Peter Lange. 1991. Political Responses to Interdependence: What's "Left" for the Left? *International Organization* 45 (4): 539–64.

Gemmill, Paul F. 1922. A Survey of Wage Systems: Compiled from the Experience of Fifty Plants. *Industrial Management* LXIV (4): 207–8.

Gemmill, Paul F. 1924. Methods of Promoting Industrial Employees: Is Hit-or-Miss Promotion Giving Way to Scientific Methods? *Industrial Management* LXVII (4): 235–47.

Gesamtverband Deutscher Metallindustrieller. 1934. *Planmäßige Lehrlingsausbildung in der Metallindustrie*. Berlin: GDM.

Gillingham, John. 1985. The "Deproletarization" of German Society: Vocational Training in the Third Reich. *Journal of Social History* 19: 423–32.

Gordon, Andrew. 1985. *The Evolution of Labor Relations in Japan: Heavy Industry, 1853–1955*. Cambridge, MA: Harvard University Press.

Görs, Dieter. 1976. Aspekte der beruflichen Bildung und Berufsbildungsreform: Ein Literaturbericht. *WSI-Mitteilungen* 29 (6): 353–61.

Gosden, P. H. J. H. 1961. *The Friendly Societies in England 1815–1875*. Manchester, UK: Manchester University Press.

Gospel, Howard F., and Reiko Okayama. 1991. Industrial Training in Britain and Japan: An Overview. In *Industrial Training and Technical Innovation: A Comparative and Historical Study*, edited by H. F. Gospel. London: Routledge.

Gottschalk, Peter, and Timothy M. Smeeding. 1997. Cross-National Comparisons of Earnings and Income Inequality. *Journal of Economic Literature* XXXV: 633–87.

Gray, Robert Q. 1976. *The Labour Aristocracy in Victorian Edinburgh*. Oxford: Clarendon.

Green, Andy, and Akiko Sakamoto. 2001. Models of High Skills in National Competition Strategies. In *High Skills*, edited by P. Brown, A. Green, and H. Lauder. Oxford: Oxford University Press.

Greif, Avner, and David Laitin. 2003. How Do Self-Enforcing Institutions Endogenously Change? Unpublished manuscript. Stanford University, Stanford, CA.

Greinert, Wolf-Dietrich. 1994. *The "German System" of Vocational Education: History, Organization, Prospects*. Vol. Band 6, *Studien zur Vergleichenden Berufspädagogik*. Baden-Baden: Nomos Verlagsgesellschaft.

Hacker, Jacob. 2002. *The Divided Welfare State: The Battle over Public and Private Social Benefits in the United States*. New York: Cambridge University Press.

Hacker, Jacob. Forthcoming. Policy Drift: The Hidden Politics of U.S. Welfare State Retrenchment. In *Change and Continuity in Institutional Analysis: Explorations in the Dynamics of Advanced Political Economies*, edited by W. Streeck and K. Thelen.

Hacker, Jacob, and Paul Pierson. 2002. Business Power and Social Policy. *Politics & Society* 30 (2): 277–325.

Hall, Peter A. 1986. *Governing the Economy: The Politics of State Intervention in Britain and France*. New York: Oxford University Press.

Hall, Peter A. 1994. Central Bank Independence and Coordinated Wage Bargaining: Their Interaction in Germany and Europe. *German Politics and Society*: 1–23.

Hall, Peter A. and Daniel Gingerich. 2001. Varieties of Capitalism and Institutional Complementarities in the Macroeconomy: An Empirical Analysis. Paper presented to the Annual Meeting of the American Political Science Association, San Francisco, August 2001.

Hall, Peter A. and Daniel Gingerich. 2004. Spielarten des Kapitalismus und institutionelle Komplementaritäten in der Makroökonomie – Eine empirische Analyse. *Berliner Journal Für Soziologie* (Winter).

Hall, Peter A., and David Soskice, eds. 2001. *Varieties of Capitalism: The Institutional Foundations of Comparative Advantage*. New York: Oxford University Press.

Hansen, Hal. 1997. Caps and Gowns. Ph.D. dissertation, Department of History, University of Wisconsin-Madison, Madison.

Harris, Howell John. 1991. Getting it Together: The Metal Manufacturers Association of Philadelphia, c. 1900–1930. In *Masters to Managers: Historical and Comparative Perspectives on American Employers*, edited by S. Jacoby. New York: Columbia University Press.

Hart, R. A., and D. I. MacKay. 1975. Engineering Earnings in Britain, 1914–68. *Journal of the Royal Statistical Society* 13 (1): 32–43.

Hattam, Victoria. 1992. Institutions and Political Change: Working-class Formation in England and the United States, 1829–1896. In *Structuring Politics: Historical Institutionalism in Comparative Analysis*, edited by S. Steinmo, K. Thelen, and F. Longstreth. New York: Cambridge University Press.

Haydu, Jeffrey. 1988. *Between Craft and Class: Skilled Workers and Factory Politics in the United States and Britain, 1890–1922*. Berkeley, CA: University of California Press.

Haydu, Jeffrey. 1997. *Making American Industry Safe for Democracy*. Urbana, IL: University of Illinois Press.

Hayes, Peter. 1987. *Industry and Ideology: IG Farben in the Nazi Era*. Cambridge, UK: Cambridge University Press.

Hayes, Peter. 2001. Industry under the Swastika. In *European Business in the Fascist Era*, edited by H. James. London: Ashgate Press.

Hazama, Hiroshi. 1964. *Nihon rōmukanri-shi kenkyū*. Tokyo: Diayamondosha.

Heinemann, Manfred, ed. 1980. *Erziehung und Schulung im Dritten Reich*. 2 vols. Vol. 1. Stuttgart: Klett-Cotta.

Helfert, Mario. 1970a. Berufliche Bildung und das Berufsbildungsgesetz. *WWI-Mitteilungen* 5: 152–9.

Helfert, Mario. 1970b. Berufliche Bildung und das Berufsbildungsgesetz II. *WWI-Mitteilungen* 7–8: 229–40.

Herber, Leo. 1930. Die Organisation des Lehrlingswesens im Handwerk und die Stellung der Handwerkervertretungen und der Gewerkschaften zu seiner Reform. Wirtschafts- und Sozialwissenschaftlichen Fakultät (Economics and Social Sciences), Universität Köln, Köln.

Herrigel, Gary. 1993. Identity and Institutions: The Social Construction of Trade Unions in the United States and Germany in the Nineteenth Century. *Studies in American Political Development* 7 (Fall): 371–94.

Herrigel, Gary. 1996a. Crisis in German Decentralized Production: Unexpected Rigidity and the Challenge of an Alternative Form of Flexible Organization in Baden Württemberg. *European Urban and Regional Studies* 3 (1): 33–52.

Herrigel, Gary. 1996b. *Industrial Constructions: The Sources of German Industrial Power*. New York: Cambridge University Press.

Herrigel, Gary. 2000. American Occupation, Market Order, and Democracy: Reconfiguring the Steel Industry in Japan and Germany after the Second World War. In *Americanization and Its Limits: Reworking US Technology and Management in Post-War Europe and Japan*, edited by J. Zeitlin and G. Herrigel. New York: Oxford University Press.

Herrigel, Gary, and Charles F. Sabel. 1999. Craft Production in Crisis: Industrial Restructuring in Germany during the 1990s. In *The German Skills Machine: Sustaining Comparative Advantage in a Global Economy*, edited by P. D. Culpepper and D. Finegold. New York: Berghahn Books.

Hinton, James. 1983. *Labour and Socialism. A History of the British Labour Movement 1867–1974*. Amherst: University of Massachusetts Press.

Hodgson, G. M. 1993. *Economics and Evolution: Bringing Life Back into Economics*. Cambridge, MA: Polity.

Hoffmann, Ernst. 1962. *Zur Geschichte der Berufsausbildung in Deutschland*. Bielefeld: W. Bertelsmann.

Homburg, Heidrun. 1982. Externer und interner Arbeitsmarkt: Zur Entstehung und Funktion des Siemens-Werkvereins, 1906–1918. In *Historische Arbeitsmarktforschung: Entstehung, Entwicklung, und Probleme der Vermarktung von*

Arbeitskraft, edited by T. Pierenkemper and R. Tilly. Göttingen: Vandenhoeck & Ruprecht.

Hopkins, Eric. 1995. *Working-class Self-help in Nineteenth-century England*. New York: St. Martin's Press.

Hounshell, David. 1984. *From the American System to Mass Production 1800–1932*. Baltimore: Johns Hopkins University Press.

Howell, Chris. Forthcomong. *Trade Unions and the State: Constructing Industrial Relations Institutions in Britain, 1890–2000*. Princeton, NJ: Princeton University Press.

Howell, George. 1877. Trade Unions, Apprentices, and Technical Education. *Contemporary Review* XXX: 833–57.

Huber, Evelyne, and John D. Stephens. 2001. *Development and Crisis of the Welfare States: Parties and Policies in Global Markets*. Chicago: University of Chicago Press.

Ikeda, Makoto. 1982. *Nihonteki kyōchōshugi no seiritsu*. Tokyo: Keibunsha.

Inoko, Takenori. 1996. *Gakkō to kōjō*. Tokyo: Yomiuri Shinbunsha.

Ipsen, Hans-Peter. 1967. *Berufsausbildungsrecht für Handel, Gewerbe, und Industrie*. Tübingen: J. C. B. Mohr.

Iversen, Torben. 2003. *Capitalism, Democracy and Welfare: The Changing Nature of Production, Elections, and Social Protection in Modern Capitalism*. Cambridge, MA: Harvard University manuscript.

Iversen, Torben, Jonas Pontusson, and David Soskice, eds. 2000. *Unions, Employers, and Central Banks: Macroeconomic Coordination and Institutional Change in Social Market Economies*. New York: Cambridge University Press.

Iversen, Torben, and David Soskice. 2001. An Asset Theory of Social Policy Preferences. *American Political Science Review* 95 (4): 875–93.

Jackson, Robert Max. 1984. *The Formation of Craft Labor Markets*. New York: Academic Press.

Jacoby, Daniel. 1991. The Transformation of Industrial Apprenticeship in the United States. *The Journal of Economic History* 51 (4): 887–910.

Jacoby, Sanford M. 1985. *Employing Bureaucracy: Managers, Unions, and the Transformation of Work in American Industry, 1900–1945*. New York: Columbia University Press.

Jacoby, Sanford, ed. 1991. *Masters to Managers: Historical and Comparative Perspectives on American Employers*. New York: Columbia University Press.

Jacoby, Sanford. 1993. Pacific Ties: Industrial Relations and Employment Systems in Japan and the United States since 1900. In *Industrial Democracy in America: The Ambiguous Promise*, edited by N. Lichtenstein and H. J. Harris. New York: Cambridge University Press.

Jacoby, Wade. 2000. *Imitation and Politics*. Ithaca, NY: Cornell University Press.

Jeffreys, James B. 1945. *The Story of the Engineers 1800–1945*. Letchworth, Hertfordshire, UK: Lawrence & Wishart.

Jevons, H. Winifred. 1908. Apprenticeship and Skilled Employment Committees. In *Continuation Schools in England & Elsewhere*, edited by M. E. Sadler. Manchester, UK: University of Manchester Press.

Kaiser, Rolf, and Hermann Loddenkemper. 1980. *Nationalsozialismus – Totale Manipulation in der beruflichen Bildung?* Frankfurt/Main: Peter Lang.

Kantorowicz, Heinz. 1930. Comments. *Industrielle Arbeitsschulung als Problem: Bericht über die "Seibente Tagung für Werkspolitik*. Frankfurt/Main: Spaeth & Linde.

Kaps, Hans Augustin. 1930. Die Beziehungen zwischen Lehrlingsvertrag und Tarifvertrag. Rechts- und Sozialwissenschaften, Schlesischen Friedrich-Wilhelms-Universität, Breslau.

Kapstein, Ethan. 1996. Workers and the World Economy. *Foreign Affairs* 75 (3): 16–37.

Katz, Harry, and Owen Darbishire. 1999. *Converging Divergences*. Ithaca, NY: Cornell University Press.

Katz, Lawrence F., and Kevin M. Murphy. 1992. Changes in Relative Wages, 1963–1987: Supply and Demand Factors. *Quarterly Journal of Economics* 107 (1): 35–78.

Katzenstein, Peter J. 1987. *Policy and Politics in West Germany: The Growth of a Semisovereign State*. Philadelphia, PA: Temple University Press.

Katznelson, Ira. 2003. Periodization and Preferences: Reflections on Purposive Action in Comparative Historical Social Science. In *Comparative Historical Analysis in the Social Sciences*, edited by J. Mahoney and D. Rueschemeyer. New York: Cambridge University Press.

Kell, Adolf. 1970. *Die Vorstellungen der Verbände zur Berufsausbildung*. Berlin: Institut für Bildungsforschung in der Max-Planck-Gesellschaft.

Kellett, J. R. 1958. The Breakdown of Gild and Corporation Control over the Handicraft and Retail Trade in London. *The Economic History Review* X (3): 381–94.

Kellner, Hans. 1930. Die Pädagogik der Facharbeiterausbildung. *Industrielle Arbeitsschulung als Problem: Bericht über die Siebente Tagung für Werkspolitik, 3./4 Oktober*. Frankfurt/Main: Spaeth & Linde.

Kelly, Roy Willmarth. 1920. *Training Industrial Workers*. New York: The Ronald Press Company.

Kelly, Thomas. 1992. *A History of Adult Education in Great Britain*. Liverpool: Liverpool University Press.

Keohane, Robert. 1984. *After Hegemony: Cooperation and Discord in the World Political Economy*. Princeton, NJ: Princeton University Press.

Kieslinger, Adolf. 1950. Berufsausbildung am Scheideweg. In *Quellen und Dokumente*, edited by G. Pätzold. Köln: Böhlau Verlag.

Kieslinger, A. 1960. Vocational Training and Education in Industry and Commerce: The Cooperation of the Chambers of Commerce and Industry. In *Berufsausbildung in Industrie, Handel, Handwerk der Bundesrepublik Deutschland*. Paderborn: Verlag Ferdinand Schöningh.

Kieslinger, Adolf. 1966. *20 Jahre Berufsausbildung in der Bundesrepublik Deutschland, 1945–1965*. Bielefeld: W. Bertelsmann Verlag.

Kikkawa, Takeo. 1988. Functions of Japanese Trade Associations before World War II: The Case of Cartel. In *Trade Associations in Business History*, edited by H. Yamazaki and M. Miyamoto. Tokyo: University of Tokyo Press.

King, Desmond. 1997. Employers, Training Policy, and the Tenacity of Voluntarism in Britain. *Twentieth Century British History* 8 (3): 383–411.

King, Desmond, and Mark Wickham-Jones. 1997. Training without the State? New Labour and Labour Markets. *Policy and Politics* 26 (4): 439–55.

King, Desmond, and Stewart Wood. 1999. Political Economy of Neoliberalism. In *Continuity and Change in Contemporary Capitalism*, edited by H. Kitschelt, P. Lange, G. Marks, and J. D. Stephens. New York: Cambridge University Press.

Kipp, Martin. 1990. 'Perfektionierung der industriellen Berufsausbildung im Dritten Reich. In *Erkundungen im Halbdunkel: Fünfzehn Studien zur Berufserziehung und Pädagogik im nationalsozialistischen Deutschland*, edited by M. Kipp and G. Miller-Kipp. Kassel, D: Gesamthochschul-Bibliothek.

Kipp, Martin, and Gisela Miller-Kipp. 1990. *Erkundungen im Halbdunkel: Fünfzehn Studien zur Berufserziehung und Pädagogik im nationalsozialistischen Deutschland.* Kassel, D: Gesamthochschul-Bibliothek.

Kitschelt, Herbert, Peter Lange, Gary Marks, and John D. Stephens, eds. 1999. *Continuity and Change in Contemporary Capitalism*. New York: Cambridge University Press.

Klug, Thomas A. 1993. The Roots of the Open Shop: Employers, Trade Unions, and Craft Labor Markets in Detroit, 1859–1907. Dissertation submitted to Department of History, Wayne State University, Detroit, MI.

Knight, Jack. 1992. *Institutions and Social Conflict*. New York: Cambridge University Press.

Knight, Jack. 1999. Explaining the Rise of Neo-Liberalism: The Mechanisms of Institutional Change. Unpublished manuscript, Washington University in St. Louis, MO.

Knowles, K. G., and D. J. Robertson. 1951. Differences between the Wages of Skilled and Unskilled Workers, 1880–1950. *Bulletin of the Oxford University Institute of Statistics* 13 (4): 109–27.

Knox, William. 1980. British Apprenticeship, 1800–1914. Ph.D. dissertation, Edinburgh University, Edinburgh.

Knox, William. 1986. Apprenticeship and De-Skilling in Britain, 1850–1914. *International Review of Social History* XXXI (Part 2): 166–84.

Kocka, Jürgen. 1984. Craft Traditions and the Labor Movement in Nineteenth Century Germany. In *The Power of the Past: Essays for Eric Hobsbawm*, edited by P. Thane, G. Crossick, and R. Floud. Cambridge, UK: Cambridge University Press.

Kocka, Jürgen. 1986a. Problems of Working-Class Formation in Germany: The Early Years, 1800–1875. In *Working-Class Formation: Nineteenth Century Patterns in Western Europe and the United States*, edited by I. Katznelson and A. R. Zolberg. Princeton, NJ: Princeton University Press.

Kocka, Jürgen. 1986b. Traditionsbindung und Klassenbildung: Zum Sozialhistorischen Ort der frühen deutschen Arbeiterbewegung. *Historische Zeitschrift* 243 (2): 331–376.

Konietzka, Dirk, and Wolfgang Lempert. 1998. Mythos und Realität der Krise der beuflichen Bildung. *Zeitschrift für Berufs- und Wirtschaftspädagogik* 94 (3): 321–9.

Kopsch, Albert. 1928. Die planmäßige Lehrlingserziehung in der Industrie und die Gewerkschaften. Economics, Philipps-Universität zu Marburg, Marburg.

Koremenos, Barbara, Charles Lipson, and Duncan Snidal. 2001. The Rational Design of International Institutions. *International Organization* 55 (4): 761–800.

Krasner, Stephen D. 1988. Sovereignty: An Institutional Perspective. *Comparative Political Studies* 21 (1): 66–94.

Kume, Ikuo. 1998. *Disparaged Success*. Ithaca, NY: Cornell University Press.

Kurzer, Paulette. 1993. *Business and Banking*. Ithaca, NY: Cornell University Press.

Labor, Ministry of. 1961. *Rōdō gyōsei-shi*. Vol. 1. Tokyo: Rōdōhōrei Kyōkai.

Lauder, Hugh. 2001. *Innovation, Skill Diffusion, and Social Exclusion*. Oxford: Oxford University Press.

Lazonick, William, and Mary O'Sullivan. 1997. Big Business and Skill Formation in the Wealthiest Nations: The Organizational Revolution in the Twentieth Century. In *Big Business and the Wealth of Nations*, edited by A. D. J. Chandler, F. Amatorim, and T. Hikino. Cambridge, UK: Cambridge University Press.

Lee, J. J. 1978. Labour in German Industrialization. In *The Cambridge Economic History of Europe Volume VII: The Industrial Economies: Capital, Labour, and Enterprise*, edited by P. Mathias and M. M. Postan. Cambridge, UK: Cambridge University Press.

Lehmbruch, Gerhard. 2001. The Rise and Change of Discourses on 'Embedded Capitalism' in Germany and Japan and their Institutional Setting. In *The Origins of Nonliberal Capitalism: Germany and Japan*, edited by W. Streeck and K. Yamamura. Ithaca, NY: Cornell University Press.

Lenger, Friedrich. 1988. *Sozialgeschichte der deutschen Handwerker seit 1800*. Frankfurt/Main: Suhrkamp.

Levine, Solomon B., and Hisashi Kawada. 1980. *Human Resources in Japanese Industrial Development*. Princeton NJ: Princeton University Press.

Levy, Frank, and Richard J. Murnane. 1992. U.S. Earnings Levels and Earnings Inequality: A Review of Recent Trends and Proposed Explanations. *Journal of Economic Literature* 30 (3): 1333–81.

Liebowitz, S. J., and Stephen E. Margolis. 1990. The Fable of the Keys. *Journal of Law and Economics* XXXIII: 1–25.

Linton, Derek S. 1991. *Who Has the Youth, Has the Future: The Campaign to Save Young Workers in Imperial Germany*. New York: Columbia University Press.

Lippart, Gottlieb Matthias. 1919. Einleitender Bericht über zukünftige Lehrlingsausbildung in der mechanischen Industrie. *Abhandlungen und Berichte über Technisches Schulwesen*. Berlin: B. G. Teubner: 1–10.

Lipset, Seymour Martin, and Stein Rokkan. 1968. Cleavage Structures, Party Systems, and Voter Alignments. In *Party System and Voter Alignments: Cross-National Perspectives*, edited by S. M. Lipset and S. Rokkan. New York: Free Press.

Lipsmeier, Antonius. 1998. Berufsbildung. In *Handbuch der deutschen Bildungsgeschichte*, edited by C. Führ and C.-L. Furck. München: C. H. Beck.

Lynch, Lisa M., ed. 1994. *Training and the Private Sector: International Comparisons*. Chicago: University of Chicago Press.

Mack, Frida. 1927. Fortschritte in der Lehrlingsausbildung in Handwerk und Industrie. Dissertation in Staatswissenschaften (Political Science), Ruprecht-Karls-Universität Heidelberg, Heidelberg.

Mahoney, James. 2000. Path Dependence in Historical Sociology. *Theory and Society* 29: 507–48.

Mahoney, James. 2002. *The Legacies of Liberalism: Path Dependence and Political Regimes in Central America*. Baltimore: Johns Hopkins University Press.

Mallmann, Luitwin. 1990. *100 Jahre Gesamtmetall: Perspektiven aus Tradition*. Edited by Gesamtverband der Metallindustriellen Arbeitgeberverbände. 2 vols. Vol. I. Köln: Deutscher Instituts-Verlag.

Manow, Philip. 1999. The Uneasy Compromise of Liberalism and Corporatism in Postwar Germany. Paper read at Workshop on "Liberalism and Change: Political Rights and Economic Capacities in Germany and the United States," (January 22–24), at Center for German and European Studies, University of California, Berkeley.

Manow, Philip. 2001a. *Social Protection, Capitalist Production: The Bismarckian Welfare State and the German Political Economy From the 1880s to the 1990s*. Habilitationsschrift, University of Konstanz, Konstanz.

Manow, Philip. 2001b. Welfare State Building and Coordinated Capitalism in Japan and Germany. In *The Origins of Nonliberal Capitalism*, edited by W. Streeck and K. Yamamura. Ithaca, NY: Cornell University Press.

Mares, Isabela. 2000. Strategic Alliances and Social Policy Reform: Unemployment Insurance in Comparative Perspective. *Politics & Society* 28 (2): 223–44.

Martin, Andrew, and George Ross, eds. 1999. *The Brave New World of European Labour: Comparing Trade Unions Responses to the New European Economy*. Oxford: Berghahn Books.

Mason, T. W. 1966. Labour in the Third Reich, 1933–1939. *Past and Present* 33: 112–41.

McKinlay, Alan. 1986. From Industrial Serf to Wage-Labourer: The 1937 Apprentice Revolt in Britain. *International Review of Social History* XXXI (1): 1–18.

McKinlay, Alan, and Jonathan Zeitlin. 1989. The Meanings of Managerial Prerogative: Industrial Relations and the Organisation of Work in British Engineering, 1880–1939. *Business History* xxxi (2): 32–47.

Mehren, E. J. 1914. A Factor in Alleviating Industrial Unrest. *Bulletin of the National Association of Corporation Schools* 3: 7–9.

Meyer, J. W., and B. Rowan. 1991. Institutionalized Organizations: Formal Structure as Myth and Ceremony. In *The New Institutionalism in Organizational Analysis*, edited by W. W. Powell and P. DiMaggio. Chicago: University of Chicago Press.

Millikan, William. 2001. *A Union against Unions: The Minneapolis Citizens' Alliance and the Fight against Organized Labor 1903–1947*. St. Paul: Minnesota Historical Society Press.

Ministry of Labour. 1928a. *Report of an Enquiry into Apprenticeship and Training for the Skilled Occupations in Great Britain and Northern Ireland, 1925–26: General Report*. Vol. VII. London: His Majesty's Stationery Office.

Ministry of Labour. 1928b. *Report of an Enquiry into Apprenticeship and Training for the Skilled Occupations in Great Britain and Northern Ireland, 1925–1926: Engineering, Shipbuilding and Ship-Repairing, and other Metal Industries*. Vol. VI. London: His Majesty's Stationery Office.

Miyamoto, Mataji. 1938. *Kabunakama no kenkyū*. Tokyo: Yūhikaku.

Moe, Terry. 2003. Power and Political Institutions. Paper read at conference on Crafting and Operating Institutions, April 11–13, 2003, at Yale University, New Haven, CT.

Moene, Karl Ove, and Michael Wallerstein. 1995. How Social Democracy Worked: Labor Market Institutions. *Politics & Society* 23 (2): 185–211.

Molitor, Erich. 1960. *Die überbetriebliche Regelung der Lehrlingsvergütung*. Stuttgart: W. Kohlhammer Verlag.

Mommsen, Wolfgang J., and Hans-Gerhard Husung, eds. 1985. *The Development of Trade Unionism in Great Britain and Germany 1880–1914*. London: Allen and Unwin.

Montgomery, David. 1989. *The Fall of the House of Labor*. New York: Cambridge University Press.

More, Charles. 1980. *Skill and the English Working Class, 1870–1914*. New York: St. Martin's Press.

Morita, Yoshio. 1926. *Wagakuni no shihonka dantai*. Tokyo: Tōyō Keizai Shinpōsha.

Morris, John van Liew. 1921. *Employee Training: A Study of Education and Training Departments in Various Corporations*. New York: McGraw-Hill.

Mosher, James. 1999. The Institutional Origins of Wage Equality: Labor Unions and their Wage Policies. Paper read at 57th Annual Meeting of the Midwest Political Science Association, at Chicago.

Mosher, James. 2001. Labor Power and Wage Equality: The Politics of Supply-Side Equality, Ph.D. dissertation, Political Science Department, University of Wisconsin-Madison, Madison, WI.

Motley, James M. 1907. *Apprenticeship in American Trade Unions*. Edited by J. M. Vincent, J. H. Hollander, and W. W. Willoughby. Vol. Series XXV, Nos. 11–12; (November–December 1907), *Johns Hopkins University Studies in Historical and Political Science*. Baltimore: Johns Hopkins University Press.

Münch, Joachim. 1991. *Vocational Training in the Federal Republic of Germany*. 3rd ed. Berlin: European Centre for the Development of Vocational Training.

Muth, Wolfgang. 1985. *Berufsausbildung in der Weimarer Republik*. Edited by H. Pohl and W. Treue. Vol. 41, *Zeitschrift für Unternehmensgeschichte*. Stuttgart: Franz Steiner.

NACS, National Association of Corporation Schools. 1914. Proceedings of the First Annual Convention, 1913. New York: The Trow Press.

Nelson, Daniel. 1975. *Managers and Workers: Origins of the New Factory System in the United States, 1880–1920*. Madison, WI: University of Wisconsin Press.

Nelson, Daniel. 1992. *A Mental Revolution: Scientific Management since Taylor*. Columbus: Ohio State University Press.

NICB, National Industrial Conference Board. 1929. *Industrial Relations Programs in Small Plants*. New York: National Industrial Conference Board.

Nielson, Klaus, Bob Jessop, and Jerzy Hausner. 1995. Institutional Change in Post-Socialism. In *Strategic Choice and Path-Dependency in Post-Socialism: Institutional Dynamics in the Transformation Process*, edited by J. Hausner, B. Jessop, and K. Nielsen. Hants, UK: Edward Elgar.

Nishinarita, Yutaka. 1995. An Overview of Japanese Labor-Employer Relations from the 1870's to the 1990's. *Hitotsubashi Journal of Economics* 36: 17–20.

Noguchi, Yukio. 1995. *1940-nen taisei*. Tokyo: Tōyō Keizai Shinpōsha.

Nolan, Mary. 1994. *Visions of Modernity: American Business and the Modernization of Germany*. New York: Oxford University Press.

Noll, Ingeborg, Ursula Beicht, Georg Böll, Wilfried Malcher, and Susanne Wiederhold-Fritz. 1983. *Nettokosten der betrieblichen Berufsausbildung*. Berlin: Beuth Verlag.

North, Douglass C. 1990. *Institutions, Institutional Change and Economic Performance*. New York: Cambridge University Press.

Odaka, Konosuke. 1984. *Rōdō shijō bunseki*. Tokyo: Iwanami Shoten.

Odaka, Konosuke. 1990. Sangyō no ninaite. In *Nihon keizaishi*, edited by S. Nishikawa and T. Abe. Tokyo: Iwanami Shoten.

Odaka, Konosuke. 1995. *Shokunin no sekai, kōjō no sekai*. Tokyo: Libro.

Ogilvie, Sheilagh C., and Markus Cerman, eds. 1996. *European Proto-Industrialization*. Cambridge, UK: Cambridge University Press.

Okazaki, Tetsuji. 1993. Kigyō shisutemu. In *Gendai Nihon keizai shisutemu no genryū*, edited by T. Okazaki and M. Okuno. Tokyo: Nihon Keizai Shinbunsha.

Olofsson, Jonas. 2001. Partsorganisationerna och industrins yrkesutbildning 1918–1971- en svensk modell för central trepartssamverkan. *Scandia* 1.

Olson, Mancur. 1982. *The Rise and Decline of Nations*. New Haven, CT: Yale University Press.

Orren, Karen, and Stephen Skowronek. 1994. Beyond the Iconography of Order: Notes for a "New" Institutionalism. In *The Dynamics of American Politics*, edited by L. C. Dodd and C. Jillson. Boulder, CO: Westview.

Orren, Karen, and Stephen Skowronek. 2002. The Study of American Political Development. In *Political Science: The State of the Discipline*, edited by I. Katznelson and H. Milner. New York: Norton.

Oulton, Nicholas, and Hilary Steedman. 1994. The British System of Youth Training: A Comparison with Germany. In *Training and the Private Sector: International Comparisons*, edited by L. M. Lynch. Chicago: University of Chicago Press.

Palier, Bruno. Forthcoming. Ambiguous Agreement, Cumulative Change: French Social Policy in the 1990s. In *Change and Continuity in Institutional Analysis: Explorations in the Dynamics of Advanced Political Economies*, edited by W. Streeck and K. Thelen.

Park, L. L. 1914. Does Modern Apprenticeship Pay? *Buelletin of the National Association of Corporation Schools* 10: 11–16.

Parker, Eric. 1996. The District Apprentice System of the Milwaukee Metalworking Sector, 1900–1930. Paper read at Social Science History Association Meeting, at New Orleans, LA.

Patten, Thomas H. 1968. *The Foreman: Forgotten Man of Management*. New York: American Management Association.

Pätzold, Günter. 1989. Berufsbildung: handwerkliche, industrielle und schulische Berufserziehung. In *Handbuch der deutschen Bildungsgeschichte. Die Weimarer*

Republik und die nationalsozialistische Diktatur, edited by D. Langewiesche and H.-E. Tenorth. München: C. H. Beck.

Pätzold, Günter, ed. 1991. *Quellen und Dokumente zur Betrieblichen Berufsbildung*. Köln: Böhlau Verlag.

Pempel, T. J. 1998. *Regime Shift: Comparative Dynamics of the Japanese Political Economy*. Ithaca, NY: Cornell University Press.

Perlman, Mark. 1961. *The Machinists: A New Study in American Trade Unionism*. Cambridge, MA: Harvard University Press.

Perry, P. J. C. 1976. *The Evolution of British Manpower Policy*. Portsmouth, UK: British Associations for Commercial and Industrial Education.

Phelps Brown, Henry. 1959. *The Growth of British Industrial Relations: A Study from the Standpoint of 1906–14*. London, New York: Macmillan, St. Martin's Press.

Pichler, Eva. 1993. Cost-Sharing of General and Specific Training with Depreciation of Human Capital. *Economics of Education Review* 12 (2): 117–24.

Pierson, Paul. 2000a. Increasing Returns, Path Dependence, and the Study of Politics. *American Political Science Review* 94 (2): 251–68.

Pierson, Paul. 2000b. The Limits of Design: Explaining Institutional Origins and Change. *Governance* 13 (4): 475–99.

Pierson, Paul. 2000c. Not Just What, But When: Timing and Sequence in Political Processes. *Studies in American Political Development* 14 (Spring): 72–92.

Pierson, Paul. 2003a. Public Policies as Institutions. Paper presented at conference on Crafting and Operating Institutions, April 11–13, 2003, Yale University, New Haven, CT.

Pierson, Paul. 2004. *Politics in Time: History, Institutions, and Political Analysis*. Princeton, NJ: Princeton University Press.

Pierson, Paul, and Theda Skocpol. 2002. Historical Institutionalism in Contemporary Political Science. In *Political Science: The State of the Discipline*, edited by I. Katznelson and H. Milner. New York: Norton.

Pigou, A. C. 1912. *Wealth and Welfare*. London: Macmillan.

Piore, Michael J., and Charles F. Sabel. 1984. *The Second Industrial Divide*. New York: Basic Books.

Pollard, Sidney. 1965. *The Genesis of Modern Management: A History of the Industrial Revolution in Great Britain*. Cambridge, MA: Harvard University Press.

Price, Richard. 1983. The Labour Process and Labour History. *Social History* 8 (1): 57–74.

Prothero, I. J. 1979. *Artisans and Politics in Early Nineteenth-Century London*. Kent, UK: Dawson.

Przeworski, Adam. 2001. *Democracy and the Market*. New York: Cambridge University Press.

Quack, Sigrid, Jacqueline O'Reilly, and Swen Hildebrandt. 1995. Structuring Change: Training and Recruitment in Retail Banking in Germany, Britain, and France. *International Journal of Human Resource Management* 6 (4): 759– 94.

Ralf, Klein, and Manfred Schlösser. 1994. Socio-Economic Structural Changes and Innovations in Vocational Training in Selected Economic Sectors. In *Vocational Training in Germany: Modernsation and Responsiveness*, edited by OECD. Paris: OECD.

Raspe, H. 1960. Vocational Training in Handicrafts: Functions of Handicrafts' Organization. In *Vocational Training for Trade, Industrie and Handicrafts in the Federal Republic of Germany*, edited by P. Behler. Paderborn: Verlag Ferdinand Schöningh.

Rathschlag, Axel. 1972. Der Anlernberuf als Ausbildungsberuf für Jugendliche: über die Entwicklung und Bedeutung einer berufspädagogisch umstrittenen Ausbildungskonzeption. Ph.D. dissertation, University of Cologne, Köln.

Reich, Robert B. 1991. *The Work of Nations: Preparing Ourselves for 21st Century Capitalism*. New York: A. A. Knopf.

Richter, Ingo. 1968. *Die Rechtsprechung zur Berufsbildung: Analyse und Entscheidungssammlung*. Stuttgart: Ernst Klett Verlag.

Richter, Julia F. 2000. *Das Ausbildungsverhalten von Betrieben: Eine Analyse der Kosten und Nutzen der betrieblichen Berufsausbildung in Westdeutschland*. Berlin: Logos Verlag.

Richter, P. S. 1950. *Die rechtliche Grundlagen des Lehrlingswesens*. Munich/Erlangen: Siemens & Halske AG, Siemens-Schuckerwerke AG, Kaufmännisches Ausbildungswesen.

Riker, William H. 1980. Implications from the Disequilibrium of Majority Rule for the Study of Institutions. *American Political Science Review* 74 (2): 432–46.

Rohlfing, Theodor. 1949. *Der handwerkliche Lehrvertrag und das Verfahren in Lehrlingsstreitigkeiten*. Bremen-Horn: Industrie- und Handeslverlag Walter Dorn GMBH.

Romer, Paul M. 1990. Endogenous Technological Change. *Journal of Political Economy* 98 (5): S71–S102.

Rorabaugh, W. J. 1986. *The Craft Apprentice: From Franklin to the Machine Age in America*. New York: Oxford University Press.

Rule, John. 1981. *The Experience of Labour in Eighteenth-Century Industry*. London: Croom Helm.

Rule, John. 1988. The Formative Years of British Trade Unionism: An Overview. In *British Trade Unionism 1750–1850: The Formative Years*, edited by J. Rule. Essex, UK: Longman.

Rupieper, Hermann-Josef. 1982. *Arbeiter und Angestellte im Zeitalter der Industrialisierung*. Frankfurt/Main: Campus.

Sabel, Charles F., and Jonathan Zeitlin, eds. 1997. *Worlds of Possibility*. New York: Cambridge University Press.

Sadler, M. E. 1908a. Compulsory Attendance at Continuation Schools in Germany. In *Continuation Schools in England & Elsewhere*, edited by M. E. Sadler. Manchester, UK: University Press.

Sadler, M. E., ed. 1908b. *Continuation Schools in England & Elsewhere*. Manchester, UK: University Press.

Sadler, M. E. 1908c. The Present Position of State-Aided Evening Schools and Classes in England and Wales. In *Continuation Schools in England & Elsewhere*, edited by M. E. Sadler. Manchester, UK: University Press.

Sadler, M. E., and Mary S. Beard. 1908. English Employers and the Education of their Workpeople. In *Continuation Schools in England & Elsewhere*, edited by M. E. Sadler. Manchester, UK: University Press.

Saegusa, Hirone et al. 1960. *Kindai Nihon sangyō gijutsu no seiōka*. Tokyo: Tōyō Keizai Shinpōsha.

Saguchi, Kazuro. 1991. *Nihon ni okeru sangyō minshushugi no zentei*. Tokyo: University of Tokyo Press.

Sako, Mari. 1995. *Skill Testing and Certification in Japan*. Washington DC: The Economic Development Institute of the World Bank.

Sakurabayashi, Makoto. 1985. *Sangyō hōkokukai no soshiki to kinō*. Tokyo: Ochanomizu Shobō.

Sandiford, Peter. 1908. The Half-time System in the Textile Trades. In *Continuation Schools in England & Elsewhere*, edited by M. E. Sadler. Manchester, UK: University Press.

Sauter, Edgar. 1996. Continuing Vocational Training in Germany. In *Continuing Vocational Training: Europe, Japan, and the United States*, edited by J. Brandsma, F. Kessler, and J. Münch. Utrecht: Lemma.

Sawai, Minoru. 1996. Kikai kōgyō. In *Nihon keizai no 200 nen*, edited by N. S. et. al. Tokyo: Nihon Hyōronsha.

Schatz, Ronald. 1977. American Electrical Workers: Work, Struggles, Aspirations, 1930–1950. University Microfilms, History, University of Pittsburgh, Pittsburgh, PA.

Schickler, Eric. 2001. *Disjointed Pluralism: Institutional Innovation and the Development of the U.S. Congress*. Princeton NJ: Princeton University Press.

Schluchter, W., and Peter Quint. 2001. *Der Vereinigungsschock*. Weilerswist: Velbrück Wissenschaft.

Schmedes, Hella. 1931. *Das Lehrlingswesen in der deutschen Eisen- und Stahlindustrie*. Muenster: Verlag August Baader.

Schneiberg, Marc, and Elisabeth Clemens. forthcoming. The Typical Tools for the Job: Research Strategies in Institutional Analysis. In *How Institutions Change*, edited by W. W. Powell and D. L. Jones. Chicago: Chicago University Press.

Schneider, Michael. 1999. *Unterm Hakenkreuz: Arbeiter und Arbeiterbewegung 1933 bis 1939*. Bonn: Verlag J. H. W. Dietz.

Schömann, Isabelle. 2001. Berufliche Bildung antizipativ gestalten: die Rolle der Belegschaftsvertretungen. Ein europäischer Vergleich. In *WZB Working Papers*. Berlin.

Schönhoven, Klaus. 1979. Gewerkschaftliches Organisationsverhalten im Wilhelminischen Deutschland. In *Arbeiter im Industrialisierungsprozeß*, edited by W. Conze and U. Engelhardt. Stuttgart, D: Klett-Cotta.

Schriewer, Jürgen. 1986. Intermediäre Instanzen, Selbstverwaltung und berufliche Ausbildungsstrukturen im historischen Vergleich. *Zeitschrift für Pädagogie* 32 (1): 69–90.

Schütte, Friedhelm. 1992. *Berufserziehung zwischen Revolution und Nationalsozialismus*. Weinheim: Deutscher Studien.

Scranton, Philip. 1997. *Endless Novelty: Specialty Production and American Industrialization 1865–1925*. Princeton, NJ: Princeton University Press.

Seubert, Rolf. 1977. *Berufserziehung und Nationalsozialismus*. Weinheim: Beltz.

Sewell, William H. 1996. Three Temporalities: Toward an Eventful Sociology. In *The Historic Turn in the Human Sciences*, edited by T. J. McDonald. Ann Arbor: University of Michigan Press.

Shefter, Martin. 1986. Trade Unions and Political Machines: The Organization and Disorganization of the American Working Class in the Late Nineteenth Century. In *Working-Class Formation: Nineteenth-Century Patterns in Western Europe and the United States*, edited by I. Katznelson and A. R. Zolberg. Princeton, NJ: Princeton University Press.

Shepsle, Kenneth A. 1986. Institutional Equilibrium and Equilibrium Institutions. In *Political Science: The Science of Politics*, edited by H. Weisberg. New York: Agathon.

Shepsle, Kenneth A., and Barry Weingast. 1981. Structure-induced Equilibrium and Legislative Choice. *Public Choice* 37: 503–19.

Skocpol, Theda. 1985. Bringing the State Back In: Strategies of Analysis in Current Research. In *Bringing the State Back In*, edited by P. B. Evans, D. Rueschemeyer, and T. Skocpol. New York: Cambridge University Press.

Skocpol, Theda. 1992. *Protecting Soldiers and Mothers: The Political Origins of Social Policy in the United States*. Cambridge, MA: Belknap.

Smith, Michael. 2000. Warning over IT skills gap. *Financial Times*, March 7, 3.

Soffer, Benson. 1960. A Theory of Trade Union Development: The Role of the 'Autonomous' Workman. *Labor History* (Spring): 141–63.

Soskice, David. 1991. The Institutional Infrastructure for International Competitiveness: A Comparative Analysis of the UK and Germany. In *The Economics of the New Europe*, edited by A. B. Atkinson and R. Brunetta. London: Macmillan.

Soskice, David. 1994. Reconciling Markets and Institutions: The German Apprenticeship System. In *Training and the Private Sector: International Comparisons*, edited by L. M. Lynch. Chicago: University of Chicago Press.

Soskice, David. 2003. Die deutschen Probleme. *WZB Mitteilungen* 99: 12–14.

Sozialen Museum E. V., ed. 1931. *Industrielle Arbeitsschulung als Problem: Fünf Beiträge über ihre Aufgaben und Grenzen*. Frankfurt/Main: Industrieverlag Spaeth & Linde.

Stark, David. 1995. Not by Design: The Myth of Designer Capitalism in Eastern Europe. In *Strategic Choice and Path-Dependency in Post-Socialism*, edited by J. Hausner, B. Jessop, and K. Nielsen. Hants, UK: Edward Elgar.

Stemme, Dr. Heinz. 1955. *Lehr- und Anlernberufe in Industrie und Handel: Lehrlingzahlen vom 31.12.1954 und Prüfergebnisse der Jahre 1949–1954 der Industrie- und Handelskammern*. Edited by DIHT, *Berufsausbildung*. Bielefeld: W. Bertelsmann Verlag.

Stevens, Margaret. 1996. Transferable Training and Poaching Externalities. In *Acquiring Skills*, edited by A. L. Booth and D. J. Snower. London: Centre for Economic Policy Research.

Stevens, Margaret. 1999. Human Capital Theory and UK Vocational Training Policy. *Oxford Review of Economic Policy* 15 (1): 16–32.

Stinchcombe, Arthur. 1968. *Constructing Social Theories*. New York: Harcourt, Brace and World.

Stockton, C. E. 1908. The Continuation Schools of Munich. In *Continuation Schools in England & Elsewhere*, edited by M. E. Sadler. Manchester, UK: University of Manchester Press.

Stratmann, Karlwilhelm. 1990. Der Kampf um die ausbildungsrechtliche und ausbildungspolitische Hoheit der Unternehmer während der Weimarer Republik und im NS-Staat – die didaktische Unterordnung der Berufsschule. In *Das duale System der Berufsbildung: Eine historische Analyse seiner Reformdebatten*, edited by K. Stratmann and M. Schlösser. Frankfurt/Main: Verlag der Gesellschaft zur Förderung arbeitsorientierter Forschung und Bildung.

Stratmann, Karlwilhelm. 1994. Das duale System der Berufsbildung: Eine historisch-systematische Analyse. In *Lernorte im dualen System der Berufsbilder*, edited by G. Pätzold and G. Walden. Berlin und Bonn: Bundesinstitut für Berufsbildung.

Stratmann, Karlwilhelm. 1999. *Berufserziehung und Sozialer Wandel*. Edited by G. Pätzold and M. Wahle. Frankfurt/Main: Verlag der Gesellschaft zur Förderung arbeitsorientierter Forschung und Bildung.

Stratmann, Karlwilhelm, and Manfred Schlösser. 1990. *Das Duale System der Berufsbildung: Eine Historische Analyse seiner Reformdebatten*. Frankfurt/Main: Verlag der Gesellschaft zur Förderung arbeitsorientierter Forschung und Bildung.

Streeck, Wolfgang. 1983. *Die Reform der beruflichen Bildung in der westdeutschen Bauwirtschaft 1969–1982: Eine Fallstudie über Verbände als Träger öffentlicher Politik*. Berlin: Wissenschaftszentrum Berlin für Sozialforschung, Discussion Paper IIM/LMP 83-23.

Streeck, Wolfgang. 1988. *Skills and the Limits of Neo-Liberalism: The Enterprise of the Future as a Place of Learning*. Berlin: WZB Discussion paper FS I 88- 16.

Streeck, Wolfgang. 1989. Skills and the Limits of Neo-Liberalism. *Work, Employment & Society* 3: 90–104.

Streeck, Wolfgang. 1991. On the Institutional Conditions of Diversified Quality Production. In *Beyond Keynesianism*, edited by E. Matzner and W. Streeck. Aldershot, UK: Edward Elgar.

Streeck, Wolfgang. 1992a. The Logics of Associative Action and the Territorial Organization of Interests: The Case of German Handwerk. In *Social Institutions and Economic Performance*, edited by W. Streeck. London: Sage.

Streeck, Wolfgang. 1992b. *Social Institutions and Economic Performance: Studies of Industrial Relations in Advanced Capitalist Economies*. London: Sage.

Streeck, Wolfgang. 1996. Lean Production in the German Automobile Industry: A Test Case for Convergence Theory. In *National Diversity and Global Capitalism*, edited by S. Berger and R. Dore. Ithaca, NY: Cornell University Press.

Streeck, Wolfgang. 2001. Introduction: Explorations into the Origins of Nonliberal Capitalism in Germany and Japan. In *The Origins of Nonliberal Capitalism: Germany and Japan*, edited by W. Streeck and K. Yamamura. Ithaca, NY: Cornell University Press.

Streeck, Wolfgang, Josef Hilbert, Karl-Heinz van Kevelaer, Frederike Maier, and Hajo Weber. 1987. *The Role of the Social Partners in Vocational Training and Further Training in the Federal Republic of Germany*. Berlin: CEDEFOP.

Streeck, Wolfgang and Kathleen Thelen. Forthcoming. Introduction: Institutional Change in Advanced Political Economies. In *Change and Continuity in Institutional Analysis: Explorations in the Dynamics of Advanced Political Economies*, edited by W. Streeck and K. Thelen.

Streeck, Wolfgang, and Kozo Yamamura. 2002. *Germany and Japan in the 21st Century: Strengths into Weaknesses?* Ithaca, NY: Cornell University Press.

Sumiya, Mikio. 1955. *Nihon chin-rōdō shiron*. Tokyo: University of Tokyo Press.

Sumiya, Mikio. 1970. *Nihon shokugyō kunren hattenshi*. Vol. 1. Tokyo: Nihon Rōdō Kyōkai.

Suzuki, Atsushi. 1992. Teppōkaji kara kikaikō e. *Nenpō kindai Nihon kenkyū* 14.

Suzuki, Tessa Morris. 1994. *The Technological Transformation of Japan: from the 17th to the 21st Centuries*. Cambridge, U.K.: Cambridge University Press.

Swenson, Peter. 2002. *Capitalists against Markets*. New York: Oxford University Press.

Swenson, Peter A. Forthcoming. Varieties of Capitalist Interests: Power, Institutions and the Regulatory Welfare State in the United States and Sweden. *Studies in American Political Development*.

Swidler, Ann. 1986. Culture in Action: Symbols and Strategies. *American Sociological Review* 51: 273–86.

Taira, Koji. 1970. *Economic Development and the Labor Market in Japan*. New York: Columbia University Press.

Taira, Koji. 1978. Factory Labour and the Industrial Revolution in Japan. In *The Cambridge Economic History of Europe: Volume VII, Part 2*, edited by P. Mathias. New York: Cambridge University Press.

Taira, Koji. 1989. Economic Development, Labor Markets and Industrial Relations in Japan, 1905–1955. In *The Cambridge History of Japan: The Twentieth Century*, edited by P. Duus. New York: Cambridge University Press.

Tawney, R. H. 1909a. The Economics of Boy Labour. *The Economic Journal* 19: 517–37.

Tawney, R. H. 1909b. Memorandum. In *Report of the Consultative Committee on Attendance, Compulsory or Otherwise, at Continuation Schools*, edited by Board of Education. London: His Majesty's Stationery Office.

Taylor, M. E. 1981. *Education and Work in the Federal Republic of Germany*. London: Anglo-American Foundation for the Study of Industrial Society.

Tekkō Kikai Kyōkai (Association of Machine and Iron Works). 1974. *Tokyo Kikai Tekkō Dōgyō Kumiai-shi*. Tokyo: Tekkō Kikai Kyōkai.

Thelen, Kathleen. 1991. *Union of Parts: Labor Politics in Postwar Germany*. Ithaca, NY: Cornell University Press.

Thelen, Kathleen. 1999. Historical Institutionalism in Comparative Politics. *The Annual Review of Political Science*, Vol. 2: 369–404.

Thelen, Kathleen. 2002a. How Institutions Evolve: Insights from Comparative-Historical Analysis. In *Comparative Historical Analysis in the Social Sciences*, edited by J. Mahoney and D. Rueschemeyer. New York: Cambridge University Press.

Thelen, Kathleen. 2002b. The Political Economy of Business and Labor in the Advanced Industrial Countries. In *Political Science: The State of the Discipline*, edited by I. Katznelson and H. Milner. New York and Washington DC: Norton Books and the American Political Science Association.

Thelen, Kathleen, and Ikuo Kume. 1999. The Effects of Globalization on Labor Revisited: Lessons from Germany and Japan. *Politics & Society* 27 (4): 476–504.

Thelen, Kathleen, and Christa van Wijnbergen. 2003. The Paradox of Globalization: Labor Relations in Germany and Beyond. *Comparative Political Studies* 36(8): 859–80.

Thompson, E. P. 1963. *The Making of the English Working Class*. New York: Vintage Books.

Tolliday, Steven. 1992. Management and Labour in Britain 1896–1939. In *Between Fordism and Flexibility*, edited by S. Tolliday and J. Zeitlin. Oxford: Berg Publishers.

Tollkühn, Gertrud. 1926. *Die planmäßige Ausbildung des gewerblichen Fabriklehrlings in der metall- und holzverarbeitenden Industrien*. Jena, D: Gustav Fischer.

Ullmann, Hans-Peter. 1988. *Interessenverbände in Deutschland*. Frankfurt/Main: Suhrkamp.

Ulman, Lloyd. 1955. *The Rise of the National Trade Union*. Cambridge, MA: Harvard University Press.

Unwin, George. 1909. *The Gilds and Companies of London*. London: Methuen.

U.S. Department of Labor, Bureau of Apprenticeship and Training. 1991. *Apprenticeship Past and Present*. Washington DC: U.S. Department of Labor.

Vereinigung der Deutschen Arbeitergeberverbände. 1922. *Geschäftsbericht über das Jahr 1921*. Berlin: VDA.

Vogel, Steven K. 2001. The Crisis of German and Japanese Capitalism: Stalled on the Road to the Liberal Market Model? *Comparative Political Studies* 34 (10): 1103–33.

Volkov, Shulamit. 1978. *The Rise of Popular Antimodernism in Germany: The Urban Master Artisans, 1873–1896*. Princeton, NJ: Princeton University Press.

von Behr, Marhild. 1981. *Die Entstehung der industriellen Lehrwerkstatt*. Frankfurt/Main: Campus.

von Rauschenplat, Helmut. 1945. *Vocational Training in Germany*. London: The Westminster Press.

von Rieppel, A. 1912. Lehrlingsausbildung und Fabrikschulen. *Abhandlungen und Berichte über technisches Schulwesen*, Bd. III. Berlin: B. G. Teubner, 1–10.

von Saldern, Adelheid. 1979. *Mittelstand im "Dritten Reich."* Frankfurt/Main: Campus.

Wagner, Karin. 1997. Costs and Other Challenges on the German Apprenticeship System. Paper read at Workshop on "Skills for the 21st Century" (January 10), at Institute for Contemporary German Studies, Washington DC.

Wagner, Karin. 1999. The German Apprenticeship System under Strain. In *The German Skills Machine: Sustaining Comparative Advantage in a Global Economy*, edited by P. D. Culpepper and D. Finegold. New York: Berghahn Books.

Walle, Bernhard. 1963. *Das Lehrlingsrecht in der Bundesrepublik Deutschland und seine Vereinheitlichung: Eine Bearbeitung des im Jahr 1962/63 von der Rechts- und Staatswissenschaftlichen Fakultät der Julius-Maximilians-Universität ausgeschriebenen*

Preisthemas unter dem Kennwort "Meisterlehre:" Würzburg: Hans Holzmann Verlag.

Wallerstein, Michael. 1999. Wage-setting Institutions and Pay Inequality in Advanced Industrial Societies. *American Journal of Political Science* 43: 649–80.

Wallerstein, Michael, and Miriam Golden. 1997. The Fragmentation of the Bargaining Society: Wage Setting in the Nordic Countries, 1950 to 1992. *Comparative Political Studies* 30 (6): 699–731.

Ware, George W. 1952. Vocational Education and Apprenticeship Training in Germany: Office of the U.S. High Commissioner For Germany, Office of Public Affairs, Division of Cultural Affairs.

Webb, Sidney, and Beatrice Webb. 1897. *Industrial Democracy*. Vols. 1, 2. London: Longmans.

Webb, Sidney, and Beatrice Webb. 1920. *The History of Trade Unionism*. Revised edition, extended to 1920. New York: Longmans.

Webb, Sidney, Beatrice Webb, and Robert Alexander Peddie. 1911. *The History of Trade Unionism*. London, New York: Longmans.

Weber, Hajo. 1991. Political Design and Systems of Interest Intermediation: Germany between the 1930s and the 1950s. In *Organising Business for War*, edited by W. Grant, J. Nekkers, and F. van Waarden. New York: Berg.

Weingast, Barry. 2002. Rational-Choice Institutionalism. In *Political Science: The State of the Discipline*, edited by I. Katznelson and H. Milner. New York: Norton.

Weingast, Barry R., and William J. Marshall. 1988. The Industrial Organization of Congress; or, Why Legislatures, Like Firms, Are Not Organized as Markets. *Journal of Political Economy* 96 (1): 132–63.

Weir, Margaret. 1992. Ideas and the Politics of Bounded Innovation. In *Structuring Politics: Historical Institutionalism in Comparative Analysis*, edited by S. Steinmo, K. Thelen, and F. Longstreth. New York: Cambridge University Press.

Weir, Margaret. 2003. Institutional Politics and Multi-Dimensional Actors: Organized Labor and America's Urban Problem. Presented at Yale Conference on Institutions. New Haven, CT.

Weiss, Linda. 1993. War, the State, and the Origins of the Japanese Employment System. *Politics & Society* 21 (3): 325–54.

Welskopp, Thomas. 2000. *Das Banner der Brüderlichkeit*. Bonn: Dietz.

Wigham, Eric L. 1973. *The Power to Manage: A History of the Engineering Employers Federation*. London: Macmillan.

Wilden, Josef. 1926. Das Prüfungswesen im Handwerk und in der Industrie. *Technische Erziehung* 1 (4): 1–2.

Wilentz, Sean. 1981. Artisan Origins of the American Working Class. *International Labor and Working Class History* 19: 1–22.

Winkler, Heinrich August. 1971. Der rückversicherte Mittelstand: Die Interessenverbände von Handwerk und Kleinhandel im deutschen Kaiserreich. In *Zur soziologischen Theorie und Analyse des 19.Jahrhunderts*, edited by W. Rüegg and O. Neuloh. Göttingen: Vandenhoeck & Ruprecht.

Wolsing, Theo. 1977. *Untersuchungen zur Berufsausbildung im Dritten Reich*. Kastellaun, D: A. Henn.

Wolsing, Theo. 1980. Die Berufsausbildung im Dritten Reich im Spannungsfeld der Beziehungen von Industrie und Handwrk zu Partei und Staat. In *Erziehung und Schulung im Dritten Reich*, edited by M. Heinemann. Stuttgart: Klett-Cotta.

Yamamoto, Kiyoshi. 1994. *Nihon ni okeru shokuba no gijutsu to rōdōshi*. Tokyo: University of Tokyo Press.

Yamamura, Kozo. 1977. Success Illgotten: The Role of Meiji Militarism in Japan's Technological Progress. *Journal of Economic History* 37 (1) March: 113–35.

Yamamura, Kozo. 1986. Japan's Deus ex Machina: Western Technology in the 1920s. *Journal of Japanese Studies* 12 (1) Winter: 65–94.

Yamazaki, Hiroaki, and Matao Miyamoto, eds. 1988. *Trade Associations in Business History: the International Conference on Business History 14: Proceedings of the Fuji Conference*. Tokyo: University of Tokyo Press.

Yokosuka, Yokosuka Kaigun Kōshō (Yokosuka Navy Factory, ed.). 1983. *Yokosuka kaigun senshō-shi*. Vol. 1. Tokyo: Hara Shobō.

Zeitlin, Jonathan. 1980. The Emergence of Shop Steward Organization and Job Control in the British Car Industry: A Review Essay. *History Workshop Journal* 10 (1980): 119–37.

Zeitlin, Jonathan. 1990. The Triumph of Adversarial Bargaining: Industrial Relations in British Engineering, 1880–1939. *Politics & Society* 18 (3): 405–26.

Zeitlin, Jonathan. 1991. The Internal Politics of Employer Organization: The Engineering Employers' Federation, 1896–1939. In *The Power to Manage*, edited by S. Tolliday and J. Zeitlin. London: Routledge.

Zeitlin, Jonathan. 1996. Re-forming Skills in British Metalworking, 1900–1940: A Contingent Failure. Paper read at 21st meeting of the Social Science History Association, October 10–13 (panel on "Skill formation in comparative-historical perspective"), at New Orleans, LA.

Zeitlin, Jonathan, ed. 2000. Special Issue on Flexibility in the 'Age of Fordism' in *Enterprise and Society*. Vol. 1, No. 1 (March 2000).

Zeitlin, Jonathan. 2001. Re-Forming Skills in British Metalworking, 1900–1940: A Contingent Failure. In *Les ouvriers qualifiés de l'industrie (XVIe–XXe siècle). Formation, emploi, migrations*, edited by G. Gayot and P. Minard. Lille: Revue du Nord.

Zysman, John. 1983. *Governments, Markets, and Growth*. Ithaca, NY: Cornell University Press.

Zysman, John. 1994. How Institutions Create Historically Rooted Trajectories of Growth. *Industrial Corporate Change* 3 (1): 243–83.

Index

Abel, Heinrich, 66, 245
Acemoglu, Daron, 14–15, 74, 138
Act Against Sedition, 97
Act for the Encouragement and Relief of Friendly Societies, 97
Adenauer, Konrad, 251, 255
Albert, Michael, 2
Alexander, Magnus, 199
Allan, William, 100, 106
Allgemeine Elektrizitätsgesellschaft (AEG), 57, 60, 69
Allied Powers in post-WWII Germany, 240, 242–248; *American Zone*, 243, 246, 247, 247n; *British Zone*, 242, 246, 247, 247n, 248, 251n, 254; *French Zone*, 243, 246, 247, 247n; *see also Occupation*
Allis-Chalmers, 196
Amalgamated Engineering Union (AEU), 137, 137n, 139, 140, 146
Amalgamated Society of Engineers (ASE), 99, 100, 103, 103n, 105–107, 107n, 108, 109, 111, 130, 131, 132, 135, 137n, 182, 183, 184n, 190, 191, 212
American Federation of Labor (AFL), 188, 195
American Management Association, 205
Amt für Berufserziehung und Betriebsführung (AfBB), Office for Vocational Training and Works Management, 232, 234, 235, 237
Apprentice strike (Britain), 113, 144
Apprentice wages, 114, 118
Apprenticeship and Skilled Employment Association, 120–121
Apprenticeship Promotion Act of 1976, *see Ausbildungsplatzförderungsgesetz*
Apprenticeship training, joint regulation through unions and employers, 132, 196
Apprenticeship training, length of, 102, 112, 114, 114t, 115, 117, 143, 178n, 283
Apprenticeship, conflicts between unions and employers, 21, 100, 113, 132–133, 145, 148, 186, 190–191, 228, 280
Arbeitsausschuß für Berufsbildung (AfB), Working Committee for Vocational Training, 88, 89, 250
Arbeitsstelle für Berufserziehung des Deutschen Industrie- und Handelstages, Office for Vocational Training of the Association of German Chambers of Industry and Commerce, 241, 249, 254n
Arbeitsstelle für Betriebliche Berufsausbildung (ABB), 249, 250, 251n, 261n

Armstrong, Whitworth and Company, 127
Arnhold, Carl [Karl], 83–85, 86, 232, 233, 234
Arthur, Brian, 26, 27
Artisans, artisanal sector (Germany), *see* Handwerk
Artisans, artisanal sector (Japan), *see* *Oyakata*
Association for Education in Industry and Commerce, 142, 143
Association for Metalworking Employers, *see Gesamtmetall*
Association for the Advancement of Education in Industry and Commerce, 135
Association of Berlin Metal Industrialists, 57, 75, 86
Association of German Employers' Organizations, *see Vereinigung der Deutschen Arbeitgeberverbände* (VDA)
Association of German Machine-Building Firms, *see Verband Deutscher Maschinenbauanstalten* (VDMA)
Association of German Metal Industrialists, (GDM), 77
Association of the German Iron and Steel Industrialists, *see Verein Deutscher Eisen- und Stahl Industrieller* (VDESI)
Association of Machine and Iron Works, 161n
Ausbildungsplatzförderungsgesetz, Apprenticeship Promotion Act of 1976, 265
Auxilliary Service Act of 1916 (Germany), 133
Axmann, Artur, 227

Baethge, Martin, 219, 263, 266, 269, 275, 276
Basic Law (Germany), 256n
Bates, Robert, 25, 293
Becker, Gary, 11–15, 21, 127, 147n, 173, 210, 211, 284
Berghoff, Hartmut, 239
Berlin Association of Metalworking Employers, 88
Booth, Charles, 103
Borsig, 55, 57, 60, 69, 88
Boyer, Robert, 1
Brandt, Willy, 264
Bray, Reginald, 115, 127, 128
Britain, *compared with Germany*, 16, 19, 21, 22, 32, 33, 46, 48, 51, 51n, 53, 64, 67, 97, 100, 104, 109, 111, 114–116, 118, 121, 125–127, 133, 135–136, 138, 140, 145–146, 279–280; *compared with Japan*, 21, 22, 32, 156, 280; *compared with United States*, 21, 38, 148, 177, 178–180, 181, 183, 184, 188, 189, 212–213, 280, 282
British Electric, 122
British Westinghouse Company, 103n, 117, 123, 125, 127, 134n
Brody, David, 212
Brown & Sharpe, 199
Bundesinstitut für Berufsbildung (BIBB), National Institute for Vocational Education, 260n, 261n, 265, 268n
Bundesinstitut für Berufsbildungsforschung (BBF), Federal Institute for Vocational Training Research, 260, 261n, 265
Bundesministerium für Wissenschaft und Forschung (BWF), Federal Ministry for Science and Research, 262
Bundesverband der Deutschen Industrie (BDI), National Confederation of German Industry, 245n, 249, 254
Bundesvereinigung der Deutschen Arbeitgeberverbände (BDA), Confederation of German Employers' Associations, 249

Carnegie Steel Works, 192
Cartels (Japan), 162, 162n
Central Office for Research and Promotion of Vocational Education, *see Zentralstelle zur Erforschung und Förderung der Berufserziehung* (ZEFB)
Christian Democratic Union (CDU), (Germany), 241, 255, 260, 261n, 264, 277n
Christian Social Union (CSU), (Germany), 261n, 264, 277n
Clayton and Shuttleworth, 122, 125
Clemens, Elizabeth, 295
Clement, Wolfgang, 277n
Codetermination as union demand in Germany, 255, 258, 259, 263, 290
Collective action problems, role in skill formation, 11, 19–20, 24, 60, 64, 111, 148, 161n, 162, 175, 179, 194, 196, 202, 269, 272, 273; *see also Employer coordination*
Collectivist system of skill formation, 19, 20, 148, 149, 151, 175–176, 281
Collier, David & Ruth, 215n
Colonial period, apprenticeship in US, 178–180
Combination Acts (1799, 1800), 96; *repeal of*, 98, 99
Company unionism, 56, 72, 74, 85, 149, 171
Congress of German Crafts and Trades, *see Deutscher Handwerks und Gewerbekammertag* (DHGT)
Congress of German Industry and Commerce, *see Deutscher Industrie und Handelskammertag* (DIHT)
Continuing vocational education and training (Germany), 270
Convergence theories, 1
Coordinated market economy, 2–4, 5, 9, 17
Corporation schools (US), 199–202
Costs of training, 17, 19
Craft control strategies, 51, 53, 62, 67, 107, 108–109, 110, 133, 136–138, 146, 168, 181–184, 195, 199, 202, 203, 212, 279
Craft labor markets, 21–22, 98
Craft unionism, 21, 156, 157, 279, 280; *Britain*, 92, 98, 98n, 100–103, 104–107, 130, 145, 279, 281, 283; *United States*, 32, 148, 149, 177, 179, 181–184, 186, 188, 189–190, 191, 193, 202–203, 280, 282, 289; *Germany*, 51n, 68, 70
Crafts Institute at the University of Cologne, 241
Credible commitment problems, 17–18, 19, 21, 24, 47, 92, 101–104, 115, 116–117, 118, 121, 129, 144, 159, 179, 182, 183, 283–285
Credit constraints as source of market failure in skill production, 12, 17, 19, 114, 127
Critical junctures, 27, 28, 29, 34, 37, 215, 215n, 218, 292
Crouch, Colin, 21n, 262, 268
Crusius, Werner, 254
Culpepper, Pepper, 269n, 275

DATSCH (*Deutscher Ausschuß für Technisches Schulwesen*), German Committee for Technical Education; *role in skill standardization*, 77–78, 134, 135, 200, 205, 223–225; *under Weimar*, 59–62, 63, 64, 73, 79, 82, 83, 84, 88; *under National Socialism*, 90, 225, 225n, 230, 231, 232, 232n, 233–234, 235n, 238, 241, 248, 249, 250, 251
David, Paul, 26
Dehen, Peter, 62
Deutscher Handwerks und *Gewerbekammertag* (DHGT), Congress of German Crafts and Trades, 89

Deutsche Arbeitsfront (DAF), German Labor Front, 219n, 220, 220n, 221, 226, 227n, 228, 231, 231n, 232, 232n, 233, 234n, 236n, 240; *conflicts with Economics Ministry over training*, 231, 234–237
Deutsche Demokratische Republik (DDR), East Germany, 216n, 240n, 259
Deutscher Gewerkschaftsbund (DGB), German Trade Union Confederation, 244n, 254, 255n, 259
Deutscher Handwerkskammertag (DHKT), German Association of Chambers of Artisans, 256n
Deutscher Industrie-und Handelskammertag (DIHT), German Congress of Industry and Trade, 82, 88, 89, 245, 246, 246n, 248, 249, 250, 253, 259, 263
Deutscher Metallarbeiterverband (DMV), German Metalworkers Union, 49–50, 52, 68–70, 71
Dilution, in Britain, WWI, 133
Dinta (*Deutsches Institut für Technische Arbeitsschulung*), German Institute for Technical Training, 83–86, 231, 232, 232n, 233, 233n, 234, 236n
Diversified quality production, 6, 9, 15n, 23
Dobbin, Frank, 37
Domanski-Davidsohn, Elisabeth, 50
Douglas, Paul, 201
Drive system (US), 191–192, 198, 203, 208

East Germany, *see* DDR
East London Apprenticing Fund for Christian Children, 119
Eastern Germany (post-unification), 271, 275–276
Economic theories of institutions, 286n
Economic theories on skills, 8, 11–15
Economics Ministry (Germany), *role under National Socialism*, 220, 224, 228, 231, 233, 234–237; *post-World War II*, 231n, 233, 234n, 240, 245, 251, 252, 257–258, 261, 277n
Elementary schools and education, 125, 125n, 126, 134
Employer associations, role in training, 269, 273
Employer coordination, 60, 62, 75, 76, 79, 87, 88, 161–162, 193, 250; *see also Collective action problems*
Engineering Employers' Federation (EEF), 108, 109, 111, 113, 133, 134, 135, 136, 137, 140, 143, 146, 212
Erhard, Ludwig, 253
Exploitation of apprentices, 46–47, 54n, 63, 94–95, 110, 111, 112n, 113, 119, 131, 144, 179, 257, 279

Fachhochschulen, technical colleges, 275
Fachvereine, 49–50
Factory schools, *Britain*, 122, 123, 142; *Germany*, 56, 85, 86; *Japan*, 154, 163–164; *United States, see Corporation schools*
Federal Institute for Vocational Training Research, *see Bundesinstitut für Berufsbildungsforschung* (BBF)
Federal Ministry for Science and Research, *see Bundesministerium für Wissenschaft und Forschung* (BWF)
Federalism, 244
Feedback effects, 27, 31, 34, 36, 37, 41, 48, 52–53, 288–290, 291, 293, 295
Feldman, Gerald, 75
Finegold, David, 10, 13, 262, 270
Fisher Act, 134, 141
Fisher, H.A.L., 134, 135
Fleming, Sir Arthur, 134n
Foreign craftsmen, as source of skills in Japan, 154, 155

Foremen, 177, 192, 198, 202, 203, 206, 207, 208, 209, 213, 282
Four Year Plan, Office of, 236
Franklin, Benjamin, 180
Free Democratic Party (FDP), (Germany), 253, 264, 265
Friderichs, Hans, 265
Friendly benefits, 51n, 92, 96–97, 98–99, 104, 105–107, 145
Friendly Union of Mechanics, 104n
Functionalism, 6, 7, 24–25, 27, 30, 32, 36, 293, 294

Gemmill, Paul, 208, 209
General Electric, 199, 200, 200n, 201, 206n, 208, 278
General skills, 11, 13, 14, 15, 17
German Association of Chambers of Artisans, *see Deutscher Handwerkskammertag* (DHKT)
German Committee for Technical Education, *see* DATSCH (*Deutscher Ausschuß für Technisches Schulwesen*)
German Congress of Industry and Trade, *see Deutscher Industrie-und Handelskammertag* (DIHT)
German Institute for Technical Training, *see* Dinta
German Labor Front, *see Deutsche Arbeitsfront* (DAF)
German Metalworkers Union, *see Deutscher Metallarbeiterverband* (DMV)
German Trade Union Confederation, *see Deutscher Gewerkschaftsbund* (DGB)
Germany, *compared with Britain*, 16, 19, 21, 22, 32, 33, 46, 48, 51, 51n, 53, 64, 67, 97, 100, 104, 109, 111, 114–116, 118, 121, 125–127, 133, 135–136, 138, 140, 145–146, 279–280; *compared with Japan*, 22–23, 38, 148, 149–151, 156, 163, 166, 172–176, 280; *compared with United States*, 32, 184, 205–206, 280
Gesamtmetall, Association for Metalworking Employers, 273
Gesetz zur vorläufigen Regelung des Rechts der Industrie- und Handelskammern (1956) (IHKG), Law for the Provisional Regulation of the Rights of the Industry and Trade Chambers, 241, 256, 258, 258n
Gewerbeordnung (1869), 248
Gewerbevereine, role in training, 44–46
Globalization, 1, 3
Gompers, Samuel, 194
Gordon, Andrew, 163
Göring, Hermann, 236
Grand Coalition (Germany, 1966–69), 241, 260, 263
Great Depression (1929), 90, 137, 211, 220
Great Lockout (1897), 191
Greif, Avner, 30
Großer Befähigungsnachweis (major [or comprehensive] certificate of competence), 228
Guilds, 21, 21n, 42, 45, 46, 51, 93–95, 152, 157, 162, 178, 181, 257; voluntary guilds in Germany, *see Innungen*
Gutehoffnungshütte (GHH), 85, 234

Hacker, Jacob, 218–219, 287–288
Hall, Peter, 2, 3, 4, 9, 16, 285
Handelsgesetzbuch 1897, 248
Handicraft chambers, role in apprenticeship training, 22, 40, 44, 46–47, 51, 81, 88–90, 229, 241, 247, 256–257, 262–263, 267–268
Handicraft Protection Law (1897), 7, 23, 33, 39–41, 42, 43–47, 53, 57, 57n, 58, 107, 175n, 281, 289, 294n
Handicrafts, handicraft sector (Germany), *see* Handwerk
Handwerk chambers, cost of training in, 54n, 268, 283

Handwerk sector, 79–81, 88, 174, 221, 224, 228–230, 246, 259, 279; *definition of*, 40n
Handwerkskammern, see Handicraft chambers
Handwerksordnung (HwO) 1953, 241, 256–257, 258n
Hansen, Hal, 19, 44, 44n, 46, 46n, 47, 82, 179, 185, 201, 237
Heavy industry, approach toward training (Germany), 237
Herrigel, Gary, 19n, 20, 45n, 49, 51, 56, 76, 245, 270
High school (enrollments in US), 180n, 210
High skill equilibrium, 5n, 10, 149
Historicist explanations, 294
Hitler Youth, 219n, 226
Hitler, Adolf, 232n
Hollingsworth, Rogers, 1
Homburg, Heidrun, 56
Huber, Evelyne, 288, 289

Immigration, as source of skills in US, 180, 181, 185, 186, 197, 203
Imperial Institute for Labor Exchange and Unemployment Insurance, *see Reichsanstalt für Arbeitsvermittlung and Arbeitslosenversicherung* (RAA)
Increasing returns effects, 26, 27, 31, 34, 289, 291, 293, 295
Indentures, 12–22, 101, 103n, 113, 115, 120, 123, 182, 200, 201, 225
Industrial Committee of the Jewish Board of Guardians, 119
Industrial Patriotic Council, 171
Industrial Training Boards, 147
Industrie und Handelskammer, see Industry and Trade Chambers
Industrielle Mittelstand, 43n, 76–77, 79
Industry and Trade Chambers, 59, 67, 79; *role in apprenticeship*, 221, 222–223, 226, 236, 241, 247n, 249, 250, 250n, 252, 256, 257–258, 259, 261, 262–263
Innungen (voluntary guilds in Germany), 43, 44, 49, 51
Inside contracting (US), 187–188, 189, 192, 213
Institutional change, xii–xiii, 3, 4, 6–8, 23–24, 28–31, 33–36, 38, 215, 216–217, 218, 278, 289, 291, 292–296; *mechanisms of*, 35–36; *political coalitions and*, 33–36; *see also Political coalitions, role in institutional stability and change*
Institutional complementarities, 3–4, 16n, 278, 285–291
Institutional conversion, 36, 37, 218, 291, 293, 295
Institutional evolution, *see* institutional change
Institutional layering, 35, 36, 37, 41, 217, 293
Institutional origins, 4–5, 278–282, 294; *political coalitions and*, xi–xii, 20–23, 31–34; *theories of*, 23, 27
Institutional reproduction, 7, 8, 34, 36, 37, 215, 216, 217, 218, 278, 292–296; *mechanisms of*, 7
Institutional stability, *see* Institutional reproduction
Internal labor markets *Germany*, 290; *Japan*, 148, 149, 165, 166, 167, 169, 171, 175, 176, 206, 213, 282, 284; *United States*, 207, 208, 209, 214
International Association of Machinists (IAM), 182, 183, 183n, 184, 184n, 190, 191, 202
International Harvester, 200
International Molders Union (IMU), 188
Iron and steel industry (Germany), 81–86

Jacoby, Sanford, 185, 187, 192, 201, 208

Japan, *compared with Britain*, 21, 22, 32, 156, 280; *compared with Germany*, 22–23, 38, 148, 149–151, 156, 163, 166, 172–176, 280; *compared with United States*, 148, 177–178, 184, 188, 206–207, 210, 213–214, 280, 282
Job classifications, 203, 203n, 206, 207, 211, 284
Job control unionism, 22, 178
Journeymen Steam Engine and Machine Makers' Friendly Society, 104
Jowitt, Kenneth, 29
Junior Technical Schools, 127, 141n

Kansai Industrial Federation, 172
Katznelson, Ira, 29, 292
Kawada, Hisashi, 152, 166
Kearney & Trecker, 196
Kelly, Roy Wilmarth, 195
Kerschensteiner, Dr. Georg, 127n
Kieslinger, Adolf, 246, 246n
King, Desmond, 147
Kleiner Befähigungsnachweis, (minor certificate of competence), 57n
Klug, Thomas, 190
Knight, Jack, 25, 32
Knox, William, 95, 96, 100, 116
Kocka, Jürgen, 40n, 48–49, 51
Krause, Erwin, 254n
Krupp, 234
Kultusministerkonferenz (KMK), Standing Conference of the [state-level] Ministries of Culture, 244, 244n

Labor, organized labor, *Britain*, 81, 99–100, 104, 130–131, 131n, 138–139, 189, 212, 280, 283; *Germany*, 48–53, 65, 66–67, 68–72, 90, 175–176, 218, 219n, 241–242, 251n, 252–255, 257, 258, 259, 262, 262n, 263, 264, 276, 290; *Japan*, 151, 166, 168, 169n, 171–176, 282; *United States*, 181–184, 189, 212, 280, 282; *comparative strategies of employers toward*, 279, 281–285
Laitin, David, 30
League of German Crafts, *see Reichsverband des Deutschen Handwerks* (RDH)
League of German Industry, *see Reichsverband der Deutschen Industry* (RDI)
Legislative reform of training (Britain), 93, 128, 129, 134, 135, 137, 141, 147
Leimig, Josef, 254–255
Leipzig Agreement, 235
Levine, Solomon, 152, 166
Ley, Robert, 220, 231n, 232, 234–235
Liberal market economy, 2–4, 5, 9, 16
Life-time employment (Japan), 160, 164–166, 167, 169, 172, 282, 284
Lockouts (Britain), 105, 106, 107, 108–109, 113, 132, 135, 140, 146, 191
Loewe, Ludwig, 55, 57, 60, 69
Low skill equilibrium, 5n, 10
Luchtenberg, Dr. Paul, 253

Machine and metalworking industries, role in training, 278; *in Britain*, 104, 122–125, 127–129, 134, 143; *in Germany*, 41, 42, 53–55, 56, 57–59, 62, 63, 72–73, 174–175, 279, 290; *in Japan*, 152–153, 155, 157, 158, 162, 174–175; *in the United States*, 186–188
Mack, Frida, 78
Mahoney, James, 27
Major [or comprehensive] certificate of competence, *see Großer Befähigungsnachweis*
Maschinenfabrik Augsburg Nürnberg (MAN), 55, 56, 57, 60, 69, 73, 278
Mason, Timothy, 220, 226
Mass production, 184, 185, 191, 192, 213

Masters and Servants Act of 1875, 113
Mather and Platt, 122, 123, 127, 128, 278
McKinlay, Alan, 137
Meiji Japan, 151, 152–154, 155, 158
Metal Manufacturers Association of Philadelphia (MMA), 193–194
Metalworkers Union (Japan), *see* Tekkō Kumiai
Military industry, role in skill formation, 152, 152n, 153, 153n, 159, 160n, 161, 171–172, 202, 220, 221, 223, 237, 238–239
Ministry of Industry (Japan), 153
Ministry of Labor (Britain), 142
Ministry of Labor (Germany), 87, 244n, 245, 252, 259, 262, 277n
Ministry of Science and Education, 264, 265
Minor certificate of competence, *see Kleiner Befähigungsnachweis*
Mitsubishi, 160, 161, 163, 164, 168, 174
Moe, Terry, 25, 32
Monitoring of training, 18, 20, 44, 46, 47, 63, 115, 118, 119, 120, 121, 144, 145, 179, 225–227, 245, 256, 279, 283
More, Charles, 125
Morris, John van Liew, 201
Mosher, Jim, 68
Motley, James, 184, 190, 212
Muth, Wolfgang, 78

Nagasaki Shipyard, 154, 165
National Apprentice Law 1937 (US), 211
National Association of Corporation Schools (NACS), 196n, 200, 201, 205
National Association of Manufacturers (NAM), 193, 193n, 194, 195, 198
National Board of Education, 129, 134, 141
National Confederation of German Industry, *see Bundesverband der Deutschen Industrie* (BDI)
National Institute for Vocational Education, *see Bundesinstitut für Berufsbildung* (BIBB)
National Institute for Vocational Training, *see Reichsinstitut für Berufsausbildung in Handel und Gewerbe* (RBHG)
National Metal Trades Association (NMTA), 191
National Socialism, 38, 90, 171, 175, 176, 232n, 281; *impact on training*, 219–222, 240, 246, 250, 252n, 255; *repression of unions*, 219n, 220n, 228, 231
National Vocational Education Act of 1917 (US), 195; *see also Smith Hughes Act*
National Vocational Skills Development Association, 173
New Institutional Economics (NIE), 24, 32
Newton, William, 105
Nolan, Mary, 74
North, Douglass, 27

Occupation of Germany, post-WWII, 38, 240, 242–251, 254; *see also Allied Powers*
Office for Vocational Training and Works Management, *see Amt für Berufserziehung und Betriebsführung* (AfBB)
Office for Vocational Training of the Association of German Chambers of Industry and Commerce, *see Arbeitsstelle für Berufserziehung des Deutschen Industrie- und Handelstages*
Olson, Mancur, 29
Open shop movement in the US, 191, 191n, 203, 205n
Orren, Karen, 37, 285

Oyakata, 23, 149, 151, 154–155, 156n, 158–159, 160, 162, 163, 164, 167, 169, 170, 172, 174, 176, 177, 187, 213, 280, 282; *Meiji government policy toward*, 151–152

Path dependence, 8, 23, 25–29, 29n, 31, 34, 36, 37, 215, 278, 289, 290, 291, 293, 294; *in economic history*, 26, 37; *theories of change in*, 28–29
Pätzold, Günter, 240, 251
Piecework, 207, 209
Pierson, Paul, 24, 24n, 25, 27, 30, 36, 287–288, 293, 294, 296
Pischke, Jörn-Steffen, 14–15, 74, 138
Poaching, 11, 12, 14, 16, 17, 19, 20, 21; *in Britain*, 127, 141, 144, 283; *in Germany*, 60, 70, 73, 82, 222, 273; *in Japan*, 158, 160, 161, 162, 162n, 164, 165, 172, 280; *in the United States*, 193, 197, 201; *see also Collective action problems*
Political coalitions, *role in institutional stability and change*, xiii, 278n, 289, 291, 293, 294; *see also Institutional change*
Poor Laws, 97
Power-distributional theories, 6, 33, 294
Premium apprenticeship, Britain, 102, 119, 123n, 124, 124n, 143
Public education and schooling, 180, 180n, 264
Public sector enterprises, role in skill formation (Japan), 159, 160
Public vocational education schooling, 193, 194–196, 210–211, 213, 260n, 268n; *see also Vocational schools*
Punctuated equilibrium models, xii, 28, 29n, 30, 31, 35, 36, 215, 216, 240, 292, 296
Putting-out system of production, 93n

Rational choice theories, 29–30, 32
Reconstruction of Germany, post WWII, 241, 242, 251–263
Red-Green Coalition, 266n, 276n
Reform of Handwerk law, 277n
Reichsanstalt für Arbeitsvermittlung and Arbeitslosenversicherung (RAA), Imperial Institute for Labor Exchange and Unemployment Insurance, 227
Reichsberufswettkampf, 226
Reichsgruppe Industrie (RGI), 220n, 225n, 235, 236
Reichsinstitut für Berufsausbildung in Handel und Gewerbe (RBHG), National Institute for Vocational Training, 224, 233, 237, 249, 251
Reichsverband der Deutschen Industrie (RDI), League of German Industry, 88
Reichsverband des Deutschen Handwerks (RDH), League of German Crafts, 89
Reichswirtschaftkammer, 246, 246n
Rhode, Helmut, 265
Royal Commission on Labour (1892), 116
RWM, *see* Economics Ministry (Germany)

Schacht, Hjalmar, 220, 231n, 234–236
Schickler, Eric, 33, 35, 41
Schmidt, Helmut, 265
Schneider, Herman, 193n
Schönhoven, Klaus, 52
Schröder, Gerhard, 276, 276n
Schütte, Friedhelm, 71
Scientific management movement, 204
Segmentalist system of skill formation, 20, 23, 38, 41, 56, 58, 82, 148, 149, 151, 158, 166, 167, 168n, 171, 175–176, 198, 213, 231, 273n, 282
Seniority system, 20, 207; *see also Life-time employment*
Shop stewards, 133, 213

Siemens, 56, 59, 69
Skill certification, 18, 19; *in Britain*, 92, 101, 102, 107, 109, 115, 116n, 118, 121, 136n, 145, 283; *in Germany*, 39, 47, 53, 57–58, 58n, 59, 60, 63, 64, 65, 73, 76, 77, 79–80, 89, 90, 145, 146, 149, 172, 174, 224, 229, 231, 238, 246, 247, 256, 279, 283 (*see also Handicraft chambers*); *in Japan*, 149, 155, 173–174; *in the United States*, 179, 182, 188, 194, 197, 201
Skill standardization, 41, 75, 77n, 78–88, 90, 145, 166, 175, 217, 221, 223–225, 230, 231, 232n, 237, 250, 281, 291
Skocpol, Theda, 37, 296
Skowronek, Stephen, 37, 286
Smith Hughes Act, 195, 210; *see also National Vocational Education Act*
Smith, Allan, 135, 137, 146
Social Democratic Party (SDP), (Germany), 87, 241, 260, 264, 281
Social democratic unions, 49–50, 52
Social Security Act, 288
Sociological theories, 6, 7, 32, 37, 286n, 288n, 295
Soffer, Benson, 188
Soskice, David, 2, 3, 4, 9, 10, 13, 14, 16, 268, 269, 271, 275
Specific skills, 11, 12, 13, 14, 16, 209
State policy, impact on skill formation, 20, 22–23, 31–32, 279; *in Britain*, 92, 94–95, 97, 98, 100, 145, 147; *in Germany*, 39, 42–44, 46, 51, 150–151, 174, 175n, 176, 217, 221, 260n, 262n, 268n, 275; *in Japan*, 150–151, 153n, 154–162, 174, 176, 184; *in the United States*, 182, 184, 196–197
Statute of Artificers (1563), 94–95, 101, 178
Stephens, John D., 288, 289
Stevens, Margaret, 13–14
Stinchcombe, Arthur, 26, 294
Stinnes-Legien Agreement (1919), 68
Streeck, Wolfgang, 2, 3, 9–10, 23, 267, 269
Sweden, 286–287, 288, 289
Swenson, Peter, 19n, 20, 93, 146, 190, 198, 205n, 286–287, 288
Swidler, Ann, 29

Taira, Koji, 157, 164, 171
Tawney, R.H., 112, 115, 116, 128, 131n
Technical Education Acts of 1939 (Japan), 172
Tekkō Kumiai (Japan), Metalworkers Union, 158
Tokugawa Shogunate, 157, 158
Tollkühn, Gertrud, 46, 78
Tōkyō Kikai Tekkō Dōgyō Kumiai, *see* Association of Machine and Iron Works
Training levy, 265–266, 266n
Transferable skills, 13, 14, 15

Unification (Germany), 216n, 270, 275–276
Unintended consequences, 36
Unions, *see Labor, organized labor*
United States, *compared with Britain*, 21, 38, 148, 177, 178–180, 181, 183, 184, 188, 189, 212–213, 280, 282; *compared with Germany*, 32, 184, 205–206, 280; *compared with Japan*, 148, 177–178, 184, 188, 206–207, 210, 213–214, 280, 282

Varieties of capitalism, xi, 2, 2n, 4–11, 278, 285
Verband Deutscher Maschinenbauanstalten (VDMA), Association of German Machine-Building Firms, 59, 60, 64, 75–78, 79, 83, 90, 111, 136, 136n, 143, 167, 205, 221n, 231
Verein Deutscher Eisen- und Stahl Industrieller (VDESI), Association of the German Iron and Steel Industrialists, 83

Index

Vereinigung der Deutschen Arbeitgeberverbände (VDA), Association of German Employers' Organizations, 88
Vestibule training, 204–205
Vickers, 122, 124
Vocational schools, *Britain*, 123, 124, 125–127, 127n, 128–129, 130–131, 141–142, 145; *Germany*, 45, 45n, 54n, 61–62, 74, 85, 225, 225n, 227, 229, 239, 240, 242–244, 250, 272n, 274; Japan, 171n; United States, 194–196, 210–211, 214
Vocational Training Act of 1969 (Germany), 91, 218, 242, 259–262, 263, 264
Vocational Training Law of 1958 (Japan), 173
Vocational training reform, failure in Weimar period, 88–90
von Dohnanyi, Klaus, 264
von Rieppel, Anton, 56, 60

W.H. Allen, Son & Co., Ltd, 123
Wage compression, 15, 15n, 17n, 68, 69–70, 74, 138–139, 140, 273
Wage coordination, 20
Wage system, skill formation and, 110n, 138n, 143, 166, 168, 170, 172, 206–208, 209, 273, 284
Wagner Act, 211
Wagner, Karin, 270, 272
Ware report, 243, 253
Webb, Sidney and Beatrice, 95, 98, 117
Weimar Republic, 15, 22, 34, 41–42, 53, 63–91, 111, 146, 166, 176, 218, 220n, 221, 222, 225n, 227, 228, 230, 231, 232, 233n, 237, 238n, 239, 246, 246n, 250, 252n, 260n, 281
Weingast, Barry, 25, 30
Weiss, Linda, 172, 176
Welfare capitalism, 198, 200n, 201, 206, 214, 284
Westinghouse Company, 199, 200, 208

Wigham, Eric L., 146
Winchester Repeating Arms Company, 192
Wisconsin model of skill formation, 196–198, 198n
Work Promotion Act, 275
Working Committee for Vocational Training, *see* Arbeitsausschuß für Berufsbildung (AfB)
Works Constitution Act (*of 1952*), 255; (*of 1972*), 263n
Works councils (Germany), 133, 263, 263n
Wright, Erik Olin, 158

Yahata steel mill, 153, 154, 165, 169
Yawata Iron and Steel Works, 168
Yokosuka, 154, 160, 165, 278

Zaibatsu, 167
Zeitlin, Jonathan, 100, 136n, 137, 139, 147
Zentralarbeitsgemeinschaft (ZAG), 65, 67, 73
Zentralstelle zur Erforschung und Förderung der Berufserziehung (ZEFB), Central Office for Research and Promotion of Vocational Education, 254

Other Books in the Series (continued from page iii)

Kanchan Chandra, *Why Ethnic Parties Succeed: Patronage and Ethnic Head Counts in India*
Ruth Berins Collier, *Paths toward Democracy: The Working Class and Elites in Western Europe and South America*
Donatella della Porta, *Social Movements, Political Violence, and the State*
Gerald Easter, *Reconstructing the State: Personal Networks and Elite Identity*
Robert J. Franzese, Jr., *Macroeconomic Policies of Developed Democracies*
Roberto Franzosi, *The Puzzle of Strikes: Class and State Strategies in Postwar Italy*
Geoffrey Garrett, *Partisan Politics in the Global Economy*
Miriam Golden, *Heroic Defeats: The Politics of Job Loss*
Jeff Goodwin, *No Other Way Out: States and Revolutionary Movements, 1945–1991*
Merilee Serrill Grindle, *Changing the State*
Anna Gryzymala-Busse, *Redeeming the Communist Past: The Regeneration of Communist Parties in East Central Europe*
Frances Hagopian, *Traditional Politics and Regime Change in Brazil*
J. Rogers Hollingsworth and Robert Boyer, eds., *Contemporary Capitalism: The Embeddedness of Institutions*
John D. Huber and Charles R. Shipan, *Deliberate Discretion?: The Institutional Foundations of Bureaucratic Autonomy*
Ellen Immergut, *Health Politics: Interests and Institutions in Western Europe*
Torben Iversen, *Contested Economic Institutions*
Torben Iversen, Jonas Pontusson, and David Soskice, eds., *Unions, Employers, and Central Banks: Macroeconomic Coordination and Institutional Change in Social Market Economics*
Thomas Janoski and Alexander M. Hicks, eds., *The Comparative Political Economy of the Welfare State*
David C. Kang, *Crony Capitalism: Corruption and Capitalism in South Korea and the Philippines*
Robert O. Keohane and Helen B. Milner, eds., *Internationalization and Domestic Politics*
Herbert Kitschelt, *The Transformation of European Social Democracy*
Herbert Kitschelt, Peter Lange, Gary Marks, and John D. Stephens, eds., *Continuity and Change in Contemporary Capitalism*
Herbert Kitschelt, Zdenka Mansfeldova, Radek Markowski, and Gabor Toka, *Post-Communist Party Systems*
David Knoke, Franz Urban Pappi, Jeffrey Broadbent, and Yutaka Tsujinaka, eds., *Comparing Policy Networks*
Allan Kornberg and Harold D. Clarke, *Citizens and Community: Political Support in a Representative Democracy*
Amie Kreppel, *The European Parliament and the Supranational Party System*
David D. Laitin, *Language Repertories and State Construction in Africa*
Fabrice E. Lehoucq and Ivan Molina, *Stuffing the Ballot Box: Electoral Fraud, Electoral Reform, and Democratization in Costa Rica*
Mark Irving Lichbach and Alan S. Zuckerman, eds., *Comparative Politics: Rationality, Culture, and Structure*
Evan S. Lieberman, *Race and Regionalism in the Politics of Taxation in Brazil and South Africa*

Pauline Jones Luong, *Institutional Change and Political Continuity in Post-Soviet Central Asia: Power, Perception, and Pacts*
Doug McAdam, John McCarthy, and Mayer Zald, eds., *Comparative Perspectives on Social Movements*
James Mahoney and Dietrich Rueschemeyer, eds., *Historical Analysis in the Social Sciences*
Scott Mainwaring and Matthew Soberg Shugart, eds., *Presidentialism and Democracy in Latin America*
Isabela Mares, *The Politics of Social Risk: Business and Welfare State Development*
Anthony W. Marx, *Making Race, Making Nations: A Comparison of South Africa, the United States, and Brazil*
Joel S. Migdal, *State and Society: Studying How States and Societies Constitute One Another*
Joel S. Migdal, Atul Kohli, and Vivienne Shue, eds., *State Power and Social Forces: Domination and Transformation in the Third World*
Scott Morgenstern and Benito Nacif, eds., *Legislative Politics in Latin America*
Layna Mosley, *Global Capital and National Governments*
Wolfgang C. Muller and Kaare Strom, *Policy, Office, or Votes?*
Maria Victoria Murillo, *Labor Unions, Partisan Coalitions, and Market Reforms in Latin America*
Ton Notermans, *Money, Markets, and the State: Social Democratic Economic Policies since 1918*
Roger D. Petersen, *Understanding Ethnic Violence: Fear, Hatred, and Resentment in Eastern Europe*
Simona Piattoni, ed., *Clientelism, Interests, and Democratic Representation*
Paul Pierson, *Dismantling the Welfare State?: Reagan, Thatcher, and the Politics of Retrenchment*
Marino Regini, *Uncertain Boundaries: The Social and Political Construction of European Economies*
Jefferey M. Sellers, *Governing from Below: Urban Regions and the Global Economy*
Yossi Shain and Juan Linz, eds., *Interim Governments and Democratic Transitions*
Beverly J. Silver, *Forces of Labor: Workers' Movement and Globalization since 1870*
Theda Skocpol, *Social Revolutions in the Modern World*
Richard Snyder, *Politics after Neoliberalism: Reregulation in Mexico*
David Stark and László Bruszt, *Postsocialist Pathways: Transforming Politics and Property in East Central Europe*
Sven Steinmo, Kathleen Thelen, and Frank Longstreth, eds., *Structuring Politics: Historical Institutionalism in Comparative Analysis*
Susan C. Stokes, *Mandates and Democracy: Neoliberalsm by Surprise in Latin America*
Susan C. Stokes, ed., *Public Support for Market Reform in New Democracies*
Duane Swank, *Global Capital, Political Institutions, and Policy Change in Developed Welfare States*
Sidney Tarrow, *Power in Movement: Social Movements and Contentious Politics*
Ashutosh Varshney, *Democracy, Development, and the Countryside*
Elisabeth Jean Wood, *Forging Democracy from Below: Insurgent Transients in South Africa and El Salvador*
Elisabeth Jean Wood, *Insurgent Collective Action in El Salvador*